Recollections of the Life of John Binns ...

John Binns

Nabu Public Domain Reprints:

You are holding a reproduction of an original work published before 1923 that is in the public domain in the United States of America, and possibly other countries. You may freely copy and distribute this work as no entity (individual or corporate) has a copyright on the body of the work. This book may contain prior copyright references, and library stamps (as most of these works were scanned from library copies). These have been scanned and retained as part of the historical artifact.

This book may have occasional imperfections such as missing or blurred pages, poor pictures, errant marks, etc. that were either part of the original artifact, or were introduced by the scanning process. We believe this work is culturally important, and despite the imperfections, have elected to bring it back into print as part of our continuing commitment to the preservation of printed works worldwide. We appreciate your understanding of the imperfections in the preservation process, and hope you enjoy this valuable book.

RECOLLECTIONS

OF THE

LIFE OF JOHN BINNS.

CT
275
.B574
.A3

RECOLLECTIONS

OF THE

LIFE OF JOHN BINNS:

TWENTY-NINE YEARS IN EUROPE AND FIFTY-THREE IN
THE UNITED STATES.

WRITTEN BY HIMSELF,

WITH

ANECDOTES, POLITICAL, HISTORICAL, AND MISCELLANEOUS.

WITH A PORTRAIT.

"I have long hesitated about a task which diffidence in my capability rendered me fearful I should not be able worthily to fulfil. In the meantime age advances, and however insufficient be my pen, I can no longer postpone giving to the world, not Memoirs, but recollections."—*Méneval*.

PHILADELPHIA:
PRINTED AND FOR SALE BY THE AUTHOR,
AND BY PARRY AND M'MILLAN.
1854.

Entered according to the Act of Congress, in the year 1854, by
JOHN BINNS,
in the Office of the Clerk of the District Court of the United States in and for the Eastern District of the State of Pennsylvania.

PHILADELPHIA:
T. K. AND P. G. COLLINS, PRINTERS.

PREFATORY ADDRESS.

INFLUENCED by the opinions of persons I esteemed, and by the persuasions of others entitled to my respect, I have written the following Recollections. I trust I have, in every instance, truly submitted every circumstance I have thought calculated to present the writer as he is, and as he has been. If a love of truth has not at all times guided and governed my pen, its wanderings, if any, have been not only without my knowledge, but against my principles and intentions.

If, at an earlier day, I had determined upon such a publication as the present, I should have previously arranged and laid away materials to have enabled me to present more facts and incidents, and thus give a more perfect representation. I have, as far as in my power, avoided noticing difficulties and misunderstandings, in which I have been involved in my political and editorial career.

Although circumstances have carried me into crowds, given me strange companions, made me a fugitive from thief-takers, and the inhabitant of many prisons, from the Bastile to the Tower of London, I can assure my female readers that, in these Recollections, there is nothing to wound their feelings, or tint their cheeks.

It is not doubted that every reasonable allowance will be made for the errors or omissions of an octogenarian. If this publication shall meet with so much public favor as to call for a second edition, care shall be taken to introduce in it whatever shall be found to have been omitted in this; thus, so far as is in the power of the writer, he will endeavor to make it more deserving of public approval, not failing to benefit by such criticisms as the present volume shall call forth.

CONTENTS.

CHAPTER I.

Birth at Dublin—Death of my father—Family of my parents—Second marriage of my mother—Early fondness for reading—Literature of my childhood—Lack of regular education—Reading in bed a dangerous practice—Incident at school—My stepfather and uncle Ambrose Binns—Dangerous amusement—My grandmother—Robbery by ruffians—Political excitement in Dublin—Project of the French government to invade Ireland—Incidents of the time—Reminiscences of Walter Blake Kirwan and of the Rev. John Summerfield 14

CHAPTER II.

Disposition of the personal property and real estate belonging to my father—My brother and myself travel to Holyhead—Gratuities to servants—We arrive in London; incidents—London Corresponding Society—Trials of Hardy, Tooke, and Thelwall—State of party feeling in 1794—Sketch of Hardy and Tooke—Character of the London police—Personal incidents—Richard Brothers—Visit to him—Sketch of Joanna Southcote—Meetings of the London Corresponding Society—Effects of the French Revolution on the public mind—Riot in London 86

CHAPTER III.

Declaration of War against France by Great Britain, not favored by William Pitt—Obstinacy of George the Third—Correspondence of the King with Charles James Fox relative to the American War—Condemnation of Kyd Wake—Scene at Covent Garden Theatre—Laws against seditious practices enacted—Action of the London Corresponding Society thereon—I am sent on a mission to Portsmouth; visit the prison at that place—My return to London—My arrest at Birmingham and confinement in "the dungeon"—The riot which occurred there in 1790–91—I visit the public house at which the riot was believed to have been planned—Scene at that house . . . 58

CHAPTER IV.

Grand-Jury of the County of Warwick find true bills against Gale Jones and myself—Conviction of the former—Interview with Mr. Rushton—I sail for Dublin, and return to Warwick in time for my trial—Sketch of Mr. Percival—My trial comes on—Acquittal—Anecdotes of Dr. Samuel Parr—Facts touching my arrest and trial—John Allen—Jeremiah Leary—Rev. James Coigley—Arthur O'Connor—My visit to Gravesend, for the purpose of securing a conveyance to France—I fail to attain my object—Danger to which Coigley and O'Connor expose themselves—We are all arrested at Margate, and conveyed to London 72

CHAPTER V.

O'Connor, Coigley, and myself are conducted to Bow Street Police Office—We are ordered to be searched—My examination before Justice Ford and Justice Addington—Committed to Clerkenwell Prison for a further hearing—Character of my jailers—My lack of accommodations—Disadvantages under which a poor criminal labors—Reflections on criminal law in Pennsylvania—I am discharged, and re-arrested on a charge of high treason—I am examined by the Privy Council, but nothing of consequence elicited—Re-examined by the Privy Council—I am sent to the Tower, where I meet O'Connor—Surveillance to which I was there subjected—Character of the place—Receive a visit from General Vernon and Colonel Smith, and from the king's messengers . 91

CHAPTER VI.

Manner of passing away my time in the Tower—Disturbance created by my yellow silk neckerchief—Removal with the other state prisoners to Maidstone jail—Imposing circumstances attending our route thither—Description of my room—Arrival of the Judges—Interview with Mr. Bonney—Counsellor Gurney appointed my counsel—I send a letter to the High Sheriff of Kent County—My indictment and trial—Unfairness of the Government; instance—My acquittal—Riot in Court—Sketch of Arthur C. O'Connor 113

CHAPTER VII.

Another storm gathers over my head, and I retire to Derby—Descend into a coal-pit—Return to London—Interview with Sir Richard Ford—Mr. Kerr—Report of Secret Committee of the House of Commons—I am again arrested, and put in Clerkenwell prison—My examinations before the Privy Council—I am joined in prison by an old acquaintance; give him some good advice; its result—My removal to Gloucester prison—Incidents—My apartments—I am visited by the Dean of Gloucester—Jealousy of my fellow-prisoners—I give them a thrashing—My letters to the Duke of Portland 139

CHAPTER VIII.

My companions in prison—Strictness of my confinement—I have been blessed through life with a happy temperament; incident—Receive a visit in prison from Secretary Dundas—My release—I embark for the United States—Jealousy of the British Government concerning the exportation of labor-saving machinery—Incidents of my voyage—Our arrival in America—Proceed to Harrisburg, and thence to Northumberland—Dr. Priestley and Thomas Cooper—Shad fisheries—Dr. Priestley's compliment to American mechanics—Condition of Pennsylvania in the early part of the present century relative to currency, manufactures, and agriculture—Northumberland in 1802; personal incidents—Politics of the period 159

CHAPTER IX.

My marriage—Character of Dr. Priestley—I engage in a duel—Simon Snyder—Dr. Leib—Wm. Duane—My visit to Philadelphia—Description of Philadelphia in 1802—I establish the "Democratic Press"—Outrage against the American frigate Chesapeake—Effects of non-intercourse and embargo 179

CHAPTER X.

A town meeting of both parties—A scene in the State Legislature—Pennsylvania politics—Pennsylvania in the war of 1812—The rights of citizens—The enemy and John O'Neill 200

CHAPTER XI.

The news, how did it come?—Honor to the brave—Fundamental difference between the Government of the United States and that of Great Britain—Some public services—The forty banks—The Declaration of Independence—Mr. Jefferson and Mr. Adams 222

CHAPTER XII.

John Randolph—A first interview—Mr. Boileau—Gen. Andrew Jackson 240

CHAPTER XIII.

The Bank of Pennsylvania—Nullification in South Carolina—Pennsylvania coal—Fire buckets—The watch-box—A somnambulist—London amusements—Country hospitality—The barber bleeder—Ann Carson and her schemes—An insurrection in prison—Public executions—Behavior of convicts 260

CHAPTER XIV.

Debased humanity—The yellow fever—Sagacity of animals—Ants at work—Bengal tiger—The paddle-wheel—Where I have lived—Troops of friends—An accident—The club—John Binns is made an alderman—A scene in an alderman's office 282

CHAPTER XV.

A deep affliction—Another accident—A compliment—Farewell to "Democratic Press"—Opinions of my capacity as a public speaker—A libel refuted—Daniel O'Connell 301

CHAPTER XVI.

Church affairs—Intolerance—Selfishness rebuked—The question put—The old Congress in 1775—Hints to immigrants—Roman Catholic discipline—State of our music—Customs and manners—A reflection—Death of my wife—A death-bed scene 325

RECOLLECTIONS

OF THE

LIFE OF JOHN BINNS.

INTRODUCTORY.

Soon after my arrival in the United States, which was on the first of September, 1801, I was urged by the late Dr. Joseph Priestley, his son Joseph, and Thos. Cooper, Esq., to write my life. These gentlemen then lived where I also resided, in Northumberland, Pa. They were among my earliest American acquaintances, and continued my zealous and faithful friends to their death. Some few American gentlemen who have subsequently, in Philadelphia, read the account of my arrest and examinations before the Privy Council in London, and of my trials for sedition and high treason in 1797 and 1798, have also urged me to publish my Recollections. Let these facts be received as an apology for this publication.

Within a few years I have, occasionally, laid away such letters and papers as have presented themselves containing matter to assist my recollection. These facts are stated, to account in some measure for omissions, want of arrangement, and other deficiencies. The lateness of the period at which these recollections have been written has its advantages. It insures a more full and frank disclosure of facts than would, probably, have been given at an earlier period. Nearly all the persons I shall name, at least in the European portion of my life, have been called hence, and their remains consigned to their silent graves; some to Westminster Abbey, and some to ignominious resting-places.

I shall write that which I know to be true of myself, and of all other persons whom I may feel called upon to name. I do not entertain unkindly feelings toward any one living, nor for the memory of any one dead. As my departed, beloved, and excellent friend, Dr. Edward Hudson, used to say: "I would not do *myself* so much wrong as to entertain such feelings." When I reflect upon the limited, irregular, and unfinished nature of my education, and the unfavorable circumstances under which I have entered upon life, in strange countries, and consequently among strangers, I am somewhat surprised, and not a little gratified, at the friends I have made, and the influence I have acquired, and exercised, over large bodies of men in Europe and in the United States.

JOHN BINNS.

CHAPTER I.

Birth at Dublin—Death of my father—Family of my parents—Second marriage of my mother—Early fondness for reading—Literature of my childhood—Lack of regular education—Reading in bed a dangerous practice—Incident at school—My stepfather and uncle Ambrose Binns—Dangerous amusement—My grandmother—Robbery by ruffians—Political excitement in Dublin—Project of the French government to invade Ireland—Incidents of the time—Reminiscences of Walter Blake Kirwan and of the Rev. John Summerfield.

I was born on the 22d of December, 1772, in the city of Dublin, Ireland. My father's name was John Binns; the maiden name of my mother was Mary Pemberton. She was the daughter of Benjamin Pemberton, a bricklayer and limeburner in the city of Dublin. The Christian name of my grandfather Binns was Jonathan. He kept an ironmongery and house-furnishing establishment in Dame Street. My father was brought up to the same business, and had a similar establishment in the same street. Although my father and all his family were members of the Moravian Church, my mother and her family were all members of the Protestant Episcopal Church. While I was an infant, two years old, my father went to England to purchase goods, and, on his return, was cast away and drowned. Although then not more than thirty years of age, he had acquired a reputation as a man of business; and, in city politics, a character for talents and integrity which justified the high expectations entertained by his friends as to his future, in public and private life. My father was accompanied to England by Alderman Forbes, who had been canvassing the city of Dublin for the office of Lord Mayor, as my father had been for the office of Sheriff. On their arrival at Holyhead, on their way home, the weather was so boisterous and threatening that the regular packet-ship declined to put to sea. From the anxiety of the above gentlemen to return and pursue their canvass, they hired a vessel and embarked for Dublin. My father's pocket-book, with some invoices of goods he had purchased, and other valuable papers, were washed ashore on the coast of Wexford, Ireland, near where the vessel had been wrecked. They were found, and carefully delivered to his family. My father left a widow and three children, two sons and a daughter; Benjamin Pemberton Binns, aged more than three years; John Binns, the writer, nearly two years; and Mary Binns, about one year old. My father, as I have understood, left a personal property of about eight thousand pounds ($40,000), and real estate worth about two thousand pounds ($10,000). At his death, my mother was not more than twenty-three or twenty-four years of age. She was tall, handsome, and gracefully formed; her understanding was of a superior order; and her deportment, in all the relations of life, such as commanded confidence and respect. She did not remain long in business after the death of her husband. So entire, however, was the confidence of all the family, the Binns and Pembertons, in her future management, and in the care of her children, that she, by common consent, took possession of all the personal property, collected the debts, settled all claims, and funded, or otherwise appropriated what came into her hands, according to her own judgment. The freehold property, by, in my opinion, the most unjust of all laws, the law of primogeniture, on our father's death became the property of his oldest son, my brother. My grandfather, Binns, was appointed his guardian, and took possession of it during my brother's minority; the rents, issues, and profits were funded, or otherwise disposed of, for his benefit. On attaining the age of twenty-one he came into full possession.

Having disposed of the stock and trade, my mother took her three children and went to board at the house of her brother, William Pemberton, a bricklayer, who, some years after, was one of the High Sheriffs of the city of Dublin; Joseph Pemberton, his cousin, was Lord Mayor of the city the same year.

My father's family were all on what was called the liberal side in politics; my mother's were on the government side. It was this circumstance which caused "the full tide of honor" to flow so bountifully in that direction.

After remaining some time at her brother's, my mother went to board at the house of my father's brother, Ambrose Binns, who had married a sister of my mother, and who carried on the business of an anchor-smith. My earliest and latest intercourse, all I have ever known or heard of this uncle, calls upon me to speak of him as one of the most amiable, upright, and kind-hearted of men. I never heard a human being speak of Ambrose Binns in any other terms than those of kindness and respect.

After remaining some time at the house of this uncle, we again returned, with our mother, to the house of my uncle William Pemberton, to board and lodge. He had been, some years before, married to a Miss McEntegart, of Drogheda. Her brother George, then rather more than twenty years of age, handsome, and well-mannered, of a good figure, and engaging address, boarded in the same family. He was at that time articled to an attorney at law, with whom he was studying. Several advantageous offers of marriage had been made to my mother, and by her declined; she, however, against the remonstrances of all my father's family, married Mr. George McEntegart. They soon after went to housekeeping, and my brother and myself were taken to live with them. My sister went to live with my uncle, John Pemberton, near Dublin, with whom she remained until her marriage with Mr. John

Browne. She has been dead some years, leaving two children, John and Rebecca; John is dead, Rebecca is in Dublin. My uncle John Pemberton's wife, Rebecca, brought him, on their marriage, a very handsome property in real estate near Dublin; some of it adjoining a property of my grandfather Pemberton's, on which he resided. John Pemberton, while yet a young man, on his marriage, and consequent easy circumstances, retired from business; he had been brought up a house-carpenter. He resided on the property obtained by his wife on their marriage. There was on it a very large, well-kept garden, in which were many wall-fruit trees. Neither in Ireland nor England do peaches or apricots grow on standard trees. The trees on which such fruits grow, except in hothouses, are those always planted against a wall, and the limbs or branches nailed against the wall with cloth, list, or other like substance. The wall itself is heated by flues at the discretion of the gardener. The price of peaches in Dublin and London varied from fourpence to sixpence a piece, according as the season was more or less abundant.

My uncle, William Pemberton, had also a country seat in the same direction, about two miles further from Dublin than that of his brother John.

In those days, schools in Ireland gave many holidays; at Christmas and Easter we never had less than six weeks, and, at Whitsuntide, four weeks. Those holidays, the junior members of the family, and they were numerous, usually spent in the country at the house of one or other of the persons I have just mentioned.

Those were joyous times; even at this day by me looked back upon with the most pleasurable feelings. At that early age my memory, which was unusually retentive, was plenteously stored with selected pieces of prose and poetry, which I was often called upon by the senior as well as the junior members of the family, to recite. I hardly ever declined to comply with such requests, having full reliance on my memory, and confidence in my elocution. Thus I won affectionate regards, beyond my compeers, and became a general favorite with old and young of the family and their friends.

I do not recollect the time when I could not read, nor

when I was not fond of reading and committing largely to memory. I have continued a great reader all my life. The books which were then read by boys were of a very different description from those which they now read; they had, however, the life and surprising adventures of "Robinson Crusoe." This book has gladdened the hearts and instructed the minds of millions. It has been translated into most of the modern languages in the course of the last century, and is, at this time, devoured with pleasure by the rising generation. Its author, Daniel Defoe, was a voluminous and popular writer; most of his other works, however, have long been scarce or out of print.

In the last century, boys—Irish boys, at least—read the "Arabian Nights' Entertainments," "The Seven Champions of Christendom," "Don Bellianis of Greece," "The Irish Rogues and Rapparees," "Fairy Tales," and other such works. The books now put into the hands of youth are of a more instructive character. It may, however, be doubted whether they are read with equal avidity.

While I was yet a small boy, I read well, and had a clear and distinct enunciation. As I advanced in years I was often called upon to read to my mother. The books I read to her were chiefly moral and historical; the "Spectator," the "Rambler," and other English classics; "Hooke's Roman History," "Hume's England," "Rollin's History of the World," &c. &c. This course of reading was of much advantage to me; my mother, herself an excellent reader, not only corrected my pronunciation, but explained many passages which I should not otherwise have understood at so early an age.

The want of a more regular education than that which was bestowed upon me, prevented me from adopting anything like a systematic or regular course of study. My reading has been very extensive, but altogether of a miscellaneous character. The circumstance which, more than any other, has most injuriously affected my advancement, and been my stumbling-block through life, has been the want of a more regular education; such a one as would have guided me to the right kind of books to read, and dictated the arrangement or order in which I should read them. If I had been thus instructed and guided, I should have laid up, in some systematic order, facts and reasoning upon which I could have safely drawn for improvement, enjoyment, and happiness. I have, from my boyhood, felt that I had an intellect capable of cultivation, and which, if cultivated, would insure to me useful knowledge, and resources against idleness and waste of time. The want of such an education, with some superior superintending mind to guide and direct me, has been no common injury to me. I have read thousands of volumes, one after another, one having no connection with, or dependence upon, another. Such reading filled my mind with information and knowledge of various kinds, but there was a total want of system or arrangement. There was, consequently, in my mind and memory the same want of connection and dependence of one subject upon another which there would have been in a room full of books, into which thousands of volumes had been thrown hap-hazard without arrangement, one after another, as they had been read. There was, if I may so express myself, a mob of information, not a disciplined army; organization was wanted.

For many years, from my boyhood until I was married, I was in the habit of reading after I went to bed; for this purpose I always selected a flat candlestick, which I took into bed with me, never extinguishing the candle until I became sleepy; and not always then. I frequently fell asleep while the candle was burning, and on more than one occasion, when I awoke in the morning, I found the candlestick in bed with me, the candle having burned into the socket. The book which I held in my hand when I fell asleep was, on more than one occasion, scorched. At one time an octavo volume of "Rollin's Ancient History," which I dropped asleep while reading, had nearly one-third of the leaves reduced to ashes in my hand while I slept. This, however, did not induce me to abandon the habit.

Reading in bed is an unprofitable and dangerous habit. Against it I would raise my warning voice; yet how am I to expect that my voice shall act as a warning, when my example, in defiance of my own personal experience, invites to the practice rather than deters from it. The experience of one individual, it seems to me, has little influence on the conduct of other individuals. Nations are more influenced by history than individuals by biography. It is not improbable that one cause for the greater influence of nation upon nation, than of individual upon individual, may be attributed to the fact that the causes of national action are more palpable than those of individuals. They are consequent upon the judgment and councils of many minds, and the statesmen with whom they originate not unfrequently publish their memoirs, these memoirs become materials for history, and, when they are carefully examined and made known to the world, are either rejected or acted upon by future statesmen ; on the other hand, the *motives* which actuate individuals are generally known only to themselves, and thus cannot be expected, and do not influence the actions of others.

To return to my narrative. My mother, on her marriage, purchased the remainder of Mr. McEntegart's time from the gentleman to whom he was articled, and obtained admission for him to practise as an attorney when he became of age. During the time my mother and her husband resided in Dublin, Benjamin and myself went to the school of Sisson Darling, an English and writing-school of high reputation, and attended by many scholars. I note these school facts as introductory to one which has had influence on me through life, and which may influence others beneficially. It was the practice at Mr. Darling's school, on every quarter-day, to read aloud in the school, and in the hearing of the pupils, the name of every scholar whose bill for schooling was more than one quarter unpaid; stating the number of quarters, and the amount due and unpaid. Notwithstanding the amount of property which, on my father's death, came into possession of my mother and subsequently passed into the hands of her husband, our bills at this school were never paid until my brother paid them, many years after, when he came of age. I shall never forget the feelings of shame and confusion of face which came over me, and always drove me to some hiding-place, out of view of the other scholars, when those quarter-days arrived and the unpaid bills were about to be read aloud. I dare affirm that my children's school-bills have, at all times, and under all circumstances, been paid with the most punctilious promptitude and exactness. No blush has ever tinged their cheeks for the same cause which so often crimsoned those of their father.

A holiday being given at school within a year after my mother's marriage, without mentioning the fact at home, my brother and I, for our pleasure, went early in the morning with some of our schoolmates into the country, and did not return home until after sundown. My mother, alarmed at our unusual and protracted absence, was weeping when we came home; Mr. McEntegart was sitting with her in the parlor. So soon as we had told our tale, he took us both into the back parlor, made us take off our upper garments, whipped us pretty severely with a light riding-whip, and sent us supperless to bed. The servant girl who put us to bed, and who had lived some years in my father's family, early next morning, of her own accord, went to my uncle, Ambrose Binns, and told him what had taken place. This uncle was, as I have before noted, married to my mother's sister, and, notwithstanding his disapprobation of my mother's second marriage, entertained for her the most affectionate regard. About noon of the day after we had been whipped, a rather loud and hurried rap was heard at the front door. My brother and I were, at the time, with our mother in the front parlor. She looked through the window toward the hall door, and saw my Uncle Ambrose waiting for admittance. She was evidently alarmed, and went herself and opened the door. My uncle, instantly on entering, said, in a hurried tone of voice: "Mrs. McEntegart, where is your husband? I understand he has been whipping my brother's children." His coat was buttoned over a riding-whip. My mother told him that Mr. McEntegart was not at home. He came hastily into the parlor, and, taking my brother and myself one on each of his knees, he pressed us to his bosom and wept. After a few minutes, he took each of us by the hand, and, without any remonstrance or opposition on the part of my mother, took us to his own house, where we remained for several weeks before we were permitted to return to that of Mr. McEntegart. That was the first and last time he ever whipped my brother or I.

I will not deny myself the pleasure of stating a circumstance which occurred at the house of this uncle. The senior members of the family, to the number of fourteen or more, certainly not less, were one evening playing cards and backgammon in the parlor; directly under it, down one flight of stairs, was the kitchen. The servants were none of them in the kitchen, but there were some six or eight of us boys. We had some gunpowder, and made squibs and crackers, and let them off one by one for our amusement. It so happened that we made some of the powder so wet that it would neither spit, sparkle, nor explode. To remedy this evil all the wet gunpowder was put into a large frying pan, which I was carefully holding over the fire and watching, when, without any expectation or thought of such a thing, all the powder in the pan exploded, and shook, not only the kitchen furniture, but the kitchen and the parlor floor over it. Instantly our lights were put out; and we, boys, tumbling one over the other in the dark, rushed up stairs. The company in the parlor, their chairs and tables, being well shook, and the smell of the gunpowder, so alarmed all the elders that they rushed out of the parlor and down the kitchen stairs until they met the boys rushing up. It would be difficult to tell whether the elders or the youngsters were most frightened. I know not how this story may read, but, I assure my readers, the remembrance of the general fright and exclamations of alarm has afforded the writer many a laugh, even when he has had no one to enjoy the fright of old and young in the midst of darkness and the smell of "villainous saltpetre."

Some months after this time, Mr. McEntegart and his family, of which my brother and I were a part, removed to the town of Drogheda, which was the place of his nativity, and of which he was, some years after, Mayor and Collector of the Port. It was twenty-two miles from Dublin. The father and mother of George McEntegart resided in the house in Drogheda with Mr. McEntegart and his family. His father, for many years, had been master of a whale ship. He was a quiet, well-tempered, good-looking old gentleman. He took pleasure and passed many hours in relating to us his "hair-breadth escapes, by flood and field," from angry whales, who had been bereft of their young, and from mountains of ice, while he was engaged in whaling. His wife, Mr. George McEntegart's mother, had charge of the house. My mother was fond of company, and her company was much sought after. She, therefore, spent her winters in Dublin with her husband and relations, resigning all control over her Drogheda household to her mother-in-law, who was smart, active, and economical. While in Drogheda, we went to Dr. Norris's Select and Classical Academy, where we were several months, with very little improvement, for want of a qualified superintendent at home.

At this school there were from one hundred and eighty to one hundred and ninety scholars. They principally boarded at Dr. Norris's, or at the houses of the two principal ushers. There were not more than twenty scholars who lived with their families in the town. We went to school at six in the morning; at eight we had fifteen minutes to play; at nine we went to breakfast, and returned at ten o'clock; at twelve, noon, we had fifteen minutes to play, and went to dinner at one. At three, in the afternoon, we again went to school; at five had fifteen minutes play; and, at six P. M., school finished for the day.

Old Mrs. McEntegart was not so indulgent as we thought she ought to be. A servant girl, who had lived with my mother during the lifetime of my father, had continued to reside in the family. This girl, desiring to return to Dublin, fostered unkind feelings in us towards old Mrs. McEntegart, and proposed to us to run away, and take us to Dublin. Benjamin was then about twelve, and I was nearly ten years of age. The girl had but a small amount of money, and we had much less; so, with fear and trembling, one morning, a little before daybreak, we started from Drogheda to walk to Dublin. We slept one night in a cabin on the roadside; started early, and, about noon the next day, arrived in Dublin, and walked into the shop of my grandfather, Binns, where we were affectionately welcomed, and the girl provided for.

In 1786, I was apprenticed to a soap-boiler. My grandfather Binns was twice married, and had thirty-two children; the last was a posthumous child, born three months after his death. His widow, many years younger than he, took his eldest son into partnership, and continued the business under the firm of Ann and George Binns. This may have been provided for in the will of my grandfather. He left me a legacy of fifty pounds; of this, thirty guineas were paid as an apprentice fee. My grandmother provided me generously with all my wearing apparel so long as I remained in Dublin. She was very fond of me, and very kind to me; at this day I am, and always have been, grateful for the affectionate liberality with which she supplied all my wants. This lady being my grandfather's second wife, and not being my father's mother, was very distantly, if at all, related to me. I therefore felt the more indebted to her liberality and kindness.

While apprentice, I was much indulged, being permitted to spend one or two evenings in every week with my relations. One evening, on my return home, passing up an alley, not more than twenty feet wide, three men seized me, pulled my hat over my face, put a pistol into each of my ears, and commanded me to be silent on pain of being shot dead. I did as I was commanded. They took my watch, breastpin, and the small amount of money I had. While this robbery was committing, I could distinctly hear the footsteps of passengers; they were very near to me.

I was, notwithstanding this circumstance, permitted to spend much time, particularly in the evenings, with my relations, by whom I was much loved, as well by those of my father's as those of my mother's family. There was not one of them, young or old, who did not always treat me most kindly. This was more especially the case with my female relations and acquaintances, to whom I read, recited poetry, told anecdotes and stories, and made myself ever welcome. My rap at the front door was well known, speedily answered, and I was hailed by one and all as their "sprightly cousin John."

My grand-uncle, John Binns, was the representative of one of the Dublin corporations, in the Common Council, and a speaker of fearless ability on the liberal political side. James Napper Tandy, Esq., and John Binns were influential, indeed leading members, in opposition to those who were the supporters of every measure proposed by those who, from their obedience to every behest of the

English government, were called "Castle Hacks." My grand-uncle was a tall man, and generally esteemed by the liberal party, by whom he was familiarly called "long John Binns;" while by the other party he was called "the devil's darning-needle." He was a man of wealth, of ability and influence, and known as a strenuous advocate of the canal system in Ireland. In his society, and that of his political friends, I became at an early age a lover of republican principles.

About the same time, Archibald Hamilton Rowan was generally esteemed for his generous heart and liberal principles. He was a lieutenant-colonel of the Independent Dublin Volunteers, of which corps the Right Hon. Henry Grattan was colonel. On the 14th of July, 1790, all the Irish volunteers near Dublin assembled in St. Stephen's Green, to fire a *feu-de-joi*, in honor of the French Revolution, and to commemorate the destruction of the Bastile. Among the transparencies carried on that occasion was a large illuminated globe, on which the New World, America, was represented as shedding a blaze of light on the Old World, Europe. This transparency was carried in front of the Independent Dublin Volunteers, who were that day under the command of Lieutenant-Colonel Rowan. As this corps, which was followed by a large crowd, were marching up the hill near the upper castle gate, some three or four sturdy ruffians seized the standard which upheld the transparency, tore it from the standard-bearers, and fled with it into the guard-house, at the castle gate. Colonel Rowan marched his company, nearly one hundred strong, drew them up in front of the guard-house, and there beat a parley. The crowd was in the rear of the volunteers; I was among them. The castle guard, I suppose about one hundred in number, under their proper officers, were soon formed in front of the guard-house. They and the volunteers, under the orders of their respective commanders, primed and loaded with ball cartridge. By this time the crowd thought proper to retire; and an officer from each company met in the centre; the volunteers demanded that those who had seized and carried away the transparency should be surrendered. The parley ended in their being put under the guard of a detachment of an equal number of the volunteers and the infantry, and taken to prison to be disposed of according to law, in the morning, which was accordingly done. The final issue I never heard.

In the year 1792 there was a meeting of some officers of the Irish Volunteers at Pardon's fencing-school in Fownes Street, Dublin, at which meeting Col. Hamilton Rowan was the presiding officer. I know not by what chance it happened, but it did so happen, that I was at the meeting in the gallery; an address to the Volunteers of Ireland was read, adopted and published, signed by the officers of the meeting. Col. Rowan was tried on a charge of having, in that address, published a seditious libel. He was defended by J. P. Curran, Esq. It was in that defence he made one of the most finished appeals he ever made to the genius of universal emancipation. It was casting pearls before swine. Rowan was found guilty and sentenced to two years' imprisonment in Newgate. He paid liberally, and was allowed several apartments in the prison, which he furnished according to his own taste, at his own expense. Near the expiration of the time for which he was sentenced, a man by the name of Jackson was sent by the French government to ascertain the state of public opinion in Ireland, in order to determine whether it would be desirable to invade that country. Before Jackson left London, on his way to Ireland, he expressed a wish to have an intelligent attorney as his secretary; a man of the name of Cockayne was recommended and engaged. This man immediately communicated to one of the agents of the government of England the nature of his engagement with Jackson, and was taken into pay as a spy of the English government. When Jackson had been some time in Ireland, he was introduced to Mr. Rowan, whom he visited in prison, sometimes alone and sometimes accompanied by Cockayne. When he had prepared his report for the French government, he went to Newgate, accompanied by his secretary, and handed over the report to Rowan, who approved of it, but said: "You have some very bad French in it." Cockayne asked him to have the goodness to correct it, handing pen and ink for that purpose. Rowan made the corrections in his own handwriting, and Cockayne had it laid before the Privy Council at the castle, taking care to point out the corrections which were in the handwriting of Mr. Rowan. Happily for Mr. Rowan, Mrs. Rowan had a friend in the council who communicated to her the information which had been given by Cockayne, and which would have been sufficient to have had Rowan tried and executed for high treason. Mrs. Rowan obtained and communicated this important fact to her husband. No time was to be lost in devising a plan for his escape. Thus it was effected. It has been already stated that Mr. Rowan had several well-furnished rooms in Newgate prison. In consequence of this, and the near termination of the period for which he was to be imprisoned, Mr. Rowan was in the habit, when visited by Mrs. Rowan, of handing her to her carriage in front of the prison. The night after the plan for his escape had been matured, Mrs. Rowan's carriage was stationed somewhat further than usual from the entrance of the prison, and she stayed later than usual at the prison. A few bonfires, lighted for the purpose, were blazing when Mr. Rowan, with Mrs. Rowan's hand in his, walked from the prison-door on their way to the carriage; on reaching it, Mrs. Rowan, followed by Mr. Rowan, stepped into the carriage. Mr. Rowan, apparently, instantly stepped back, shut the carriage door and stood close to it, seeming to be earnestly conversing with Mrs. Rowan. The jailer all this time was standing on the elevated door-way of the prison, keeping, as he thought, the prisoner and his lady constantly in view. Thinking, however, that Mr. Rowan stayed too long, he went to the coach-door and put his hand on the shoulder of the gentleman, who, to his great alarm, he discovered was not Mr. Rowan, but a gentleman about his size, and dressed exactly as Mr. Rowan was when he left the door of the prison. The gentleman now made his bow to Mrs. Rowan and departed, the carriage at the same time driving off.

On the morning of that day a small house had been rented on the Hill of Howth, in the bay of Dublin, about seven miles from the city. So soon as Mr. Rowan handed Mrs. Rowan into the carriage, and stepped into it himself, another gentleman, dressed like him, and of the same stature and proportions, stepped out, shut the carriage door, and, with the windows down, began a conversation with Mrs. Rowan; Mr. Rowan having, as agreed upon, found the other door of the carriage open, and a horse saddled and bridled standing at it. He mounted the horse, and rode to Howth, where he found a house in good order ready for his reception, and a faithful servant in waiting. On that island he remained until he hired a fishing-smack to take him to Dunkirk. A few hours after he had embarked he saw the three seamen, whom he had hired, looking with much earnestness at a printed paper, and from that paper at him. He stepped to where they were and saw that they had spread before them a proclamation offering a thousand pounds [$5,000] for his apprehension. He however soon found that the men were honest, they faithfully performed their contract, and landed him at Dunkirk, where he soon found his way to the United States, the sure and certain refuge of every friend of freedom and every honest man. If I am rightly informed, and I think I am, he worked hard in Wilmington and Philadelphia some time before it was known where he was, and his relatives in Ireland enabled to remit to him. After some time, permission was obtained for Mr. Rowan to return to Ireland, on condition of publicly pleading his Majesty's pardon and acknowledging his political errors. His family affections and love of country induced Mr. Rowan to comply with these humiliating conditions. He returned and lived many years, not, according to my advices, very happily.

Many were the embraces given and the tears shed when, in April, 1794, I left Dublin for London, in company with my brother.

WALTER BLAKE KIRWAN.

About the year 1790-91, the Rev. Walter Blake Kirwan, a Roman Catholic clergyman, in the city of Dublin, read his recantation from that church, and was, as a Christian minister, received into the Protestant Episcopal Church. He was soon after appointed Minister of the Parish of St. Nicholas Without, and one of the Chaplains in Ordinary to the Lord Lieutenant. His eloquence, and the effects produced on those who heard him, were subjects of general conversation. The sums collected, when he preached charity sermons, were large without precedent. These collections ranged from four to six thousand dollars at a time, including the sums which were subsequently sent to redeem—watches, rings, breast-pins, and other articles of jewelry which, under the influence of his eloquence, had been freely placed in the collection-plates which had been carried from pew to pew, and through the crowded aisles and passages by ladies of the first rank and fashion in Ireland, who proudly volunteered their services on such occasions.

I was in my twentieth year when I first went to hear Mr. Kirwan preach a charity sermon; it was in St. Peter's Church, Dublin; I went early and alone. I was in front of one of the principal entrances to the church, at least an hour before the gates were opened, and two hours before service was to commence. I was determined, if it were at all possible, to obtain admittance. I found a strong post and rail fence on each side of the entrances to the church through the churchyard and over the flagged way of the street, so that persons who came in carriages could step from their carriage-steps on the inclosed flagway, and then walk, without annoyance, into the church doors. The post and rail fence was about four feet six inches high, inclosing a passage from twelve to fourteen feet wide at each entrance, to prevent persons from clambering or vaulting over the fence, or getting between the rails, and thus finding access to the church. There were also many police officers stationed on duty. Many gentlemen also, interested in the charity, stood with long white rods in their hands, giving facility to the entrance of ladies and gentlemen who came in carriages, and from whom liberal contributions might be expected. Similar arrangements were made at all the entrances to the church, and were adopted whenever and wherever he preached for charitable purposes. The object was to give facilities to the entrance of the wealthy.

I had never before, nor have I at any time since, seen a Christian church, of any denomination or description, under any circumstances, so fortified and guarded against the entrance of those who were anxious to enter, and who gave unmistakable evidence of their desire so to do. At length I obtained admission into the church, and had the good fortune to obtain a seat in the gallery, nearly opposite to, and within twenty-five or thirty feet of the front of the pulpit from which Mr. Kirwan was to preach. The Right Hon. Henry Grattan—one of the most, if not *the* most eloquent, patriotic, and argumentative orators of all the great orators which Ireland has a right to claim—was in the next pew to that in which I sat. Filled, as all the pews were, with the rank and fashion, the talent and wealth of Dublin, I should not mention the presence of even Mr. Grattan, if I did not now, after the lapse of more than half a century, see and feel the extraordinary, I should say extravagant, manifestations of delight which he then exhibited as vividly as I then saw and felt them. His countenance was irradiated by, and expressive of, the highest intellectual enjoyment. His eye never wandered from the speaker, yet he was scarcely ever quiet in his seat. His body moved with a rocking motion towards, and then, as retreating from, the preacher. His feet, or rather his toes, rested on the floor of the pew, his person sometimes attaining nearly an erect position, and immediately falling back on the seat from which he had just risen. When speaking of Mr. Kirwan in the Irish House of Commons, Mr. Grattan said: "He is a man, Mr. Speaker, who has nearly exhausted the lamp of life in feeding the lamp of charity."

The pews, the aisles, the passages, the window-seats, every part of the church, where there was sitting or standing room, was crowded. It was a large church and had many windows. The time of which I am writing was in the summer season; every window in the church, up stairs and down stairs, was open, and every window on the outside as well as the inside was crowded, some standing on the outside on ladders. It rained pretty smartly while Mr. Kirwan was preaching, but I did not see that the rain compelled any person, even among those most exposed, to leave their places. They were willing to be wet to the skin and to take all consequences, but they were not willing to risk the loss of a word which should fall from the lips of the preacher, or to lose the sound of his voice, even though they should hear it indistinctly. I have no recollection of having seen Mr. Kirwan ascend the steps and take his seat in the pulpit, although he did so after I was in the gallery. He was seated in the back of the pulpit when I first saw him. I can never forget the solemn stillness of that large assemblage when the minister rose and knelt down to pray the Lord's Prayer. I had repeated it myself thousands of times, and heard it read and prayed thousands of times by others, in church and out of church. But there was a fulness, a richness, a pathos, a reverential tenderness in the voice of Mr. Kirwan which carried every word he uttered to the heart of the hearer so as to affect it, as it had never before been affected, even on hearing that most sacred, impressive, and affecting of all prayers. The solemn fulness of his voice and the impressiveness of his manner carried his text to the heart and impressed it deeply on the memory of his hearers. This was followed by a gentle rustling of clothes, caused by the crowded audience endeavoring to settle themselves down in their well-filled pews. Every eye was directed towards the preacher, who was fully, may I not truly say proudly, conscious of his commanding influence. Throughout the sermon the deepest silence pervaded the congregation; coughing and sneezing, and the use of pocket-handkerchiefs seemed forbidden by the highest authority, common consent. When the sermon was concluded, a collection was taken up in the usual manner and of the usual amount.

Mr. Kirwan seemed conscious that his sermons produced their effects principally from his delivery, his tones, his emphasis, his looks and actions, and was apprehensive that they would not read well. He never published a sermon, and always refused a copy for publication. Stenographers were then but little known. The art of reporting was then in its infancy. Since that time it has proved itself an able auxiliary to telegraphs, railroads, and steam-engines, in the rapidity with which it embodies and circulates information.

After Mr. Kirwan's death, some one announced that he had taken down some of his sermons, and published what he called a volume of them. It fell stillborn from the press. Those who spoke of it, said the sermons had but little merit, and attributed their success wholly to the manner in which they had been delivered. I feel confident, however, that there was much force and beauty in the language, independent of all extraneous circumstances. I remember two passages which, imperfectly as I recollect them, will give, to those who never heard Mr. Kirwan, some idea of the beauty and brilliancy of his style, and the grandeur of his illustrations. The parish of which Dr. Kirwan had charge, was one of the largest and poorest in the city. An annual charity sermon was deemed essential to procure for the poor, the sick, and the helpless the necessaries of life. Dr. Kirwan, the most powerful and effective advocate of the indigent I ever heard, or ever expect to hear, had, at all times and on all occasions, to be solicited and besought by the high and the mighty to induce him to preach for the benefit of the poor. He had even at that time but little credit with the public for that warmth of feeling and tenderness of heart which appertains to genuine charity. "Do you," said he on one occasion, when asked by some ladies of merit and distinction to preach for the poor of his parish, "Do you suppose, ladies, that charity sermons spring up like mushrooms? if you do, let me tell you you are very much mistaken."

The ladies took their leave. Mr. Kirwan did not that year preach the annual charity sermon. The poor widows and orphans felt the want of it severely.

I was present, full in front of the pulpit, the following year when Mr. Kirwan did his duty, and did preach in aid of the poor of his parish. The Charity School children, two hundred more in number, were ranged, in their peculiar dress, in the gallery on his left hand. Having nearly exhausted all pleas in their behalf, he seemed to feel that he was called upon, and that it was his duty, to tender some apology for former neglect. As he approached the subject, he appeared to labor under the weight of public opinion, and anxious to lighten or cast off the burden. After a solemn pause, and evidently an anxious, silent survey of the congregation, in a low, deep, yet distinctly heard tone of voice, he said: "I know it has been said that I have been the cause of additional suffering having been heaped upon the heads of these poor children"—at the same time turning one half his person toward them, extending his arms, and pointing with both his hands in the direction of the children—his open hands elevated and his fingers extended on each side, he threw his head back, and imploringly raising his eyes to heaven, said: "If I have, may God forgive me." As he delivered these last four words, tears sprang from his eyes; he cast his head into his hands, sobbed audibly, and fell into the pulpit cushion. The effect was electric, and the contribution unusually large.

Soon after the declaration of war in 1793, by Great Britain and Ireland against France, there was great and general distress in the commercial and manufacturing districts, and many bankruptcies. When this distress was at its height in Dublin, Mr. Kirwan was addressing a very crowded church in behalf of the suffering poor. The general distress, scarcity of money, and other causes, induced a belief that even the eloquence of Kirwan would fail to bring much relief. I was present when he preached this sermon. He concluded it, as well as I can recollect, with the following splendid figure: "Why should I anticipate a collection less liberal than on former occasions? The times, melancholy and distressing as they are, have not taken one ray from the sun of pleasure, why then should they snatch a pillar from the throne of mercy?"

The following paragraph I select from "Madden's Revelations of Ireland." It is deeply interesting as a picture of the death-bed of a man so celebrated as the Rev. Mr. Kirwan: "I have heard," says Mr. Madden, "from good authority, that in the latter part of his life he was a firm believer in the truth of revelation, and that he adopted strictly spiritual views of religion. He was low in spirits as he drew near his death, and suffered much from general depression. A brother clergyman, a minister of the Established Church, tried to comfort him, reminding him of all the good he had done by preaching so often and so powerfully in the cause of charity. 'Ah!' said the dying Dean, 'those sermons were inspired only by human feelings—they were merely the blossoms of religious sentiment—but if I have now the least wish that my life should be prolonged, and that I should be allowed to return again into the world, it is that I may be enabled to put forth not merely the blossom or the flower, but to manifest the ripe and solid fruit of mature and deeply-felt conviction.' 'He must,' said I to the reverend gentleman who told me these particulars, 'he must have been a consummate actor.' 'Ay, sir,' was the reply, 'but he died a still more consummate Christian.'"

THE REV. MR. SUMMERFIELD.

About the year 1827, I was called upon in Philadelphia by a friend, who informed me the Rev. Mr. Summerfield was expected the next morning (Sunday) to preach in the Methodist church in Fourth Street. "He is," said he, "a young but a very extraordinary man; come early, or I fear you will not get even standing room." I went early, as requested; but even then, early as it was, and unexpected as had been the arrival of the preacher, the church was filling fast. The people, men and women, on a quick step, and in large masses, were pressing forward and eagerly entering into the house of prayer. All descriptions of persons hurried forward, and were alike fearful lest they should be crowded out. There was no complimentary holding back; no precedence given. Those who were in advance endeavored to keep so, and those in the rear did not scruple to *kibe the heels* of those before them, if they could thereby more certainly attain a place in the church. I had the good fortune to obtain a front seat in the gallery. When standing in the pulpit, the preacher appeared to be rather below than above where I sat. Mr. Summerfield, I understand, was then not more than two or three and twenty years of age, and looked much younger. There was nothing light, vain, or worldly in his appearance. Among the finest specimens of the British arts is one of Flaxman's, illustrative of the words —"Thy will be done." It is an exquisitely beautiful female figure, seated with open, elevated hands, the palms gently laid together, and upraised eyes; the very folds in her garment seem expressive of entire resignation to the behests of her Divine Master. Yet the impression made by the figure and countenance of Mr. Summerfield set at naught this most perfect embodiment of heavenly resignation which genius had ever executed. He brought before the mind's eye the figure usually given of that disciple whom Christ loved. There were three or four other ministers in the pulpit with Mr. Summerfield. While they went through the service, preparatory to the sermon, I could, and did, at my leisure, note him who was "the observed of all observers." The youthful, saint-like expression, not only of his face, but of his whole delicate figure, and the high reputation which had preceded him, and prepossessed the minds and hearts, yea, the very spirits, of all beholders, insomuch that they waited in breathless anxiety, watching his every movement, anxiously waiting to hear the sound of his voice. I am not portraying individual feelings, but shadowing forth those of a large congregation. It seems, even to me, that what I have just written savors of exaggeration; yet I am certain that, if I had sketched my feelings thirty years ago, the picture would have had more warmth of coloring, and been more life-like. Every eye was inquiringly and expectingly directed toward the pulpit, and many an eye was bedewed with religious feeling. Every look, every motion of Mr. Summerfield's gave birth to new and undefinable expectations. The church-service, in which Mr. Summerfield took no part, being concluded, there was a gentle restlessness in the congregation, a settling of themselves quietly in their seats, and a putting of themselves in the best possible position to see and to hear. A wave-like motion passing over the whole congregation gave strong indications of the feelings of the mass who were before and on each side of him. All anxious hopes, all intensity of feeling must fade before the fervency which is felt by a congregation of sincere and warm-hearted Christians when assembled to pray, to praise and to glorify the God of their salvation; they look as though they had a foretaste of the bread of eternal life, and were enjoying that highest of earthly enjoyments—they being borne on angel's wings while they give ear to the fervently pious and hope-inspiring language which flows from the lips of a highly-gifted and eloquent minister of the Living God. Such were the hopes and feelings agitating the bosoms of that congregation of which I was one. I have heard pulpit orators of the first order, of many religious denominations, and have at times been more moved, more awfully impressed—shall I say more spiritually awakened—than I was on this occasion in the Methodist church. Yet I was there in a tranquil, hopeful, delightful frame of mind. My best feelings, my highest anticipations and most blissful hopes, all that was good and promising within me, was in the highest state of enjoyment. It does not often happen that congregations, large assemblies of men and women are so entirely spiritualized as was that congregation while listening to the mild, sweet, and persuasive eloquence of this young divine. He died within a few months after he had thus been heard, and seen, and felt.

CHAPTER II.

Disposition of the personal property and real estate belonging to my father—My brother and myself travel to Holyhead—Gratuities to servants—We arrive in London; incidents—London Corresponding Society—Trials of Hardy, Tooke, and Thelwall—State of party feeling in 1794—Sketch of Hardy and Tooke—Character of the London police—Personal incidents—Richard Brothers—Visit to him—Sketch of Joanna Southcote—Meeting of the London Corresponding Society—Effects of the French Revolution on the public mind—Riot in London.

I HAVE before stated that the personal property of my father, which was considerable, my mother took possession of. On her marriage it passed to her husband, and was never accounted for. I cannot allow this apparently harsh sentence to appear without accompanying it with the statement that at all times, even to her death, I loved my mother dearly. She was highly gifted, had engaging manners, was well educated, well read, and generally loved and esteemed. I shall never forget, nor ever cease to be thankful for, or uninfluenced by, the sound advice on morals and manners which she, most judiciously, and on well-selected occasions, bestowed upon me, long after her marriage with Mr. McEntegart.

My brother, as the eldest son, was put in possession of what real estate my father left, and its income while he was a minor. In his company, and at his request and expense, I sailed with him in a packet-boat for Holyhead. We had a severe blow of wind; all hands at the pump, and a drunken captain; in despite of all which, we arrived in safety. We travelled post through Wales to Chester. The high mountains, hard and steep roads, and rapid streams, as well as the goats and many begging children, engaged our attention, as did the venerable harpers at the several stage-houses at which we stopped. The small sweet mutton, peculiar to the country, we very much enjoyed. The flavor of this mutton is attributed to the active exercise of their sheep traversing the steep mountains, which were covered with a variety of sweet herbs, on which the sheep fed. We travelled leisurely up to London, stopping wherever there were paintings, statuary, the seats of noblemen and gentlemen, or public buildings, old or new, which were represented as worthy of notice, and to which we were allowed, or could purchase, access.

At that time the custom of making presents to servants, of every description, was universal in England. Access to public places, and the houses, gardens, and parks of noblemen and gentlemen, was attainable, by strangers, in no other way; when, as was frequently the case, the owner of the estate and his family were at home, they would go from the room in which they were sitting to other rooms, or walk out, to give strangers admittance. The presents, at that time given to servants, were not only expected by them, but by their masters; they were understood to be taken into consideration by masters and servants when they agreed as to the amount of wages to be paid and received. In the same spirit and custom, travellers in stage-coaches, post-chaises, &c. &c., were expected, at every stage at which they stopped to change horses, &c., to make presents to every person who claimed to have rendered them service. For example, when the stage or carriage stopped all night at a tavern, when the passengers were about to depart in the morning, the servants would range themselves in the hall through which the passengers were to pass, and with extended hands exclaim: "Remember the boots, the chambermaid, the waiter, the coachman, the guard, the hostler," &c. &c., and each of these persons confidently expected money, all of them declining to take less than silver coin. It is proper to state that this custom has been wholly abolished in England; such presents have not been given nor expected there for many years.

Mr. Cole says: "When I sat to Hogarth, the custom of giving vails to servants was not discontinued. On taking leave of the painter, at the door, I offered his servant a small gratuity, but the man politely refused it, telling me it would be as much as the loss of his place if his master knew it. This was so uncommon and so liberal in a man of Hogarth's profession, at that time, that it much struck me that nothing of the kind had happened before."

"Nor is it likely," says Spooner, in his "Curiosities of Art," "that such a thing would happen again. Sir Joshua Reynolds gave his servant six pounds ($30) annually, as wages, and offered him one hundred pounds ($500) a year for the door."

In a recent conversation with a friend, on this subject, he assured me that when he was in England, so late as 1852, he found that the same presents were then expected from strangers and visitors as had been usual half a century ago. "I assure you," said he, "I paid a guinea and a half ($7 50) to the servants for their trouble in showing me through the house and domain of the Duke of Devonshire."

In Mrs. Mowatt's very interesting "Autobiography," she gives us an account of the custom respecting *vales* in Germany:—

"On leaving the house, it is customary for each person to present the servant, stationed at the street door, with a piece of money equal to five or six shillings, and this 'drink geld,' as it is called, which is obtained in various ways from the guests of the master, is always carried to the mistress of the mansion, and kept by her until the end of the year, when it is distributed amongst all the domestics of the family, and often amounts to so considerable a sum that a servant, before making an engagement, regularly asks whether much company is received, that an estimate may be formed of the lucrativeness of the situation."

To resume: In this way we leisurely travelled to the capital. On our arrival in London, we devoted some weeks to the examination of all that was deemed curious or particularly worthy of observation. The Tower, the Monument, St. Paul's, Westminster Abbey, Westminster Hall, and both Houses of Parliament, the Courts of Law, St. James's Palace, Carlton House, the Museum, the Opera House, the Theatres, Vauxhall, &c. &c., were all visited, and filled us with wonder and admiration. I presume, in a few weeks we saw more of the curiosities and antiquities of the great city and its environs, than ever engaged the attention of millions who were born and lived and died in that immense metropolis.

In 1794, I saw the Turkish ambassador and suite make their grand entrance into London, on their way to St. James's Palace. They had no wheel carriage of any kind. They were dressed in the costume of their country, and their horses were equipped in the same manner. The Turks rode with long, loose, white linen trousers; remarkably short stirrups, of thin metal, shaped like slippers, into which they thrust their feet, or rather their loose boots or slippers of rich bright red or yellow morocco leather. The large slipper-shaped stirrups were made of brass gilt. In St. James's Park, some days after, I saw the Turkish suite perform such daring feats of horsemanship as would put young Astley, the most daring and graceful rider of his day, to the blush. They would, in squadron, gallop say one hundred yards toward a stone wall, and when within a few inches of the wall, by a word of command and a check of their bridles, with a large, peculiar shaped, powerful iron bit, they would throw their horses upright on their haunches, and thus face them round as if they turned on a pivot, and gallop back to the place whence they had started. A few days after, at a grand masquerade at Ranelagh, Lady Wallace sported her person in the same dress which had been worn by the Turkish ambassador when he was presented at court. Nearly all standards have been lowered to the half moon. It is, at this time (1854), upheld and advanced with much skill and courage against the Russians.

About this time there was so dense a fog in London that

few foot-passengers ventured into the street without carrying a light. Carriages of every description ran foul of each other, and much damage was done. There were lights burning in every shop; no business could be transacted without artificial light. On the Thames, boats, yachts, and crafts of all sorts and sizes dashed against, overset and damaged each other so that many people were drowned. Such fogs are not unfrequent in London.

Snow Hill was a narrow, steep lane, extending from the end of Fleet Market to the Old Bailey. On one side of it was a barber's shop of so peculiar a character as to claim a description. So soon as candles were lighted, a man took his station, near the door of the shop, who passed his expanded hand occasionally over his chin, and with a loud voice exclaimed, "Shave, shave." Those who desired to be shaved, and the shop was generally pretty full, walked in, when they were assisted to take off their hat and coat, which were hung on a peg; a chair was then set out on which the customer was seated; another person placed a towel under his chin and about his neck; a fourth person came forward and lathered the customer; a fifth advanced and shaved him; he was by a sixth shown to the wash-stand, where, having washed, a seventh person handed the customer a towel, and with a low bow received a *penny;* his coat and hat were handed to him by a boy, after which he departed, having been waited upon by no less than eight persons, for all which services he paid a penny, equal to nearly two cents. Adam Smith, who has written so much on the advantages of a division of labor, would have been delighted to be passed through so many hands at so low a price.

My brother and I lodged together. So long as he received remittances from Dublin, he furnished me with the means of subsistence and enjoyment. When his funds ran out he worked at the plumbing business, to which he had served an apprenticeship in Dublin. After some time, and obtaining no better employment, I was, for months, his assistant. I was in that humble situation when I was chairman of the general Ward Committee of the London Corresponding Society, and at the time I was chairman of the great meeting near Copenhagen House, in 1795.

At the close of the year 1794, I became a member of the London Corresponding Society. This event gave color to my future life. While I was their deputy, travelling on their business, they paid my expenses liberally. Subsequently, in 1796 and '97, John Gale Jones and William Wright, both excellent and popular public speakers, proposed to me to join them and open a Debating Room. I agreed. We hired a large public room in the Strand, London, and proposed, for debate, questions of a popular and exciting character. The room was open at least one evening, and sometimes two, in every week. There were many volunteer speakers; some of them we furnished with free tickets, and occasionally invited to supper, &c. The admittance to the room was a shilling ($\$\frac{25}{100}$) each person. After paying all expenses, such as rent, advertisements, hand and posting bills, suppers, &c., each of the three proprietors, Jones, Wright, and I, received from a guinea to two guineas a week. I have thought it best thus early, once for all, to settle my account for board, &c. &c., before I enter upon the wide field of politics, lest my readers should unnecessarily puzzle their brains guessing how I found means to meet my personal expenses.

In the year 1794, Thos. Hardy, Jno. Horne Tooke, John Thelwall, and others (Hardy and Thelwall were members of the London Corresponding Society), were tried, at the Old Bailey, London, for high treason, and acquitted. The London Corresponding Society became, soon after, not only the most numerous and influential political association in London, but in Great Britain. It occupied the public mind, and the attention of the Government, more than any other popular political association, save only the Whig Club. This society originated with Thos. Hardy, in 1791. He was then a boot and shoemaker, and resided in Westminster. At the Bell public house, in Exeter Street, he and eight of his acquaintances, whose political opinions were congenial with his own, frequently met together. He, at length, detailed to them a plan of an association to advocate Parliamentary Reform. They, all but one, concurred. A committee was appointed to draft a constitution, and each of them agreed to pay a penny a week to defray the expenses of the society. Thus birth was given to the London Corresponding Society, of which Thomas Hardy was the first Secretary. After his acquittal, in 1794, Hardy opened a boot store in Fleet Street, London. The friends of Parliamentary Reform, and the Radicals, liberally patronized him, and he acquired considerable property. This made no change in his principles, character, or deportment. He was always polite and obliging; never obsequious. He was about 5 ft. 9 in. high, of a moderate frame, dressed plainly, talked frankly, never, at any time, assuming airs or making pretensions. He was firm in his principles, and of a sound understanding. After his acquittal, at the Old Bailey, he never, to my knowledge, attended any political meetings. He continued, however, to be popular and esteemed by the members of those associations.

I will here state some facts at once illustrative of the political feelings of the times and the political standing of Hardy. I think it was in 1795-6, a naval victory had been obtained over the French, and a general illumination was ordered by the proper authorities. The houses of foreign ministers, and of all public officers, the shops of all the tradesmen of the royal family, and the several places of public amusement, &c. &c., vied with each other as to the number and disposition of their lights, their colored lamps and transparencies. The brilliancy of their displays was regarded as tests of their loyalty. Those who were opposed to the war then waging against the French Republic, and to the administration of Mr. Pitt, put few, if any, lights in their windows, which were usually broken by the loyal mobs, street-walkers, and glaziers' boys. On the night to which I refer, Hardy would not allow his windows to be illuminated, and they were not only threatened to be broken, but the more violent royalists declared they would sack his house. These threatenings were noised abroad, and about 100 men, chiefly members of the society, many of them Irish, armed with good shillelahs, took post early in the evening in front of, and close to, the front of Hardy's house. As night approached an immense crowd gathered in the street; many and violent were the attacks and efforts made to get possession of the house, and many were the wounds inflicted by fists and sticks. There were no fire-arms used nor stones thrown, except at the windows. About 11 o'clock at night, a troop of horse were sent to keep the peace, and soon after the crowd dispersed. I never was in so long-continued and well-conducted a fight as was that night made by those who defended Hardy's house against such overwhelming numbers.

I have stated that after his acquittal, Hardy never attended the meetings of any political society. The same remark is equally true of Horne Tooke, John Thelwall, Thomas Holcroft, and William Godwin; they had been all indicted for high treason at the same time that Hardy, Tooke, and Thelwall were indicted, tried, and acquitted. Holcroft and Godwin were liberated without trial. The law laid down on those trials, not only by the law-officers of the Crown, but by the judges, was: "That every *member* of a political society was *answerable*, not only for all the acts of the society, but for all the acts of all the members of the society, done in pursuance of any order or resolution of the society, or of any of its constituted committees or authorities." This authoritative judicial decision deterred many persons from associating, and induced many, who had associated for political purposes, to withdraw.

Horne Tooke has filled too large a space in the political world, and had too many anecdotes, notices, and biographies of him published, by friends and foes (he had a host of both), to leave anything untold essential to a thorough understanding and a fair estimate of his character. He was a remarkable, indeed, a very peculiar public speaker. I have heard him frequently, at public dinners and meetings, at the Crown and Anchor, and London taverns, and at the Hustings at Covent Garden, when he was a candidate for a seat in Parliament, to represent Westminster. He spoke slowly, and accompanied what he said with scarcely any action. A rich vein of wit and sarcasm flowed through his political and personal remarks, which told more effectually than those of any other speaker I ever heard. I have, on more than one occasion, heard him illustrate his subject with such genuine English humor as to convulse his whole auditory, gentle and simple, men and women; all would be laughing heartily while the face of the speaker would look cold and unconscious as a metal rapper. The words dropped from his mouth, and his face gave no indication whatever of any consciousness, in the speaker, as to what he was saying or the effect he was producing. He was especially agreeable and instructive at his own house, a few miles from London, where, for many years, on set days, he entertained select parties of his friends. The other three gentlemen I have named with Tooke were literary men. They have all passed away, as indeed have nearly all the men who, at that time, were active in London as statesmen or politicians. I may almost say of myself what Horace Walpole said of himself, toward the close of a long life: "I seem to be intruding myself upon a new generation."

John Thelwall was one of the boldest political writers, speakers, and lecturers of his time. In his lecture-room, in a debating or political society, or at his desk, he was fearless; yet, in private, he was one of the most timid alarmists I ever associated with. If he went into an oyster-house, or an *a-la-mode* beef-shop, he would conceit that one-half of the boxes in the room had Government spies in them, whose especial business it was to watch and report, as far as possible, all he said and all he did. Going home at night, he would prefer to walk in the middle of the street, and took special care never to go down dark or narrow streets, for fear of assassins. London was not then, as it is now, lighted with gas, and its peace preserved by a body of well-organized patrol. Every American who has visited London for the last thirty years, speaks in high terms of the attention, civility, and efficiency of their police. We neither hear nor read of rioting or street fights, much less of murders committed even in the broad daylight. Be it remembered and especially kept in mind by our city-constituted authorities, that the police of London are not intrusted with blunderbusses, pistols, or bowie-knives; they are simply armed with a stout walking-stick, and when they see any sign of a disturbance of the public peace, they blow no horns, ring no alarm-bells, nor spring no rattles; they simply strike the end of their sticks against the footway, and soon assemble a sufficient force without awakening the neighborhood, or disturbing instead of keeping the public peace. Might not our constituted authorities take a hint from the experience of those of London?

William Godwin and Thomas Holcroft were among the most powerful and admired writers of their day. Their style (for example, read Caleb Williams and Hugh Trevor) was vigorous and captivating; yet were they among the most diffuse and tiresome of speakers. I was one of an association, "The Philomathean Society," of which they were both members. The number was limited to twenty-one. The society met once a fortnight, to debate a subject previously proposed. So prolix were both these gentlemen, that a committee of the society was instructed to buy, and did buy, two fifteen minute glasses, the society having adopted a rule, that no member should speak for a longer time. I have no recollection ever to have seen either of those glasses turned when any member, other than Godwin or Holcroft rose to speak.

The London Corresponding Society met and was organized in divisions in various parts of London, Westminster, and Southwark. Its organization was very complete and efficient. Each division was authorized to elect one delegate. The delegates so elected, when assembled, were called "The General Committee of the London Corresponding Society." They met in Thelwall's lecture-room, Beaufort's Buildings, near the Strand. It was a very large room fitted up with seats and desks, pens, ink, and paper, for the accommodation of the delegates. I was for six months Chairman of this committee, at which time the number of delegates was from 160 to 180. The avowed object of the society was to obtain a reform in the Commons House of Parliament, on the plan of universal suffrage and annual Parliaments. I say their avowed object, but the wishes and hopes of many of its influential members carried them to the overthrow of the monarchy and the establishment of a republic. The regular contribution to be paid by each member, was one penny (nearly two cents) a week. The income of the society for three or four years was more than fifty pounds sterling (say $250) a week. To collect that amount would require the regular attendance of 12,000 members, who should punctually pay and have paid over to the treasurer, a penny a week. Those who have any knowledge of political societies, here, or in England, know that many of the members seldom contribute, or contribute very irregularly. I think it probable that, for years, the average number of attending members in the several divisions in London, Westminster, and Southwark could not be less than eighteen or twenty thousand. The great mass of the members were shopkeepers, artisans, mechanics, and laborers. Few professional or wealthy men could be numbered among its members. Those among the wealthy who were friendly to parliamentary reform, associated with the Whig Club, the Friends of the Constitution, &c. &c.

There are two circumstances consequent upon my going to and returning from the general committee of this society, which seem to me of sufficient interest to claim an insertion.

One night, returning home in company with John Fenwick, who afterwards attended poor Coigley to the place of execution, and wrote and published an account of that sad spectacle, as we passed along Holborn, about 11 o'clock at night, our attention was arrested by loud cries of "Stop thief! Stop thief." A crowd quickly gathered, in the centre of which, we found a well-dressed young man in custody, charged with having stolen a public house pewter pint measure. He violently persisted in asserting his innocence, and was as violently accused of the theft. Fenwick and myself became interested, and accompanied the accused, one on each side of him, to the watch-house. The captain of the watch ordered him to be searched. Nothing of the kind charged, or in any way suspicious, being found upon the young man, he was discharged and promptly departed. Fenwick and I had scarcely walked forty yards from the watch-house, congratulating ourselves on having in some measure contributed to the liberation of an innocent person, when Mr. Fenwick, putting his hand into his coat pocket, to take out his handkerchief, laid it on the stolen pewter pot, which the thief, on our way to the watch-house, had very adroitly contrived to slip into Mr. Fenwick's outside coat pocket. He threw the pot from him, and we rejoiced at our good fortune in not having, from the interest we manifested, been searched by order of the captain of the watch.

What paragraphs it would have furnished for the ministerial newspapers, if the Chairman of the General Ward Committee of the London Corresponding Society, and his friend, had been arrested and committed on a charge of pot stealing!!! It is within the scope of possibility that, at that time, on such presumptive evidence, both Fenwick and the writer might have been indicted, if not convicted and sentenced to be imprisoned or transported to Botany Bay. Such an issue to such an adventure will seem not improbable, to those who recollect that Thomas Muir, a distinguished advocate at the Scottish bar, was tried and convicted at Edinburgh, on a charge of having loaned Paine's "Rights of Man" to his hairdresser, and was sentenced to be transported to Botany Bay for fourteen years. In pursuance of that sentence, he was sent, in a convict-ship, to live among convicts, and lost his life in an attempt to escape. Many and bitter were the prosecutions instituted by the administration of William Pitt, for treason, treasonable conspiracies, libels, and sedition. The freedom of speech and of the press in England, from the days of Jeffreys, have been mainly indebted for their preservation to the intelligence and independence of English jurors.

I remember meeting Horne Tooke, a short time before I embarked for the United States, at a public dinner at the Crown and Anchor; when shaking me by the hand he said: "Mr. Binns, I am glad to see you; you and I are the only two men in England who have been tried for treason and sedition; and I think we have been in more jails than any two horse-thieves in England. I wish you well with all my heart."

One of those false prophets, who, in so many ages of the church, have succeeded in obtaining thousands of credulous followers, was, in 1795–6, at the acme of his popularity in England. His name was Richard Brothers. Soon after the mightiest of all popular outbreaks—the French Revolution, in 1789, Brothers published two small pamphlets of explanations and applications of Bible prophecies, which he avowed had been, by the Deity, revealed to him. In those pamphlets, with the most undoubting confidence, he predicted, as revelations to him, from the Supreme Being, the certain triumph of the armies of the Republic over all its enemies. The scriptural style of those pamphlets, the success of the French armies, and the appearance and imposing manners of the author of the pamphlets, caused much sensation throughout England. Some idea may be formed of the abiding steadfastness of belief in the divine mission of this man, from two facts. In the British Parliament, in the session of 1795–6, Nathaniel Brassey Halhed, believed to be the most profound oriental scholar in Great Britain, declared, on the floor of the British House of Commons, of which he was a member, "I believe heaven and earth may pass away, but that not one word which Richard Brothers has prophesied, shall pass away unfulfilled." Mr. Sharpe, the intimate friend of Horne Tooke, Sir Francis Burdett, and other eminent men also believed in the divine mission of Brothers. Mr. Sharpe, at that time, certainly the best line engraver in England, engraved and published a very fine quarto head of Brothers (an admirable likeness it was), under which he engraved the following words : "This is the portrait of Richard Brothers, in whom I firmly believe as a man sent from God. J. SHARPE."

Early in the year 1795, Richard Brothers wrote and published, ought I not to say prophesied and published, that on the evening of the 4th of June, of that year, the king's birthday, London would be destroyed by an earthquake, for its wickedness and crimes, and that the destruction would be so entire that not one stone should be left upon another. It would be difficult, even in these days of Millerism and Mormonism, to convey an adequate idea of the nature and extent of the fears and apprehensions to which this prediction gave birth, among the millions of various descriptions and nations, who inhabited that great city. Many thousands left London, from fear of the destruction to which it was said to be doomed. "Incredible numbers of people," says the London "Gentleman's Magazine," left their houses and walked in the fields, or lay in boats all night; many persons of fashion in the neighboring villages sat in their coaches till daybreak; others went to a great distance, so that the roads were never more thronged."

In 1750, Horace Walpole wrote that, in consequence of the *then* predicted earthquake, within three days, "seven hundred and thirty carriages were counted passing Hyde Park Corner, then one of the extreme western outlets of London, with whole parties removing into the country." Such is and ever has been the superstitious credulity of men in all ages and countries.

On the evening of the day on which Brothers's earthquake was predicted to take place, about dusk, I was walking down the Strand, to the lecture-room in Beaufort's Buildings, when a most violent storm of wind and rain, thunder and lightning, swept that great thoroughfare, and every street in London in that direction, of every living thing. I hastened for shelter into the bar-room of a large hotel. In it, I found fifty or sixty (there may have been more) men and women, with their children, huddling together for shelter. It seemed to me that every one in the room knew something of Brothers's prophecy, and of the time at which it was to be fulfilled. No one seemed to regard the storm as one of a common character. Many a tongue talked of the prophet and his prophecy, and many a greedy ear devoured up their discourse. There was a general feeling and expression of alarm. Some were drinking at the bar—some were swearing profanely —some were laughing at the fears of those around them, while their own cheeks were blanched; not a few were devoutly praying on their bended knees, and with uplifted hands, and some were crying aloud for mercy. I have a clear and distinct recollection of the whole scene, although I cannot recall my own particular feelings. I do not recollect that any one spoke to me or that I spoke to any one in the room. I presume I was not much alarmed, for so soon as the storm had abated, which was in fifteen or twenty minutes, I went on my way to the committee room. There, in a short time, a quorum of members assembled, and the committee organized; little business however, was transacted. Nearly the whole time they were in session, sheets of liquid fire, heavy thunder and rain, were descending. Never before had I witnessed so awful, vivid, and protracted a storm. I have seen and been awed by many, more terrific, since I have been in the United States.

A few days after the day of the storm, I called on Richard Brothers. He then resided at Pentonville, near London. It was my first visit, and I had no introduction; he received me civilly, and we had much conversation. He assured me, with all solemnity and placidity of manner, that the earthquake had, at his earnest and oft-repeated intercession, been, by the Almighty, postponed, and the destruction of London averted. No person but he and I were in his room, which was large and genteelly furnished. He had an elderly, respectable-looking woman as a servant, and an errand-boy. It was apparent that he was in the enjoyment of not only all the necessaries, but the comforts of life. Whence he derived means, I know not, unless it was from the sale of his prophecies, which had been extensive; they were printed and sold in moderate-sized pamphlets. At that time, I supposed his age to be about forty-five; I was three and twenty. He was not less than six feet high, of large and well-proportioned frame; his face was ashy pale; his features harmonious and pleasing; on one of his cheeks was a large, dark-colored mole; his manners were mild and winning; his tone of voice soft, and his language persuasive and well-chosen. It was on the sandy foundation of this man, and his reception from the public, that Joanna Southcote built up her pretensions to divine inspirations, which I shall notice hereafter. I visited Brothers, occasionally, for some months; he never availed himself of my repeated invitations to call on me; he never inquired as to my motives, objects, or circumstances; he always received me with kindness, conversed freely, and, as I thought, unreservedly. At this distance of time—it is more than half a century since I last saw him—I think of him as a man without a wish to offend or injure; laboring under an hallucination of mind, and incapable of harboring a wish to impose himself upon the world for anything but what he really thought he was. I have sat with him for hours, listening to him with deep interest, regarding him as insane on the one subject, sane on all others, and intelligent on many. He had served in the British Navy, and attained the rank of a lieutenant. He died some years after. I last saw him in a lunatic asylum, where he had been confined by order of the British Government.

I never saw Joanna Southcote, but I was intimately acquainted with a gentleman who frequently visited her. She first went to London in 1803; I finally left it early in 1801. For many years preceding her arrival in London, she had been preaching, publishing, and proclaiming, through various parts of England, notices of her divine mission. In the sixty-fifth year of her age, Dr. Reese, and other medical men, believers in her mission, declared that she was then pregnant, and she, with never-failing confidence, insisted she would soon be the mother of the Messiah. The exact period at which she was to be confined she said had never been revealed to her. Those who believed her to be what she said she was, furnished her money, with which she caused a small, but neat and rather elegant place of worship to be built and fitted up. They provided for her apartments furnished in handsome style. They also purchased for her superb baby linen, a silver cradle, with expensive bedding; a white silk bedquilt, with silver fringe, and all things else deemed suitable for the expected stranger. She thus lived, and was thus accredited and maintained, for several years, the faith of her followers continuing unshaken. The accounts published in England, concurred in stating that many hundreds believed her to be what she represented herself to be, even to the time of her death. She died in London; her death-bed was surrounded by many of her most devoted female followers, who were in hourly expectation, as she herself appears to have been, that a miracle would be wrought. The chill of death, however, came, and, according to a pamphlet then published, she declared that she certainly had been inspired, but whether by the Supreme Being or the Prince of Darkness, she was unable to say. That nothing might be wanting to cap the climax of this superstitious mania, even death did not cut down the hopes of her followers so close, but that they are still said to cherish the expectation that, though dead and buried, Joanna will, in some mysterious way, present to them the Messiah. On the 28th of August, 1847, I copied the following article from a London paper:

"The remains of the celebrated Joanna Southcote are deposited in the very pretty cemetery which is attached to St. John's Wood Chapel, near the Regent's Park."

To return from this digression: On the 29th of June, 1794, a general meeting of the members and friends of the London Corresponding Society, called by posting-bills, hand-bills, &c. &c., was held in St. George's Fields. John Gale Jones was appointed chairman, and John Ashley secretary of the meeting. It is a fact strongly indicative of the times, and the political views of the society, that, when the chairman was proposed, it was, as it is of record in the printed proceedings of the meeting, as "*Citizen* John Gale Jones." The meeting adopted "an address to the nation," an address "to the King's most excellent Majesty," and several resolutions. In one of these, it was "resolved that *Citizen* Earl Stanhope be requested to present the address to the King, George III." In another of the resolutions the meeting expressed its approbation of the public conduct of "*Citizens* Earl Stanhope and R. B. Sheridan." These few words, extracted from the doings of a public meeting, whose proceedings were published, give some notion of the early and continued effects of the Revolution in France on the people of England.

It seems scarcely possible for the people of the present century to form a correct idea of the enthusiastic rejoicings and powerful sympathy of a large portion of the human family on the outbreak of the French Revolution of 1789. In Ireland and Great Britain it was ardent and universal. All ranks and degrees, all classes and descriptions of persons, the high and the low, the rich and the poor, the learned and the ignorant, the old, the young, and the middle-aged, all rejoiced and were exceeding glad. The ministerial, the Whig and the Reform parties, the pulpits and the printing presses, vied with each other in their manifestations of joy. The people and the press emulated each other in their congratulations, and in their praises and glorifications of France, and of the French people. Spirited and expensive scenic representations of the "Destruction of the Bastile," were performed at all the theatres and circuses, to crowded and applauding houses, not only in London, but in all the cities and large towns in Great

Britain and Ireland. In them were introduced, sung, and danced, the popular French airs, *Ca Ira, Carmagnole*, &c., which were rapturously applauded and encored, ay, even by the King and Royal Family, to the very echo. I speak of what I have seen and heard many times. The nations of the earth, in no age of the world, had ever before exhibited such wild, enthusiastic, and general rejoicings. Assuredly, there were no such manifestations of public feeling, even in England, at the time of the Revolution of 1688. The whole civilized world rejoiced that grass would grow where the Bastile stood; and that an enslaved people had arisen, in the majesty of manhood, and had tumbled its frowning towers into its fetid ditches.

These feelings, however, were damped, chilled, I had almost said, trodden under foot, when the constituted authorities of France abolished the keeping of the Sabbath, established a Tenth instead of a Seventh day of rest; paraded to the Champ de Mars through the streets of Paris after a triumphal car, in which was a courtesan representing the Goddess of Liberty, and did all things else in their power to extirpate the Christian religion.

On the 26th of October, 1795, another public meeting of the London Corresponding Society and the friends of its political principles was held near Copenhagen House, about two miles from London. An account of the proceedings of that meeting, and its consequences, is now before me in a large octavo volume, entitled the "History of the Two Acts." London, printed 1796. It is there stated that "About half an hour after 12 o'clock, the people assembled on the ground, according to the concurring calculations of several persons, amounted to more than a hundred and fifty thousand persons, at the same time that the roads, in all directions, were still covered with people thronging to the meeting." There were, on different parts of the ground, at stated distances, wooden platforms, raised and railed, from which the meeting "was addressed by the Chairman, John Gale Jones, John Thelwall, Frs. Place, Wm. Friend, Richard Hodgson, and other able and well-known popular speakers." I can never forget the enthusiasm and the good order which pervaded that immense multitude. No language I can command would convey an adequate idea of my own feelings, when, as Chairman of the meeting, I was about to take their opinions on the several questions by them to be passed upon. Every face, every eye, was directed toward me; every voice cheeringly responded, and all who could make room raised their hands and clapped them heartily together. No one could imagine, unless he had been in a similar situation, my feelings, much less feel, as I then felt. The scene was deeply impressive, and I felt it to my heart's core. John Gale Jones opened the business of the day by informing the meeting that the committee, to whom the Society at large had delegated the trust, recommended " Citizen John Binns, a well-known and long-tried patriot, to be Chairman during the meeting of the day," which proposition " being unanimously approved, citizen John Binns took the Chair." "At the close of the meeting, thanks were voted to the Chairman for his manly, spirited, and judicious conduct throughout the business of the day. He was then conducted to a carriage, from which the horses being unharnessed and led away, he was, to his very great annoyance, and against his oft-repeated protests, by an immense crowd, drawn a distance of about three miles to Covent Garden Hotel, where, from the balcony, he addressed them," and, to continue the language of the " Annual Register" of 1795, " the multitude dispersed in the utmost quietness."

On the 29th of October, three days after the meeting at Copenhagen House, the session of Parliament was opened by George III. in a speech from the throne in the House of Lords. On his way from St. James's Palace to the Parliament House, a distance of less than a mile, in his state carriage, drawn by eight led horses, followed by many other state carriages, guarded by horse and foot, he and the whole cortege were assailed by an immense mass of people with hootings and hissings. Several sticks and stones were flung at the procession, nine of which reached the carriage in which the king sat, and in which two of the large plate glass pannels were broken. One of the leaders of the carriage horses was beaten down by the crowd and trampled to death. The crowd, which, upon the king's return to St. James's Palace from the House of Lords, followed the state coach on its way to the stables and nearly demolished it. The prompt arrival of some of the Horse Guards saved it from utter destruction. One newspaper account, published the next day, stated, that " when the king was in the carriage going from St. James's Palace to Buckingham House, a short distance, not a hundred yards, the mob *again* rushed upon the carriage, and one miscreant, in a green coat, endeavored to open the door of the carriage."

Deeming the facts of this riot important, strongly manifesting the then state of public opinion and public feeling in London, I have been careful to select my account from the most authentic and impartial contemporary publications, and I have severely taxed the truth of my own recollections. It is evident, from the want of preparation and arrangement, the exposed state of the King, the Lord Chancellor, the Prime Minister, and indeed all the Cabinet who were in the procession in carriages, that the Government had not the slightest apprehension that such a multitude of people would assemble, or that, if it did assemble, it would be under the influence of such angry and hostile feelings as were manifested, even to the endangering the life of the king and his ministers. There were at that time, in and near London, thousands of troops, constables, and police officers, of every description, of whom a superabundance could and would have been under arms, attending the procession, if any the most remote apprehension of a riot had been entertained by the constituted authorities. It is reasonably clear that there was no arrangement on either side for attack or for defence. There were on duty only the Guards, horse and foot, and the people acted under the influence of strong feeling. I saw nothing of this outbreak. A suggestion that something of the kind might take place, induced me, under the advice of friends, to remain at home, in the belief that, if the Chairman of the meeting at Copenhagen House should be seen in the crowd, no matter how peaceably he might demean himself, an effort would be made to connect that meeting and the outbreak as cause and effect.

On the evening of the day on which the king had been

thus assailed, at a meeting of a division of the London Corresponding Society, at the sign of the Green Dragon, Cheswick Street, Moorfield, I heard one of the members—I know him well, although his name I cannot now recollect—in the most public manner state, in the presence of fifty or more persons, that when the king was in his carriage, surrounded by the crowd in St. James's Park, the door of the carriage being forced open, he, the narrator, seized the king by the collar of his coat, he having in his alarm slipped down to the bottom of the carriage, and "I was," said the miscreant in the green coat, dragging him out of the carriage, when a troop of the guards galloped up and dispersed the crowd. "I have never had a doubt but this man was the miscreant in the green coat," of whom so much was said in the newspapers of the day, and for whose discovery, arrest, and conviction, a reward of a thousand pounds ($5,000) was offered by the Government. No information was given, and consequently no reward was ever claimed.

If this man had accomplished his object, and dragged the king out of the carriage, he, and many of his cabinet ministers, would, in all human probability, have been trampled to death. Who can conjecture what would have been the consequence, if such a tragic scene had been acted in the then excited state of the public mind, not only in Great Britain, but in all Europe. The unpopularity of the war with the French Republic, the general dissemination of republican principles; the unprecedented high price of bread, breadstuffs, and malt liquors, not only in London, but throughout Great Britain and Ireland? It might have overthrown the Government; caused the establishment of a Republic; led to a peace with France, and affected the condition of all the governments and people in Europe. What mighty events would have followed the trampling to death of George III. and his ministers by an infuriated mob, in the then state of the public mind of Europe, no human being could then, nor can now, reasonably conjecture. That I may not be thought to have overcharged the sayings and doings of the people, or the dangers to which the king and his ministers were exposed, I shall furnish some extracts from the "Annual Register," of 1795.

I prefer to quote from that periodical, because it was distinguished for the accuracy of its reports, its freedom from exaggeration, and the moderation of its language.

"On the occasion of his Majesty going to the House of Lords, to open the Parliament, the Mall, the parade of St. James's Park and Parliament Street, were completely choked up with spectators. They amounted at least to 200,000. The Earl of Chatham, Duke of Gloucester, &c. &c., were hissed, and the Duke of Portland was very much hooted; about twenty minutes afterwards the king left Buckingham House; he was violently hissed and hooted and groaned at, till he arrived opposite the ordnance office, when a small pebble, marble, or bullet, broke one of the windows. The crowd pressed closely round the wheels, and his Majesty, in considerable agitation, signified, by waving his hands to the Horse Guards on each side, his anxiety that the multitude should be kept at a distance. A few minutes after his Majesty had entered the palace, the mob attacked the state coach with stones and did it great injury. After a short time the king went in his private coach from St. James to Buckingham House, but on his way through the Park, the mob surrounded the carriage and prevented it from proceeding, crying out 'Bread! bread!' 'Peace! peace!' The Guards were speedily brought up, and they protected the carriage till his Majesty got safe to Buckingham House. Lord Westmoreland, who rode in the carriage with the king, stated that the glass of the coach had been broken by a ball from an air-gun with a view to assassinate the king. This attack upon the king and his ministers being, by Lord Grenville, communicated to the House of Lords, and by Mr. Secretary Dundas to the House of Commons, witnesses in relation to it were examined at the bar of each House, and a joint committee of conference to ascertain and report the facts, and the cause and character of the outbreak, was appointed. From the report of that committee, it appeared that the cries of 'Down with George,' 'No Pitt,' and 'No war,' were the most frequent and clamorous; the words 'No king' being occasionally heard. The first words uttered by George the Third on entering the House of Peers, show his extreme alarm, and *his* estimate of the dangers from which he had just been rescued; the words were: 'My Lord, I have been shot at.' These words he addressed to the Lord Chancellor."

CHAPTER III.

Declaration of War against France by Great Britain, not favored by William Pitt—Obstinacy of George the Third—Correspondence of the King with Charles James Fox relative to the American War—Condemnation of Kyd Wake—Scene at Covent Garden Theatre—Laws against seditious practices enacted—Action of the London Corresponding Society thereon—I am sent on a mission to Portsmouth; visit the prison at this place—My return to London—My arrest at Birmingham and confinement in "the dungeon"—The riot which occurred here in 1790-91—I visit the public house at which the riot was believed to have been planned—Scene at this house.

In 1791, and for many years after, it was the general opinion that the then Prime Minister, William Pitt, was mainly instrumental in causing war to be declared by Great Britain against France; and that such was his rabid hostility to the Republic, his fear of the spread of its political principles, and of their triumph over monarchy, that he united with Edmund Burke, not only in waging the war, but in the determination that it should be a war of extermination, if not of the people, at least of those professing the principles of republicanism. Subsequent authentic information shows that these widespread and long-entertained opinions, respecting Mr. Pitt, had but little or no foundation in truth. This has been demonstrated by a statesman who was personally intimate, and in the confidence of Mr. Pitt—I mean, Lord Malmesbury. In his "Life and Times," written and published by himself, he informs us, that William Pitt was opposed to the declaration of war, and always prompt to treat for peace, without regard to the form of Government in France, or by whom, or in what manner it was administered. His Lordship not only vouches for the truth of these statements, but fortifies them by showing that Mr. Pitt actually opened negotiations for peace whenever it was thought attainable. The better opinion now is, that it was George the Third, who insisted upon the war with France, and the war against this country which issued in the establishment of Independence, and that he thus insisted and prevailed against the opinions of his then Prime Ministers Lord North, and the Right Honorable William Pitt. Sir N. W. Wraxall, in his "Memoirs of his Own Times," details many interesting facts relative to the American War, particularly as to the debates and management of the House of Commons during that period. Both those English writers incontrovertibly prove that George the Third was an obstinate, self-willed king, one who much more frequently compelled his ministers to adopt *his* opinions and carry out *his* measures, than they succeeded in inducing him to adopt theirs. The truth of this opinion is now matter of historic record and general belief.

I am indebted to Lord John Russell's "Memoirs of the Right Honorable Charles James Fox," for the following extracts. They proclaim, in the strongest and clearest language, the obstinacy with which George the Third persisted in opposing the Independence of the United States. In a letter from Mr. Fox, then Secretary of State, to George the Third, dated July 18, 1783, acquainting him with the difficulty of obtaining a satisfactory treaty with Spain, and asking the opinion of the king on the subject, George the Third sent to Mr. Fox the following letter:—

"WINDSOR, *July* 19, 1783, 40 min. past 7 A. M.

"It is a very untoward circumstance that a definite treaty cannot be concluded without leaving clear ground for fresh disputes; but I do not mean by this reflection to object to the opinion of the Cabinet, that the Spanish treaty should not, on account of the sixth article, be longer delayed. Every difficulty in concluding peace, this country has alone *itself* to blame. *After the extraordinary and never to be forgotten vote of February*, 1782,* and the hurry for negotiation that after ensued, it is no wonder that our enemies, seeing our spirit so fallen, have taken advantage of it."

---

* On the 22d of February, 1782, on motion of General Conway, the British House of Commons adopted a resolution that an address be presented to His Majesty (George the Third) to implore His Majesty to listen to the advice of his faithful Commons, that the war in course might no

On the 6th of August, Mr. Fox writes a letter to the king, to know "whether it would be agreeable to his Majesty to receive a minister from the United States," to which the king sends the following answer:—

"As to the question whether I wish to receive a minister from America, I certainly can *never* express its being agreeable to me; and, indeed, I should think it wisest for both parties to have only *agents*, who can settle any matters of commerce; but so far, I cannot help adding that I shall ever have a *bad* opinion of *any* Englishman who would accept of being an accredited minister for that revolted State, and which certainly for years cannot establish a stable government."

At the sittings, after Hilary Term, 1796, Kyd Wake was convicted of having, on Snow Hill, London, used the seditious expressions: "No George, no war." On the 10th of November, 1796, for this offence, the following sentence was passed upon him: "That he be imprisoned and kept to hard labor in Gloucester jail during the term of five years; that, during the first three months of his imprisonment, that he do stand for one hour, between the hours of eleven and two, in the Pillory, in one of the public streets of Gloucester, on a market day; and that, at the expiration of his imprisonment, he do find security in one thousand pounds for his good behavior for ten years." The man thus sentenced for this offence was a journeyman bookbinder; an industrious, harmless, inoffensive man in all his relations in life, and in his deportment in society. It was not even attempted to be shown, nor was it alleged, that he was or had ever been a member of any political society, or had ever given offence or indicated unkindly feelings in any way, save only in uttering the words, "No George, no war." Yet was this very severe, nay, I should say cruel sentence, not only passed upon Kyd Wake, but carried out to its full extent. There was no pardon, no

longer be persevered in for the impracticable purpose of reducing to obedience by force, and to express their hopes that his Majesty's desire to restore public tranquillity might be founded and made effectual by a happy reconciliation with the revolted colonies. On the 27th of February, 1782, near two o'clock in the morning, an address to the effect of General Conway's motion was carried without a division; present, 449 members; and an address, founded on the motion, was ordered to be presented to the king by the whole House."

For this note, I am indebted to the "Annual Register" for 1782.

mitigation of punishment. Not a provision of the sentence was abated or ameliorated. I state this as a matter which fell pretty much within my own personal knowledge. I was, *on suspicion* of " treasonable practices," confined, under a suspension of the Habeas Corpus Act, in Gloucester jail more than eighteen months during the time Kyd Wake was in the same prison under the above sentence. I made frequent inquiries, and well know how rigidly this poor man was treated. I left him there in January, 1801, when I was liberated, and soon after came to the United States.

The evening after the attack upon George the Third, on his way to the House of Lords, he commanded a play at Covent Garden Theatre, which, as usual when a play is thus commanded, was honored by the presence of the king, queen, and royal family. The crowds on the streets through which the royal carriages passed to the theatre were unusually great. Care, however, had been taken, and more than the customary number of Horse Guards attended the royal family while on their way to, and returning from, the theatre. The theatre itself, and it was immensely large, was crowded in a very short time after the usual doors of admittance had been opened. The pit was nearly half filled with police officers, constables, and special constables, who had been admitted by the stage and other doors before any of the usual entrances to the audience part of the house were opened. Notwithstanding the royal visitors occupied the stage box, and it was known they would be there, yet there were but few ladies in the boxes other than those in attendance. The fear of a riot was prevalent in the upper ranks, and prevented their crowding the boxes as, on such occasions, had been always customary.

The established custom on such nights was, when the royal family entered the boxes, decorated with the king's arms, and curtained, festooned, and prepared for them, that the orchestra should be full of musicians; that the stage curtain, behind which were arranged all the players and chorus singers, should rise, and the audience, in every part of the house, stand up, the men waving their hats, and the ladies their fans and handkerchiefs; the tune of "God save the King" being played by all the musicians, and the words being sung at the top of their voices, not only by the performers, but by nearly every human being in every part of the house. *Such* had been the *customary* reception of the royal family.

It was very different, however, on this occasion. Notwithstanding the trouble and expense incurred by the Government, the police, and the managers, to have the house filled with loyal subjects, officers, and partisans, the result was not what was desired and expected. There was so much hissing and hooting, clamoring and clapping, and all sorts of noises, with whistles, penny trumpets, catcalls, and rattles, that it was hardly possible, with any tolerable certainty, to ascertain whether it was "God save the King" or "Yankee Doodle" which was being played and sung. 'Twas a sad discordant melody. I was one of those who had, through the ordinary entrances, squeezed my way into the pit, where, as well as in the lobbies and galleries, there were numberless quarrels and fights; angry words and hard hits were, from time to time, as occasion and opportunity presented, freely interchanged. The Bow Street officers, police, and constables, and special constables, plied their sticks, staves, and fists nimbly and vigorously, while others in opposition, were not idle nor sparing of hisses, cuffs, and hard knocks. Several persons were dragged out of the pit for hissing and shouting, and otherwise manifesting hatred and ill-will towards the royal family. Those persons, however, had friends and partisans in the pit, who followed them into the lobbies, some of which were rather dimly lighted. There the fights were vigorously renewed; many persons were rescued, and many officers and others were well beaten. Many a head was cut and many a black eye given and received.

On the first of February, 1794, three months after the above affray, similar angry and hostile feelings were again manifested. On that night, the state carriage in which their majesties and their accompaniments were returning from the theatre, it was, as stated in the royal proclamation, attacked, &c., "a stone was flung against it with such force as to break one of the plate glass panels of the coach, and strike her Most Sacred Majesty, the Queen, on the cheek." A reward of a thousand pounds ($5,000) was, on this occasion, also, offered for information as to who threw the stone, but it was offered without success. There was no information obtained. These facts show how intensely the popular feeling was, at that time, directed against the royal family; yet they were, even then, more popular than the leading members of the administration.

Whoever has read the foregoing statements must be satisfied that before the application of the theatrical touchstone to public sentiment, the Horse Guards, the police departments, and constabulary were put in requisition to protect the royal family, and insure the public tranquillity. The extent and violence of the outbreak, when the king went to meet his Parliament, must in some measure have put the authorities upon their guard; yet it is evident that all the official departments underrated the hostility which was felt and subsequently manifested on the public streets and within the walls of the theatre.

On the thirty-first of October, 1795, four days after the meeting near Copenhagen House, a royal proclamation "by and with the advice of the Privy Council," was issued, stating that, immediately before the opening of the present session of Parliament, a great number of persons were collected in the fields in the neighborhood of the metropolis; and divers inflammatory speeches were delivered, &c. &c., and forbidding any such seditious and unlawful assemblies. Two bills were submitted to Parliament by the ministers, one "for the preservation of his Majesty's person and Government, and against treasonable and seditious practices and attempts," and the other "for more effectually preventing seditious meetings and assemblies." These bills, after an unusually-general violent and protracted opposition, passed both houses of Parliament, received the royal assent, and became laws.

Every effort was made by the societies associated to obtain a reform in Parliament, by innumerable public meetings; by the municipal corporations throughout the kingdom; and by the Whig party in and out of Parliament, to modify or prevent the passage of those bills. They were, however, in defiance of all opposition, passed, by large majorities in both houses. Among the provisions in those laws, was one prohibiting any meeting for political purposes of more than fifty persons at one time and place, unless the meeting was called by the sheriffs or other legally constituted authorities. On the passage of these bills into laws, the London Corresponding Society sent circulars to all the societies with which they were in correspondence, and to influential friends in the large towns in England, detailing a plan by which meetings in favor of Parliamentary reform might be held, without subjecting those who assembled to the pains and penalties of the law. Finding that these communications did not produce the effects desired, the society resolved to send delegates to some of the large towns in England, to awaken public spirit, and organize societies for parliamentary reform. I was the first delegate appointed, and Portsmouth the place selected as the town to which I should go. Portsmouth was then, and I believe is now, the principal naval station and dock-yard establishment, and the most strongly fortified town in England. Why it was selected as the first place to send a delegate, I do not recollect ever to have heard. I went, attended to the duties assigned me, visited the dock-yards, naval depots, and some of the largest ships afloat and on the stocks, naval and mercantile. Owing to contrary winds, a large fleet of West India merchant ships, more than two hundred and fifty sail, waiting for convoy, were then assembled in the port. I saw this fleet, under convoy of several ships of the line, frigates, and sloops of war leave the station under a favorable breeze. It was a most imposing and beautiful sight. It was so considered even by the people of Portsmouth, who crowded the piers and wharves to view the departure of the fleet and convoy.

While on this mission I visited Portchester Castle. It was a short distance from Portsmouth, and at that time the principal depot for French prisoners of war. Two of the principal shopkeepers of Portsmouth accompanied me. On application for admission at the castle gate, we were told by the sentinel and officer on guard, that we could not be admitted without an order from the governor. One of the gentlemen who accompanied me said, "Why, that is something new." "Yes," said the officer, "it is in consequence of some delegate from London, who has been sent to Portsmouth to set fire to the dock-yards and liberate the prisoners. You must have an order from the governor before you can be admitted." We went to the governor, and obtained the order without difficulty.

On our entrance, we found the prisoners, some thousands of them, in the large yards of the prison. They were thinly clad; their clothing was in poor condition. It was then the month of March, and the weather was cold. They were confined in large post and rail inclosures. Every prisoner, no matter how he was clad, had on his head a cap of liberty; which was a high red woollen cap, hanging down on one side of the head with a red tassel on the top; on the side of the cap was the French national cockade, colors, red, white, and blue. In the centre of each of these inclosures (there were four of them) was a lofty pole or "tree of liberty," round which the prisoners, hand in hand, in concentric circles, were dancing and singing *Ca Ira, La Carmagnole, the Marseillaise Hymn*, and other popular French patriotic airs.

In the hospital for sick and wounded French prisoners, at Gosport, a fortified town on the west side of Portsmouth, I found a young French lieutenant, lying sick on a cot-bed. In addition to his sufferings from a gunshot wound, he was languishing under a low fever, and was much emaciated. His face was thin, pale, and sickly; yet it was of a peculiarly interesting character. I talked kindly with him; he seemed gratified, and freely unbosomed himself. "When I left my native village, a conscript, the girl I love," said he, "placed this cockade in my cap; for the first time she saluted me, and said: 'Jean, never return, or return victorious.' We embraced and parted. Since my capture, I have always worn this cockade next my heart." As he spoke, a faint smile irradiated his wan and languid countenance, and his eye brightened and dimmed at the scenes brought before him. "Thus," thought I, the French armies are filled, and their enthusiasm, as much as their bravery, conducts them to victory." We have no record of a more devoted national enthusiasm, or a more total overthrow of all enemies, foreign and domestic. There is no such page in human history as that on which are recorded the events of the French Revolution of 1789. It is the brightest, and yet the bloodiest, page in the annals of man; it is, to this hour, the page of deepest interest; it is, even yet, read and talked of, by all the world, and in all its tongues.

After I had been about a week at Portsmouth, I was surprised by a visit from two members of the Executive Committee of the London Corresponding Society. They informed me they had been sent to direct my immediate return, in consequence of information, on which they could depend, that orders had been given to have me impressed and sent on board one of the receiving-ships. On consultation, it was thought best that I should fulfil the engagements I had made for that evening, and depart for London the next day. This was accordingly done.

Soon after my return to London, the society appointed me a delegate to the town of Birmingham, to be accompanied by John Gale Jones, as my colleague. We were very cordially welcomed by the friends of reform in Birmingham, and were in the prosperous discharge of our duties, when, on the evening of the 11th of March, 1796, we were both arrested, at different hotels, and taken to the town-prison called "The Dungeon," on a charge of having delivered seditious and inflammatory lectures. In a few days we were liberated, giving bail to appear at the next Court of Quarter Sessions at Warwick. While in this prison, our rooms were enlivened by the company of very many friends of much respectability, ladies and gentlemen.

I cannot prevail upon myself to leave this dungeon, which was anything but a dungeon to me, without noting that the keeper was civil and obliging; his wife, a kind, motherly, well-behaved, well-dressed woman, and their two daughters, from seventeen to nineteen years of age, pretty, amiable, and educated. My time passed so agreeably that I visited the keeper's family several times after my liberation.

The "Dungeon" was a lock-up house for prisoners arrested in Birmingham, previously to their being bailed out, committed for trial, or sent to Warwick jail. A portion of it was well furnished, and occupied by the keeper and his family. Into their apartments I was conducted.

The wife of the keeper, her daughters, and a female relation were taking tea when I was introduced. I was politely invited to join them, and accepted the invitation. The freedom of the tea-table, in a few minutes, put us perfectly at ease. The young ladies sang and played on a spinet, which was an inferior kind of musical stringed instrument then in use, which has long since been superseded by the harpsichord, and that by the piano-forte. As I could neither play nor sing, I told stories, spouted speeches, and made myself as agreeable as I could. At length a tall, fat old man, with a lantern and a candle lighted in it in one hand, and a formidable bunch of large keys in the other, advanced slowly into the room, and in the most unharmonious tone of voice, and in the most ungracious manner, loudly announced, "It's time to lock up." I was in high spirits, threw myself into an attitude, and in high tragedy-style said to the old man: "Lead me to my straw, 'tis not the first time I have lodged hard to do the state a service." Poor old man! he started and stared as though there was an insurrection in the prison. Finding, however, that I had made my bow to the ladies, and was following him with all due humility, he walked up stairs. After unlocking divers locks and padlocks, and pushing back sundry bars and bolts, we entered a bed-room, furnished somewhat in the Elizabethan style, having a very large, high four-post bedstead, with heavy, dark-colored moreen hangings, two large arm-chairs, covered with the same material, a basin-stand, water jugs, basin, &c. He left with me a lighted candle, which, in about fifteen minutes, he returned and carried away. In the mean time I had carefully examined the closely iron-barred windows and doors, and satisfied myself that, however urgent might be the necessity, from fire or any other cause, to escape would be impossible. These examinations and considerations did not much alarm me, but when alone I shed many and bitter tears in the knowledge of the affliction and feelings of disgrace which my arrest and imprisonment would bring upon my relations. I felt this the more keenly, because I had abundant cause to be assured how very dear I was to them, to the young and to the old, to the male and to the female members. It is, at this time—it has been all my life, and in all situations—a source of joy and gratification that I had cause to believe that I was more generally and tenderly loved than any of the junior members of the family. In a short time, however, in the twenty-third year of my age, I was fast asleep in a prison.

A few years before the time of which I am writing, say 1790–91, there had been very serious Government riots, known as "Church and King Riots," in the town of Birmingham. During their continuance, several places of worship, dwelling-houses, and manufactories, the properties of persons obnoxious to the Government, were burned down and many lives lost. The owners of the property destroyed were all Protestant dissenters. The amount of damages was subsequently assessed on the district, and paid to the persons whose property had been burnt. The persons against whom the rage of the mob had been directed, and to whom no protection was afforded by the town magistrates, or any of the constituted authorities, were denounced as "Jacobins," a term applied to all who were known at that day to approve of the French Revolution, or were suspected of being favorable to a reform in the government of England. Among the most distinguished leaders of that "Church and King" mob, was a Mr. Barber, a master manufacturer, and a clergyman named Spencer. The riot was believed to have been planned at a public house, which, at the time I was in Birmingham, continued to be the favorite resort of the "Church and King" party. There they, daily after dinner, and nightly, after tea, drank their ale and spirituous liquors, and talked over the news of the day. Such was the furious loyalty and entire devotion to "Church and King" of the frequenters of that house, that they had, on many occasions, insulted and abused, cuffed and kicked, several respectable housekeepers because they declined to drink every toast which those loyal toast-makers thought proper to propose. A few weeks before the occurrence took place which I am about to narrate, a Mr. Bissett, a wealthy inhabitant of the town, and an extensive manufacturer of fancy articles, was pushed out of the door and dragged down the outer stone steps of that public house, because he refused to drink as a toast: "Damn all Presbyterians;" those who proposed the toast and inflicted the penalty well knowing that Mr. Bissett himself was a member of that church, the whole of whose members were thus profanely and unceremoniously condemned and sentenced. This public house was on the corner of the street on which was situated the house of my friend Edward Corn, with whom I resided some time before my trial at Warwick. I had a strong desire to visit this head-quarters of royalty, trusting, not so much to the liberality and good-manners of its customers, as to their curiosity, for my escape from insult or ill usage. I mentioned my intention to a few of my Birmingham friends, who took no small trouble to point out the dangers I should encounter, and their conviction that I should, without any chance of redress, be thrown out of doors. If I would not give up my intention, they prayed me to inform them when I would go, that some friends might be there to protect me. This I declared I would not do. "If I go," said I, " I shall go alone, without mentioning the time to any one." Through life I have manifested much self-reliance.

After the lapse of some days, I went after dinner to this tavern. I selected a market day, knowing that on that day there would be some country people present, who, whatever might be their zeal, their loyalty, or their prejudices, would not be so devoted to riot and violence as the town's people, who had a character for consistency to maintain. I went, and found three large rough granite steps on the street to be ascended before you could enter the tavern door, which was on the left hand, and gave entrance to a large room about three times as long as it was wide. This room, when I entered it, was tolerably crowded. In the centre of the entrance-door to that room was a large oval frame in which was a panel of plate glass, on which was displayed in large polished gilt letters the words, "*No Jacobins admitted here.*" I opened this warning door, and it gave me entrance to a room about sixty feet long and twenty feet wide. On each side of this room were arranged, close to the walls, a number of small tables with chairs by their sides, leaving a passage for the waiters in the centre. Most of the tables were covered with pipes, tobacco, and pewter pots with malt liquor, and glasses with wine or spirituous liquor and water. On the right-hand side of the room, within a few yards of the door, was a table and a vacant chair: on this chair I sat down, and told the waiter to bring me a paper of tobacco, a pipe (cigars were *then* unknown in England), and a small glass of ale. A newspaper was lying on the table, which I took up, not so much to read as to give me the appearance of being occupied. On casting my eyes to the upper end of the room, I saw a large unoccupied arm-chair, gilt, fringed, canopied, and decorated in high style—over it, in bright burnished gilt letters, each letter being not less than nine inches long, were the warning words, "*No Jacobins admitted here.*" My heart did not palpitate, nor did I feel any regret for having visited this anti-jacobin association.

The ale was set on my table, my pipe was lighted, my newspaper displayed, and my eyes directed sidelong to the canopied chair, round which there was evidently very soon after my entrance, some commotion. There I saw the celebrated Mr. Barber, of whom I have before made mention. He was apparently in some trepidation; there was much whispering, not only there, but throughout the room, and persons were passing to and fro into and out of a retiring room on the right hand of the great chair. The alarm, however, did not seem to extend far below the chair of state. In a few minutes, Mr. Barber took possession of the post of honor. Soon after, standing up and looking down the room, to see that his myrmidons were in readiness, he said in a loud voice: "Gentlemen, I will give you a toast." Those who were near him roared lustily: "A toast from Mr. Barber—a toast from Mr. Barber!" He then gave, in a stentorian voice, "Church and King;" which toast I drank, taking care to have it observed that I did drink it. So soon as the thunder of applause which followed this toast had been quieted, Mr. Barber rose, and loudly demanded: "Has everybody drunk the toast?" This question being answered in the affirmative, a stillness pervaded the room, there was a quiet crowding together, and a new consultation among those who were near the chair. After a few minutes, those persons cried out: "Another toast from Mr. Barber." All this time I felt no apprehension of ill-usage, yet were all my senses and faculties upon the alert, and I kept, what sailors would call, "a good lookout." Nothing escaped my notice. It was clear to me that I was known to those at the upper end of the room, and known as a delegate from the London Corresponding Society, and that the information was rapidly passing from one to another. All this introductory matter prepared me for the coming scene. Presently, the hammer of Mr. Barber was heard commanding silence, which was promptly obtained. Mr. Barber then said: "Gentlemen, I will give another toast!" Many voices roared out: "Another toast from Mr. Barber." He rose and said: "*Damn all Jacobins.*" This toast was loudly cheered and promptly drunk, with all its blushing honors. The mugs and jugs, goblets and glasses, having quietly re-established themselves in their respective places, and the hearty cheers having subsided, Mr. Barber demanded: "Have you all drunk the toast?" "All, all," said many voices; "except," said some one, "this young man," pointing to me, "he has not drunk it." "Why don't you drink the toast?" I immediately rose, and said, in rather a loud voice, "I don't understand it! I don't know whom you mean by Jacobins." This again called Mr. Barber to his feet, who was pleased to describe "Jacobins" in such hateful terms, that I kept my seat. This caused some excitement at the head of the room, and the words "Turn him out, turn him out," rolled down the room in such loud and angry tones, that I felt called upon to do something to avert, if in my power, the rising storm.

I accordingly stood up, and in a mild and persuasive tone of voice requested to be permitted to state not only my objections to the toast, but why I came to Birmingham, and what were the political principles and objects of the society which it was known I represented. The cry of "Turn him out," came from the leaders near the chair; but the market people and others as loudly cried, "Hear'em, hear'em" (hear him, hear him). I kept standing, and at length curiosity triumphed; the noisy knot at the head of the room were compelled to be quiet, and I obtained a hearing. I had much cause to be gratified. I was heard with attention; my language, manner, tone of voice, and whole deportment were as conciliatory as I could make them. I spoke about twenty minutes; many of my auditors who were near me, when I had concluded, kindly shook me by the hand and wished me well, and I then retired. It would be difficult to estimate the effects produced by this visit, not only upon the people present, and those in the town of Birmingham, but on those in the country whence the jurors to try me for sedition were to be selected. It was not only talked of, but a report of it found its way into the newspapers. By one party it was denounced as a piece of consummate impudence, and by the other represented as a bold and well-conducted sortie into the camp of the enemy, from which I was permitted, in my own good time, to retire unmolested.

CHAPTER IV.

Grand-Jury of the County of Warwick find true bills against Gale Jones and myself—Conviction of the former—Interview with Mr. Rushton—I sail for Dublin, and return to Warwick in time for my trial—Sketch of Mr. Percival—My trial comes on—Acquittal—Anecdotes of Dr. Samuel Parr—Facts touching my arrest and trial—John Allen—Jeremiah Leary—Rev. James Coigley—Arthur O'Connor—My visit to Gravesend, with the object of securing conveyance to France—I fail to attain my object—Danger to which Coigley and O'Connor expose themselves—We are all arrested at Margate, and conveyed to London.

THE grand-jury of the county of Warwick, in which county Birmingham is situated, found a true bill against Gale Jones, and one against me. He was tried and found guilty at Warwick, April 9, 1797. My trial, on account of the absence of some special jurors, was postponed until the next session of the court in August. Having settled what business it was necessary for me to arrange, I determined to visit Ireland, in the knowledge that all the prosecutions which the Government had instituted for sedition, &c., had issued in the conviction of the persons prosecuted. I had no right to calculate upon an acquittal.

While in Liverpool, about to embark for Ireland, I lounged into the bookseller's shop of Mr. Rushton. He was a blind man, aged, I suppose, about sixty years, an ardent friend of liberty, and a poet of some celebrity. He was the author of "Mary le More." We had much conversation on public affairs. I told him I was about to sail in the next packet for Dublin. "I should be glad," said he, "to prevail on you to spend the evening with me, but I am engaged with a few friends who have invited a young man, who is under prosecution for sedition, to take supper with them. He is going to Ireland the first packet which sails." "And his name," said I; "is John Binns," said he. I then introduced myself, and went with the old gentleman to the supper.

At that supper I was prevailed upon to sit for my portrait to Mr. Houghton. I sat, and Mr. Houghton painted the portrait, which his son engraved. After I had been about ten years in the United States, some person brought over and forwarded to me about fifty copies of that engraving. I have one of them now before me, which induces me to state a few particulars in relation to myself before I embarked for the United States. To acquire what knowledge I could of the people and the country to which I was about to embark, I read what travels or other books had then been published relating to the United States. The books were few in number, and did not contain much correct information, as may be inferred from the impression made upon me as to the people and the country. I expected that among the people, even in the large towns, I should occasionally meet one of our red brethren with his squaw leaning lovingly on his arm. I expected that I should find the white men so plain and quakerly in their dress that I had the lace ripped from my neckerchiefs, and the ruffles from my shirts. If I had been better informed I should have saved myself a great deal of trouble, and not found myself at all finer if as fine as the people I came to live among and associate with. At that time, 1801, there were fifteen United States, now there are more than twice that number of States, and we are threatened or promised, I don't know which would be the better word, with as many more States if the people will but put certain persons in high places.

In the half century which I have resided in the United

States, she has purchased many millions of acres of land, and by conquest obtained many more millions of land. All the land thus purchased, and all the land thus acquired by blood and treasure, has been to the South; thus enriching and transferring power to the South at the expense of the North. Is it not time, would it be anything but sheer justice, to turn our eyes to the North? Why not look to the Canadas, with their three millions of white inhabitants? to say nothing of Nova Scotia, &c.

Lest, upon reading the last paragraph, the reader should conclude I was a zealous, active abolitionist, I take the liberty to inform him that, soon after the insurrection of the slaves in South Carolina had been quelled, the then Governor of that State, J. Hamilton, came to my office, and making known who he was, said: " Mr. Binns, on my own behalf, and on that of the people of Charleston, I call to express to you our thanks for the notices you from time to time published in relation to the late insurrection. I feel," said he, "the more bound to do so, inasmuch as your paper was the only newspaper north of Mason and Dixon's line, which ever published a sentence in defence of the conduct of the authorities of the State and City during that alarming period."

But to resume. On my way from Birmingham to Liverpool, after that supper, I passed in a packet-boat over the Duke of Bridgewater's Canal. In the canal is a tunnel, through which the boat is put forward by the boatmen lying on their backs on the deck, and thus pushing the boat forward with their feet against the brick arch which forms the roof of the canal. I am unable to say the length of the canal thus arched and lighted by torches, but from the time we were passing under it, according to my watch; from the time we lost daylight under the arch, until we again came to it, was one hour and forty minutes, in which time I think we travelled three miles.

In a few days I sailed from Liverpool for Dublin, where, with relatives and friends, I spent the time which intervened between that period and the time when my attendance at Warwick was required; at which time I returned to England.

The 15th of August, the same year, my trial at Warwick was called on before Mr. Justice Ashurst and a special jury. The counsel for the prosecution were the Hon. Spencer Percival, assisted by Messrs. Balguy and Clark. For the defence, Mr. (afterwards Sir Samuel) Romilly, Mr. Reader, and Mr. Fletcher.

Mr. Percival, a few years later, was Prime Minister, first Lord of the Treasury, and Chancellor of the Exchequer. He was shot dead, May 11, 1810, in the lobby of the British House of Commons, by a man named Bellingham, who thought himself aggrieved by the official conduct of the Prime Minister. On the following Monday, the dead body of the assassin, who was generally believed to be insane, lay exposed in the dissecting-room. Within seven days he had been examined before the magistrate, committed to Newgate, a true bill had been found against him; he had been tried at the Old Bailey, convicted of murder, sentenced, and executed at 8 o'clock on the Monday morning that next succeeded the murder. A writer of high character inquired: "Was not this a cruel, unrighteous, intemperate haste; an eager thirst for retribution; not slaked, certainly, at the fountain of justice?"

Mr. Percival was one of the most extraordinary, and least prepossessing looking gentlemen I recollect to have seen. There was nothing strikingly intellectual in his countenance or manly in his personal appearance. However, notwithstanding his appearance, Mr. Percival was a gentleman much esteemed and beloved; of unquestionable talents, and an able public speaker. His face, in shape and color, struck me, when I first saw it, as being just such an exhibition as might be expected if a piece of thin, damp, yellowish-colored parchment had been drawn tight over the bony structure of his face and there allowed to dry; the parchment adhering tightly to the bones in every way it could, and in every part. His eyes were large, dark-colored, and deep-set in his head; his mouth was prominent, his teeth large and white.

In the indictment against me, I was charged with having uttered seditious and inflammatory language; with having called upon the people to be ready, not only to take the field, if necessary, but to suffer death on the scaffold, in their struggle to obtain universal suffrage and annual parliaments. The first portion of the language charged, had been used by me; not, however, in reference to obtaining a reform in Parliament, but in reference to a defence of the trial by jury. I therefore determined, on the trial, to admit that the words charged had been spoken, but to prove the subject to which they related, and the order in which they had been delivered. The trial was fixed for August 18, 1797. On that day the jury was sworn at 8 o'clock A. M. The witnesses, on both sides, were ordered out of court, and so remained until called and examined. Mr. Romilly having, in his defence, stated to the jury that he felt confident of my acquittal, from the contradictions of the witnesses for the Crown, and the consequent uncertainty of ascertaining what were the words actually spoken, and the order in which they were spoken. Mr. Romilly then concluded his address and sat down. In a few minutes he again rose and said: "Gentlemen, were I to exercise my own judgment, I should rest my defence here, but my client is not satisfied to obtain a verdict of acquittal on the contradictions of the Crown evidence, but desires—I speak it to his honor—to be acquitted solely on the merits of his cause, the justice of his principles, and the purity of his intentions. He desires me to prove exactly what he has said. I shall, therefore, call all the witnesses. [I am indebted for this extract, and other facts here stated, which, after a lapse of half a century, had escaped my memory, to the report of the trial in "Howell's State Trials," vol. xxii.] At eight o'clock P. M. the jury, under the charge of the court, retired to consider of their verdict. At eleven o'clock they went to the judges' chambers and returned a verdict of "not guilty."

It would be regarded as a display of vanity if I were to set forth the interest taken in this trial, as well by the Government as by the friends of reform. Mr. White, the solicitor of the treasury, came from London to Warwick, nearly 100 miles, attended the whole trial, and, after the jury had retired, he had his horses put to his post-carriage to start for London, express, as soon as the verdict should be rendered, not presuming an acquittal to be within the range of probability.

As a powerful representative of the friends of reform, I select the celebrated Dr. Samuel Parr. He has been dead many years. Some of the most eminent men of the age have written eulogiums on his scholarship, his intellect, his independence of mind, and his virtues. At the time of the trial, I think he was at least fifty years of age. He was a dignitary of the church, and kept a select classical boarding school, in Warwickshire. In height, he was about five feet nine inches, inclining to corpulency. He wore a full suit of black: a black silk bib and apron, a large well-powdered clerical wig, and black silk shovel hat. I can never forget the keen and anxious interest which he publicly manifested, and the inconvenience to which he, uncomplainingly, submitted throughout the whole trial. During the examination of the witnesses, he sat at the council-table. His ivory-headed cane was placed between his knees, upright before him; he held it in his left hand, near the top, and on the top was placed his open right hand. When the testimony, delivering, was in favor of the defence, his face beamed with satisfaction; he pressed the palm of his hand upon the ivory head of his cane, raised his fingers, gently inclined his head toward the jury, and spoke, as plain as outward and visible signs could speak: "*That*, gentlemen of the jury, you may depend upon; that *is* the truth." On the contrary, when the witnesses for the Crown were bearing hard upon the defendant, the Doctor assumed a grave, doubting expression of countenance, and his large white wig would move slowly, from side to side, seeming to say: "That I do not believe—that is not credible." When the judge was about to charge the jury, the high sheriff, a friend of reform, purposely left his seat on the bench, which was forthwith occupied by Dr. Parr, who, after saluting the judge, turned half round toward him, with that sort of expression which was generally interpreted to mean: "If you misrepresent the evidence, or misstate the law, I shall write a pamphlet and review the whole case." When I recollect the importance which, at that time in England, and more especially in the county of Warwick, was attached to everything said and everything done by Dr. Parr—the Dr. Johnson of his age—I cannot entertain a doubt but his deportment influenced the opinions of some of the jury. I am very certain he thought so himself; indeed, he did not scruple to say so. When the eloquent *Joseph Gerald* was in Edinburgh, convicted of sedition, and sentenced to be transported to Botany Bay for fourteen years, the sentence was regarded as one of great severity, and caused much animadversion. Soon after it was passed, it became a subject of conversation in a company in which Dr. Parr and the Hon. Richard B. Sheridan were present. Mr. Gerald and Mr. Sheridan had both been pupils under Dr. Parr. Mr. Sheridan rather flippantly remarked, addressing himself to the Doctor: "Gerald was a fine scholar and a very clever fellow." "Yes, sir," said the Doctor, "he was the cleverest fellow I ever educated." Dr. Parr, like many gentlemen advanced in life, in easy circumstances, and of sedentary habits, was a little peculiar, not to say eccentric in his habits at table. I had the honor to dine in his company at Mr. Toms's, at Warwick, with a large party. Mrs. Toms, so soon as she had taken the head of the table, addressed herself to the Doctor, saying: "Doctor, I think I have before me a shoulder of very fine mutton, cooked exactly to suit your taste; shall I have the pleasure to send you a slice from the blade bone?" "If," said the Doctor, "you will do me the honor to allow one of the servants to bring me the mutton, I will help myself." The dish was soon placed before the Doctor, when he took the carving-knife and cut from the centre of the blade-bone a circular piece of mutton, which, having placed on his plate, he took a gravy-spoon, and with it carefully transferred every drop of gravy from the circular hole he had made on the blade-bone, to his own plate; then, politely bowing to Mrs. Toms, returned the dish.

FACTS TOUCHING MY ARREST AND TRIAL FOR HIGH TREASON, IN 1798.

James Coigley and Arthur O'Connor are so identified with me in regard to the trial at Maidstone, that I shall introduce them at once, and take some notice of the other two persons who were arrested and tried at the same time: John Allen and Jeremiah Leary.

I do not remember ever to have seen ALLEN before I saw

him at Margate, where he was arrested in February, 1798. He was an Irishman, and came from London, in company with Coigley, to obtain a passage to France, to find shelter from the persecutions of the Irish government. His age, at that time, I presume, was about twenty-three years. I have a letter from him dated the twenty-first of February, 1842, which is the latest account I have of him. Immediately after his acquittal and liberation at Maidstone, he found his way to Holland and then to France, where he was appointed a third lieutenant in the French service. He was subsequently distinguished for bravery and good conduct, insomuch that he was promoted to the rank of colonel. My friend, Colonel Lawless, who was an aid to his uncle, the Duke of Feltré, at the battle of Waterloo, told me in 1846, at Philadelphia, that Allen commanded one of the storming parties at Badajoz, and was the first in the breach. When Allen wrote to me in 1842, he was living at Caen, in Normandy, on his half-pay and a pension from the French government. His two sisters, whom he had invited from Ireland, were living with him.

I have a letter from a friend which is too honorable to my old associate, and too characteristic of the government of England, and of the Bourbons, to be withheld. It is dated

"BALTIMORE, August 30, 1841.

"Colonel Allen has suffered much. After the campaign of 1806, the battles of Jena, of Eylau, and Friedland, and those of 1810, his regiment was ordered to Spain. He was severely wounded at Badajoz, afterwards made prisoner, and remained so during the Prussian campaign of 1812, the privations of which were scarcely more severe than those of Spain. He made the campaign of 1813 in Germany, one perhaps not less dreadful in the retreat from Leipsic, than that of 1812. After the return of the Emperor Napoleon from Elba, his defeat at Waterloo, and the restoration of the Bourbons in 1815, he (Allen) was demanded by the British government, who, as you know, never forgives or spares political offenders. Allen was given up by the Bourbons, and marched from Paris to the frontier, but the *gens d'armes*, who conducted him, would not deliver him to the tender mercies of English executioners; the old soldiers of the empire allowed him to escape at their peril, the night before that on which he was to be delivered up to the English brigade stationed at Metz, to receive him."

JEREMIAH LEARY was the body servant of Arthur O'Connor. I can say nothing of him after his acquittal and liberation, which it would gratify me to record; I therefore prefer to be silent. He died in Philadelphia about the year 1806.

The Rev. JAMES COIGLEY I first knew in London, in 1797. He was then on his way to France. I presumed him to be, at that time, nearly thirty-five years of age. I saw him again in London on his return to Ireland. It was understood among his Irish political friends, that his mission to France was political, secret, and important. Although he and I were entirely confidential, I never asked him nor did he ever communicate to me any particulars of his journeyings, his motives, or his objects; by whom he was sent, or with whom he was authorized to communicate in France; yet, he left in my care his most valuable papers. Among them was the passport he had obtained in Paris, in 1797, which was countersigned by the authorities from that city to Dunkirk, whence Coigley came to England, in a smuggled vessel. He had many personal friends in Paris, where he was educated at the Irish College.

Mr. Coigley was nearly six feet high, of a large frame, gray eyes and gray hair. His family, an old Irish Catholic family, had suffered much from the persecutions of the English government, which the family had always met by open and manly opposition. The tone of his voice was mild and of a subdued character. His deportment and demeanor were grave. He was slow of speech, of respectable classical and literary acquirements, and his understanding above mediocrity. His attachment to country, to principles and friends, was firm and steadfast. I never knew him hesitate, as to the performance of what he deemed a duty, although I have known him greatly to err in judgment, as he assuredly did in taking with him and carelessly exposing a treasonable paper, which might, and which did endanger the lives of men who had no knowledge of its existence, but were anxiously endeavoring to get him beyond the reach of that Government by which he was persecuted, and which he had always opposed. It is true the efforts made to have him landed on the continent of Europe, were not altogether personal, they were stimulated by the expectation that in so doing they were serving the cause of Ireland's independence. Under these circumstances it was the duty of Coigley to have acquainted O'Connor and I, that he had with him a paper which, if by any chance discovered, would endanger our lives, so that we might exercise our judgments as to accompanying a man who carried about him so dangerous a document. His usual dress, whenever I saw him, was that of a respectable tradesman; there was no peculiarity in the color, cut, or fashion of his garments, which indicated a profession. Notwithstanding the general sobriety of his manner and sedateness of his deportment, I should not, at any time, have taken him for a clergyman, if the fact had not been made known to me. When he embarked for Whitestable, and was subsequently arrested, at Margate, he wore a military undress, and went by the name of Captain Jones.

From the arrest, trial, and execution of the Rev. James Coigley, even to this time, various opinions touching his guilt have been entertained. But two persons, Arthur O'Connor and I were competent to state the facts which caused his arrest, trial, and execution. Every individual is entitled to justice, and James Coigley is entitled to a full measure of justice, even to pressing down and running over, from Arthur O'Connor and John Binns. When in Maidstone prison, awaiting his trial, he was by courtly ministers of religion—of that religion of which he was himself a minister—tempted and besought, by all the arguments they could urge, strengthened by the promise of life, to turn informer. He spurned the offer, and was executed as a traitor.

I have no doubt Coigley saw Dr. Crossfield, with whom he was intimate, the night before he left London in February, 1798. I have repeatedly heard it asserted that Dr. Crossfield was the author of the paper found in Coigley's greatcoat pocket at Margate. I never heard it either from Coigley or Crossfield, nor did I ever inquire as to the truth of the assertion. My brother, some years after, 1798, told me that he was told by Crossfield, that he wrote that paper and handed it to Coigley the night before he left London on his way to France, and that, after the paper had been written and delivered, they passed the balance of the night together.*

While in London, Coigley manifested no apprehension of being arrested. When there in 1797-8, he went, I believe, every evening to Furnival's Inn Cellar, Holborn, which, at that time, was a very general resort of the most radical Jacobinical politicians in London, and there was generally in attendance, one or more spies of the Government. I was in London from 1794 to February, 1798, when I was arrested. I was an active member and officer of the Society of United Irishmen, and of the London Corresponding Society. I never saw Coigley at any meeting of either of those Societies, nor was there, during that time, any communications between either of those Societies, and the United Irish Societies in Ireland.

I saw the Rev. James Coigley in his room in Maidstone jail, about eight o'clock the same morning on which, between twelve and one o'clock, he had been found guilty of high treason, and sentenced to death. He was then standing close to me in the dock on my right hand, when the verdict was brought in and sentence passed. The other

* That address after the trial at Maidstone, in 1798, was carefully preserved by the officers of the British government. Its agents knew the handwriting of Dr. Crossfield, and a reward of £1,500 ($7,500) was offered by the Government for his apprehension. He was warned of his danger and escaped to France, where he was immediately arrested by the Government as an Englishman, and imprisoned with a number of other Englishmen. While there, he made a confidant of one of his fellow-prisoners, and communicated to him his having written the treasonable paper, which was found in Coigley's greatcoat pocket. This confidence awakened the avarice of the Doctor's confidant, and he burned with the desire to obtain the reward. After an imprisonment of about two years, Dr. Crossfield and his confidential friend and three other Englishmen, escaped to England in a yacht. Crossfield's friend, on their arrival, ascertained who was the nearest justice of the peace, gave information, and had the Doctor arrested. He was carried to London, and, as the author of the address found on Coigley, arraigned for high treason. At the trial, on the cross-examination of the informer, he was asked if he had ever seen a witch, to which he answered that he had many times, and, more than once, he had had glorious sport in hunting them. This staggered all belief in his evidence, and the other three men who came in the yacht, being called as evidence, swore that Dr. Crossfield had been indefatigable in his attention to the sick and maimed of the English prisoners. The consequence of these things was, the acquittal of Crossfield. He had many years before been acquitted of the charge of high treason, for what Mr. Sheridan called the "Popgun Plot."

prisoners, including myself, were acquitted, but on account of a riot in the court, we were recommitted to prison. Allen, Leary, and myself, were liberated next morning. O'Connor remained in custody, and was, on a charge of high treason, sent to Ireland. On my way to the front door of the Maidstone prison, accompanied by the jailer, the passage from the room in which I had been confined to the outer door of the prison, took me past the room in which Coigley was confined. All the rooms in that prison that I ever saw were small. The door of Coigley's room, as we were passing was open, and there were three or four men in it, occupied about his person. They were changing his dress and putting heavier irons on him. No objection being made, I entered the room, and found Coigley, in manner, tone of voice, and general deportment, the same I had ever found him. His language was full of hope as to the establishment of Ireland's independence, a cause for which he said he was about to suffer death. He desired friendly and affectionate greetings to his friends, more especially to my brother. He pressed my hand between both his hands—my eyes were full of tears; he prayed to God to bless me; I came out of the room and never saw him more. He was executed a few days after. I presume it is unnecessary to say he died as became a man conscious that he suffered in the cause of his country's Freedom and Independence.*

ARTHUR O'CONNOR was introduced to me by Sir Francis Burdett, at his house in Piccadilly, London, early in February, 1798. I saw him there in his private rooms frequently. He had arrived from Dublin the same day on which I first saw him. At that time he was the ostensible editor of the "Dublin Press." Engaged as we were in a

* In Twiss's "Life of Lord Eldon," in a note, I find the following anecdote: "Soon after the execution of the Rev. James Coigley, Sir James Mackintosh observed to Dr. Samuel Parr, 'There was never a worse man than Coigley.' The doctor retorted: 'You are wrong, Jammy, you are wrong; he *was* an Irishman; he *might* have been a Scotchman; he *was* a priest; he *might* have been a *Lawyer;* he was a *Traitor;* he might have been an *Apostate.*" When it is remembered that Sir James *was* a Scotchman, a Lawyer, and an Apostate, it will hardly be denied that the Doctor sharply rebuked his uncalled for illiberality.

common cause, and for a common country, we at our first interview became entirely confidential. He mentioned his anxiety to get to France to see Napoleon Bonaparte and General Hoche, who, it was understood, was to command the army which was expected to invade Ireland, the movements of which O'Connor expected to hasten, and in some measure direct. The difficulties thrown in the way of getting to France, by the existing war between that country and England, and the prohibition, by law, of all intercourse without a Government license, between the people of the two countries, made the obtaining a passage from England to France a very difficult matter. The idea of applying to Government for a license was never entertained. We agreed that I should undertake to procure O'Connor a passage to France, or some port on the continent. I had no acquaintance with any one in Kent County, much less had I any with smugglers or persons of their character. All that I had ever heard or read of them, was calculated to impress me with the belief that they were a desperate, lawless, wicked race of men. My undertaking to find, to negotiate, and to bargain with such men, inexperienced as I was, is a proof of the readiness with which I embarked in any measure, however dangerous, which promised to assist in emancipating Ireland from the thraldom and oppression of England. For this purpose I left London, and went to the several towns in the County of Kent which were opposite to the coast of France.

At that time Arthur O'Connor must have been thirty-five years of age, about five feet nine inches high, stout built, dark eyes and eyebrows, black hair and whiskers. His features were handsome, expressive, and manly; his manners fascinating, and his information, especially upon Irish affairs, extensive. His conversational powers were of the first order; his family respectable and influential, and for the most part supporters of the English government. He had himself been high sheriff of the County of Cork, about 1791, and in 1797 was a member of the Irish House of Commons. He was an eloquent public speaker, and his society courted by the most talented public men of the Democratic and Whig parties in Ireland

and Great Britain. It is in my knowledge, indeed it is a matter of notoriety, that he made great pecuniary sacrifices, and declined high public stations from devotion to Ireland and her interests. Had he been as willing to barter the independence of his country, as was my Lord Castlereagh, he was quite as likely to have become Prime Minister of the United Kingdom.

I know, from the lips of Arthur O'Connor, that the following extract from Madden's "Revelations of Ireland," is substantially true:—

"When General Arthur Condorcet O'Connor, nephew to Lord Longueville, joined the extreme popular party in Ireland, he was offered by his noble relative the reversion of his estates and title, *provided*, he would abandon his democratic principles, and support the government of England. Arthur O'Connor refused the offer, and never swerved from the profession of his principles. In the month of November, 1847, the veteran democrat, upright and consistent, presided at a meeting in *France*, for electoral reform. Lord Longueville possessed the power of returning sixteen members to the Irish House of Commons." [His annual income was something less than £20,000 ($100,000).]

[The greater portion of the manuscript of the following pages was written in Maidstone jail, when the facts, which it narrates, were fresh in my memory. Immediately previous to my trial for high treason, this was sent to my friend, Edward Corn, of Birmingham. From that time to the 30th of August, 1817, nearly twenty years, I never saw the manuscript. On that day it was handed to me in Philadelphia by Mr. Henry Cobbett, a son of Wm. Cobbett, who brought it direct from New York city, where he had received it from Mr. William Clark, who had brought it from England, where it was given to him by Mr. Corn, to be given to me.

The additions I have made to it, since 1817, have been such as to elucidate the facts it narrates. At the advanced age at which I am preparing this statement for the press, I have erased some incidents, which, when I wrote them, I thought of moment, but which now appear even to me of little interest, as I doubt not a portion of what is suffered to remain will appear to many of my readers.]

February 21, 1798, I left London in a Gravesend packet. My object was to engage a conveyance to France for Arthur O'Connor, who was going there as the accredited agent of the United Irishmen, to hasten and direct an invasion of Ireland by the government of France.

It may not be irrelevant to remark that at no period of his life was Napoleon Bonaparte known to favor a descent on Ireland. The cause of this disinclination was believed to be because the Executive Directory of the United Irishmen would never agree that Ireland should become a dependency of France. All their negotiations were based upon the principle that Ireland was to be aided and regarded as an ally, and when independent, and recognized in that character, the French government to be paid for whatever aid of men or money it should have furnished.*

Having arrived at Gravesend, a town in Kent, on the River Thames, twenty-two miles from London, I took coach for Rochester, a town seven miles in the interior. There

---

* In 1804, Napoleon affected to be determined on the invasion of Ireland. This affectation was for the purpose of invigorating the arms of the many thousand Irish troops which were then, and had been, in the service of France, at all times, since the outbreak of the Revolution in 1789. A French gentleman, who for several years served as a conscript in the French army, assured me that there was at all times a considerable amount of Irish attached to the armies of France. In 1804, Marshal Augereau was appointed Lieutenant-General of the troops said to be destined for the invasion of Ireland, and was ordered to the coast, whither he repaired to make arrangements. Arthur Condorcet O'Connor was appointed Lieut.-General and ordered to the coast, whither he repaired. Suspecting, however, that Napoleon did not seriously contemplate an invasion, O'Connor, without orders, returned to Paris. For this disobedience he was not brought to trial. O'Connor, however, presuming that he had offended beyond forgiveness, never after presented himself at the levees of the First Consul or Emperor, and refrained from demanding his pay for some months, when he received a communication from the Minister of War that it would be convenient if he would call at the office for his appointments. This he did, and continued to receive his pay to the day of his death. He was, however, never again called into service. General O'Connor was the only superior officer in France who had not been honored with the cross of the Legion of Honor. I doubt not but this slight was put upon General O'Connor in consequence of his having, at Paris, presided at a public meeting at which the desire of the First Consul to become Emperor was canvassed with more freedom than was deemed altogether decorous. The proceedings were published, signed by "Arthur Condorcet O'Connor," as the presiding officer. Subsequent orders state that Marshal Augereau was appointed to command the expedition, and Marshal Marmont, with 25,000 men, to serve under him. I need not add that no invasion was, at any time, countenanced or undertaken by order of Napoleon.

I saw some persons from whom I got information, and slept there that night. Next morning I took a seat in the stage for Canterbury, distant twenty-seven miles. Thence I walked to Whitstable, a small town, distant about five miles from Canterbury, on the coast, much inhabited and frequented by smugglers, who made trips to France and Holland. I saw, and conversed with, several of them; to some of them I had obtained letters. Some had small craft, and others yachts and boats at their command. I talked with several of them, separately, as to furnishing a vessel to make a trip to the continent; sometimes talked of going myself, and sometimes talked of wanting a vessel for others. The price, the dangers, and all probable contingencies were spoken of, but nothing in the nature of a bargain was concluded. They had their suspicions of me, and I wanted confidence in them. I returned to Canterbury on the 24th. I went from that ancient city to Deal, by the stage-coach, thirteen miles. There I found I had no prospect of accomplishing my object. I hired a horse and rode to Margate, seventeen miles, where I found a pilot in whom I placed entire confidence, and with whom I made an agreement, and returned well satisfied to Deal, promising to be at Margate again in less than a week, ready to fulfil the contract we had made. I took the stage at Deal for London, a distance of seventy-two miles. On my arrival in London, about seven o'clock in the morning, I went to the house of Hugh Bell, in Charter House Square, where, to my extreme mortification, and against my express injunctions, in my daily letters to O'Connor, I ascertained that he and Coigley had, that morning at six o'clock, embarked in a hoy for Whitstable—that very town, some of the inhabitants of which I had sounded, and found unworthy of trust. This information filled me with sad forebodings. I immediately jumped into a hack, and ordered the man, with all speed, to drive to Tower stairs, on the Thames, whence the hoy, in which were O'Connor and Coigley, had sailed about fifteen minutes before I arrived. I hired a wherry in the hope of overtaking the hoy, which was yet in sight. I was disappointed. I then got from the wherry on board a Gravesend packet, and there landed. Without delay I proceeded to Canterbury, where

I slept that night. Judge Buller, in his charge to the jury, speaking of the writer, said: "This man was also using great expedition, and taking journeys with great haste; he is proved to have gone from one place to another with as much expedition as a man could well travel."

Early the next morning I left Canterbury, on foot, for Whitstable, to find O'Connor and Coigley, feeling no little alarm at their having gone there. On the road, about five miles from Canterbury, I met O'Connor on his way from Whitstable to Canterbury in search of me. On our way to Canterbury, I expressed my regret at their having arrived at Whitstable, and acquainted him with all I had done since we parted in London. On our arrival in Canterbury, we ordered a post-chaise and posted to Deal, where we slept that night. The next morning we posted to Sandwich, where we discharged the post-chaise and walked a few miles across the country to the town of Margate, where we expected to meet, and did, a few hours after our arrival, meet Coigley, with whom were Allen and Leary, with a cart heavily laden with baggage. Not a syllable was uttered by any of them to induce O'Connor or me to suppose that any obstruction or difficulty had then presented itself, or that any suspicion or alarm had been excited at Whitstable or anywhere on the road, as we subsequently found was the fact. These suspicions and alarms arose from the immense quantity of baggage, mahogany cases, swords, pistols, military accoutrements and equipments of all sorts, which O'Connor had brought with him to Whitstable. Had these statements been made as they ought to have been, we should, necessarily, have talked the matter over, and our conversation, in all probability, would have awakened caution, if it did not excite alarm, which would have caused Coigley to think if not to speak of the dangerous paper he had about him, and thus have induced him to dispose of it in some safe place, if he did not utterly destroy it. I think he must have forgotten it; in no other way can I account for the careless and exposed manner in which he had disposed of it. Coigley, O'Connor, and I supped together and retired to bed early. I then entertained no doubt whatever but they would embark for France the next forenoon, in a first-rate packet which

I had engaged, and which was commanded by a trusty friend; and that I should then joyously return to London. I was sadly mistaken.

In the morning, I was going down stairs from my bedroom, when, on the dark stairway, I was seized by the collar by Fugion, a Bow Street officer. He was attended by a party of dismounted light-horsemen, who had been stationed on the stairs with their swords drawn. Fugion demanded my name, and I demanded his authority. He insisted I should tell my name, which I persisted in refusing. He then conducted me down stairs into a parlor, on a level with the street. In that room, with a large quantity of luggage, were Allen and Leary. Coigley, accompanied by a local magistrate, was soon after brought by some of the military into the room. The officers carefully examined my clothes, took off my neckerchief; in fine, closely searched me from head to foot; taking a ring from my finger, my watch from my fob, and my money. In a word, they took whatever they thought proper, and nothing that they took was ever returned. Mr. O'Connor and Mr. Coigley were now brought into the room in which I was. They were in custody of Rivett, another Bow Street officer, and some dismounted troops. These Bow Street officers had been sent down from London in consequence, as we afterwards ascertained, of information sent from Whitstable, after the arrival there of O'Connor, &c., and their baggage of swords, pistols, chapeaus, military boots, brass-bound mahogany boxes, &c. &c.

In half an hour we were removed, under a military guard, from the King's Head to Benson's Hotel. We were not allowed to interchange a word with each other. Breakfast was provided, soon after which I was handed into a post-chaise with Mr. Coigley and Fugion, who sat between us, and peremptorily forbade all conversation. There were three other post-chaises, and a troop of light-horse under the orders of a justice of the peace. Surrounded and attended, in this manner, all the prisoners and their baggage left Margate. About 4 o'clock, that day, we arrived at Canterbury and drove to the principal hotel, the King's Head. We, the prisoners, and our immediate guard, were ushered into a very large parlor or bar-room. Two soldiers were placed at the door, and other policemen and constables were constantly moving about the room to prevent the prisoners from conversing with strangers or with each other. There was a vast crowd of people in the yard and in the street, more especially at the street windows of the hotel. People of every description, opinions, and feelings, entered the room and crowded about the windows; all, so far as we could ascertain, equally ignorant and inquisitive. Various, confident, and contradictory were their conjectures; the loudest and most general which reached our ears seemed to be that we were French spies taken in the act of drawing plans of the forts, &c. Officers of the British army and navy were occasionally admitted; one of them politely volunteered as an interpreter, presuming we could not speak English. In this room we were kept all night. What with prisoners, and civil and military guards, there could not have been less than thirty persons in the room throughout the night. Through the courtesy of Lord Paget we were furnished with mattresses to sleep on. "There are plenty of beds in the hotel," said the waiter, "but the justice will not order them." The justice declined to visit us, although we repeatedly requested that honor.

On Wednesday, March 1, at six o'clock in the morning, our post-chaises and escort being ready, we left Canterbury in the same order, and with pretty much the same attendants, civil and military, which we had when we made our entrance. The rear of the procession was brought up by a post-chaise and four filled with witnesses picked up at Margate, on the road, and at Canterbury. Some of them, smugglers, made such a display of loyalty by abusing the prisoners that they were ordered out of the room in which we were. There was nothing remarkable on the road except the multitude of people which were, at every favorable position, gathered together to see the procession. The government express, which was sent forward to announce our arrest and provide carriages and a guard, by making known our approach, gave the people time to assemble, which they did in great numbers. We reached London about half-past three o'clock P. M. As we passed through the Strand we met a procession of carriages in which were a number of Welsh gentlemen going to the Crown and Anchor Tavern to dine, it being St. David's day. The people who had assembled to see them followed us, and by the time we got to the police office, in Bow Street, our attendants were very numerous.

As the carriages passed through the streets, I sat as forward as I could, in the hope of seeing, as I fortunately did, a friend, who would have sense and courage enough to go to my lodgings, make known my arrest, and take charge of my papers, &c. To this foresight I was, in some measure, indebted for my acquittal. Most of the things, then at my lodgings, were subsequently seized and taken before the Privy Council; but the time which had elapsed before they were seized, the place where they were seized, and the personal friendship of the person in whose care they were found, made it impossible for the government, notwithstanding all their care and trouble, to prove that the things so removed, or any of them, belonged to me. I was well content to lose them all; none of them were ever returned to me.

CHAPTER V.

O'Connor, Coigley, and myself are conducted to Bow Street Police Office—We are ordered to be searched—My examination before Justice Ford and Justice Addington—Committed to Clerkwell Prison for further hearing—Character of my jailers—My lack of accommodations—Disadvantages under which a poor criminal labors—Reflections on criminal law in Pennsylvania—I am discharged, and rearrested on a charge of high treason—I am examined by the Privy Council, but nothing of consequence elicited—Re-examined by the Privy Council—I am sent to the Tower, where I meet O'Connor—Surveillance to which I was there subjected—Character of the place—Receive a visit from General Vernon and Colonel Smith, and from the king's messengers.

WHEN we arrived at the police office, Bow Street, Coigley, O'Connor, and myself were hurried into a large back room in which the police business was usually transacted, but which, at the time of our arrival, was only occupied by a few constables and runners. The magistrates were sitting in a front room up stairs. When we had waited about half an hour, Mr. Justice Addington and Fugion, one of the officers by whom we had been arrested came into the room where we were, in search, as they said, of the silk handkerchief in which, at Margate, the attorney had tied up the papers found on or with the prisoners. This bundle, by some mismanagement, was now said to be lost or mislaid. Justice Addington rudely ordered us to be searched for the handkerchief, the recovery of which he had so much at heart; although at that time they did not, to our knowledge, know its contents. So soon as we three prisoners were left alone, Coigley, in a tone and with a look of the deepest concern, informed O'Connor and myself that in his greatcoat pocket, which had been taken by the officers at Margate, there was a treasonable address to the Executive Directory of France. It was too late to remonstrate, and useless to complain or reproach. The deed was done; our lives jeopardized, and the evidence was in possession of those who would neither be slow nor unwilling to use it.

In the short time we were thus together, it was agreed, upon a suggestion of mine, that it was the part of prudence to decline to answer any questions which should be put to us by any of the officers of the Government, but more especially to be silent and decline to answer all questions which should be put by the Privy Council or any of its members. After some time, I was desired to walk up stairs. I did so, accompanied by an officer. In the room into which I was conducted, I found Mr. King, the Under Secretary of State, Mr. Justice Addington, and Mr. Justice Ford.

Ford.—"Pray, be seated." I complied.

Ford.—"You must be fatigued; will you take a little wine and water?" Having tasted nothing since ten o'clock at Rochester, I very willingly accepted the offer.

Addington.—"I know you very well; your name is Binns. I remember you last summer."

Binns.—"You are mistaken, sir, you do not know me; nor do I know that you ever saw me before to-day. My name is John Binns." The last sentence I addressed to Mr. Justice Ford.

Ford.—"I think it my duty to inform you of what I

doubt not you are already aware, that you may answer, or decline to answer, any question you think proper."

Binns.—"I am aware, sir, that no prisoner is bound to answer unless he thinks proper."

Ford.—"Then, I presume, you decline answering?"

Binns.—"It is an unfortunate situation in which a person accused of crime is placed on an examination of this nature. Whatever he might state in his own favor, however true, would probably be considered the effect of ingenuity or the offspring of falsehood; but should an accusatory expression, or an ill-chosen phrase, fall from his lips, it would be set down as the truth, which had unguardedly escaped when his intention was to have confined it."

Ford.—"I shall not press you further. Your name is John Binns?"

Binns.—"It is. I beg, before I leave the room, to state that no part of the baggage seized is mine."

Ford.—"We do not believe it is. At present, Mr. Binns, you stand charged with an attempt to leave the kingdom without the necessary passports."

Conscious as I was that I had no such intention, I declined saying anything on the subject, lest I might injuriously affect those who were arrested with me. I bowed, was conducted down stairs, and given in charge of two officers, with orders to prevent any conversation between the prisoners. After the other prisoners had been examined, I requested to see Mr. Ford. I was shown into his room, and asked permission to write to Council to attend my examination, which, I was told, would take place at Bow Street, at 12 o'clock the next day. The request was granted, and I wrote a note to Counsellor Vaughan. About half-past six o'clock, it being then dark, I was handed into a carriage with three officers, and committed for a further hearing to Clerkenwell prison, where Mr. Ford told me I should have every accommodation. I did not then know what was done with the other prisoners. I subsequently ascertained they were sent to other prisons.

As soon as I entered Clerkenwell jail, the turnkey measured me from head to foot, and from front to rear, with a most inquisitorial eye. Ill-nature and angry passions were strongly impressed upon his forbidding carbuncled countenance. He was tall and unhealthily fat. His legs and whole body seemed bloated by disease, the effects of intemperance and dissipation. His age was about sixty. He stooped with the weight of many large keys and a lantern at his girdle, and other keys in his hands. The Bow Street officers delivered to him their commitment, and left me in the prison in this man's care and custody, to be dealt with according to his tender mercies. With becoming humility, and a proper sense of my own situation, I requested to have something to eat. "I have got nothing for you to eat," said he; "had no orders; you must now pay me two shillings, or go into the yard among the common felons." These words were uttered in the most unfeeling and harsh tone, and I angrily said: "I will do neither." The fellow seemed provoked, but soon after directed me to be taken into a room in which there was a fire. The only hangings on the walls of that room were irons of every size and description for pinioning the arms and legs of prisoners, and chains to which heavy logs of wood were fastened. Patiently as I could, I sat down to wait the arrival of the deputy jailer, who, I was told, was soon expected, and was superior in authority to the turnkey. In the mean time, I looked at the prisoners by whom I was surrounded. One of them was a youth about twenty years of age; I was five-and-twenty. He attracted my especial notice; he seemed indifferent to everything but playing mischievous and vicious tricks, and telling loose tales. He had a wonderful flow of spirits; his youth, volubility, and gayety of manner arrested general attention. At eight o'clock the prisoners were all, except myself, taken to other places to be locked up for the night. A few minutes after their departure, the deputy-keeper announced his approach by an authoritative rap on the outer prison gate. His appearance was not prepossessing; he talked some time with the turnkey, and as he entered the room, the door of which was open, he eyed me with that kind of suspicion with which, Sterne says, "every man looks at another with whom he is going to make a bargain." He examined my commitment, then whispered with the turnkey; then re-examined me, and then the commitment, preserving a profound and dignified silence.

I have mentioned that on my arrest, my watch and everything of value were taken by the Bow Street officers, and never returned. I had accepted a loan of five guineas while at Bow Street. "Sir," said I, addressing the deputy-keeper, "Mr. Justice Ford informed me that, when I came here, I should be furnished with a bed and something to eat!" "There is no mention of any such thing in the commitment," said he, keeping his eye, Shylock-like, fixed on the commitment, without deigning to honor me with even a look. "Probably not," said I; "but he said so, notwithstanding. I did not go to bed at all last night, nor have I eaten a morsel since I left Rochester. I will pay whatever may be demanded." He was deaf to my requests and entreaties; kindly feelings had long before departed from him. He then ordered me to be locked up. I was forthwith walked through a small portion of the prison yard, to a high flight of irregular loose stone steps, which, with the aid of a lantern, my guide and I ascended; we then walked along a dreary passage—an iron door was unlocked and opened, and I was told to walk in. I did so, and being given a small piece of lighted candle, the doors were then locked, bolted, and barred.

The dreary apartment in which I now found myself was about thirty feet long, eight feet wide, and fourteen feet high. There were two windows in it; one was to admit light from the yard, the other was in the side wall; it was merely an iron window frame, without any glass. They were both nearer to the roof than the floor. That one which was in the side wall separated the room in which I was from a room in which I soon ascertained, from their conversation, there were a number of untried prisoners.—The lower part of the iron frame was at least eight feet from the floor. In the room were three large iron bedsteads, on each of which were what were called a bed and bedclothes. The bedsteads had no posts, and were all turned up against the side wall. This was all the furniture, and I was now the only person in that miserable, dirty, cold room. I turned down one of the bedsteads, threw myself on the dirty bed, and crept, for warmth, between the still dirtier bedclothes, without, in any way, undressing. The straw bed and the bedclothes were, indeed, most uninviting; they were neither soft nor clean; it was the most filthy sleeping establishment on which, by any chance, at any time, I ever lay. I loathed it, but what could I do? I had no choice; I was hungry and sleepy; I must either sit up or lie down on one or other of those bundles of dirty clothes; I made my election, and down I lay.

Overcome as I was, by fatigue, hunger, and thirst, I soon sank into a deep sleep, from which I awoke about daylight on the morning of Friday, March 2. The only comfort I had was in ascertaining that I was still alone; companions, conformable to the beds, would have been detestable. Notwithstanding the filth and wretchedness by which I was surrounded, and the want of food and drink, I awoke refreshed by "nature's sweet restorer, balmy sleep." The sounds which first assailed my ears were from the adjoining room, which I ascertained was a lockup for prisoners who were to be taken before police magistrates, in the morning. The prisoners were cursing, swearing, blaspheming, and giving accounts of crimes of almost every kind, of cheating, and robbing, which they eagerly, and in loud voices, claimed to have committed; claiming, I doubt not, to be more vicious, and greater knaves, than, in truth, they were, hoping thus to win the confidence and regard of their fellow-prisoners. It was evident, from the order in which they proceeded, that they had a mock tribunal, representing that before which they expected to be examined, and before it they exercised all their ingenuity and villany, in devising defences against the charges which they presumed would be brought against them. Among the loudest, and most boastful of the voices, I could clearly distinguish that of the young man, who, on the preceding evening, had attracted my attention; he distinguished himself by recounting the villany of his exploits, and the ingenuity of his defences, deceptions, and escapes. What is the usual treatment of a person accused of crime, but who is, according to the maxim of the law, to be presumed to be innocent, until proved, and, according to law, found guilty? He is brought before a magistrate, and charged, on oath, with having stolen a loaf of bread, or a garment to shield him or his child from the inclemency of the weather. All the magistrate has to require, is probable proof; he has that in the oath of the complainant; and the person charged, being unable to give bail, is sent to prison. While there, a bill of indictment is sent to the grand-jury, before whom the complainant again appears, and, on oath, makes the same statement he had made before the magistrate. As the grand-jury require only probable cause, they find a true bill. After some time, the prisoner is brought before the court, to be tried for the larceny he is charged with having committed. In the mean time, what has the law, or society, done in order to have justice done to this poor, imprisoned man, whom the law, the judges, and jurors are bound to believe innocent until he is, what he has not yet been, *proved* to be guilty. Have they provided him with what he is unable to procure? No, sir! but they have provided an attorney-general, and all other things necessary to insure his condemnation. Let our legislators ponder upon these truths, and devise some means, which, while it protects the wealthy, shall also make some provision for the defence of the poor, who, although accused, may be, and is presumed to be, innocent.

Jails are now greatly improved in their construction, and the treatment of the persons confined is more accordant with the principles of justice than they were. The voice of humanity is found to be more persuasive and imperative than it has heretofore been. It is of much moment that it should be so, and that *all* those, who are known and called officers of justice, should be especially careful to be honest in all their dealings with those who are charged with crime. For example, it is the law, in some cases, in Pennsylvania, that prisoners committed to prison, should be regularly furnished with a certain quantity of a certain kind of food, of which, and an account of their earnings in prison, is ordered to be kept. At the expiration of the time, for which the prisoner was sentenced to be confined, a balance is, by law, to be struck, and all that the prisoner shall have earned, over and above what had been furnished to him, at the expense of the prison, shall, on his discharge, be paid to the prisoner. I have never yet heard of the payment of any such surplus being made to any prisoner; but I have often heard, and sometimes seen, work of the most ingenious and expensive kind, executed by prisoners, in possession of inspectors, for which they never paid a cent. Other articles, such as clothing, shoes, &c., manufactured and made by the prisoners, out of stuff found by the public, have, in like manner, been appropriated to the use of inspectors, for which they never paid. I would ask, is this the way to effect a reformation of the prisoners, or is it the way to teach them new modes of cheating those, who, under pretence of law and authority, scruple not to cheat those committed to their care for reformation?

But recently, it was stated in the public papers, in such a way as to command belief, that prisoners have been brought before our courts on a charge of having attempted to break out of prison, and others on charges of having actually broken out of prison, and been rearrested. For these attempts to escape, and for having escaped, the offenders have been recommitted, and sentenced for longer terms of imprisonment than those for which they had been originally sentenced and committed. May I be allowed to question the justice of such sentences? May I go a step further, and question the *right* to pass such a sentence? The protection of persons and property require the imprisonment of certain convicted offenders. Does not justice, also, require that when persons are so sentenced, the laws shall provide prisons of sufficient strength, and keepers of sufficient honesty and vigilance, to prevent escapes?

May I presume, with all respect, to ask the consideration of our legislators to these subjects. They are worthy of it, and the consideration of them could not but be attended with benefit to society. If the authorities, legislative, executive, and judicial, do consider, the result, I doubt not, will be creditable to the State which has already had the honor of having led the way in some of the most useful and humane improvements in criminal law. That our prisons demand legislative influences, is daily made more manifest and imperative. Since the above was written, a detailed account has been published, setting forth that one of the officers of Moyamensing prison has defrauded it of more than five thousand dollars. If there are such knaves among us let them be exposed, and the penalty of the law inflicted on them.

At eight o'clock in the morning, the turnkey unlocked, unbolted, unchained, and unbarred the door of my filthy apartment. I followed him, "nothing loath," down the rough and unsteady stone steps, and soon found myself in the room in which I had, for some time, sat on the preceding evening. There were several persons in it, men, women, and children, waiting to be taken before police magistrates. I sat down, and, with no little curiosity, observed the conduct, and listened to the strange language, of those around me.

After some time, perhaps an hour, the keeper, not the deputy, entered the gate of the prison. He impressed me more favorably than any one I had yet seen in that receptacle for the accused. He soon came to me. In as few words as I could, I made him acquainted with my situation, and the treatment I had received. He heard me patiently; he said nothing, but left the room. In about a quarter of an hour a turnkey came and begged to know "what I would be pleased to wish to have to eat."

Binns.—"By whose orders do you inquire?"

Turnkey.—"By my master's, sir."

He went away, and in a few minutes a table-cloth was spread, and a beefsteak, tea, and bread and butter, were set before me. It was now near noon, and I was really so faint, discontented, and out of temper from my treatment, that I did not eat much; the little I did eat refreshed me. Just as I had finished, a carriage, in which were three Bow Street officers, drew up inside the outward gate of the prison. They produced a discharge for me, and they and I stepped into the carriage, and were soon driven round the New Clerkenwell prison, then universally known in London by the name of the Bastile. It was so called on the floor of the House of Commons by Mr. Sheridan. We had not ridden much further when we were stopped by a Government express, who ordered the driver to drive back to the prison from which he had just driven us. The gate being opened, the carriage drove in, and I was reconducted to the room which I had not long before left. As I knew not how long I should be kept, I obtained writing materials, and wrote to Mr. Justice Ford, informing him I had been kept twenty-six hours without refreshment, and requesting he would give orders to prevent such treatment in future. The keeper saw the officer go out of the jail with a letter in his hand, and returned into the prison to know to whom it had been sent. Having ascertained that it was written by me, and addressed to Mr. Justice Ford, he took a key from the turnkey, came into the room in which I was sitting, and requested me to walk up stairs, "where," said he, "you can be better accommodated." I bowed, and followed him. He imagined, and I told him, the contents of the letter I had written. He apologized for the conduct of his deputy and turnkey, and assured me he had no knowledge of my arrival until just before my wants had been supplied. "Will you," said he, "have a fire made in this room? shall I order coffee? perhaps you would prefer wine," &c. I declined all further accommodation, saying that I did not expect to remain long under his care. On my return to the yard, I heard the keeper, in no gentle phrase, reprimanding his deputy and turnkey.

At one o'clock the same day, a carriage, with two Bow Street officers, drove into the prison yard. They were accompanied by a tall, genteel-looking, elderly man. His name, I afterwards ascertained, was Mason. I knew, from the silver grayhound suspended at his breast, that he was a king's messenger. He drew from his pocket a slip of paper, which he courteously handed me to read. It was a warrant to arrest the body of John Binns, with all his papers, &c., "upon a charge of high treason;" signed "Portland;" his Grace, the Duke of Portland, being, at that time, Secretary of State for the Home Department.

It will be remembered that, when at Bow Street, the charge was for an attempt to leave the kingdom without a passport. I instantly concluded that, since that time, the papers found, when the prisoners were arrested at Margate, had been carefully examined, and that among them was found the "Address to the Executive Directory of France," upon which was laid the foundation, broad and deep, for the charge of high treason.

Soon after two o'clock, I went in the carriage with Mr.

Mason and the Bow Street officers. We went up stairs into a large room, in a large marble building, to the south of the Horse Guards, near the office of the Prime Minister. After waiting about three hours, I was required to go before the Privy Council, which was sitting in the same building, in another room. I was shown into an apartment where there were from fifteen to twenty Privy Councillors, seated at the Council Board, which was a long table covered with green cloth, on which were writing materials, papers, maps, charts, and books, of various kinds and sizes. In the room, some near and others more distant, from the table, were messengers and other officers. The room was perfectly quiet; whoever spoke, spoke in a low voice. As I came forward, accompanied by the messenger, he announced my name; instantly every eye was turned upon me. I bowed respectfully, and slowly advanced to the table round which were seated the principal members of the administration of the British government. I felt, momentarily, somewhat awed by their presence, and from their looks and attention being rather inquisitorially and unkindly directed toward me. Soon, however, I felt disembarrassed, at least sufficiently so to have the command of all my faculties. Among those most attentive to all that was said and done, were the Duke of Portland, the Lord Chancellor, Mr. Pitt, Mr. Dundas, and the Attorney-General, Sir John Scott. More than one clerk was, apparently, employed in writing down everything which was said, and noting everything which was done. The Lord Chancellor was Lord Loughborough (Wedderburne) proverbial for his devotion to the Court, and his rudeness to his opponents. Lord Brougham, in his "Statesmen of George III.," says that that monarch, on the resignation of the seals, by Lord Loughborough, said: "He has not left a greater rogue behind him." Such was the reward of his obsequiousness. He turned to me, and, in rather an authoritative and overawing tone, said: "You are brought here, Mr. Binns, on charges which may affect your life; you may refuse to answer, if the answer will criminate yourself."

Binns.—"Pray, my Lord, what are those charges?"
Lord Chancellor.—"You are charged with the crime

of high treason. You may answer what questions you please."

Binns.—"My Lord, high treason is so general and indefinite a charge, that I am as much as ever at a loss."

Lord Chancellor.—"We cannot help that. Did you ever go by the name of Williams?" I remained silent.

Duke of Portland.—"You have not attended to the question his Lordship has asked you."

Binns.—"I have, sir; and I have been considering whether I should answer or remain silent."

Lord Chancellor.—"Well, sir!"

Binns.—"I have determined to remain silent."

Lord Chancellor.—"Were you at Whitstable on the 23d of February?"

This is always the course pursued by those Right Honorable gentlemen. They endeavor to entrap the examinant into giving answers before he is aware of their artifice, and upon the answers thus obtained they put other questions and obtain other answers, and a clue to which may lead to useful information, often at the expense of the witness who is the means of their obtaining it.

Binns.—"I have already informed your Lordship that I will answer no question until I am acquainted with the nature of the charge brought against me."

Lord Chancellor.—"An innocent man has nothing to fear from answering."

Binns.—"I am not so sure of that, my Lord; and as I am ignorant what may be deemed high treason, I do not know how far I may commit myself by an indiscreet answer."

Lord Chancellor.—"Pray, were you at Canterbury on the 23d of February?"

Binns.—"My Lord, you give yourself unnecessary trouble in asking me questions, unless you give me leave to judge of their relation to the crime which I am charged with having committed."

Mr. Pitt, the Earl of Liverpool, and other members of the Council, politely and mildly advised me to answer, as, they said, it would be better for me. I heard them with becoming respect, but declined following their advice. A king's messenger was called; I was delivered into his custody, and conducted into another room. In a little more than an hour I was again taken before the Council; but, persisting in the same course of conduct, I was again given in charge to the same king's messenger.

Duke of Portland.—"Messenger, take Mr. Binns to your house; keep him safe and close till you have further orders; let him have whatever he may wish consistent with his safety."

The messenger and I walked across St. James's Park, followed, at some distance, by two Bow Street runners. The messenger's house was not more than three hundred yards from where the Privy Council sat. The house was small and neatly furnished. I was introduced to an agreeable young lady, Miss Mason, and allowed to go up or down stairs, and from one room to another, as was most agreeable to myself. Every attention was paid to my wants and wishes. I ate and drank at the same table with the messenger and his daughter. If a stranger had come into the house he would have thought me one of the family, or a friend on a visit. Not a word was said in my hearing in relation to my arrest, from the time I entered the house until I finally left it. The idea of my being a prisoner would never have entered the mind of any one who had come to visit the family.

Hearing the sound of the newsboys' horns, "with a full and particular account of the arrest of the traitors, &c." I requested to have a copy of the paper, which was purchased and handed to me. I found in it a long and garbled account of our arrest and alleged treasonable conduct. It was a strange mixture of truth and falsehood. I was, however, gratified by its perusal, in the expectation that what I there read would be of some advantage when I should next be taken before the Privy Council. I retired early to bed; my room was handsomely furnished; my bed and bedclothes sweet and clean, and I slept soundly.

When I awoke in the morning, I was surprised to find that the wearing apparel I had taken off and laid on a chair-back near my bed had been taken away while I slept. I rang the bell, and they were forthwith returned. I made no inquiries why they had been taken, and nothing was said to me on the subject. Why they had been taken

I promptly discovered on their return. The collar and cuffs of my coat, the soles of my boots, and the padding of my neckerchief had all been ripped open, examined, and sewed up. Papers of value, perhaps treasonable, were presumed to be hidden and expected to be found; therefore Mr. Mason had been directed to do as he had done. No such papers were found. I had no such papers.

We breakfasted about nine o'clock, and at twelve the messenger and I walked to the office of the Secretary of State. This day I was not honored by the Privy Council with an audience. The concourse of people on the great stairway on our entrance was so great as to induce the messenger on our return, to take me down a private stairway into St. James's Park, through which we reached his house unobserved by the crowd.

On Tuesday, March 6, I was again taken before the Privy Council. The room was furnished and occupied pretty much in the same manner, and by the same persons and things, as on a former occasion; the only difference I remarked, was the attendance of a greater number of Privy Councillors.

Lord Chancellor.—"Pray, Mr. Binns, have you considered the propriety of answering such questions as shall be put to you?"

Binns.—"My Lord, it did not require consideration; if your Lordship will inform me what acts of my life are charged as treasonable, I will answer; but upon no other consideration."

Lord Chancellor.—"You cannot be told that!"

His Lordship manifested some displeasure; I was content. Mr. White, the Solicitor of the Treasury, now brought into the room three persons, smugglers, with whom I had talked at Whitstable about hiring a vessel to go to France. I declined asking them any questions. They were dismissed, and a fourth person brought into the Council Chamber. To him I said: "Who told you, my friend, that I wished to hang you?" My reason for asking him the question was that he had used such language to me when under arrest at Canterbury.

As soon as I spoke, Mr. Pitt spoke to Mr. White, who immediately got ready his pen, ink, and paper. This awakened my faculties, and I instantly came to the determination to fall back upon silence, inasmuch as I saw that my examination of their witnesses would necessarily lead to the admission of facts which I had better not disclose; I therefore declined to ask any question. Mr. Pitt, however, was not disposed to acquiesce in such a determination; he therefore stepped forward, and with a polite bow and a courtly smile, inquired why I had asked the man the question, and said: "You are at liberty, Mr. Binns, to ask him, or any other person, whatever questions you may think proper."

Binns.—"So I understood, sir; but it is no use to ask questions of a man who is intoxicated." Mr. Pitt was disappointed, and rather angrily said: "Oh no, sir; he is not intoxicated; it is his way. I dare say you know his way."

Binns.—"Then, sir, you dare say for me what I dare not say for myself; I do *not* know his way."

Men who are unused to retort or contradiction, bear them with an ill grace. Mr. Pitt turned on his heel, gave orders, and the man was taken out of the room. In the mean time, I continued standing. The landlord of the Sun Inn, Canterbury, where I slept one night, was then brought forward: "That," said he, pointing to me, "is the gentleman who slept at my house by the name of Williams."

Binns.—"Give me leave to ask you, sir; did you ever hear me say my name was Williams, or did you ever hear any person address me by that name?"

Landlord.—"No."

Binns.—"Then why do you say that is my name?"

Landlord.—"Because, while at my house, you sent my servant to the Fountain Inn to inquire for letters by that name."

Mr. Pitt again came forward, and rather rudely said: "Well, sir, what do you say to that fact?"

Binns.—"Do you know, sir, that it is a fact?"

Mr. Pitt retired and talked with Sir John Scott, the Attorney-General. The woman who washed for me in London was next introduced. She came pertly forward, courtesied, and said: "How do you do, Mr. Binns?" I did not take any notice of her. The Lord Chancellor said to her: "That's the person you spoke of." "Yes, sir; the gentleman's name is John Binns."

Lord Chancellor.—"Ask this woman any questions."

Binns.—"My Lord, I have already promptly acknowledged who I am, and if I wished to conceal it there are thousands who could identify me. I shall ask her no questions."

Three other persons were brought forward; and after them the landlord of the Inn at Rochester returned and said: "Sir, I have got a horse of yours; what shall I do with him?"

Binns.—"If you have got one, take care of him."

Lord Chancellor.—"Where did you get that horse, Mr. Binns?"

Binns.—"I don't think proper to tell, my Lord."

Lord Chancellor.—"So unimportant a question as that, I can see no impropriety in answering."

Binns.—"Perhaps not; but while your Lordship keeps me ignorant of the precise offence with which I am charged, I cannot judge what is important. I do not see the consequences which may follow, or how one question and answer may bear upon another."

Lord Chancellor.—"Your own conscience must point out the crime you have committed, and your judgment must satisfy you how clearly it will be proved against you."

Binns.—"I do not think I have done anything I ought not to have done, and my conscience acquits me of any crime."

His Lordship perceiving that what he was pleased to call my obstinacy was immovable, gave orders to the messenger, and turning to me, said: "A jury must determine this business."

Binns.—"Nothing, my Lord, will give me greater pleasure."

I then bowed respectfully, was delivered into the custody of Mr. Mason, and returned with him to his house. At seven o'clock, he again went to the Privy Council, from which he did not return until near midnight. I sat up with some anxiety, and on his return said: "Well, Mr. Mason, what news?"

Mason.—"Why, sir, you must be up before six o'clock in the morning, so that I think you had better go to bed."

Binns.—"Why, where am I going, so early?"

Mason.—"Can't tell you, sir."

I then went to bed; my clothes were taken away, and the room-door locked as usual. A little before six o'clock, next morning, my clothes were brought, and I was called upon to dress. I did so, and in a few minutes was seated at the breakfast-table.

Binns.—"May I now ask, Mr. Mason, where I am to be taken?"

Mason.—"If you will promise me not to be alarmed."

Binns.—"That I will, most readily."

Mason.—"Then, sir, we are going to the Tower."

Breakfast being over, we stepped into a carriage and drove direct to what was called the Governor's House, which was some distance within the outer wall of the Tower. There are twelve acres and five rods within the Tower wall, outside of which there is a deep and wide ditch. The circuit on the outside of the ditch is 1,052 feet. Within those walls as much crime has been committed, and as much cruelty inflicted, as within the walls of the Bastile, and as much magnificence and splendor displayed as at Versailles.

At the door of the Governor's House we were met by the gentleman jailer, a man about sixty years of age. He had for many years been a sergeant in the Guards, and had all that prompt obedience of manner consequent upon such stations. He was, however, a good-natured, kindly man. He conducted the messenger and myself into a parlor, where we were received by the governor (Colonel Smith). Arthur O'Connor, who had just arrived, was in the same room. We were mutually gratified at the interview, and engaged in conversation while the governor gave to the messenger receipts for our persons. Colonel Smith's stature was below the middle size; his complexion sallow, and his eyes gray, keen, and anxious; he frequently bit his nether lip, and looked anything but kindly at Mr. O'Connor and me. The messenger having obtained his receipt for my person from Colonel Smith, I made acknowledgments for his uniform kindness, and he departed.

A military guard under a commissioned officer, and some half-dozen yeomen of the Guards, being mustered under the command of Colonel Smith, Mr. O'Connor and myself, in their charge, left the house. Mr. O'Connor was soon disposed of in an apartment on the ground floor of a house near the governor's. I was marched some distance, say 80 or 100 yards to the foot of a tower, nearer to the entrance of the fortification. At this time there was a brigade of 800 men stationed within the Tower walls; outside of which was a moat, deep and wide, supplied with water from the Thames, and defended by many pieces of heavy cannon.

We, the governor, his guards, and myself, entered a round tower near the Thames. It was one of the four round towers of white stone built by William the Conqueror. It was the northeast tower in which, accompanied by Colonel Smith, we ascended three high flights of narrow, dark, circular stone stairs, which conducted to the room in which I was to be confined. A soldier from an accompanying guard, was stationed by Colonel Smith, as a sentinel on every platform or landing-place on the stairs, at which we arrived. A sentinel was also stationed immediately outside the door of the room which had been selected as my place of confinement.

The warders, or yeomen of the Tower, wore the same rich, ungainly, heavy uniforms which their predecessors wore in the reign of Henry the Eighth, by whom the warders were first uniformed and organized. They were, I believe, the first standing army, if army they might be called, established in England. There were, originally, fifty of them. I do not know that the number has ever been altered.

Speaking of the warders of the Tower, from my own experience, I should say they were well-behaved, respectable, obliging, elderly men. They have generally been upper servants in noblemen and gentlemen's families, and have obtained those quiet, easy situations, through the influence of their former masters.

Some of the warders were in the habit of washing their heads in cold water every morning, as contributing to their general health. I adopted the practice, and from that time to this, in all seasons and situations, have washed my head the first thing when I get out of bed, and the last when I return to bed, with a sponge saturated in clear cold water. At the time I am writing this, I am more than eighty-one years old. I read or write every day, on an average, eight hours, and do not use glasses, and never have, to read or write. I attribute this clear-sightedness to the use of the sponge and cold water, which I have indulged in for fifty-six years. I have no doubt that this habit has also preserved my sense of hearing, which is reasonably acute.

Seeing that Colonel Smith was about to leave me, I inquired if I should be allowed the use of books, pens, ink, and paper.

"You can be allowed no indulgence, sir," said the colonel, "without permission from the Lords of his Majesty's most Honorable Privy Council."

Binns.—"And how, sir, is that permission to be obtained, if I am denied pen, ink, and paper?"

Smith.—"You shall have pen, ink, and paper to write when you wish to address the Lords of his Majesty's most Honorable Privy Council; but, without their permission, for no other purpose." He then turned from me to two of the warders, and said: "You are to remain in this room night and day; you are to hold no conversation with your prisoner, nor suffer him to go out of the length of your swords" (which were about eighteen inches long). "You shall answer for his appearance at the peril of your lives." These orders, I thought, would have answered the purpose just as well, and been equally well observed, if they had been given out of my hearing. I, however, presumed that the orders were thus given as much to impress me with a proper idea of the consequence of Colonel Smith, as rules to govern the conduct of the warders.

The colonel ceremoniously bowing and taking leave, I made my best bow and he departed. As the door shut after him, it seemed to cut me off from all communication with the world. My heart was heavy; a damp came over my spirits, and melancholy thoughts took entire possession of me. "Are, then," thought I, "my friends and relations to be left wholly to conjecture, and to receive from me no information to relieve their anxieties, and still the troubles of their hearts! If such is to be their condition, it shall not be my fault. I will ask permission to write to some of them; to my mother or my sister."

The next morning I determined I would make the request for writing materials, &c. "You will oblige me," said I, turning to one of the warders, "if you will apply to Colonel Smith for pen, ink, and paper, that I may write to the Privy Council." After some hesitation and consultation, one of the warders went to Colonel Smith, and returned with one sheet of paper, a pen and ink, all of which he was ordered to take back so soon as I had written my letter. In the letter to the Privy Council, I asked permission to walk abroad, when and where, and under such restrictions as the Privy Council should think proper; to be allowed a razor, &c. to shave, and requested to be permitted the use of books, and to write to Ireland, to my sister. I dispatched a warder with my letter and writing materials to Colonel Smith, from whom, in due time, I learned that, at present, none of my requests could be granted, but that a barber should be sent daily to shave me. This favor I declined, thinking that if I could not be trusted with my own throat, I would not trust it to another. I was not shaved from the time I was committed until the morning I was about to leave the Tower for Maidstone. Having thus, in some measure, tranquillized my mind, I examined the apartment in which I was placed. It was a large-sized room, the southern end, that nearest the River Thames, being semicircular, and having two windows with iron sashes and outside iron bars. The iron doors of the windows opened inwardly and longitudinally. There were two doors to each window. There was a bedstead and bed, &c. for myself, and two closets in which were cots for the warders; a cupboard for provisions; a mahogany bureau, table, washstand, and chairs. The two windows, in a modern-built house, would be regarded as small, but in a prison might be regarded as of the largest dimensions. The iron bars on the outside were about four inches apart. One of the windows opened southeasterly, and the other to southwesterly. Before each of them was an ever-changing panorama, an extensive and delightful prospect up and down the Thames: Merchant ships, barges, wherries, and boats nearly of every nation and description, were continually passing and repassing. The fluctuations of the tide; the rising and the setting sun; the moon's pale, silver light, and the infinite variety of business which was daily transacting on the river, formed an ever-varying and ever-pleasing scene. The Custom-House on the Thames was only a few perches further west than the Tower; the front of those buildings were not more than one hundred feet back from the water's edge. The principal docks for the accommodation of the larger merchant ships, were considerably lower down the river on the north side.

Having reconnoitered my room, I made occasional inquiries as to its former inhabitants. The eldest of the warders said: "This room was once occupied by Lord Balmerino, one of the Scotch Lords who was active in the rebellion of 1745, and since by Lord Ferrars. In the year 1780, Mons. De la Motte was here, and in 1794, Mr. Thelwall was confined in this room."

On Friday, March 9th, Major-General Vernon, the Lieutenant-General of the Tower, attended by Col. Smith, without any previous notice, entered my room. He was a tall, gray-haired, venerable-looking gentleman. The Marquis Cornwallis was at that time the constable, or senior officer, a sinecure office of about £5,000 [$25,000] a year. General Vernon was in full uniform. The introduction being over, the general politely inquired as to my accommodations, and talked upon indifferent subjects with politeness and candor. I made such answers as I deemed proper to a gentleman of his rank, age, and deportment. He remained about half an hour. We interchanged salutations, and the general retired.

After I had been in custody about four weeks, the gentleman jailer introduced two king's messengers. They had, each of them, a large green bombazine bag in his hand. I was somewhat surprised at their appearance, but much more so when they had emptied the contents of their bags on the table. They were filled with linen and woollen clothing of mine, which I had left locked up in my trunks at my lodgings. In these trunks, in a pocket-book I had left, was Coigley's passport and other papers, which I was anxious should not fall into the hands of the Government. I knew the clothing and other articles the moment they were spread before me; but I had gained some experience, and had so far profited as not to be in a hurry, and, therefore, did not utter a syllable. I looked on, with all calmness, until the bags were emptied and their contents spread before me; I then said: "What are all those things brought here for? Whom are they sent by? For whom are they intended? Where did you get them?"

Messenger.—"They are sent to you, sir, by order of the Privy Council, and were taken out of a trunk belonging to you, sir."

Binns.—"Pray, gentlemen, where was that trunk found?"

Messenger.—"Why, sir, it was traced from some place where you left it, to some other place where it was found, and the people there had no key for it."

Binns.—"Consequently, it must be mine." The messenger did not notice the interruption, but proceeded: "So, sir, when it was brought before the Privy Council, they had it broken open, and all the things taken out of it."

Binns.—"Are these *all* the things which were found in it?"

Messenger.—"No, sir, there were two pocket-books with papers in them in the trunks; these the Privy Council thought proper to keep, together with some other things."

Binns.—"You, gentlemen, may take those things back to the Privy Council, that they may have an opportunity to return all the things together, when they find the owner."

The messengers appeared much disconcerted, and at a loss what to do when I refused to take the clothing. They talked together for some time, when, at length, one of them said: "Then, sir, you won't take them?"

Binns.—Certainly not as a matter of right, not as my property; but if the Privy Council shall think proper to make me a present of those things, I will accept them, as I have already, by letter, informed the Privy Council I am in want of such things."

The messengers seemed unprepared for a refusal, and again consulted together as to what they should do. "We will," said one of them, "leave the bags, and the things in them, in the Tower, at the Governor's House; perhaps the Privy Council will order them to be given to you, without your acknowledging them to be yours."

Binns.—"You may do as you please, gentlemen; but if the Privy Council shall order me the things, in the way you suggest, it will somewhat surprise me."

The messengers refilled their bags and carried them away. I never saw either them, the bags, or the clothes, or any of them afterwards.*

CHAPTER VI.

Manner of passing away my time in the Tower—Disturbance created by my yellow silk neckerchief—Removal with the other state prisoners to Maidstone jail—Imposing circumstances attending our route thither—Description of my cell—Arrival of the Judges—Interview with Mr. Bonney—Counsellor Gurney appointed my counsel—I send a letter to the High Sheriff of Kent County—My indictment and trial—Unfairness of the Government; instance—My acquittal—Riot in Court—Sketch of Arthur C. O'Connor.

A FEW days after the occurrence mentioned in the last chapter, and after repeated applications, I obtained from

* I have reason to know that the clothing thus taken out of my trunks was replaced in them, and the trunks and their contents, except the pocket-books and papers kept by the Privy Council, sent to the police office at Bow Street, and put in the care of Mr. Justice Ford. Early in the year 1801, when I was about to leave England for the United States, I called at the Bow Street office to inquire if I could obtain a protection, as there was then war between the United States and Tripoli. Mr. Ford said I might have one if I sailed under the flag of Great Britain, but not if I went under that of the United States. He then took occasion to tell me he had two trunks full of clothing and books, which had been sent from the office of the Duke of Portland, to be delivered to me or my order. I told him, that with all respect for his friendly assurances, I did not dare to take them lest they should lead me into fresh trouble. I have never seen them or any portion of their contents since. The loss of the clothing has given me no concern, but there were several books in them which I had read with care, and in which I had, according to my custom, written many notes; their loss I have many times regretted.

the Secretary of State for the Home Department, permission to walk on the Grand Parade for two hours every day; one hour in the forenoon and one hour in the afternoon, always to be accompanied by the two attending warders. Pen and ink prohibited. Books, such as the Government approved, I was permitted to have. Under this permission, I obtained and carefully read all the English State trials.* Colonel Smith was, indeed, a vigilant spy, so vigilant that he read even my notes to the washerwoman, and carefully examined all my foul linen. He told me so himself. "Nothing," he said, "must come to or be taken from you without first undergoing my inspection." He seemed delighted to give trouble and raise objections. He was, in every sense of the word, a small, time-serving officer.

The first intimation I had of my brother's arrival in England was a knowledge of his arrest. He was soon after liberated. This information, and much more, I obtained, notwithstanding the double-distilled vigilance of Colonel Smith.

On Sunday, March 25, 1798, I walked as usual on the Grand Parade, the place for that purpose appointed by the authorities. It was a broad flagged way, not less than fifty feet wide, and of considerable length. There, on the afternoon of fine days, the ladies and gentlemen, who live within the Tower walls, and those of the neighborhood, who have permission, usually sport their persons. On this particular afternoon, I remarked a group of army officers in full uniform, walking, arm-in-arm, up and down the parade, viewing me with a curiosity bordering on impertinence. If they remain silent, thought I, I shall not notice the rudeness of their manner. The warders, who accompanied me, noticed their conduct, the cause of which I soon after ascertained to be the color of the silk neckerchief which I wore round my neck. When, how, and through whom, I obtained this offensive article, I shall now state. Soon

---

* It is due not only to my personal friends, but to many liberal-minded men to whom I had not the honor to be personally known, to acknowledge that, from the hour of my arrest to my liberation, every attention and care was paid to supply not only books, but everything I desired, which it was the pleasure of the Government to permit to be brought to me.

after my commitment to the Tower, and permission had been given that I might walk on the parade, I remarked that the window of Coigley's room overlooked my road to and from the parade. I frequently saw him bow to me at his window; and in return I bowed to him. I also ascertained that, on my road to the Grand Parade, I passed at right angles the row of trees under which O'Connor was allowed to walk. Occasionally I saw him, and we interchanged mute salutations. These things made me desirous to devise some means by which, unsuspected by others, I could show my fellow-prisoners that I was in good spirits. Green, the national color of Ireland, for years before our arrest, had been adopted and worn as a party badge by the Society of United Irishmen. Just, however, before Coigley and O'Connor left Ireland, the green had been laid aside, and yellow, not orange, had been adopted instead of green. After my commitment, through the agency of Colonel Smith, I obtained a yellow silk handkerchief, which I wore on my neck when I walked out. The colonel, of course, was ignorant as to the motive which induced me to obtain and wear that particular color.

Monday, March 26.—About noon this day, while walking on the parade, accompanied by the warders, the gentleman jailer advanced towards us, as I thought, with intention to address me; his age commanded my respect, and his office my prompt attention. We stopped until he came near; when, addressing himself to me, he said: "I am come, sir, by order of the governor, to desire you will take off that yellow silk handkerchief."

Binns.—"For what reason, pray sir, does the governor undertake to direct what colors I shall be allowed to wear?"

Gentleman Jailer.—"He says, sir, that it is the badge of the United Irishmen."

Binns.—"I know that green was the color worn by the United Irishmen, and I also know, to the dishonor of Englishmen to do, and of Irishmen to suffer, many Irish women were grossly insulted for wearing it."

Gentleman Jailer.—"Sir, the governor says the green has been laid aside, and the yellow adopted in the place of it."

Binns.—"If I might form an opinion from the governor's message, I should presume the United Irishmen have hoisted the standard of revolt against the Government."

Gentleman Jailer.—"Shall I tell the governor, sir, that you will put away the yellow handkerchief?"

Binns.—"You may tell the governor that I know no country where the people are so abject as to be divided into classes and colors appropriated to each class, except it be China. Assure the governor that so degrading a badge of slavery shall not be introduced into England by a compliance, on my part, with so unjustifiable an order."

The gentleman jailer, with great kindness, begged that I would not irritate the governor, which I would do if I did not comply with what he desired. He then took his leave. This message accounted for the conduct of the army officers on the parade. They had recently come from Ireland, and doubtless told the governor how much their loyalty and sensibilities had been shocked at the sight of a yellow handkerchief parading before his Majesty's small armory. I had on two former occasions received messages from Col. Smith, through the gentleman jailer, desiring that I would not walk so fast. I treated them as they deserved, always taking care to walk according to the ability and wishes of the warders, who walked one on each side of me. Colonel Smith was one of those men who have no comfort in authority without they are constantly exercising it to the annoyance of others.

On the afternoon of the same day I again walked the parade, neckerchief as before. It was very much crowded; nothing unusual took place, and I returned to my apartment. I could not, however, fail to remark that every eye was turned in search of the prohibited color. On my return from walking, I took off the neckerchief, laid it in a drawer, and put on a white one. I felt assured, from the large company on the parade, that the message of Colonel Smith, and my answer, had been noised abroad, and that the unusual attendance was to see whether I did, or did not, obey his order, and, if I did not, to mark the consequences.

The gentleman jailer came that night to lock the door of my room at nine o'clock; which he did every night, although five sentinels were stationed on the several platforms of the stone stairway; a battalion of eight hundred men were on duty within the Tower walls, and two warders slept in my room every night. "Sir," said the gentleman jailer, immediately on entering the room, "the governor says you must give me that yellow silk handkerchief which you wore." My blood boiled with indignation. Rising from my chair, and laying my hand on my left breast, I said, "I will give him my heart's blood first."

Gentleman Jailer.—"Sir, I am ordered not to return without it; do not oblige me to call a guard."

Binns.—"Mr. Kinghorn, whatever observations I may make, "I beg you not to consider them as personal; I intend them for the governor, to whom I hope you will report them. The law does not forbid yellow. If I were walking at liberty, the governor, nor no man, dare desire me to take off a neckerchief, or any other article of dress; if he did, it should not be with impunity. Do you know, sir, is he authorized in these proceedings?"

Gentleman Jailer.—"Sir, he was at the Privy Council this day; will you tell me, Mr. Binns, where you have put the handkerchief?"

I made no reply; a guard was called and entered, the room was searched, the object sought was found and taken away. I shall probably be accused of rashness or obstinate folly for this determined resistance in so small a matter, but I assert that no man is competent to pass upon my conduct without at least imagining himself in my situation. I did not regard it as a small matter. I knew the demand and the refusal were known to hundreds, and would soon be known to thousands. Such was the fact, and the whole matter found its way into the daily newspapers. Prisoners in the town charged with high crimes usually occupy a share of public attention; their conduct and treatment in confinement become matters of public conversation, of accusation and defence. They should never, therefore, quietly submit to insolence or injustice.

Binns.—"Before you depart, Mr. Kinghorn, let me again ask you to tell the governor what I have said; and further, that I solemnly protest against his conduct as a gross violation of law, and a wanton abuse of the authority with which he is intrusted."

He bowed and left the room, attended by the guard.

I felt excessively mortified, and in a rather impatient temper reviewed the busy events of the day; I laid me down, however, quietly to rest, and soon was dead to "the whips and scorns of the proud man's contumely," and "the insolence of office."

When I awoke in the morning, my thoughts were so entirely occupied by "the handkerchief," that I determined to send and request a personal interview with Colonel Smith. It was yet too early to send, and I impatiently waited for the time to arrive when I might, with propriety, send for him. I sent one of the warders at ten o'clock, and at twelve in came Colonel Smith, attended by the gentleman jailer. More than the usual ceremonies and salutations being gone through, I said: "I am concerned, governor, to give you this trouble, but I hope that it will prevent future trouble, and feeling it to be a duty, not only to myself, but to ———."

Governor.—"Mr. Binns, I cannot enter into conversation. I should have come whether you sent for me or not. The letters which you yesterday sent, I took to the Privy Council, and they were much displeased at the liberty you took in mentioning names disrespectfully. Sir, you positively must not enter into any kind of correspondence; name the things you want, and mention nothing further."

Binns.—"I did not intend, sir, that that letter should be taken to the Privy Council, it was addressed to the washerwoman. I only meant them to get the one in which I requested to be allowed newspapers, pen, ink, and paper."

Governor.—"I thought proper to take both letters to the Lords of his Majesty's Honorable Privy Council."

Binns.—"I principally wish, governor, to speak to you relative to a transaction which took place yesterday, which I consider unwarrantable, and ———."

Governor.—"Mr. Binns, I cannot enter into conversation. Whatever has been done, has been done by my orders. I am not young in the office which I hold here.

I have long been a magistrate for this county, and I am Colonel of the Tower Hamlets militia.

Binns.—"Pray, colonel, was the yellow handkerchief taken from me solely by your order, unsupported by an order from the Privy Council?"

Governor.—"They know and approve of my conduct."

Binns.—"Which in my opinion is most extraordinary. I wrote for that handkerchief, and named the particular color; you read my note, inspected the bundle in which it came, and sent it to me; and now, after I have repeatedly worn it, and walked abroad with it on my neck, to your knowledge, sir, it has suddenly become an offence of a very high nature."

Governor.—"You know, sir, that yellow is the color worn by the United Irishmen."

Binns.—"I know that green was their color, and I have a green silk neckerchief, for which I did not send, because I thought it might give offence."

Governor.—"You are not ignorant, Mr. Binns, that the yellow has been substituted for the green."

Binns.—"I have been a close prisoner several weeks, during which time I have had no intercourse with the world; how then is it *possible* that I should be acquainted with a fact of which the governor of the Tower appears to have been ignorant until yesterday?"

Governor.—"You know their proceedings, sir, better than I do, but thank God!" and he turned his little gray eyes upwards with what he desired to have regarded as an expression of pious gratitude—"everything has been happily discovered, and the necks of ——." Here he abruptly broke off, hoping he had left me something to ponder on.

Binns.—"I suppose if I had a green handkerchief you would take it!"

Governor.—"Certainly I should. Everything remarkable, that's worn by you, Mr. Binns, is taken notice of." As he spoke these words, he looked with some earnestness at a pair of dark green pantaloons in which I had been arrested, and which I then wore. He was about to leave me, when I said: "Yellow and green being prohibited, may I ask, sir, what colors are licensed?"

Governor.—" That's a very improper expression."

Binns.—" Very likely, sir; a man is apt to use improper expressions, when he is insulted and his property ——"

Governor.—" Sir, I hold myself answerable for the handkerchief. You may wear black or white." He bowed and retired. When the door was closed, I said :—

> " Man, proud man!
> Dress'd in a little brief authority,
> Plays such fantastic tricks before high heaven
> As make the angels weep."

April 4.—I received a letter from Mr. White, Solicitor of the Treasury, informing me that a special commission had been issued for the trial of the state prisoners, then confined in the Tower, which commission would be opened at Maidstone, on the tenth inst. The person who handed me the letter either was, or affected to be ignorant of the object in sending it, and left me to draw my own conclusions, which were that I should soon be removed.

On Friday night, April 6, when the gentleman jailer, who was a " good, easy man "—on all occasions the mouthpiece of the governor—came to lock up, he informed me that the governor had received his Majesty's *habeas corpus* to remove me and the other state prisoners, Messrs. Coigley and O'Connor, early next morning.

My wardrobe was soon in order for travelling, and I went to bed. At five o'clock the next morning, before daylight, the gentleman jailer unlocked my room-door and awoke me, saying: " I am sent, sir, to pay you twelve shillings for the four days which have elapsed since you received your weekly allowance." I have not before mentioned that I was weekly paid, since my commitment to the Tower, by order of the Government, twenty-one shillings [$4 $\frac{67}{100}$] subsistence money. I daily ordered, and payed for, whatever I chose to eat and drink. While I was washing and dressing, the girl, who daily made the fire and the bed, and swept and cleaned the room, having had her orders, came much earlier than usual; she made the fire, boiled the kettle, and soon had breakfast ready. She refused the money I offered her, and burst into tears. The girl was not handsome, nor witty, indeed, scarcely good-humored; she was a "fat, foolish scullion;" yet did I heartily wish she were in her native county of Hereford, when she thus awoke feelings which I wished to remain tranquil. I soon overcame her scruples; she took the money, and was tolerably reconciled, when Col. Smith, of the Tower Hamlets militia, justice of the peace, acting governor, &c., &c., made his appearance, and said: "Are you ready, Mr. Binns?" "I am, sir." "Then I am not," said he, and, turning on his heel, left the room.

About six o'clock I was, with due formality, under a guard, conducted down the stone stairs of my Norman Tower, and, with all politeness and dispatch, crowded into a postchaise which was close as it could come to the door at the foot of the round tower. I was placed in the centre of the seat, and on each side of me was a warder, with a brace of pistols in his girdle. There was, also, a strong military guard, horse and foot, under arms within the outer wall of the Tower, the outer gates of which, at this time, were shut. There appeared to me to be much confusion and crowding together of the authorities between the foot of the tower, in which I had been confined, and the principal gate, or entrance, in the Tower wall. "If you will give me leave," said I to the warders, "I will sit a little more forward, and we shall then be all more at ease." "We will, Mr. Binns," said one of the warders, "when we have passed the governor, but he directed us to sit before you, to prevent the people from seeing you."

About half-past six o'clock the whole cavalcade moved slowly forward, and passed the outer gate of the Tower, the other state prisoners, Coigley and O'Connor, being accompanied and disposed of in separate postchaises. At the outer Tower gate we were received by fifty of the London Yeomen Cavalry. The governor, Smith, pointed out, and by name introduced each prisoner to the commander of the escort. The concourse of people was prodigious, considering that our removal was intended to be kept secret, and the early hour at which it had been got under way. The procession consisted of five postchaises, with Yeomen Cavalry before, behind, and on each side.

In this order we sat off for Maidstone, thirty-six miles from London.

Innumerable were the disadvantages I apprehended from this removal. London abounds with zealous friends; solicitors and counsellors are there to be promptly had, who may be freely consulted and safely confided in; above all, the firmness and discrimination of the jurors of Middlesex were proverbial. I thought of the thousands and tens of thousands who daily and nightly gathered together in front of the Old Bailey, when Hardy, Tooke, and Thelwall were on trial, and of the joyous and hearty cheers with which they greeted counsellors Erskine and Gibbs and the jurors. The parade at our removal, the selection of Yeomenry as the guard, were all in my mind but drops in the cup which was to prejudice and poison the public mind, and especially the minds of those who were to be our jurors. The people, thought I, in the country and towns through which we pass, will be confounded and astonished at the cavalcade, and come to the conclusion that we must be men of the most desperate characters, whose guilt can, and will, be proved clear as the light of heaven.

About fifteen miles from London, we were met by a troop of the Kent Co. Cavalry, to whom we were given in charge; and nine miles further, they were relieved by another party of the same corps. Thus men from every part of the country, farmers and others, were taken from their usual occupations to guard us to prison; these men, on their return, through every part of the country whence our jurors were to be selected, would spread abroad exaggerated accounts of our guilt, and the clearness of the proof against us. It is a fact not unworthy of note, that the two captains who commanded the two divisions of the Kent Yeomenry, which formed our guard, were both on the grand-jury which found the bill of indictment against us.

In every parish through which we passed, the Minister of the Established Church was to be seen in some conspicuous place, where he was easily distinguished, not only by his peculiar dress, but by the joy which lighted up his countenance, and marked his deportment. This is one of the evil effects of a union of Church and State; it makes clergymen, church-wardens, beadles, &c., officers, I might say partisan officers, of the Government. "Church and King," was the cry in England, in 1793, under which houses of worship were desecrated and destroyed, manufactories and private houses burned, and their owners turned naked wanderers from their own heretofore comfortable, well-furnished dwellings.

It was near four o'clock in the afternoon when we arrived at Maidstone, the county town of Kent. We were expected, and the crowd in the streets was very great. From our entrance into the town to the place where the jail stands, the street on which we rode was all the way up hill. As we moved slowly, the people had abundant opportunity to gratify their curiosity. The prison is situated on a narrow street. As we made our way into that street, I heard several women scream; their curiosity and the elbowing of the multitude had squeezed them into situations almost beyond endurance. Some of them had children in their arms, and were in momentary danger of being trodden under the hoofs of the horses of the cavalry, or run over by the carriages. An accident which happened on the road is here brought to mind. One of the London Yeomenry riding too near the postchaise, just before me, was unfortunately caught by the metal scabbard of his sword getting between the spokes of the wheel; luckily, the sword-belt snapped and promptly relieved him from rather a perilous situation. The suddenness of the shock made him bow down, and the flat side of the sword, which he held upright in his hand, struck and cut him under the eye, which swelled and became black.

We are arrived at the door of the prison. I was promptly handed out of the chaise, and, with the assistance of some persons' arms under each of mine, I made my way up some awkward narrow stone steps, and was taken through several doorways and narrow passages into a room in which I was with all dispatch locked, bolted, and left by myself. The suddenness of the change affected my spirits. One instant surrounded and pressed upon by a multitude, each of whose expressive countenance was a study, but which, owing to "the buzz and bustle of the field before me," I could not examine; the next moment alone, immured in a small dark room, in a prison, without an object worthy of attention, or which could amuse or instruct. To get to this very mean habitation I had passed through five heavy doors, all of them strengthened and fastened by iron bolts and bars, chains, and locks. We had ascended a flight of stairs, passed through a narrow passage, turned to the left, and thence through a door and another passage into the room in which I was confined.

The gentleman jailer and the warders, who had come with us from London, were my first visitors in this wretched room; they came to wish me health. Three of the warders expressed the kindest wishes for my liberation. I did not doubt their sincerity. They, one and all, kindly and cordially shook me by the hand and took their leave. I did not allow them to go without making acknowledgments for their uniform kindness. Their conduct towards me was more that of fellow-prisoners than guards. Their company and good offices I very much regretted. I am now the lonely tenant of a small dark room.

The size of the room is about fourteen feet by twelve, and eight feet high. The walls about four feet thick, as I calculated, from the depth of the window in the wall of the room, which had recently been plastered and whitewashed. Over the door-case are six square holes in an iron frame, which is let into the wall; in the door itself is one larger hole, or rather small door, which opens on hinges, and is about six inches long and four wide. Through this little door I sometimes received my victuals and sometimes other communications, and held short conversations and exchanged notes with Coigley and O'Connor, who were each confined in rooms about the same size and on the same platform. The door is secured on the outside by a large strong iron lock, and two large iron bolts secured by padlocks, staples, &c. The window—there was but one—consisted of sixteen squares of glass, each square about eight inches by five; eight of these squares opened obliquely to admit air to refresh the room. The window-frame and sash are iron. How widely different is the prospect from this dismal window to those which I enjoyed from the windows in the Tower. Immediately under this window is the felon's yard. When the little door of my window is open, my ears are compelled to receive the poisonous breath of—

"Vulgar ribaldry,
The ill-bred question, and the lewd reply."

If I look forward, with all earnestness, through the open sash, I cannot, from its obliquity, look up or down. I can only see horizontally, where dead walls and roofs of houses are the uninteresting objects which everywhere present themselves. "The rising and the setting sun," which, in the Tower, beguiled many a tedious hour, are now lost to me as objects of admiration—

"The firmanent on high,
With all the blue ethereal sky,"

are almost wholly excluded from my sight.

The furniture of the room—and it is my chamber, my hall of audience, my kitchen, and my parlor—consists of a small, low, field-bedstead, bed, and bed-covering, and curtains, three rush-bottomed chairs, a small table, a looking-glass, a basin-stand, basin, soap, a water-jug, sponge, tooth-brush, and towel. There is, set in the wall, a very small grate; no fire-irons, of any kind, are allowed. I am allowed, as a very special favor, a slender stick, to stir the fire; of this little stick I am especially careful; if I were not, I should soon have my poker reduced to ashes. In this room, thus furnished, lighted, and aired, I am to be found $22\frac{1}{2}$ hours in every 24. The yard, in which I walk, is about 40 feet long, and 25 feet wide. The walls are very high, insomuch that the air I breathe is not often changed, nor by any means of the purest kind. In this yard, I have occasionally picked up a green leaf, and a white blossom, and heard the birds chirping and singing, which caused involuntary sighs. Ah! thought I, while all nature is exulting, bursting into, and enjoying, life; while the fields are green, and the trees covered with many colored, fragrant blossoms, and sweet-smelling flowers are everywhere presenting themselves, I am not permitted to share in the general reinvigorations and rejoicings; while every production of nature seems starting into life, mine drags slowly on, and is threatened with dissolution.

The jail, in addition to its usual guards and turnkeys, is nightly surrounded by a detachment of the Maidstone Volunteers, the commanding officer of which, every night, accompanies the jailer to see that we are all safe in our respective beds, fires extinguished, &c. &c. Our meals here, are whatever we think proper to order from a neighboring hotel, and are paid for by the Government. I breakfast at ten, dine at four, take bread and milk at eight, and go to bed before ten o'clock. I rise before eight, perform my ablutions, and read the remainder of the day, save the short time I am in the yard. My appetite is not so good as usual; my general health is tolerable, and if it were not for out-of-door remembrances, I could, even here, be content, if not cheerful.

On Tuesday, the 10th of April, I heard the town bells ringing a merry peal, and the trumpets sounding glad tidings, to announce the entrance into Maidstone of the judges who were appointed to hold the court for our trial. My heart bounded with joy at the sound; the hour advances, the decisive hour which is to restore me to the embraces of friends, or forever deprive me of the power of inflicting on them future anguish. This day the judges went to church, to hear what was called an assize sermon preached, and the next day they were to proceed to business.*

About eight o'clock the following evening, Mr. Bonney, an attorney, from London, entered my room. His was the first friendly voice that, for seven long weeks, had reached my ear; his was the first friendly hand which had been outstretched to me, in all that time; "nor had the voice of friend or kinsman breathed through my lattice." While confined in the Tower, Mr. Bonney had sent me whatever books, &c. I required, and offered his services as

---

* Dean Swift having preached an assize sermon, was, as is customary, invited to dine with the judges and members of the bar; at and after dinner, many professional gentlemen spoke of the extreme severity with which the Dean had spoken of the members of the bar, and took occasion to retort upon the clergy. One of them, in rather a loud voice, and addressing himself to the Dean, said: "For my part, sir, I believe that if the Prince of Darkness were dead, we could get a clergyman to preach his funeral sermon." "Certainly you could," said the Dean, "and I would willingly be the man, and I would then take care to give the devil his due, as I have this day his children."

solicitor; he came now to inform me the court had assigned him to that office. The grand-jury having returned a true bill for high treason, against my fellow-prisoners and myself, Mr. Bonney was permitted to visit me. I anxiously inquired after my friends. All, who had recently been in custody, on suspicion of conspiring against the Government, had been liberated, my brother among the rest. He, however, was obliged to give bond in the sum of £200 to appear, if required, at the trial at Maidstone, as a witness.

Mr. Bonney did not remain long, but said he would see me in the morning. I went to bed, was soon under the influence of the leaden god, and did not hear the officials when they came to see that all was safe. The jailer, however, awoke me to say that I must be in the court-house before eight o'clock in the morning. I said: "I shall be ready." They departed; I turned on the other side, and was soon asleep.

What took place in court, is reported in the newspapers of the day, therefore I detail it not. On our return to prison, Mr. Bonney said: "You were well spoken of by many, in court; many said your appearance indicated conscious innocence, while others said your boldness showed how hardened you were in crime." Preconceived opinions brought men to different conclusions, from the same premises.

If a man, possessed of ordinary powers of mind, has time to collect them, and knows how far they are to be tested, he can readily summon sufficient fortitude to support him in any situation, or under any circumstances, in which he can be placed. I can truly say, I never felt fear, nor was overawed by any man or association of men. I believe I always knew what I ought to say, and what I ought to do. Whatever resources or powers I had I could draw upon, and they would answer at a moment's notice. How can any man, with manly feelings, cower down or appear a coward, when he is an object of attention to his fellow-men. It rarely, very rarely indeed, ever happens.

Men who have been guilty of the basest crimes; whose whole lives have been a series of actions more or less dishonorable and dishonest; yea, whose crimes have been of so deep and deadly a dye that their fellow-men, from a sense of self-preservation have felt called upon, and deem it their duty, in self-defence, to try, condemn, and publicly execute them; yet, the very beings thus infamous, and conscious not only of the wrongs they have inflicted, but of the horror and detestation in which they are held by their fellow-beings; even such wretches, when, after a trial, and in pursuance of law, they are about to die an ignominious death; when they appear in public, even when under the gallows, summon up all their energies to enable them, even on the platform of death, to look and to behave so as in some measure to command the pity, if they cannot hope for any better feeling from their fellow-beings.

Counsellor Gurney was the person I named and the court assigned, as my counsel. On the evening of his appointment he came to me, and in short-hand wrote down my account of my whole journey, even to minute circumstances, from the time I left London, to hire a vessel, to the time I arrived there in custody. It was just eight days; in which time I had transacted much business, talked with many and strange people, travelled on foot, on horseback, in coaches, postchaises, and in ships, boats, and barges, a distance of four hundred miles. There was then neither steamboats nor railroads. Such was the earnestness and zeal with which I had devoted myself to the business I had undertaken. I thought of writing a detail of my journey, but the list of witnesses which I have just received from the law officers of the Crown prevents the necessity. I feel certain they will prove, in their own way, colored by their opinions and situations, almost every step I have taken, if not every word, and many more than I have spoken. They will give in evidence pretty nearly all I have been doing, at least all they can gather, to prove my hostility to the Government.

This day, for the first time since my arrest, I was allowed the use of pen, ink, and paper; but, to use the language of the Attorney-General, in court, when the permission was granted, "*not* for communication with all the world;" which I understood to mean that I should make no use of them, but for the purpose of preparing for my defence. This book, in which I am now writing, I always take with me wherever I go; it has constantly been under my pillow or in my bosom, except when I have been writing in it, and it must be thus guarded until an opportunity offers to send it to the friend for whom it is intended.

On Saturday I sent the High Sheriff of Kent county a letter, of which the following is a copy:—

"SIR: Knowing there are many inconveniences, privations, and hardships, to which every person who is confined in a common jail must submit, and not wishing to trouble you, unnecessarily, I have hitherto forborne to write. The object of the present letter is not so much to complain of past evils as to prevent future.

"When confined in the Tower, my room had two large windows, which opened to admit air; my present apartment has only two small holes about five inches square. In the Tower, I had also two hours a day allowed me to walk abroad.

"A complaint which caused a difficulty of breathing, makes me desirous of embracing every opportunity to take air and exercise. Since my arrival in this place, I feel that this difficulty has increased, and I am persuaded that any additional privation of air or exercise would be extremely injurious to my health, if it did not endanger my life. I should not do my duty, to you, sir, nor justice to myself, if I neglected to acquaint you with some facts which have taken place recently. Two days ago the small hole in the door of my room was shut and padlocked, and thus I was deprived of a part of the air which changed, and, in some measure, refreshed my apartment. This morning I made application to be permitted to go down stairs, upon a natural and unavoidable occasion, and received for answer, that *I must not leave my room on any account, only one hour in the day.* If, in addition to the closeness of the room, the air is to be thus rendered fetid—but I will not offend your delicacy by attempting to set before you the inevitable consequences of such unnecessary severity; your own discretion will lead you to the only true and rational conclusion. So far have I been from giving any *pretence* for further severity, that I have, with the most scrupulous exactness, conformed to everything which has been enjoined. I take the freedom to suggest the following arrangement as calculated to give as little suspicion of intercourse between the state prisoners, and to give them as much air and exercise as is attainable.

"There are five state prisoners, and twelve hours daylight, from six in the morning to six in the evening. If we were each allowed to walk one hour every morning and one hour every afternoon, there would exist no necessity for any two to be in the yard at the same time.

"In hopes that my situation will be considered as ample apology for this communication, and that you will favor me with your determination,
I remain, sir, yours, &c.,
JOHN BINNS."

On the Tuesday following, I was visited by the under sheriff. He brought me a polite message from the sheriff, which, however, has caused no alteration in my treatment, nor in the condition of my room. He then informed me, that in a few minutes he would have the honor of introducing Colonel Watson, and the commissioned officers of the Seventh Light Dragoons. I had scarce time to reflect upon so extraordinary a procedure when he left the room, and promptly returned, introducing, I cannot tell how many, but my room was soon full of military officers. The colonel, under sheriff, and myself talked of how indifferently I was accommodated, &c., &c., and at the end of half an hour they bowed and retired, to pay a like visit to the other state prisoners. They apologized for their intrusion, and said it was under orders. This visit gave birth to a multitude of conjectures and some meditation.

Tuesday, April 17, Mr. White, the Solicitor of the Treasury, sent one of his clerks to my room about nine in the evening, with a copy of the indictment, a list of witnesses, and a list of petit jurors. The indictment consisted of seventeen sheets of closely written pages of folio paper. The list of jurors embraced upwards of two hundred names, and the list of witnesses for the Crown upwards of one hundred.

On Thursday, May 19, Mr. Bonney went to London to make some necessary inquiries. I gave him letters and instructions to people in London, who would cheerfully aid him in relation to all matters touching my defence.

On Sunday, O'Connor whispered through the keyhole of my door, that my brother and some twenty or thirty other persons had been arrested for treasonable practices. While the Government were thus laboring to overawe our friends, they were endeavoring also by promises to win others to their purposes. For some weeks a Catholic priest was closeted daily, and for hours, every day, locked in the room with the Rev. Mr. Coigley, promising him that his life should be spared if he would make a full discovery of all he knew touching my brother's late visit to Ireland, and give evidence against O'Connor and I.

Take the following extract from a note I received from Coigley, through the hole in my door. It should be borne in mind that Mr. Coigley was himself a Catholic priest in good standing. "I applied," he writes, "for a clergyman. Some of the ministerial tools sent for Dr. Douglass, the superior of the priests in London; he appointed, and he instructed Mr. Griffiths, also a priest, who waited on Mr. Wickham, under Secretary of State, for a letter to the jailer, here; and *there*, I believe, he got another lesson. He told me he had sufficient ground, from what he heard from Dr. Douglass and Mr. Wickham, to say that my life would be spared, if I would make a full and candid disclosure of what I knew, and that they did not wish to hang me, on account of my being in orders."

In another note from Mr. Coigley, he thus wrote: ("The priest, the Rev. Mr. Griffiths,) used every means that cunning, unbounded zeal, or pretended piety and religion could invent to induce me to make an entire confession to Government of everything I knew; asked if I would swear against my fellow-prisoners, O'Connor and you in particular." Thus did the Government of Great Britain resort to every base means to take our lives. Innocence itself was but a slender safeguard against the arts and influence of such a Government. On the return from London of Mr. Bonney, I learned that my brother, and those who had been arrested, had been liberated. The postponement of the trial at Maidstone, was to give time to obtain the attendance of witnesses, some of them in Ireland, who were deemed essential to the defence of Coigley and O'Connor, who both made oath to that effect.

Tuesday, May 15.—Since my imprisonment here, my life has been so invariably the same; the acts of one day are so like the acts of another, that the doings and thoughts of one day, if narrated, would be so like the doings and thoughts of another, that one day would scarcely be distinguishable from another. Reading, writing, walking, eating, drinking, and sleeping, each formed a part, and together formed the whole of my doings. It is verily the life of a horse in a mill, save only that the man has more apprehensions and anxieties. Pen, ink, and paper were so long withheld, and when granted, the use so restricted, that many circumstances, some of them doubtless of moment, have been forgotten; while others, it may be of little value, have been minutely, if not tediously detailed.

On the 31st of May, 1798, the judges, the counsel, the jurors, and the prisoners were in the court when Mr.

Plumer, one of the counsel for the prisoners, stated to the court that a most flagitious attempt had been made to poison the fountain of justice. He then read a letter, written and forwarded to a friend by the Rev. Arthur Young, in which he informed his friend that he had for some time been using all his influence to convince the jurors of the Blackburn hundred how absolutely necessary it was at the present moment, for the security of the realm, that the felons (the prisoners) should swing. "I urged them," said he, "by all possible means in my power, to hang them, through mercy, with a view that they should go into court, avowedly determined in their verdict, no matter what was the evidence." This letter, the Rev. Arthur Young admitted was written by him to insure the hanging of five men of whom he knew nothing but from common report. For this atrocious offence he was tried and acquitted. Is not such an acquittal a reproach to the administration of justice? With such dark and deep stains upon their judicial escutcheon, how can, how dare, England boast of the purity of her judicial ermine?

It is the opinion of professional men, that at the Maidstone trial for high treason, in 1798, there was as much legal talent, ingenuity, and research displayed, and as much business done, as at any state trial in England. On the 21st of May, 1798, the judges were on the bench, the counsel were at the bar, and the prisoners in the dock at eight o'clock in the morning. The court did not adjourn till twelve o'clock that night. All that time, sixteen hours, the several parties never left their places more than for a few minutes at a time; whatever they ate or drunk, was eaten and drunk by the judges, the jury, the bar, and the prisoners, in the several places where they were severally stationed. The next day the several parties were in their several places at eight o'clock in the morning, and did not adjourn until twenty-five minutes after one the next morning—seventeen hours and thirty-five minutes, subject to certain duties and privations. The audience part of the court was always crowded and guarded, not only by police officers of the court, but by a military force.

THE RIOT IN COURT.

Judge Buller finished charging the jury at ten minutes before one o'clock on the morning of the 24th of May, 1798. The jury came into court at twenty-five minutes after one o'clock of the 25th. They brought in a verdict of *guilty* against Jas. Coigley, and *not guilty* as to the other prisoners. The court remained in session while the jury were out, the prisoners being in the bar. Few persons left the court-house. The bar was directly opposite to the bench, at a distance of from twenty-five to thirty feet. I had a commanding view of everything which was done in front of the bar. I was attentive to all that was said, and all that was done during the riot. Behind the prisoners, a little elevated, sat the keeper of the Maidstone prison and some constables. The crowd in the court-house was at all times excluded from the business part of the house.

When the jury retired to consider of their verdict, O'Connor called my attention to a king's messenger and some police officers who were sitting to the right, nearly under us, on the seat appropriated for the gentlemen of the bar. He expressed the belief that on his acquittal it would be found that these men had authority to arrest and take him to Ireland. This belief gained ground, and its truth was soon reduced to a certainty. Watson, the jailer, addressing himself to the person named, said: "Mr. O'Connor, you are not discharged, though you are acquitted."

O'Connor.—"Why?"

Watson.—"Because I have no authority to discharge you, and therefore you must not go."

Immediately after sentence had been passed on Coigley, some persons under the bar, in which were the prisoners, said: "O'Connor, you are acquitted. What do you stand there for? Why don't you jump over?" O'Connor made answer: "Mr. Watson says I am not to go." The person below said: "Pshaw! you are acquitted; what do you stay there for? Jump over." O'Connor then jumped over the bar, which was nearly breast-high, and Watson cried out: "Stop him! stop him!" O'Connor ran toward the hatch-door on his left hand, which, at a distance of twenty or thirty feet, opened into the audience part of the court-house. Midnight as it was, that portion of the house was crowded, and the large doors, or rather gates, opening to the street on each side, were open for the ingress and egress of the people, and to admit fresh air into the court-house. These gates were guarded by the Maidstone Infantry, some of whom were stationed between the gate and the hatch-door to which O'Connor ran, but through which he was unable to make his way. He was there seized, brought back, and replaced in the bar, where he remained with the other prisoners until they were all taken back to the prison.

I do not think I can convey to my readers an adequate idea of the confusion and noise consequent upon this attempt of O'Connor. The Maidstone volunteers rushed through the doorway where O'Connor had been endeavoring to escape; a cry was raised by many voices, of "Shoot the prisoners." Coigley, on my right, was perfectly still. He looked on quietly, neither stirring hand nor foot. Some persons behind seized my arms, drew them behind me, and put a mace across my back, between my back and my arms. I was thus promptly and safely pinioned. I could not see, but I could hear the noise behind, and could distinctly see and hear all that took place in front. The judges all exhibited fear. They did not, like Roman senators, keep their seats and face the danger; they rose up and opened the doors to the passage-way behind them on their retreat from the bench. The clerk of the court, whose official seat was immediately under, and in front, of the judges, jumped on the barrister's table, instantly drew one of the splendid military swords which were on the table, and, flourishing it round his head, cried aloud: "Defend the court," and forthwith, in his fright and hurry, cut down several of the patent lamps (there were then no gas-lights) which were suspended over the table on which he stood. This partial extinction of the light increased the noise and confusion.

At the time O'Connor jumped over the bar, two of the London police, who were seated at the barrister's table, pushed violently forward to seize him. Earl Thanet was sitting between them and the outlet from the bar-end, and either from accident or design obstructed their egress, upon which they pushed him down, with his face to the table, where, with good stout sticks, and a hearty good-will, they gave him some half a score of reasonably heavy blows on his back, which presented the most favorable part on which they could exercise themselves.

Counsellor Ferguson also made some demonstrations of friendliness to O'Connor. He and Earl Thanet were tried and found guilty of being concerned in the riot. Lord Thanet was sentenced to pay a fine of a thousand pounds, [$5,000,] to be imprisoned one year in the Tower, and give security in twenty thousand pounds [$100,000] for his good behavior for seven years. Mr. Ferguson was sentenced to pay a fine of a hundred pounds, [$500,] to be imprisoned in the King's Bench prison one year, and give security in one hundred pounds [$500] for his good behavior for seven years.

Both sentences were inflicted on these gentlemen to the utmost extent, while the Rev. Arthur Young, when tried for a strenuous and deliberate effort to have five men hung, "No matter what the evidence," was acquitted and promoted in the church. It is quite probable that, if alive, he is now a bishop. Such is the "even-handed justice" of the British government on state trials. Judge Buller said from the bench: "This clergyman ought to be punished, and very heavily." Judge Heath said: "It is a very grave offence."*

It is now (1854) two years since a friend in Paris advised me of the death of General Arthur C. O'Connor, in the eighty-ninth year of his age. The same friend assured me the general had completed, in five volumes, his "Life and Times," and left them with his wife for publication; and that she had taken them to Switzerland. On receiving this information, I ordered, through a bookseller here, a copy of the work so soon as published in Europe, well knowing the superior opportunities and talent of the writer,

---

* Howett's State Trials, vol. xxvi. p. 122.

and that he was intimately acquainted with all the relations, intercourse, and negotiations which had taken place between the would-be Irish rebels and the Government of France. To my extreme disappointment, regret, and mortification, my order was returned to the bookseller here, with the information that Mrs. General O'Connor had printed the work in Dublin; that the Government had seized the whole edition, and suppressed the publication. I am unable to say whether a copy, printed or manuscript, remains in possession of the relations or friends of the deceased. I fervently hope there may be. Thus circumstanced, I feel called upon to write in relation to my departed friend whatever may have come to my knowledge.

In "Fraser's Magazine," for April, 1852, is the following extract from Lord Holland's "History of the Whig Party:" "Few pitied Mr. Arthur O'Connor. He had betrayed, at Maidstone, an anxiety for his own safety hardly honorable to any man, and quite unpardonable in one who had involved others as well as himself in very dangerous transactions."

It will not be disputed that my opportunities of knowing the conduct of "Mr. Arthur O'Connor" were very superior to those of my Lord Holland; and I affirm that the conduct of Arthur O'Connor never did, at any time, or under any circumstances, exhibit any other than an honorable and warrantable *anxiety* for his personal safety.

In the same Magazine, p. 443, we are assured that, in 1802, four years after the trial at Maidstone, the uncle of Lord Holland, the Right Honorable Charles James Fox, a man of riper judgment than his nephew, invited Arthur O'Connor to take dinner with him at Quilbac's Hotel, in Calais.

Mr. Adolphus, whose ultra Tory opinions are well known, says in a note to his history: "I have been told by a gentleman, whose information I know to have been correct [why not give his name], and on whose word I can implicitly rely, that this statement [about the Executive Directory of France] is true. The letter [the address] was never intended to be communicated to the French Directory; but that at a tavern in London, the well-known resort of inferior agents of sedition, a person deeply engaged in their proceedings, produced the letter to O'Coigley, proposing that copies should be scattered about to frighten Pitt. O'Coigley did not recollect putting the letter [the address] into his pocket, nor had ever mentioned it to his companions, except in a short conversation at Canterbury."

There is not a word of truth in this statement of the Tory Historian of England.

Lord Holland, p. 22, says: "O'Coigley, feeling that he had endangered the companions that he had with him, generously entreated them to sacrifice him without scruple, if in any way it could contribute to their defence. With this request, Mr. O'Connor religiously complied."

Mr. Coigley, at all times, behaved himself as became an honorable man; but he never, at any time, or upon any occasion, made any such proposal, much less entreaty, as my Lord Holland has been pleased to manufacture for him. I feel warranted in saying that his lordship invented the above slander, solely for the purpose of casting upon Mr. O'Connor the foul imputation which he has done.

Having charged and *proved* my Lord Holland guilty of falsehood on many occasions, I feel called upon, indeed bound, to state, that he has stated one truth; but not of Arthur O'Connor. Thus it reads, in his History, p. 124: "When Judge Buller, in passing judgment [sentence], enlarged in commonplace eloquence, on the mercy and virtues of George the Third, the poor man, Coigley, with great composure, but with a smile of contempt, took a pinch of snuff and cried 'Hem.'"

This is most true; he stood close to me at the time sentence was passed, and I know it to be true. He took his snuff with all possible deliberation, and made so loud a noise in taking it as to attract very general attention and the eyes of the whole court, and the expression of his face and his whole manner was indicative of entire disbelief in the praises lavished by Judge Buller on George the Third.

In 1828, I wrote the following letter to Mr. O'Connor:—

PHILADELPHIA, *August* 25, 1828.

DEAR SIR: I just learn from a friend of mine (Mr. Canonge, a merchant of New York), that he will leave this city on Tuesday next for Paris. He has obligingly offered to take any small packet I may wish.

I embrace the occasion, after a silence of thirty years, to write to one whose esteem I was ambitious to obtain, and whose friendship I had flattered myself I had merited. Why I have not written to you before I can give no other reason than that I have had a feeling that I was forgotten or neglected. My friend, and your friend, Dr. Hudson, had, as I learned from your frank and manly letter to him of the 3d of December, 1811, informed you of the bitter and malignant persecution set on foot against me, in a charge so detestable that I could not make up my mind to the degradation of denying or confuting it. I thought that, with this knowledge, I had a right to expect from you, who knew all about it, a communication. I do not now undertake to justify that expectation, or my silence, much less can I prevail upon myself to think I was much to blame. This picture of my feelings and motives I present as the true cause why I have not written; and now, allow me to say why the current of my feelings is changed, and I am now writing to you.

A few days ago our common friend, General Devereux, called on me and said: "I saw our friend Arthur O'Connor, at Paris, and he desired to be affectionately remembered to our friend Hudson, and to you." I expressed my gratification at the interesting account he gave me of your family and domestic felicity. The next time I saw Hudson we had a conversation about you, as we had had many times before; and, having mentioned what Devereux had said, I said, I think I will write to O'Connor the first opportunity. This thought is now being carried into execution, and I frankly confess that I feel much satisfied in, to use an American phrase, finding myself employed in brightening the chain of friendship with a man for whom I have so strongly and keenly felt as I have for you.

I accompany this letter with a small pamphlet, published a few months ago, on the subject of the Coigley charge. I need not ask for it your serious attention. May I recall to your memory a few facts connected with that memorable enterprise by which our lives were so eminently jeopardized by the indiscretion, to call it by no harsher name, of unfortunate Coigley.

You will remember that you and I walked from Deal to Margate, that there we found Coigley, Allen, and Leary, who had come across the country from Whitstable; on the road from which place, on your road to Canterbury, I had met you the day before. We went together to Margate, to which place, in a Whitstable hoy, you had come with Coigley, &c., from London. I never saw Coigley, as you know, from the time he left London until I saw him at Margate, where we were all arrested. You will also remember, that, after having been kept in separate postchaises from the time we left Margate until our arrival at the police office in Bow Street, we, that is, Coigley, you, and I, were all put into a back room, where, for the first time, to our utter consternation and amazement, we learned from Coigley the existence and nature of the paper he had left in his coat pocket. This was the first intimation we had of the existence of the paper which jeopardized our lives.

There are many particulars which will present themselves to your mind, which, even at this distance of time, will enable you to bear willing and honorable testimony to the fearlessness and disinterestedness which marked my whole conduct.

I am at this time an Alderman of this city, and a Judge of one of our Criminal Courts, and it is desirable that no speck or spot should stain the ermine; therefore, as well as from personal and family considerations, I should wish to have a letter from you.

I herewith send for you and for General Lafayette each a copy of a splendid edition, which I have recently published, of the Declaration of Independence. It may occasionally remind you of one who has long had the liveliest esteem and respect for you, and holds your services and devotion to our common country in grateful remembrance. Take the trouble to have the other copy, and a letter you will find inclosed, conveyed to General Lafayette.

You and the General will be surprised to learn that this is the *first* CORRECT *copy* of the Declaration *ever published*. It is not even correctly printed on the journal of Congress of 1776. The caption, as printed in the journal of Congress, is as follows: "The Declaration of the thirteen United States of America." On the original parchment, and in the correct copy I have published, it is in these words: "The UNANIMOUS Declaration of the thirteen United States of America."

It is somewhat remarkable that one of the most effective words in one of the most important state papers, should never have been published correctly until twenty-five years after the Independence, which that paper proclaimed, had been acknowledged by the whole world, yea, even by him who most obstinately opposed it, George the Third, King of Great Britain and Ireland.

Affectionately and respectfully, I am your friend,
JOHN BINNS.

MAJOR-GENERAL ARTHUR CONDORCET O'CONNOR,
(MR. CANONGE.) *Paris.*

CHAPTER VIII.

Another storm gathers over my head, and I retire to Derby—Descend into a coal-pit—Return to London—Interview with Sir Richard Ford—Mr. Kerr—Report of Secret Committee of the House of Commons—I am again arrested, and put in Clerkenwell prison—My examination before Privy Council—I am joined in prison by an old acquaintance; give him some good advice; its result—My removal to Gloucester prison—Incidents—My apartments—I am visited by the Dean of Gloucester—Jealousy of my fellow-prisoners—I give them a thrashing—My letters to the Duke of Portland.

A. D. 1798. The morning after my acquittal and liberation, I left Maidstone on my return to London. On my way, while dining at a tavern where the stage stopped, I saw at the dinner-table Mr. Mason, the king's messenger, in whose custody I had been, and at whose house I was for some days before my commitment to the Tower. He was on his way from Maidstone to London. As we rose from table, he said: "Mr. Binns, I wish to speak with you." I followed him into another room, thinking, nay, not doubting, but he had a warrant for my arrest on some new charge of hostility to the Government. I was mistaken. He had information to communicate which he knew would be agreeable. I thanked him and we parted.

A few days after my arrival in London from Maidstone, I had information from a person, upon whom I had cause to rely, that a warrant for my arrest on a charge of high treason had been issued. This information, unwelcome and vexatious as it was unexpected, determined me to retire into the country until the political storm should somewhat abate. I went into the counties of Derby and Nottingham, where I had many friends, and there remained several weeks under the name of Pemberton, my mother's maiden name, and passed my time very agreeably.

While in Derbyshire, I had the curiosity to descend, dressed altogether in flannel, in a large wooden bucket attached to a windlass, into a coal-pit. The well-like excavation through which I descended, was of very considerable depth, probably two hundred and fifty or three hundred feet. While descending in the bucket, the springs, after I had descended a certain depth, showered water on me like a heavy cold rain; when near the bottom, casting my eyes up, I saw the stars in the firmament as bright as in a clear blue sky at midnight. The average height of the centre of the coal-arches under which I passed into the mine, where several men with pickaxes were picking out the earth, while others with iron wedges and sledge-hammers were setting the upper strata of coal at liberty, was not five feet high. This imposed upon me the necessity of stooping all the time I was in the mine. The flannel in which I was clothed was quite wet with spring water in my descent, and was soon after wet with perspiration, insomuch that I well remember it gave me such a pain in my back, that I was unable to stand upright for several days. Children are born, and hundreds of people live and die, in such miserable habitations.

In November, 1798, I left Nottingham, and arrived in London on the same day. The following morning I waited on Sir Richard Ford; he was one of the Bow Street police magistrates, and also Secretary to the Duke of Portland, who was Secretary of State for the Home Department. From that quarter I felt assured I could obtain the information I required. I had an interview with Sir Richard Ford, to whom I mentioned the information I had received, and inquired if it were true, stating that I would much rather surrender myself than be arrested. "What are you now doing, Mr. Binns?" I said I was about entering into business as superintendent with Mr. Peter Kerr, a steam-engine manufacturer and contractor with Government for gun-carriages, &c.; but this information, I said, had deranged all my plans, and therefore it was I sought to ascertain the truth from authority. The answer was in substance, if not in words, what follows: "Why, Mr. Binns, circumstances have recently so much changed, and so favorably for the Government, that I do not think it probable there is any intention of arresting you. However," continued he, after a short and thoughtful pause, "I will mention at Whitehall your visit, and I shall then be able to give you a decisive answer." I retired, and in a few days, by appointment, again saw Sir Richard, who said he had communicated what I said to the Duke of Portland, and felt authorized to say that, if I was not found to interfere with the Administration, I should not be molested. I gave my address, and took my leave.

I went to and continued for some time at my friend Mr. Kerr's manufactory. He was one of the most extraordinary men I ever knew. He had received so little education, that he wrote slowly, awkwardly, and with difficulty; as to orthography, it was an art with which he had but slight acquaintance. It was from the sound of the word that he guessed at, and put together letters to form it, whenever he found himself under the necessity of joining letters to make words. He had, however, a warm heart, and a remarkably clear head, eminently so as to machinery and mechanics. He had obtained several patents, one for an improvement in the steam-engine, and one for a self-oiling coach and wagon axletree-box. Before the patent was granted for the box, he inserted a set of the boxes in the hubs of the wheels of a mail stage-coach, which, without any other supply of oil, ran from London to Edinburgh, three hundred and seventy miles, and back. On its return to London, the boxes were found in good order, the supply of oil unexhausted, and a patent was granted. This performance would at this time, 1854, be regarded as that of a slow wagon. Then there were no railroads, save only for short distances, to drag on them small roller-moving carriages laden with marble, iron, coal, or other heavy substances from the quarries and pits to the yard and places of sale and consumption. Such railroads were always made down hill; the cars were strong and heavily built, such as a few years ago, and probably now, may be seen at the Lehigh and other coal mines in Pennsylvania. They did not, I think, carry more than about two hundred pounds each. Such railroads and carriages were in use for at least half a century before lengthened railroads with steam-engines to draw carriages, and burden-cars laden with many tons, were to be seen; such cars are now drawn at the rate of twenty, thirty, forty, and even fifty miles an hour; whereas the small burden-cars, of which I have just spoken, did not go, when laden, at the rate of more than a mile or two an hour.

Deficient, however, as my friend, Mr. Kerr, was of knowledge extracted from books, he had a fund of practical common sense. He understood mankind, and discerned their motives and their springs of action, with a quickness and correctness which was admirable. Notwithstanding his avowed republican principles, he was constantly under contract, making improved gun-carriages for the English Government. More than once, with all frankness, he stated to me his early life. He was a native of Scotland, and had a brae, broad, national brogue, which he carefully cultivated. His parents were poor; he was sometimes an errand-boy, for their benefit; he ran away from them, however, at an early age, having become enamored of a strolling company of showmen. Under their instruction, he became an expert ground and lofty tumbler, and at length attained the honor to become a clown. He was afterwards a gardener, a waiter, a coachman, and, at length, found himself in London, in his proper element, in a blacksmith shop. He had previously worked as a locksmith and bell-hanger; soon after, he put his mechanical head to work, and commenced as a mechanician in iron work, on his own account. When I knew him, he had about fifty men, and a steam-engine, at work. He was a man of property, and enjoyed much respect and confidence. My residence was distant from the factory about three-quarters of a mile, near Pentonville, three miles from London. The factory was inclosed by a high wall, gateway, and side-doors.

A report, from a secret committee, was made to the House of Commons, by Mr. Secretary Dundas, chairman of the committee, and, by order of the House, printed in pamphlet form, for the use of the members, under date of the 15th of March, 1799. In that report—extracts from which I was early favored with—my name was several times mentioned as that of a person particularly zealous and influential in organizing political associations, in opposition to the Government. This report, coming from so distinguished a cabinet minister as Mr. Secretary Dundas, and bearing the imprimatur of the House of Commons, excited in me strong apprehensions. How could it fail? I knew how powerless would be my most solemn asseverations, when met by the feeblest whisperings of authority. "Attempts," says this report, "were made to form, in London, upon the plan of the United Irishmen, the Society of United Englishmen, or United Britons, and O'Coigley and John Binns appear to have been leading persons in that design." It is now more than half a century since that report was published, and I declare that, until I read the report, I had never even heard of any society or societies, such as those named in the report. In another part of that report, is the following passage: "About the same time, February 1, 1798, a most seditious paper, from the London Corresponding Society to the Society of United Irishmen, signed J. T. Crossfield, President, Thomas Evans, Secretary, dated 30th January, 1798, was published in Ireland, in a paper called the 'Press,' and the original seized in March, 1798, in consequence of the apprehension of Arthur O'Connor, in England." The address, here spoken of, was written by the same hand which is writing these lines. The date of it shows that it was written and published more than a year before Mr. Secretary Dundas made his report.

On the 16th of March, 1799, the next day after the report had been made to the House of Commons, and before it was published in the newspapers, having dined at my boarding-house, I had not proceeded far, on my return to the factory, when, a few yards in front of me, I saw Revitt, one of the officers by whom I had been arrested at Margate, and another police officer, with their eyes fixed on me, and walking fast toward me. I promptly conjectured their business, turned short to the right, and ran up a narrow street which led into the country. I ran swiftly, and the officers did their best in pursuit. The longer we continued to run, the greater was their distance. Despairing of overtaking me, they raised a loud cry of "Stop thief! stop thief!" I had just leaped a fence, and would soon have cleared myself, had not a respectable-looking man, hearing the cry of "Stop thief," and seeing me running, struck me, with a heavy stick, a violent blow across the breast, which knocked me down, and I was captured. Both the officers were fat, and the day being warm, they were bathed in sweat, and out of breath. I have rarely seen two men more exhausted than they were when they reached and made me prisoner. I demanded their authority; they produced a warrant, signed by the Duke of Portland, commanding them to arrest the body of John Binns, on a charge of "treasonable practices." "If I had known," said the man who had just knocked me down, "what your warrant was for, I should have been pretty clear of busying myself." Having ascertained the charge, I told the officers I would accompany them to my lodgings, give them my keys, and they might take what they thought proper, and mark what they took, in my presence. They did as I suggested, called the coach they had in waiting, and took me, and a trunk which they had filled with selected articles, books, and papers, to where the Privy Council was sitting. I was conducted into a large room, where I remained about two hours, but was not that day taken before the Council, or by any one examined. I was committed to Clerkenwell prison. The prison-gate being opened, and the commitment and I delivered to a jailer, the Bow Street officers took their leave. It was then about five o'clock in the afternoon. I was shown into a moderate-sized room, in which was a table, some chairs, a bedstead, bed, and furniture. Dinner was served, tea, &c. soon followed, and then to bed, care having been taken to throw a heavy iron chain across the door, and to lock and bolt it.

The next day, soon after breakfast, accompanied with the usual retinue of officers, I was taken in a carriage to near the Horse Guards, and soon after shown into a large room, in which the Privy Council were sitting. The members were seated round a large long table, covered with a green cloth; Mr. Pitt was conversing earnestly with another gentleman; sometimes they stood still and sometimes they slowly paced the carpet.

The room was perfectly still, when the Duke of Portland, addressing himself to me, politely said: "I am sorry, Mr. Binns, that I have been under the necessity of again requiring your attendance."

Binns.—"I am very sure your Grace is not so sorry as I am, and I am also very sure I have given no cause for my arrest."

Duke of Portland.—"How can any one doubt the necessity of your arrest, who has read the report made to the House of Commons by Mr. Secretary Dundas?"

Binns.—"Very true, your Grace, if they credit it; but I know, so far as I am concerned, that it is without foundation in truth."

Mr. Dundas then stepped forward and said, looking me full in the face, "I beg your pardon; it is all in evidence under oath."

Binns.—"I do not doubt it, sir; but I *know* it to be untrue so far as relates to myself."

The bell was rung, and I was taken into another room. After a lapse of some hours, without being again taken before the Council, I was taken back to Clerkenwell, to the room from which I had been taken in the forenoon. I had finished my tea, and was about to retire to bed, when another prisoner was brought into the room. A cot-bed, &c., was brought for him to sleep on, and we were locked up. The man, thus made my room-mate, I quickly recognized as a countryman of mine, who kept a public house in Oxford Street, where I had occasionally, within the last year, met a division of United Irishmen. He told me, he did not know for what he had been arrested; that he had not been asked any questions; but had, by Rivett, been brought from his own house to this jail and put into my room. I found him well disposed, and sat up talking with him about two hours. I put to him all such questions as I thought it probable, from my own experience, would be asked him at the Privy Council, suggesting and impressing upon him such answers as he ought to make to effect his own liberation, and best serve his political friends. He was intelligent, and entered thoroughly into my views, which he was anxious to carry out. In the morning, for about the same length of time, I put him through the same questions, and impressed upon him the same answers, so that when the officer came, at noon, to take him to the Privy Council, I considered he was well prepared to be questioned, and to answer. I did not see him for some considerable time after, when he told me what took place at Whitehall, in, as near as I can recollect, the words following: "In troth, Mr. Binns, it's myself that's right glad to see you. I have been longing to tell you all that passed when they took me fornent Mr. Pitt, and the rest of the lords and gentry. They asked me a power of questions, and just such questions as you said they would, and as you had put to me before; so I did my best, and gave them, as near as I could, all the answers, as you told me to give them. They appeared to be surprised, looked at one another, and seemed to be asking questions one of another, although they said nothing at all that I could hear, the devil a word. After a while I heard a bell ring pretty fast and pretty loud, and a man came in, and the Bow Street officer that had took me up was sent for; he was quite near at hand, and when he came in, Mr. Pitt pointed his finger at me, and said, 'Where was that man confined?' 'In Clerkenwell,' says the officer. 'Who was in the room with him?' says Pitt. 'John Binns,' says the officer. 'I knew it,' says Pitt. 'There's Binns's very words coming out of that fellow's mouth.' I said nothing, but said I didn't know Mr. Binns at all at all, and only just saw him that one night in the jail. After a couple of days more they sent me home, and tould me they would keep a good watch over me."

Some days passed before I was again taken to the Privy Council, and when I was, they held toward me a milder tone than they had done before. It was then at least tacitly admitted that I had broken no promise; but they said they could not trust me; how could they, and believe Mr. Dundas's report? and therefore I must be confined. This declaration was, in some measure, softened by the assurance that I might select the place in which I should be confined. I named the Tower, made my bow, and was reconducted to Clerkenwell prison. About ten days after, the keeper of the prison told me that he understood I would soon be removed; he did not know where, or at least did not inform me. I accordingly made what preparations and arrangements I deemed necessary, not entertaining a doubt but I should be sent to the Tower. I was miserably mistaken. "Put not your trust in princes," nor in their ministers. One morning, early in May, before daylight, two officials came into my room, and by force, put on my wrists a pair of light handcuffs. My trunks were made fast behind a postchaise, I was handed in, and the officials took seats beside me. To my surprise I was told I was on my way to Gloucester prison. A "copy of instructions," dated "Whitehall, May, 1799," signed "Portland," and addressed to the keeper of the prison, was sent with me. It stated that I was "committed for treasonable practices," "to be confined alone;" "to be, on no account, permitted to hold any intercourse, or communication, with any person whatever, within or without the prison, without authority from one of his Majesty's principal Secretaries of State;" "to be allowed the use of pen, ink and paper, in presence of some confidential person appointed by the keeper," and my "correspondence to be submitted to one or more of the visiting magistrates;" "to be permitted to read such books as may be approved by the visiting magistrates;" "his money to be taken, if you think he has more than sufficient, giving him a regular receipt for it." "The sum of thirteen shillings and four pence, sterling, weekly ($3,$\frac{8}{100}$), exclusive of coal, will be allowed him for his maintenance, to be laid out as he shall direct, subject to the visiting magistrates, excepting that he must not be allowed the use of spirituous liquors."

I was received at the gate of the jail by the governor;

that is the title bestowed upon the principal keeper of the prison. His name was Cunningham, a retired half-pay officer in the army of his Britannic Majesty. He was well known in Philadelphia in 1777, while it was in possession of the British army. At that time, and in that service, Cunningham was Provost Marshal at Walnut Street prison. He married an American lady. She was an intelligent, good-looking, well-bred woman, younger than he was some years. She was living with him in the governor's apartments, at the time I was confined. He was, at the period at which I am writing, about fifty years of age, five feet seven inches high, well made and well mannered. So long as I was in the prison, which was until February, 1801, I never had an angry word with him, nor any reasonable cause of complaint against him.

The prison was built of granite, upon the penitentiary system, superintended and governed by a board of magistrates. It covered several acres of ground, and was surrounded by a heavy stone wall, twenty or more feet high. The jail itself was not less than eighty or ninety feet from the outer or surrounding wall of the prison. The governor's house, which was large and lofty, was of brick, and exactly faced the entrance to the prison. Over and around this entrance-gate were rooms, in which resided the gate-keeper and his family. There were also bathing-rooms, in which the penitentiary prisoners, on their entrance, were washed, their clothes were taken from them, and they were then dressed in the uniform of the prison. One half of the outside of these prison garments was yellow, and the other half brown. The object of thus clothing the prisoners, in party-colored garments, was to facilitate their recapture, if they should by any plan or any chance escape. The roof of this outer building over the entrance-gate was about twenty or twenty-five feet from the ground. It was square, flat roofed, and had a strong iron railing round it. On a gallows erected, as occasion required, on that roof, all those who suffered death by sentence of the law in that county were hung. That platform, on which the condemned were executed, was directly opposite, and nearly on a level with the windows of the day room in which I was confined. On that roof I saw several men hung, for highway robbery and horse-stealing, and one for murder. This last was a remarkable case. This man was, from his appearance on the platform, threescore and ten years of age, low in stature and slight in person. There was a chair on the platform, on which he sat. He was dressed in a suit of fine light brown woollen clothes, and silk stockings of the same color. His right leg was thrown across his left thigh, near to his knee. His left side was toward the prison. It appeared to me that he was troubled with an itchy humor in his right leg, which, as it rested on his left thigh, he gently rubbed with his left hand, apparently unconscious or indifferent to his position and prospects. The sheriff, and a few gentlemen, were on the platform, and the executioner was making the necessary arrangements to perform his duty. The same calm indifference, I might say apparent unconsciousness of his situation, and of the persons and things about him, marked the conduct of this aged man to the latest period of his life. It was a scene of deep interest. I had made inquiry as to the cause of his execution, and had the same statement from the governor and turnkey. He was a gentleman of large fortune, but avaricious habits. He was, however, in association with the gentlemen of his county. The year before his execution, when paying the collector the income tax assessed upon his estate, he found much fault with the tax, said it was unjust and unequal, and at length advised the man, as he valued his life, never again to call on him to collect that tax, threatening, if he did, that he would surely shoot him. The man, unfortunately for them both, disregarded the warning given him, and he who gave it kept his word to the letter. The next year, this aged man, sitting in one of the front rooms of his house, looking down the long avenue of trees, and seeing the doomed tax-gatherer walking toward the house, with his tax-book under his arm, promptly took a gun, which he kept charged, and shot the unfortunate man dead. He did not attempt to escape, was forthwith arrested, and imprisoned. Soon after he was tried, convicted, and sentenced to be hung. I saw the sentence carried into execution. I never was able to ascertain, and I made many inquiries, that he complained of any of the proceedings against him, or murmured against the sentence under which he was executed. While in prison, before and after his trial and conviction, he submitted, unmurmuringly, to all the privations and restrictions to which he was subjected. I never understood that he was visited by relations or friends while in prison, nor did it appear that any the slightest attention was paid to him while on the platform.

Soon after my entrance into Gloucester prison, I was ushered into a large room, to be used by me as a day room. All the time I remained in that prison, which was from May, 1799, until February, 1801, I occupied one bedroom, if room it might be called. It was, correctly speaking, an arched stone cell. Its dimensions about eight feet long, four or five feet wide, and its circular, or vault-like roof, about eight feet high, in the centre. Over the iron door or entrance was a small iron window-sash, and a large-sized one in the wall opposite the door, which opened on one of the interior yards of the prison. The frame of the larger window was also iron, and, by an iron handle, might be opened to an angle of forty-five degrees. This little place was whitewashed, and constantly so kept. Perhaps it was every way a few inches, certainly not many, larger than I have stated. The furniture consisted of a small iron camp bedstead, on which was a mattress and necessary bedding, and in winter, there were curtains to the bedstead. A square block of granite to be used as a seat, a small looking-glass, a basin stand, basin, towels, &c., &c. I was locked up in this sleeping place every night, I think about nine o'clock, and let into the day room in summer, at six, and in winter, at eight o'clock in the morning. In the day room was all necessary plain furniture. I was allowed the use of a yard abundantly large, to walk in, three or four hours a day. The rest of the day I was locked up in the day room. After I had been confined a few months, I was allowed two plats of ground, about thirty feet square each, to cultivate as a garden. They were strongly railed in and opened on the flag-way, where I was permitted to walk. I cultivated the ground with some care, and raised many vegetables such as peas, beans, lettuces, radishes, &c., &c., for my own use.

In the summer of 1799, which was an unusually warm summer in England, I planted two sound grains of maize, or Indian corn, in a small, rich bed of ground near a wall, for the benefit of the sun; I tended them carefully. The stalk of the healthiest and strongest plant grew to about four feet high. On it there were three or four small cobs, imperfectly covered with corn, which never ripened or grew to the proper size. I do not think that any care or attention, which the most intelligent agriculturist, with the very best ground, and the greatest care, could bestow upon this vegetable, would ever induce it to come to its proper size, and ripen, in England. There is not sun nor warmth enough of climate.

The board of visiting magistrates, who acted as inspectors of the prison, met twice every week. At their first meeting after my commitment, I was introduced to them in their sessions room. The usual inquiries on such occasions were made; I had no complaints to offer, which they could remedy, and we soon parted. I will here take occasion to say that, upon all occasions, and on every opportunity which presented itself, this board, and the individuals composing it, behaved to me not only with politeness, but with friendly attention, some of them supplying me with books, &c. from their own libraries, from which, for a short time, I procured what books I read. I occasionally resorted to a circulating library in Gloucester, but it had nothing but trash to loan. I then sent to London for books; the distance, say two hundred miles, and the loss of time, &c. made this an expensive and unsatisfactory mode of supply. I had a microscope, which afforded me pleasure and improvement. After having been in prison some months, the governor introduced to me a tall, mild, dignified-looking gentleman, as the "Dean of Gloucester." After an interchange of civilities, the Dean said: "I am told you read a great deal, Mr. Binns." I answered in the affirmative. In the course of conversation, he said: "I have but recently been promoted to the Deanery, and my library has not yet arrived; I have rather an extensive one; I will send you a catalogue when it arrives, and I shall be gratified by your using it freely; send for as many sets as you think proper, and keep them as long as you please." I made my acknowledgments, and, during my imprisonment, the Dean proved his offer to be as sincere as it was promptly made, and heartily fulfilled. I had an enviable and abundant supply, after he undertook to furnish me, for which I was very thankful. It may be proper, after these acknowledgments, to say that, in no instance, was I indulged more than the instructions of the Duke of Portland permitted. The inspectors were all loyal gentlemen; the Dean was one.

It has been to me a source of regret that I had no musical education. Music would, in my several confinements, have been a source of much enjoyment; I have always been fond of music, particularly sacred and military music. It seems to me that a musical cultivation of the ear is equivalent to the creation of a new sense. Do we not, however, usually overestimate the pleasures which we are unable duly to appreciate?

Some weeks after my settlement in Gloucester prison, two persons, members of the London Corresponding Society, whom I had known in the Society, were arrested and committed, for "treasonable practices," to the same prison with me. During the day, we were all in the same room; they had sleeping-places near, and similar to that in which I slept; we took daily lessons in French, and mathematics, together, without any assistance, other than what books afforded, and passed our time, for two or three months, agreeably enough. It was, however, their pleasure to become jealous, and to conspire against me, which issued in our separation. Thus it broke out:—

We were one day exercising ourselves whipping tops, in the usual flagged parade on which we walked, when my companions were sent for, and left the yard, to go before the board of magistrates, who were then sitting in the governor's house. In about three-quarters of an hour they were brought back to the yard, and I was told the magistrates wished to see me. I went to the board, the chairman of which addressed me in words to this effect: "Mr. Binns, we have sent for you to acquaint you that we received a request, from your fellow-prisoners, to be heard on a complaint of a serious character, which they had to make, in regard to violations of the discipline of the prison, to which you were a party." It is here proper to say that I had early that morning, before I went into the day room, been privately given to understand, not only that my fellow-prisoners were going to complain, but a clear intimation was given me as to the nature of the charges they were about to make. Neither of those prisoners, at any time, or on any occasion, had in any way apprised me of their mean suspicions or petty jealousies, nor warned me that they had, or thought they had, cause of complaint against me, or in relation to me; much less did they, by any hint, or coldness of manner, give me reason to surmise that they were about to lodge a formal complaint before the magistrates. If I had not, from a well-informed quarter, been thus apprised of their intentions, I might have felt at a loss, when so grave a charge was made by the inspectors. So soon, however, as the chairman of the board, Sir George O. Paul, had stated the complaint, I expressed my surprise; could not imagine what could be the cause of it. The chairman proceeded: "They have just been examined by the board, and they declare that, for some time past, two or more evenings in every week, after they are locked up for the night, you, instead of being left locked up in your sleeping-room, are taken into the castle, and allowed to remain there, in the governor's rooms, in company with his lady, and occasionally his niece, until they have notice that the governor has rung the outer prison bell, upon hearing of which, you are carefully returned to, and locked in, your sleeping-room." At all this statement I expressed my astonishment, branded it as "a weak invention," indeed, a naked untruth, maliciously got up by my fellow-prisoners, whose motives I was at a loss to conjecture. Some conversation, in an undertone, took place among the magistrates, and I was conducted back to the yard from whence I came, in the full persuasion, from what I saw and what I heard, that my story, and not that of my fellow-prisoners, had full credit. I afterwards learned, indeed that same evening, that two of the turnkeys were examined, and a maid-servant, without any fact being ascertained to support the accusation.

I no sooner found myself in the yard, on my return from the board, and within striking distance of my worthy compeers, than I began thrashing them soundly; while they, to do them justice, "ran and roared" lustily, until the turnkeys came and took them out of the yard into the prison. I never saw them after, although they were confined in the same jail with me until my liberation, in March 1801, at which time all the state prisoners in England in confinement, under the suspension of the *habeas corpus* act, were liberated.

While in Gloucester prison, I wrote, at their dates, the following letters. I insert them that, from their perusal, my readers may be enabled to form a tolerably accurate opinion of the manner in which I bore my imprisonment and its privations. A perusal of these letters will also make the reader acquainted with the language I held towards the rulers of the land by whom I was persecuted.

The first line of the following letter informs the reader that other letters had preceded the one he is about to read, and he may inquire, why are those other letters withheld? I answer because, when those other letters were written, I had not made friends enough to enable me to make and keep copies of the letters I wrote. If I had them, they should not be withheld.

HIS GRACE THE DUKE OF PORTLAND,
Secretary of State for the Home Department, London.
"HEAR, AND BE JUST."

MY LORD DUKE: After a silence of nearly a year, I trust I shall not be thought importunate in submitting a few observations to your consideration. I write not to complain of the *manner* of my imprisonment, but to remonstrate against my imprisonment itself.

The only legal provision by which I could demand justice being no more, and a discretionary power lodged in the Executive Government, I think it my duty to appeal to your Grace, as the ostensible minister under whose authority I am confined, to do me that justice, and afford me that protection, which I can no longer hope legally to claim as a matter of right. It may not be irrelevant to remark, that if the *habeas corpus* act is to be suspended, during pleasure, upon the pretended, real, or supposed discovery of a traitorous conspiracy, that part of the act which was designed as a protection to the subject from the persecutions of evil ministers, becomes null and void. It is only under such circumstances that persons can be arrested; and for want of legal defence subjected to all the hardships of arbitrary imprisonment. If the act was irreversibly established, or wholly repealed, there would at least be certainty; at present, it too much resembles professional friendship—while we want not assistance, it is profusely and ostentatiously offered; but when the hour of calamity arrives, the protection on which we relied is withdrawn, and we are left, exposed and unsheltered, to encounter the pitiless storm of adversity. To condemn a prisoner upon a law passed after the commission of the offence charged, is a proceeding so pregnant with mischief, that it is prohibited by every code of jurisprudence, however otherwise imperfect or unjust. For my own part, I confess I cannot perceive the distinction between punishing a man by a law passed after the offence; and subjecting him to penalties by the abrogation of those laws which, if existing, would exonerate him from punishment. Both are, in my judgment, equally subversive of every principle of sound policy, and repugnant to every feeling of humanity.

I shall forbear noticing the hardships which others have suffered (though a beloved brother be of the number), and proceed to a statement of my own case, in which I hope to prove that I have in no instance shrunk from the responsibility I owe to the laws of the country:—

In the month of February, 1798, I was arrested, and on the 7th of March following, committed prisoner to the Tower. From my commitment to my trial, the most active and unremitted endeavors were made to procure evidence of my guilt. After the collection of a mass of evidence, for which both kingdoms had been ransacked, I was, on the 22d of May, brought to trial, and, on the morning of the 24th, ACQUITTED. I am aware that a Right Honorable member of the House of Commons has in that House declared: "That the acquittal of the persons tried at Maidstone for high treason was not evidence of their innocence." Be it remembered, that if my acquittal is not to be received as evidence of my innocence, by no just mode of reasoning can the conviction of Mr. O'Coigley, by a verdict of the same jury, delivered at the same time, on the same indictment, and upon the same testimony, be considered as a proof of his guilt. Yet, upon that verdict, he was condemned and *executed!* I do your Grace more justice than to suppose you concur in an opinion which is a most gross and scandalous libel upon the most venerable and sacred institution which the wisdom of man has devised. If, after a patient investigation of thirty-six hours, a jury is incompetent to the discharge of their duty, I know no procedure by which the guilt or innocence of a prisoner can be evinced. Immediately after my acquittal I returned to London, in the hope that I should be permitted to follow my ordinary avocations. Delusive hope! I had not been three days in London, when I received repeated assurances that a warrant was issued for my apprehension. Although I was without fear as to the ultimate consequences of such an arrest, I entertained well-grounded alarm as to the length of time I might be compelled to languish in the solitude of a prison. I therefore listened to the advice of friends and retired into the country, where, in the bosom of friendship and the lap of nature, I recovered the health I had lost in the closeness of a jail. I returned to London in November of the same year. I arrived on Sunday evening, and on Monday morning presented myself to a magistrate for the purpose of ascertaining what were the intentions of Government respecting me. In a few days after, I waited on the same gentleman at Whitehall. Those interviews, I presume to think, were not unknown to your Grace. I left my address, and promised, upon the receipt of an order, to appear at Whitehall and surrender myself prisoner if so required, but intreated I might not again be seized by ruffian thief-takers. The confident security I felt, discharged from my mind every doubt; I enjoyed the hours as they fled, and looked forward to yet happier days. Thus tranquil I remained a few months. My apprehensions for the loss of liberty were, however, powerfully excited on reading the report of the Secret Committee of the House of Commons, when I found in the reports my name frequently introduced for the purpose of loading me with obloquy, and pointing me out as a proper object of public abhorrence. A consciousness of my own innocence would not have stilled my anxiety, but when that consciousness was strengthened by the assurances of safety I had received from such respectable authority, I could not suffer my fears to disquiet my repose. I continued in public as usual. Some weeks passed away, and my friends began to indulge in mirth at the expense of my suspicions. Short-lived was their triumph and my freedom! I was once more dragged like a malefactor and entombed in a prison. After a few weeks' confinement, I was called from my bed at four o'clock in the morning, manacled like the vilest felon, and conveyed to the place from whence I now have the honor to address your Grace.

The papers on which the report of the Secret Committee is founded, and of which it chiefly consists, were presented to the House of Commons on the 23d January, 1799. How long they were previously in possession of his Majesty's ministers, I am unable to determine. The report was ordered to be printed on the 15th March, and I—who am therein denounced a principal conspirator—who was daily in the most public places of the metropolis—whose address was known to Government—who might almost at any hour have been arrested, was permitted to be at large until the 16th of April. The public mind has been too much harassed by rumors of plots and conspiracies, to find time to trace their inconsistencies, or attend to the concerns of particular persons, else it would easily have discovered how irreconcilable has been the conduct of ministers towards individuals, when compared with their publicly professed opinions. My simple narrative will justify me to your Grace in drawing such a conclusion. Pardon me, my Lord Duke, if I repeat what I represented in a letter to you, dated April, 1799, and again declare that the report of the Secret Committee is not warranted by facts. It is not necessary here to inquire whether the assertions there made originated in ignorance or design, it is sufficient for me that they have bereaved me of every enjoyment, and cut me off from every comfort. In the most solemn and unequivocal manner, I declare that Report (which has been made the instrument of depriving me wholly of freedom, and abridging that of the nation) IS FALSE. I cannot be mistaken, my Lord, as it regards my own actions; and upon the truth of this declaration I cheerfully stake all that is dear to me in life; nay, life itself. If the report can be substantiated, why am I not called upon to answer for my crimes? If I am a traitor, let me be proven so! Let the sanguinary sentence of the law be executed—let my panting heart be flung in my face—let my streaming head be held up as a terror to evil-doers—let my limbs be left to bleach in the winds of heaven; but suffer me not, unheard, to pine in solitude and fall a victim to disappointed expectation. In the name of justice, my Lord Duke, why am I shut out from all the blessings of society? I have violated none of its institutions. I review my life, and my cheek is untinged with the blush of shame. I examine my heart, and it exults in the pride of conscious integrity—yet am I, in the morning of my days, consigned to the miseries of a prison, distant from all those whose affectionate solicitude might soothe my sorrows. The tender offices of friendship are not permitted me to alleviate affliction—to the gentle voice of affection I am now a stranger—the cheerful sound of mirth never reaches me; but my ear is pained with the clanking of chains, the wailings of wretchedness, and the groans of despair. How long, my Lord Duke, am I doomed to this miserable life? How long am I destined to be the bondslave of those who (contrary to every maxim of law and justice) are at once my accusers and my judges, and the executioners of their own judgments!!!

This is not a time, nor is this a place, for me, from motives of delicacy, to forbear laying open my whole thoughts upon this subject. I wish to persuade, it is therefore not my interest to offend; but I must be excused if I cannot dissemble. I am persuaded administration have propagated an alarm which they did not feel, and circulated reports they did not credit. I believe they have thereby answered their purposes. The nation, appalled by its fears, has silently acquiesced in all their measures, and complaisantly echoed back the terrors which were disseminated on every side. It is possible to propagate falsehood and excite alarm until "even-handed justice returns the poisoned chalice to our own lips." I admit, therefore, that administration may at some period have felt the terrors they have so lavishly insinuated into the breasts of others. It is time to awaken from the delirium—the visions of affrighted fancy have too long usurped the throne of reason, and rendered the heart callous to the cries of suffering humanity, and the wounds of bleeding justice! May their united claims find access to your Grace's heart, and restore me to the joys of social life!

If justice be sought, upon what principle am I so long withheld from its bar? It cannot be supposed that a vigorous government, with unlimited powers, can have failed, in upwards of two years, to have collected every iota of evidence which exists, to prove their charge; nor can it be imagined that the laws are insufficient to protect the Government, or the Government unable to execute the laws. If I am guilty, let my guilt be made manifest—if innocent, what retribution will be made for the losses I have sustained, and the injuries I have suffered. I hope I shall not be deemed unreasonable in cherishing an expectation that your Grace will accede to one of the following proposals: That I shall immediately be brought to trial, or liberated on bail. Let me be perfectly understood: I will give bail for my appearance, to answer to whatever charges may be exhibited against me. But *I will not* give bail for what the law terms good behavior. I am, in common with every member of society, bound by its general laws, and subject to their penalties. I will not tacitly acknowledge guilt by imposing peculiar restrictions upon myself. Should your Grace (contrary to my expectations) reject my proposals, I must submit; but shall esteem it a singular favor, if you will afford me an idea how long it is probable I may be here a resident inhabitant. I ask not from useless curiosity; such information would assist me in arranging my mind and concerns: so that the interval should not be wholly lost; and preserve me from "that kind of sickness of the heart, which arises from hope deferred."

Truly, my Lord Duke, it is a gloomy lot for a young man to be severed from every endearing connection that was entwined around his heart to waste in a prison that season of life which ought to be devoted to its enjoyments, or the providing for its necessities. My mind is deeply sensible of the evils I endure. I have found some relief in having unburdened it by this communication. Your Grace will pardon my addressing you so much at length. To complain, is the melancholy privilege of the unhappy—to relieve, the enviable fortune of the powerful and wealthy. I have exercised my right, and flatter myself you will not be slow to exercise that which situation has intrusted to your care.

In the hope that I shall be made acquainted with your receipt of the present letter, and honored with a knowledge of your resolves, I remain, with due respect,

Your Grace's most obedient humble servant,
JOHN BINNS.
Gloucester Jail, March 14, 1800.

His Grace, the DUKE OF PORTLAND, Secretary of State
for the Home Department, Whitehall, London.

SIR: Your delivering the inclosed letter to the Duke of Portland, and taking the trouble to acquaint me with his sentiments, on perusal, will be esteemed a particular favor. It gives me pleasure to address you without complaint, for which, I am happy to acknowledge, there is no just ground, except what I have stated in the letter to his Grace. I am, sir, with gratitude, for every mark of your attention,

Your obliged and grateful humble servant,
JOHN BINNS.
Gloucester Jail, March 15, 1800.

RICHARD FORD, Esq., Whitehall, London.

SIR: Your forwarding the accompanying letter to the Privy Council, will confer an obligation on,

Sir, your obliged humble servant,
JOHN BINNS.

RICHARD FORD, Esq., Whitehall.

MAY IT PLEASE YOUR LORDSHIPS: A sense of my own unimportance would prevent me from occupying one moment of your time, if I did not flatter myself that, in addressing you, I not only open brighter prospects for myself, but gratify your Lordships, by presenting you with an opportunity of doing an act of justice. I shall not detain you with a detail of my case. I have sketched it in a letter to his Grace, the Duke of Portland, dated 14th March, to which, should your Lordships feel a sufficient interest, I beg leave to refer. I have therein stated my claims to freedom, and solicited to be made acquainted with my expectations. My letter, however, has not been honored even by an acknowledgment of its receipt, though I have every reason to believe it has been duly forwarded. If my request were of less import to my happiness, I might be discouraged by such a repulse; but the hope of liberation is too animating to be crushed by a single effort. My most ardent wish, my Lords, is to be brought to a public trial; should this be inconsistent with the plans of Government, I desire to be liberated on bail. If it shall be thought proper to admit me to bail, I hope to offer such persons, for that purpose, as shall be wholly unexceptionable.

I remain, with due respect,
Your Lordships' most obedient,
Humble servant,
JOHN BINNS.
Gloucester Jail, March 21, 1800.

Right Honorable, the Lords of the
Privy Council, Whitehall.

CHAPTER VIII.

My companions in prison—Strictness of my confinement—I have been blessed through life with a happy temperament: incident—Receive a visit in prison from Secretary Dundas—My release—I embark for the United States—Jealousy of the British Government concerning the exportation of labor-saving machinery—Incidents of my voyage—Our arrival in America—Proceed to Harrisburg, and thence to Northumberland—Dr. Priestley and Thomas Cooper—Shad fisheries—Dr. Priestley's compliment to American mechanics—Condition of Pennsylvania in the early part of the present century relative to currency, manufactures, and agriculture—Northumberland in 1802; personal incidents—Politics of the period.

I HAD two pets while I was in prison; one was a cat, the other a toad. Few will admire my taste; but if they were situated as I was, they would, in all probability, be pleased even with such pets. They both knew their names, and gave attention so soon as called. The cat followed me like a dog, up stairs and down stairs, into my sleeping place, and into the yard. When I left Gloucester, I took the cat to London, and provided her with comfortable and kindly quarters.

My toad I kept in a large clean glass globe, which I had suspended in my day room, and in which I fed him with worms, flies, &c. &c. I could take him on my finger, carry him about the room, near the walls, and thus he would catch insects. I was of opinion, from long and close observation, that so long as the flies or other insects remained still, without stirring, he did not notice them, but the instant they stirred he caught them in his mouth, with a rapidity not to be expected from an animal so sluggishly formed. I set him at liberty when I was myself liberated. About nine months before that time, I had put another toad into a small stone jar, put a cork tight in the mouth of it, tied a bladder over it, waxed it well, closely sealed, and buried it, about three feet under ground. The day I left the jail, I dug it up and took the cork out of the jar, upon which the toad jumped out apparently as large and as active as when he was inclosed and buried. Nothing could be more clear to me than that, while he was buried in the jar, no air ever found its way into his prison-house.

About eighteen months of the time I was in Gloucester jail, I ate no animal food, nor did I drink any vinous, spirituous, or fermented liquor, save only six bottles of port wine, at a time when I was ordered to do so by a physician. During the whole time I was in that prison I never saw a *newspaper*, nor had any information in relation to public affairs, or the state of public opinion. What a privation must that have been to an active politician; one whose days, and almost his nights, when at large, were devoted to reading and hearing the news, can not be easily imagined. No man, without similar training and privations, could believe how entirely and unmurmuringly he could submit himself to the total privation of what he had heretofore regarded as absolute necessaries of life.

During the time referred to, the war against France had been carried on by England; Holland had been invaded, overrun, and the republic annihilated. Napoleon Bonaparte had become one of the Directory, and the armies of France had overrun many countries, overthrown their governments, and changed their boundaries and their dynasties; yet, of all, or any of those mighty events, I never heard a syllable until after I was liberated. Those in the prison, who took pleasure in contributing to my comfort, were afraid to hand me a newspaper or to communicate its contents, for fear they might escape, excite suspicion, and cut off all intercourse.

This patient submission to all privations, is one of the circumstances which induce the belief that I was of rather an uncomplaining nature, one who could, and did, contentedly submit himself to whatever might be his lot in life.

I will illustrate the strictness of the order that I should, while imprisoned in Gloucester, be kept from all association or conversation with any person who was not part and parcel of the prison. The slave of Alladin was not more willing to obey his commands than were the keepers to obey the inspectors. During the twenty-two months I was in Gloucester jail, I was not permitted, by the Government, or any of its obedient underlings, to interchange a word with anybody who did not appertain to that authority. A lady, an esteemed friend, whose residence was in London, being on a visit, within a post of the jail, obtained, after much trouble and intercession, an order from the Duke of Portland to have an interview with me, "subject to the prison rules." When she came, I was informed that a lady from London was in the castle and desired to see me. I went; I had an interview with her; I saw her, and she saw me; I shook her by the hand; I heard the sound of her voice and she heard the sound of mine, *in the presence of a third person*, a man in authority; again we shook hands, and parted. Few circumstances more deeply wounded my feelings than that visit. I never wished, nor would permit, another friend to visit me, because I felt assured it must be under the same painful restrictions.

This is probably as appropriate a place as I shall find to make the remark, or, more properly speaking, to state the fact, that in whatever situation I have been placed, whether in prison or out of prison; whether living in the country or in a country town, or in a city; whether editing a newspaper or as an alderman administering justice; in whatever place, condition, or station in life, Providence has placed me, I have been content and reasonably happy. I never knew what envy was, nor have I ever cherished personal ill-will or unkindly feelings. To me it has been a gratification to mark the well-doing and prosperity of others. I was of a quick and rather passionate temperament, but the wave passed over with wonderful rapidity, and left no rough traces behind.

This temperament was quickened and tested on several occasions while I was editor of the "Democratic Press." At that time, a more personal and less polished style generally prevailed than does now, or for very many years has prevailed, among the editors of American newspapers. That some tolerably accurate opinion may be formed as to the style then used, I assure my readers that some of the Federal papers, at that time, did not scruple to assert that the President of the United States, James Madison, as pure a man as ever filled the office, was but a pensioner, and the obedient servant of Napoleon Bonaparte!

Taking, as I certainly did, a decided, an uncompromising part as the advocate of republican principles, men, and measures, I was sometimes less choice, less scrupulous, or, if you please, less decorous, in my personal animadversions than I could now approve, or than the individuals animadverted upon were at all times disposed patiently to submit to. On such occasions, a gentleman and his friend would call at the office, inquire for the editor, and be shown into my private office. The person offended usually, under the influence of passion, holding in his hand a copy of the "Democratic Press," would say: "You, I am told, sir, are the editor of this paper."—*Binns.* "I am, sir."—*Complainant.* "Then, sir, you have published a scandalous libel of me."—*Binns.* "I hope not; may I ask, sir, what is your name?"—*Complainant.* "My name is ———." *Binns.* "Of what publication, sir, do you complain?"—*Complainant.* "Of this," pointing to the offensive article, "and I demand the name of the author."—*Binns.* "It has always been a rule with me to correct any error or misrepresentation which may have found its way into my paper, and I will do so now with pleasure."—*Complainant.* "That's not what I came for, sir; I want to know the name of the author."—*Binns.* "There is no impeachment of character in that article; nothing of such a nature as to warrant you in demanding, or me in surrendering, the name of the writer."—*Complainant.* "I think there is, and if you do not give me the name, I shall consider you the author."—*Binns.* "You are at liberty so to do, and having now, sir, made this a personal matter, you may adopt what course you please, but you must now leave the office." —*Complainant.* "I shall leave, sir, when I think proper." *Binns.* "No, sir! you shall leave forthwith." A few angry words, probably threats, would follow; the complainant would leave the office, and I rarely ever heard more of the matter.

It is a truth, which may be stated as extenuatory of the language admitted to have been used, that previous to, and during the war of 1812, and for some years after, the bitterness, the rudeness, and in some instances the persecuting spirit of party, and the rude personal hostility of partisans, were beyond all comparison greater than they have ever been since.

To return to Gloucester prison. Governor Cunningham, about noon, one day, in the summer of 1800, came into my room, and said: "Mr. Binns, Mr. Secretary Dundas, his wife, Lady Jane, his daughters and two gentlemen are in the castle, and Mr. Dundas has sent me to know if you have any objection to their paying you a visit."—*Binns.* "Not any; I shall feel pleased." Chairs were brought, and in a few minutes the room was prepared, and the party named made their entrance. Mr. Dundas, a well-looking, gentleman-like person, advanced first into the room, and, making a courteous bow, said: "Mr. Binns, as I am the only one in the company personally known to you, I will do the honors."—*Binns.* "Nobody, I am sure, sir, can do them better." The introductions being over, and the company, Right Hon. Henry Dundas, his wife, Lady Jane, and his two daughters, both a few years older than Lady Jane, being seated, inquiries were made as to the state of my health, my wants, accommodations, &c., all of which being answered, I said: "Mr. Dundas, I have now been here more than a year, and all the novelty of the place being worn off, I should be under obligations if you would let me know how soon I may expect to be liberated."—*Dundas.* "I really cannot tell any more than you. It depends upon so many things, that nobody can tell."—*Binns*, turning to the ladies, then said: "I am sure Lady Jane will readily agree that it is a sad thing to keep a young man shut up in prison when he might be so much better employed, if he were at liberty."—*Lady Jane.* "I assure you, Mr. Binns, I know nothing about these matters. I am no politician, and I cannot see the necessity for keeping you here."—*Dundas.* "Why, my dear, if he were at liberty, he would only be doing mischief."—*Binns.* "I am determined to go to the United States so soon as I am liberated."—*Dundas.* "Well, you would only be doing mischief there."—*Binns.* "Well, sir, if I were, I should not be doing mischief to you or your friends."—*Dundas*, after a momentary pause, in a very emphatic manner said: "I am not so sure of that." My company soon after took their departure. I have thought of this declaration of Mr. Dundas when, some years after, in the "Democratic Press," I devoted all the energies of my mind to encourage domestic manufactures (even the press had not then assumed courage to talk of American manufactures); to exposing the turpitude and injustice of the British orders in council; and to cause their insolent and brutal impressment of our seamen to be fully known and keenly felt and resented by the people and Government of the United States; and when with all my heart and all my strength I made war upon the "British party" in the United States. It was, indeed, a far-seeing observation of the Secretary.

I hope that no one will do me the injustice to suppose that my paper was silent in regard to the French decrees. I represented them as being equally hostile to the law of nations as the British orders in council. It was, however, admitted—it could not be denied—that the French decrees were consequent upon, if not the legitimate offspring, of the British orders in council, and were never attempted to be enforced with the insolence which marked the conduct of the British in the overhauling of our papers and cargoes, and in the mustering the crews and impressing American seamen on the pretence that they were British subjects. We shall hereafter have occasion to show that this pretence was resisted, protested against, and punished by the legislative and executive authorities of the United States.

On the first of July, 1801, I embarked at Liverpool for Baltimore on board the ship Orion, of Boston, Captain Chew, that being as early a day as I could obtain a comfortable passage. Packets did not then sail from Liverpool as they do now, almost daily, for the United States. I well remember the frequent visits and watchfulness of the English custom-house officers, not more in reference to duties and port charges to be paid, than for the purpose of ascertaining whether, among the baggage, there were any labor-saving machines, or patterns, or drawings from which such machines might be constructed. Strict search and inquiry were also made whether, among the passengers, there were not some mechanics.

At that time all such exports, the mechanics as well as machinery, patterns or drawings of machinery, were by law prohibited, under heavy penalties, from being taken out of the kingdom. Such mechanics as wished to leave the country, shipped, dressed and represented themselves as common laborers. It is reasonable, from these facts, to conclude that the British Government presumed that they then enjoyed, and had in Great Britain, a monopoly of labor-saving machinery, and of those persons who understood how to make and to work such machinery, of which the Government was determined, if possible, to continue to be the monopolizers. Mechanics detected in an attempt to leave the kingdom, without special permission of the Government—which was rarely given—were, on conviction of such intention, subject to fine, imprisonment, and transportation. A few years have made a wonderful change. Such are *now* the improvements and superiority of labor-saving machinery in the United States, that the British manufacturers have constantly competent persons employed, in the United States, to note, and transmit to England, drawings and descriptions of all the improvements made in American machinery, in order to introduce them into the machinery of Great Britain.

After the war of 1812, when our manufacturers had mastered all the difficulties in spinning, weaving, and dyeing, the goods they manufactured were found to be more durable, and thus became more in demand here than imported British goods; it then became a common practice with the British agents in the United States closely to imitate the models and numbers of American manufacturers, and send these models and numbers to Great Britain, to be put on their inferior goods, which, when thus marked and numbered, were sent to the British agents here, and by them to be sold as *American* manufactures. This fraud was more than once exposed in our newspapers, and thus became of little or no value.

At the time of which I have just been writing, all labor-saving machinery was rude, imperfect, and in its infancy, yet, it was regarded by mechanics and laboring men as likely to throw them out of employ, and otherwise be so seriously injurious to their interests, that they used to assemble in England and in other countries, in riotous mobs, to break, burn, and destroy all such improvements, when introduced, or about to be introduced into use, not only at the hazard of imprisonment and transportation, but of death. What a wonderful change has taken place in fifty years! How blind were these men to their own interests.

At this time, the steam-engine, *one* of those labor-saving machines, does more work than all the men, women, and children in the countries where these labor-saving machines are in successful operation—as in the United States; and what is the consequence as to mechanics and laboring men, and their wives and children? It is—that they are *better* educated, *better* fed, *better* clad, *better* housed, *better* paid, and work *fewer* hours, than at any former period in the history of the world of which I have any knowledge. Notwithstanding all the work done by the steam-engine, and all other labor-saving machinery, there is work enough required to be done to keep every man, woman, and child employed who desires employment. It may not be improper to remark, that our census of 1850 makes us acquainted with the fact that, in defiance of all the labor done by men, women, children, and labor-saving machinery, we have in our employ a greater number of horses, mules, asses, oxen, and other cattle, than we had at any former time. Such is the spread of information, such are the fruits of experience and public schools, that no laboring man, no mechanic, now grumbles, quarrels, or makes war upon labor-saving machinery. Every one now acts as if conscious that the greater the progress of science, and the more extensive the improvements in labor-saving machinery, the better it is for the whole human family. What a wonderful improvement. It has carried knowledge, health, and happiness into nearly all human habitations.

That these rapid advances on the road to human happiness are consequent upon the religious and political rights enjoyed by the people in the United States, is, I think, demonstrable. A small treatise, well and clearly written, on this subject, and extensively circulated, could not fail to be eminently and generally useful. Among the publications printed and broad-cast over England, by the London Corresponding Society, was a short but admirable treatise on the subject of juries and jurymen. To the information thus, and by other and like publications, spread over the land, are the people of England indebted for the intelligence and stubborn independence manifested on many important occasions by their juries.

On our voyage to Baltimore, no unusual event occurred. We had the customary large number of porpoises jumping and tumbling over each other, close to and about the bow of the vessel. They seemed to have a superabundance of muscular power, and to use it without stint, or fear that it would ever be exhausted. I never before saw so large an animal, who appeared so much and so entirely to enjoy life. They were as playful as so many squirrels. We passed many whales of various sizes, some of them near the vessel and some at a distance; some spouting water to a great height, others lazily floating wheresoever the waves or the current were pleased to take them, while some were driving furiously through the ocean. When it was dark, myriads of bright sparks, like small fire-flies, floated on the spray and over the surface of the ocean. There are various opinions as to the cause of these small but very brilliant lights, which illumine the water of the ocean whenever it is agitated. I believe the light to be emitted from a living animalcule, something in the nature of the fire-fly. The captain, at my request, had some of the bilge water pumped out of the hold into a bucket, and we ascertained that no agitation of the bilge water caused it to exhibit any sparks or signs of vitality; whereas, a bucket of water, taken from the ocean over the ship's side, upon being agitated, gave sparks in abundance. It gave the idea of a salt water fire-fly, showing no light except when in motion.

On the Banks of Newfoundland, we tried, with hook and line, out of the cabin windows, to catch codfish, but were not so fortunate. I do not believe we ever saw one, although the water was so clear that we could plainly see the many-colored dolphins approaching and nibbling at our bait. At length we caught one and saw it die; bright, brilliant and beautiful were the colors which it vividly displayed. It was cooked and served up at dinner. It was assuredly the driest and most tasteless animal food I ever ate. It is a custom on shipboard for the cook to put a silver spoon into the fish-kettle in which he cooks a dolphin; if the spoon, when taken out, shall appear black or dingy, the conclusion is, that the fish is poisonous, and the sailors decline to eat it.

The wind, for some days, was scarcely perceptible; neither whistling nor coaxing could prevail upon it to fill, or even shake, our sails; "we lay like a painted ship upon a painted ocean." On one of those days the captain had his skiff launched, and, with four oarsmen, got into her to ascertain the current; he took the helm, and invited me to a seat. I accepted the invitation, and well remember the solemnity of my feelings when our boat was so distant from the ship that we could see no part of her; nothing was to be seen but sea and sky. I cannot think I was frightened, but I am sure I was well satisfied when I had climbed the ship's side, and was standing on her deck. I could not but feel how different, and comparatively how safe, was my then situation to what it had been but a few minutes before, when, with nothing but sea and sky in view, there was but an inch and a half plank between me and almost certain death.

The Orion did not reach America until the first of September, after a passage of nine weeks. There were reports brought by those who boarded us as we neared the port, which caused some alarm and anxiety among the passengers, lest the yellow fever should be making its ravages in the city. The ship anchored near Fell's Point. The cabin passengers determined to get carriages, drive through Baltimore, and stop at a hotel which was a mile or more beyond the city. It was nearly dark as we drove through the streets and over the commons which lay between the city and the hotel. What with bull-frogs, common frogs, tidetids, &c. &c., and negro huts, in which there was much shouting, screaming, and clapping of hands, my ears never before had been assailed by such a multitude of confused, unusual, and unmusical sounds. The whole scene, however, was splendidly illuminated by millions of fire-flies, a display which I had never before witnessed, and which I have never since beheld but with admiration.* At the hotel where we stopped, for the first time I eat cakes made of that delicious vegetable, Indian corn.

Having ascertained that there was no yellow fever in the city, we shifted our quarters, the next day, to a hotel in Baltimore, and got our goods landed. I brought over some London and Liverpool newspapers, and, although we had been sixty days on the passage, these newspapers brought to the United States the latest advices from Europe! The ocean, bays, and rivers, were not then, as now, covered with steamships; the roads swiftly passed over by the aid of steam-engines and railroads, and the land everywhere overrun with telegraph lines, stations, and offices. Having obtained everything required, from the customhouse, hired three wagons, and loaded them, I set out, on foot, to accompany them to Northumberland, Pa., my destined home. As I walked by the wagon side, many and various were the guesses, inquiries, and remarks of the wagoners and tavern-keepers. They guessed I was from the old country; guessed I was going to keep store; guessed I wanted to buy a farm, &c. &c. As an instance of their determination that nothing I had seen in the "old country" should exceed or excel anything in the new, I will mention that, being asked the size of London, I said it was between seven and eight miles long; one of the wagoners, with an air of affected surprise, said: "Is that all? Why, Philadelphia is bigger than that; it's nine miles from Chestnut Hill down to Southwark." I did not express any doubt or surprise further than by exclaiming, "Indeed!"

We passed through much miserable-looking country,

* About five years ago, a very much esteemed friend of mine received from Cuba two or more fire-flies, of that island. I saw, and could not fail to admire them. They were, each of them, about the size of the upper joint of a man's thumb, and gave a light proportionally greater than our fire-fly.

which I was told was land that had been exhausted by the growth of tobacco, which returns no manure to the land which it impoverishes. In several fields, in which wheat and corn were growing, there were many lofty girdled pine and other trees, which, having no leaves, exhibited a most forlorn appearance, which was in nowise improved by the occasional noise of the falling of the dry wood, and the rattling together of the branches, caused by the wind. The practice of girdling has so long been abandoned, that it may be well to give an extract from Webster: "*Girdle.*—In America, to make a circular incision, like a belt, through the bark and alburnum of the tree, to kill it."

On my arrival at Harrisburg, then a small town, now a wealthy and populous city, the capital of the State of Pennsylvania, I hired a boat to take the goods, and myself as a passenger, to Northumberland. At that time, little had been done by the State to clear the Susquehanna for navigation, and what had been done was done at the lower end of the river, having a tendency to divert the internal trade of the State to the capital of Maryland rather than to the capital of Pennsylvania. Susquehanna is the Indian name of the river; the meaning of the word is said to be "the river with the rocky bottom;" never was a river more correctly named. It is to be much regretted that so few of the Indian names have been retained. They are agreeable to the ear, and characteristically expressive of the places, persons, or things, named. I have, hundreds of times, poled a canoe on the Susquehanna, and never struck at the bottom anything but rock. At that time, there was no bridge of any kind anywhere over the Susquehanna; there are now several. Above Harrisburg, for the first time, I saw a canoe, and was daring, or foolish, enough to think I could paddle and pole one as I saw them paddled and poled by others. I tried the experiment as we went up the stream; the pole slipped, and I was pitched heels over head into the river, to the no small merriment of the boatmen. After some days, we arrived at the beautifully situated town of Northumberland. The town, at that time, was a much more populous and trading town than it is now, or has been for many years. There then resided the venerable Dr. Joseph Priestley, son, and family, and Thomas Cooper, Esq., afterwards a President Judge in Pennsylvania, and also President of the State College of South Carolina. He was fined and imprisoned for a libel on President John Adams. The fine, with interest, was, on a petition of Dr. Cooper's, refunded by a vote of Congress, many years after; I think when General Jackson was President. The Doctor had wielded a powerful pen in favor of the General's election, and he was a man who rarely forgot to repay both partisans and opponents. During that electioneering campaign, Dr. Cooper wrote me a letter, which is now before me, and from which I now, for the first time, publish an extract: "I am as zealous, and labor as hard to insure the election of General Jackson as you do to prevent it. I regret your opposition, but do not the less esteem you. It is with regret I read the abuse which is poured upon you in some of the Jackson papers. If they knew you, as I have known you for more than twenty years, they would not thus abuse you. I can assure them, and they will surely believe me when I assert that you are amiable in all the relations of private life; an affectionate husband, and a good father." Before Mr. Cooper came to the United States, he, accompanied by Mr. Watt, of steam-engine memory, went to Paris and took their seats in the French Convention, as the chosen representatives of the Manchester Philosophical Society. This, I think, was in the year 1793. Dr. Joseph Priestley was, about the same time, elected to a seat in the same Convention by several districts in France, but he never took a seat in that body. I have no knowledge of the reason why the Doctor never took his seat, but conjecture it may have been from an unwillingness to renounce his allegiance to his native country. I know that that consideration prevented his becoming a citizen of the United States.

The two gentlemen I have just mentioned, were among the most industrious, learned, and distinguished men of their age. Other respectable Irish and English families resided there, and carried on business in the town. Many of them removed and many have died. The situation of Northumberland, cut off, as it is, by Montour's Ridge from the surrounding country, was a heavy barrier against her having intercourse and business with the farming interests of the country. This tended not a little to prevent its improvement. There were, at that time, many and valuable shad fisheries on the Susquehanna and its branches, above, below, and at Northumberland, at many of which thousands of the finest shad were nightly caught. They used then to sell, at the Northumberland fisheries, for six dollars a hundred. The coming of the shad was usually late in April or early in May, varying according to the height and warmth of the river water. Their arrival was preceded by what was called the shad-fly, which was a long, thin, dark, brown-colored fly, in shape somewhat like a horse-fly, but larger. All these fisheries have been destroyed by dams and canals, erected in the river for the improvement and promotion of trade and intercourse. The people, living on and near the banks of the Susquehanna and its tributary streams, have thus been annually deprived of millions of pounds weight of good, wholesome food. This would probably, to a great extent, have been prevented, if a scheme, seriously talked of in 1801-2, in the town of Northumberland, had been successfully carried into operation. It is asserted, and believed, that the fish produced from spawn always ascend the river whence the spawn itself had descended. It was, at the time of which I am writing, seriously contemplated, in Northumberland, to send fishermen to the Lakes, near the head-waters of the Susquehanna, to convey thither, from the Lakes, red salmon with spawn, and put them into the head-waters of the north branch of the river, in the confident expectation that the salmon produced from that spawn would return, ascend, and become naturalized to the river, and that, in a few years, the red salmon would thus become abundant. Had this scheme been successfully carried out, the salmon would not, like the shad, have been shut out by the dams; it would have overleaped many of them. I have seen salmon, at Leislip, in the river Leffey, Ireland, bound to a greater height, say from eight to ten feet.

I wish I could now feel, and make others feel, the glow of joy, the heart-warm enthusiastic gratitude which filled my bosom when, on my way through the country, I first saw mustering in the fields and towns the awkward squads of the Pennsylvania militia, armed with muskets and rifles, clubs, sticks and cornstalks, while the banner of freedom waved over them, on which my delighted eyes read the words: "Virtue, Liberty, and Independence;" when, also, for the first time, I heard their "spirit-stirring drums," and saw them also begirt with the glorious motto: "Virtue, Liberty, and Independence." It was then, under the broad expanse of heaven, without the adoption of any form of words, I took my first oath of allegiance and fidelity to the United States; an oath which, according to my best judgment, I have faithfully kept, at all times, in all places, and under all circumstances, in peace and in war.

Northumberland was made a post-town soon after Dr. Priestley and his family had settled there. It was so made by President John Adams in compliment to Dr. Priestley. His house and garden, outhouses and orchards, were extensive, and on a larger scale than any other establishment at that time in the interior of the State. It was in 1794 he came to the United States. His valuable and extensive library, and well-furnished laboratory were under the same roof, and adjoining his dwelling. The first remark I heard complimentary to the mechanical heads and hands of Americans I heard from the lips of Dr. Priestley. It was to this effect: "The American people have a wonderful tact at making small tools, from even imperfect descriptions. Birmingham, where I resided many years, was one of the greatest towns to manufacture iron, tin and papier-mache in the world, yet I assure you, the various tools and instruments which I require in my chemical experiments, I can, from my description, get made here with more facility and accuracy than I could get them made in Birmingham."

In 1801, there were no banks in Pennsylvania, out of the city of Philadelphia, in which there were, then, the old United States Bank, the Bank of Pennsylvania, and the Bank of North America. The city banks had branches for discount and deposit at Lancaster, Reading and Pittsburg. These were the only banking-houses then in Philadelphia and Pennsylvania. When the country storekeepers, at that time, used to be preparing to start for Philadelphia to purchase goods, in the spring and fall, it was customary for them to exchange their silver money for bank notes, they being lighter and more convenient to carry, the storekeeper riding to Philadelphia on horseback, and with his saddlebags, in which were the bank notes he had collected. There was then no American gold coin, but a small portion of American silver coin. The circulating medium was chiefly Spanish and Portuguese gold and Spanish silver coin. The first deposit of California gold was made at our mint December 8, 1848. In Philadelphia, gold dollars were first coined in 1849.*

When I came to reside in Philadelphia, 1807, when our China ships—and at that time we had several regular ships trading to Canton—would be about to sail, Spanish dollars commanded a premium of from six to ten per cent., to take to Canton. It was many years after, before the Chinese would take American silver dollars. They now receive our cotton and other American manufactured goods in return for their teas, Canton goods, China and Japan ware, silks, &c.

We then imported large quantities of coarse cotton goods from Canton, called Baftas. Some time after the declaration of war, in 1812, there continued to be among the standing committees of Congress one called the Committee on Commerce and Manufactures. The mercantile interest was so much more concentrated and influential than the manufacturing influence, that the attention of the Committee was devoted to commerce, and but little, if any, was given to manufactures. When the want of manufactured goods was so sensibly felt that difficulty was found in obtaining, even at high prices, clothing for the army, the navy, volunteers, and militia employed in that war, Congress appointed a Committee on Manufac-

---

* Upper California was discovered in 1596 by Sir Francis Drake, and named New Albion. The Spaniards had possession of it for some time, but were expelled by the natives. In 1697, it was granted by Charles II. to the Jesuits. In 1824, it became a province of Mexico, and was ceded to the United States by treaty with Mexico in 1848. Thus it appears that Upper California had been in possession of the English, the Spaniards, and the Mexicans before it became one of the United States; yet, in all that time, two centuries and a half, no gold had been discovered in the country. It has been now not quite six years in possession of the United States, and there has from thence been brought to the Atlantic States more than sixty millions of gold every year!

tures; then, for the first time, attention was paid to encourage manufactures, and a small duty was laid upon Baftas. The consequence was the erection of many small manufacturing establishments where coarse cotton goods were made. Thus was laid the foundation of American manufactures.

The first encouragement given to manufactured domestic cotton goods by individuals, was in 1811. Thomas Leiper, Paul Cox, and Hugh Ferguson rented a store in Third Street near Market, where they received from the weavers such goods as they had ready for sale, at their own valuation, advanced them one-half the value of the goods, sold them at such prices as the weavers had fixed, and paid them the balance when the goods were sold. This establishment was of great value in the then infant state of our manufactures.

The agriculturists now complain that their interests are not sufficiently guarded and encouraged. Congress, I think, has no Committee on Agriculture. It is to be apprehended that this great and leading interest of the country will not receive that attention which it requires, and which it would richly repay, until Congress shall establish a standing Committee on Agriculture. There are too few agriculturists and too many lawyers in Congress. Will the agriculturists be pleased to correct this state of things? The remedy is in their own hands—will they apply it? Let them attend the primary meetings for the election of the delegates which select the party candidates, and their influence will be felt and their interests attended to in Congress.

While I am thus touching upon things unknown to many of the present generation, I had better note a few country facts of a no less interesting character. At the time I went to Northumberland (1801), it was common to see large fields without any fence, or the fence lying prostrate on the ground; upon inquiring the cause, you were told it was *worn-out land*. The stables for horses and cattle, sheep and pigs were then small log buildings, with a loft over them for fodder. The excrement of the horses and cattle, &c., which should have been spread, as manure, upon the " worn-out land," to enrich it, was allowed to accumulate in such heaps about the stables, that access to them became daily more and more difficult to men, horses, and cattle. A young farmer, of the present day, has no idea how this difficulty was overcome, and will greatly marvel, if not doubt the fact, when informed that the owner of the premises thus encumbered would remove the stable, or, to speak more accurately, he would erect a new one in another place, and leave the old stable and the manure to rot together, removing neither the one nor the other. This custom, in some measure, accounts for the "worn-out land."

On the fourth of July, 1802, a number of the inhabitants of Northumberland agreed to dine together in the large room over the market-house. At the request of a committee of that company, I agreed to deliver, and did deliver an oration. That was the first time I addressed a public meeting in the United States. The room was crowded, and I had the gratification to hear the discourse favorably spoken of by many, whose good opinion was valued and valuable.

The only newspaper at that time published in the county of Northumberland, was called the "Northumberland Gazette." Of that paper, Mr. Andrew Kennedy was the proprietor and publisher. At his request, I wrote occasional articles for it. Political parties were then, and long after, known as Republicans and Federalists. The politics of the Gazette were those of the Federal party, of which party there were many bitter partisans in the towns of Sunbury and Northumberland, and throughout the country. He, Mr. Kennedy, called on me, and said that if I would occasionally write for his paper, my contributions should be published without any alteration. I did as he requested, and on this same fourth of July, 1802, a long, and, what I thought, appropriate address, for the birthday of Independence, was written by me, and published in the Gazette. In the next week's Gazette, were published some angry animadversions on my article, to which, in the next Gazette, I made answer. This controversy continued for some weeks, when the editor of the Gazette told me that what I had written had given offence to his political friends, and that he could not publish any more of my writing on politics. I thought this unfair and unjust, and soon after issued proposals to print, in Northumberland, a weekly paper, under the title of "The Republican Argus," with the motto, "Equal and exact justice to all men, of whatever sect or persuasion, religious or political." The proposals were circulated, and the establishment of the paper advocated by the most influential Republicans in the county. The subscription and general patronage extended to the Argus were beyond my expectation. I soon got types and printing materials, and issued the first number of the paper early in 1802. In a short time I acquired the confidence of the Republican party, not only of Northumberland, but of the neighboring counties.

His Excellency, Thomas McKean, was at that time Governor of Pennsylvania. In the session (1804–5) of the General Assembly of Pennsylvania, Governor McKean gave his opinion on many subjects, but more intemperately than any other on the subject of the introduction into our system of State laws the principle of compulsory arbitration. Towards the close of the session, the language of the governor towards several members of the General Assembly became unbecoming the station he held, and that which was held by the persons to whom he was pleased to apply it. From the rude language thus addressed to the representatives of the people, the governor went a step lower, and applied to the people the vulgar epithets of clodhoppers and clodpoles. This language, in letters from Lancaster to editors of newspapers, found its way to the people, with such comments as caused those who had elected the governor to become exceedingly dissatisfied, and to turn their attention to the selection of a republican whose standing in the State would give a reasonable prospect of his success. The governor was well acquainted with the state of public opinion, and attentive to the adoption of such measures as would increase his friends and enfeeble his opponents. As the session of the General Assembly for 1804-5 drew to a close, the members turned their thoughts to the selection of a candidate whose popularity would give him a reasonable prospect of success. Simon Snyder, of Northumberland County, had, for some sessions, filled the speaker's chair in the House of Representatives with no common ability. He was intimately acquainted with the rules of the House, had a promptitude in the discharge of his duties, and a suavity of manners which caused him to be much esteemed; and his knowledge of the German language, it was thought, would make him particularly acceptable to many of the members. At that time, the Democratic members were the influence which insured a nomination for governor, and they exercised it in this instance by sustaining the nomination of Simon Snyder.

Governor McKean was well advised as to the movements making to get him in the legislature, out of their disposition to nominate Mr. Snyder. In order, so far as the governor could do, to reduce the number of members who should attend the caucus, he gave several of them commissions as justices of the peace, on condition that they would not go to the caucus. All, however, would not induce the republican members to support governor McKean at the election in 1805.

It should be borne in mind that governor McKean had been for many years Chief Justice of the State, and that it was the Republicans who had selected him as their candidate for governor in 1799, and that they had elected him. All the State officers in 1805 had been appointed by him. It was therefore a fearful undertaking to turn him out of the office into which they had put him. However, they were determined to try, and they nominated Simon Snyder as their candidate.

The Republicans calculated strongly upon the votes of the Germans, in favor of Mr. Snyder. In this they miscalculated, inasmuch as some of the heavy German counties for the most part went in favor of Governor McKean. The vote in 1805 was:—

Thomas McKean	43,544
Simon Snyder	38,483
Majority for Thomas McKean,	5,061

In 1807, Simon Snyder was again returned to the House of Representatives, and elected speaker. The defeat of Mr. Snyder in 1805 was caused by the party called Quids, who were the first seceders from the Republican party. When the time of Governor McKean was about expiring, the Republicans, well pleased with the votes which Mr. Snyder had received in 1805, again nominated him as their candidate in 1808. Mr. Snyder had no family influence; he had to rely upon his own merits.

During that contest, under the signature of "One of the People," I wrote a series of letters, addressed to Governor M'Kean, which were republished in all the Democratic papers in the State; thousands of them were printed in pamphlet form, and several Republican county meetings returned thanks to the anonymous writer of those letters. These things extended the circulation and the influence of "The Republican Argus" and of its friends, so that I was enabled to erect a large printing-office and house, and to print books and open a bookstore.

CHAPTER IX.

My marriage—Character of Dr. Priestley—I engage in a duel—Simon Snyder—Dr. Leib—Wm. Duane—My visit to Philadelphia—Description of Philadelphia in 1802—I establish the "Democratic Press"—Outrage against the American frigate Chesapeake—Effects of non-intercourse and embargo.

ON the 16th of March, 1806, Dr. Joseph Priestley married me to Mary Ann Bagster, a native of Shropshire, England. By her I have had ten children, five boys and five girls, of whom but two, Benjamin Franklin Binns, and Matilda Pemberton Binns, now the wife of John W. Simes, Jr., are now living. My wife is now (A. D. 1851) sixty-eight years of age, and I am seventy-eight; we are both in as good health as can reasonably be expected, at those ages. She has ever been a faithful, prudent, and affectionate wife, and an anxious and devoted mother. For the last twenty years I have had an annual attack of gout, which usually commences early in the spring, and puts me on crutches for six, eight, ten, or twelve weeks, as the case may be; otherwise I have enjoyed excellent health.

Dr. Joseph Priestley was one of the most voluminous writers of the eighteenth century. He published nearly a hundred moderate sized octavo volumes on a great variety of subjects, including Education, Religion, Chemistry, Metaphysics, History, Politics, &c. &c. He had an extensive library and chemical laboratory. He rose early, and retired to rest usually about ten o'clock. He slept on a cot-bed in his library. He was pleased, almost daily, to play a few games of chess or backgammon. Some time before his death, when he was very ill, and but slender hopes were entertained of his recovery, I occasionally sat with him during the night in a large arm chair by his cot side. At that time, he was writing, and I was printing his "History of the Christian Church." It was to be published in six volumes. At the time of which I am writing, between four and five volumes were printed. The doctor was quiet and patient, under his affliction, as man could be. "I should," said he, "have been gratified if it had pleased God to spare me to finish my History of the Church. If that were finished, my worldly labors would be ended. I should have nothing more on earth to do, or to regret at leaving undone." "But, my dear sir," said I, "if you were now spared, and the history finished, would you not, at a future time, have something else unfinished, which you would desire to be spared to complete?" "No," said he, "I do not think I should."

Dr. Priestley recovered so far as to finish, and correct the proof of, his Church History. Some months after his recovery, as he lay sick and feeble on the cot in his library, I was sitting by his side, and a small light burning near us. In the dead hour of the night, the doctor turned a little on one side toward me, and said: "Mr. Binns?" "Sir?" "Do you recollect the conversation we had some months ago, when I lay very sick on this cot, and you were sitting about where you are now sitting?" "Do you mean about the Church History, sir?" "I do; I remind you of it," said he, "to say that I have now nothing unfinished; nothing that I feel uneasy about, and I am ready to depart when called hence." Some hours after, surrounded by his family, he departed. I have severely taxed my memory, under a feeling of deep responsibility to the great and good man of whom I have been writing, and I verily believe that the language I have used was the language which was used at the times I have referred to. He died in the 71st year of his age, on the 6th of February, 1804.

Dr. Priestley, in his intercourse with the world, on all occasions, and to all persons, exhibited a tender regard for the feelings of everybody, the old and the young, the rich and the poor, the learned and the ignorant. It was his pleasure daily to play an hour or more at backgammon, draughts, or chess. I never saw him play cards. I frequently played with him. He was greatly my superior at all games of skill, but it was his constant practice to allow me to win the last game. Further to illustrate his kindly respect for the feelings of others, I would state that one evening, Dr. Thos. Cooper and Dr. Wm. Young played a rubber at chess, which Dr. Cooper won, and then declined to play any more, though much urged by Dr. Young. Dr. Young was sensitive, and mortified at not being indulged. I have never seen a well-tempered man —and Dr. Young was a well-tempered man—who suffered so much as he did when conquered, even at a game of chance. I have heard Dr. Priestley, on more occasions than one, complain to Dr. Cooper of his not indulging Dr. Young. "I have no idea," Dr. Cooper would say, "of indulging a man in such childish fancies."

In a conversation with Dr. Priestley, when sick on his cot, he expressed some opinions, in relation to a future state, such as I had not before heard. I wish it were in my power to communicate exactly what he said, in his own language; but that I cannot do. The force and beauty of his language, and the tenderness of his tone and manner, are forever lost. The substance was to this effect: "Reflecting," said he, "on the divine love of the Creator, and the felicities of a future state, prepared for those deemed, in some measure, worthy, I have thought that when the immortal portion of the human frame should be called hence, to be no more seen of men, that it would be conveyed to a region of blissful enjoyment, proportioned to its capacity and preparation, there to remain until, from its superior opportunities, and consequent superior acquirements, it should become better prepared and more capable of yet sublimer and more spiritual enjoyments, whence, through divine mercy and love, it would, from time to time, be removed from one region of bliss to a higher, and yet a higher, until it should attain the most sublime and perfect state of felicity of which our most improved nature should be made susceptible; enjoyments becoming more and more blissful in worlds without end."

As the private secretary of Lord Sheffield, Dr. Priestley was early introduced to Dr. Benjamin Franklin, and that introduction soon ripened into friendship. Dr. Priestley went with Dr. Franklin on his way to the Privy Council, where he was going, by appointment, to state the grievances which were most seriously felt and protested against by the people of America. On the return of Dr. Franklin, he complained bitterly of the insolence of Mr. Wedderburne, the then Attorney-General, and expressed his deep conviction that America had nothing to expect from the justice of England. The friends walked to the apartments of Dr. Franklin; he unlocked one of the drawers of his bureau, took off the silk coat and vest he had worn at the Privy Council, and laid then carefully in the drawer. "I will never," said he, "put those clothes on again, until I put them on to sign a treaty in which this Government shall so far acknowledge its error as to acknowledge the independence of America." After a few years, having assisted to negotiate the treaty in which England acknowledged the independence of the United States, the doctor signed it, dressed in the silk coat and vest which he had laid away for that purpose. Dr. Franklin returned to the United States, and died in Philadelphia in 1790, in the 84th year of his age. Few men have lived a more useful life, or descended to a more honorable grave, than Benjamin Franklin.

Forty years ago, there was a tavern in Walnut Street, on the north side, a short distance below Fifth Street, which had for a sign a particularly well-painted half length of Dr. Franklin, as large as life. He was painted with spectacles on his nose, supporting his head by leaning his chin on his right thumb. I have heard more than one of his descendants say that that sign was acknowledged, by the family, to be the best and most characteristic likeness of the doctor, that had ever been painted. It has been removed, and the tavern closed, many years. What has become of that best of all likenesses of one of the first of Americans?

I remember to have heard Dr. Priestley say he had written, and had nearly ready for the press, four volumes of "Commentaries on the Laws of England," which were burned with his other property, by the "Church and King" mob, in Birmingham, in 1791-2. It is also certain that Lord Mansfield had written, and prepared for press, some volumes on the same subject, which, together with his house and furniture, were burned in 1780 by Lord George Gordon's "Anti-Catholic mob." Such are the bitter fruits of religious intolerance, and of a union of Church and State. Undoubtedly both the works, thus ruthlessly destroyed, would have been highly valued by the statesmen, the judges, and the bar of Great Britain, and elsewhere.

Before I assumed the responsibilities of a husband, I was engaged in an affair, which, I have often thanked God, ended without bloodshed. It had been preceded by a variety of threats, of rudeness and persecutions, from members of the Federal party, not only those of them who resided in the county of Northumberland, but by men of that party who came from other counties to the Northumberland County Court. There was a manifest determination on their part to get rid of me and my paper, in one way or other. For example, one of them prosecuted me for a libel. I attended the court regularly. The bill of indictment was before the grand jury; they had come into court, for the third time, to report that they could not agree, and were about returning to their room, by order of the judge, when one of the grand jurors said: "We think it very hard, your honor, to be kept together, because eleven men insist upon finding a bill." Judge Jacob Rush was on the bench; I was sitting at the counsel-table, and immediately rose and said: "If your honor please, I believe it requires twelve grand jurors to find a bill?" "Certainly it does," said the judge. The grand jury promptly retired, and soon after returned, when their foreman reported that they had no further business, and prayed that they should be discharged, which was accordingly done. The disappointment and mortification of this defeat were so great that, so soon as the court met in the morning, a motion was made, and the court, in consequence, made an order that no person should be allowed to sit at the counsel-table but lawyers, and their clients, and students at law. To meet this order, I entered the next morning as a student of law, with Jonathan Walker, Esq., who then resided in the town of Northumberland. The next day, I was, as usual, in the court-house, at the counsel-table. This gave birth to a new scheme among the lawyers; they were then all Federalists. Mr. Walker was given to understand that so long as he retained John Binns as a student, the members of the bar would not be concerned in any cause in which he was engaged. These proceedings, originating and carried out in the persecuting spirit of Federalism, had, as was to be expected, the effect of insuring to me more generally and actively than ever the hatred of the Federal, and the support of the Republican party.

I will submit another evidence of the hostility of the Federal party, and its effects. In August, 1802, I was appointed adjutant of the 102d regiment, Pennsylvania Militia, and promptly entered upon the discharge of its duties at the fall regimental muster of that year at Sunbury. The appointment gave great offence to those who were politically opposed to me and to the Republican party. It was said to be illegal, as I had only declared my intention, and had not yet become a citizen. Many Federalists protested, and published that they would not serve under me, nor obey any orders I might give. The colonel and the two majors, or a majority of them, then were by law authorized to appoint the staff-officers. My appointment was signed by the two majors, but not by the colonel. Soon after, an election was ordered by the brigade-inspector, for field-officers of the regiment. One of the majors having removed out of the regimental bounds, new tickets were agreed upon by both parties. The Federalists headed their ticket with the name of the then colonel, who had not signed my appointment. They succeeded in electing their candidates, who were, by the governor, commissioned. The first-fruits of this victory was confidently expected to be to oust John Binns. The colonel, for that purpose, was waited upon by his Federal friends, by whom he had been elected, and joyously hailed and toasted. He was the Samson, who was to strike down the Philistine, and restore the reign of law and order. But, alas! and alackaday! the hopes of Federalism again were blighted, and, on the next regimental parade, the victorious party had to muster, and to march under the orders of Adjutant Binns, who now appeared under the authority of an appointment, signed, not only by the two majors, but also by the colonel. "This was the unkindest cut of all," and the defeated victors had to recruit their spirits—as many of them did—by toasting "the wooden walls of old England," at a time when those very wooden walls were firing upon, boarding, and robbing our ships, carrying our seamen into captivity, and, under the lash, compelling them to assist in heaping disgrace upon the flag of their own country.

It would not be easy for the people of the present day to imagine the extreme violence of the political parties of that time, and for many years after. It has happily given way to milder feelings, if not more patriotic principles and wiser counsels.

In the then state of things, it is not to be wondered at if the warfare I have been stating ended in violence, and was only put down when it was ascertained that the man sought to be prostrated was not to be overawed or intimidated.

On Saturday, November 2, 1805, while I was in the public ball-alley, in Sunbury, with a yellow pine bat in my right hand, tossing a ball against the wall, waiting for Major Charles Maclay to play a game, a very tall, stout stranger came to me and said: "My name is Sam. Stewart, of Lycoming County; your name, I understand, is John Binns, and that you are the editor of the 'Republican Argus.'" I answered: "You have been correctly informed." "I wish," said he, "to know who is the author of the letters published in that paper, signed 'One of the People.'" "For what purpose?" said I. "Because," said he, "there are some remarks in one of them which reflect upon my character, and I must know the author." With this demand I declined to comply, but said: "If there be anything in them untrue, it shall be corrected." Stewart, who was standing at my left side, instantly threw his left arm across my breast, and with it held both my arms tight above the elbows, and at the same time threw his right arm across the back of my head, violently pushing the end of his forefinger into the corner of my right eye, evidently with intent to tear it out of my head. Upon the instant I struck him, with all the strength I could command, over the shin with the edge of the heavy yellow pine bat, which I fortunately had in my right hand. This severe blow made Stewart instantly snatch his finger from my eye, and seizing me around the waist with both arms, lifted me from the ground and endeavored to throw me down. This he did not accomplish; we struggled for some time, and were separated by Major Maclay and others who came into the ball-alley. In his effort to gouge my eye out, he tore up the skin of my upper eyelid, and left a scar which will accompany me to my grave.

This attack and struggle took place in the ball-alley of Henry Schaffer, into whose hotel I went and wrote a note, which was forthwith, by Major Maclay, handed to Mr. Stewart:—

SUNBURY, November 2, 1805.

After threatening me like a bravo, you have attacked me like a ruffian. Some satisfaction ought to be rendered for such conduct. If you have the spirit and the courage to meet me as a gentleman, and will appoint time and place and meet me with pistols, accompanied by a friend, what has passed shall be overlooked by

JOHN BINNS.

SAMUEL STEWART, Esq.

To this note Mr. Stewart returned a verbal answer, by Major Maclay, that he was going to the city, but would be back in two or three weeks, when he would acquaint Mr. Binns of his arrival, and give him time to send to Buffalo for Major Maclay, who, he presumed, would attend Mr. Binns as his friend on the occasion.

Charles Maclay was about twenty-eight years of age, and of much promise. He died soon after the settlement of this affair. He was a son of the Hon. Samuel Maclay, at that time one of the United States senators from Pennsylvania.

On the day of its date I received a note, of which the following is a copy, from Mr. Andrew Kennedy, the printer of the "Northumberland Gazette," who informed me Mr. Stewart was at his house, and requested that any answer I thought proper to send should be sent there.

NORTHUMBERLAND, December 13, 1805.

When I received your challenge, I was at that time on my way to the city, and had it not in my power to meet you, but now I am here, ready to see you. You will, therefore, mention the time and place, and you will have it in your power to try my spirits, that you so much doubted; it must be immediately; let me hear from you.

SAMUEL STEWART.

JOHN BINNS.

To this note I forthwith returned the following answer:—

NORTHUMBERLAND, December 13, 1805.

Yours I have just received. You are aware that my friend Major Maclay is to attend me; so soon as he arrives, I shall be ready. I shall send for him immediately, and expect he will lose no time in coming to Northumberland, in which case I presume every necessary arrangement can be made between him and your friend this evening, and we can meet to-morrow morning.

JOHN BINNS.

SAMUEL STEWART.

About fifteen minutes after the delivery of this note, the following was handed to me by one of Mr. Kennedy's boys:—

I have been a long time from home, and cannot conveniently be detained much longer; should your friend, Major Maclay, be down this evening, I will wait; otherwise, I must return to Lycoming County, where I have business of importance to attend to; your answer I expect immediately.

SAMUEL STEWART.

JOHN BINNS.

To this note the following reply was sent:—

Your second note I have received. In answer, it is impossible for me to know whether Mr. Maclay will, or will not, be here this evening. I have sent an express for him. If, however, you think proper to leave town rather than wait my friend's arrival, you will, I presume, have no objection to name a place in Lycoming, where Mr. Maclay and myself shall await your arrival. He shall wait on you as soon as he arrives.

JOHN BINNS.

SAMUEL STEWART.

On the evening of the 15th, a friend informed me that application had been made to a magistrate, and it was probable a warrant would be issued for my arrest to bind me over to keep the peace. Alarmed at this information, I sent the following note:—

SATURDAY MORNING.

SIR: I have just heard that application has been made to a magistrate to prevent our meeting. I write to request you will instantly appoint some other place than this neighborhood, say Derrstown, Milton, or any other place more convenient to you, where my friend and myself will attend.

JOHN BINNS.

SAMUEL STEWART.

Immediately after writing the above note, I wrapped a pair of pistols in my greatcoat-pocket, and walked about half a mile to the house of Mr. Wm. Bonham, where I had directed that my horse, and any answer sent to my note, should be forwarded. While waiting at Bonham's, Major Maclay arrived. I made to him a statement of all that had passed between Mr. Stewart and myself, put him in full possession of my opinions and wishes, and he went to Northumberland to settle time and place. While we were talking in a back room, the constable rapped, and inquired if I was in the house. He was told I had gone up the road; he departed. Soon after, the boy brought me my horse, and the following note:—

SIR: I have just received your note. You say you cannot determine our dispute here, as application has been made to a magistrate. How any person could have any knowledge of this business appears very mysterious to me, as I am confident neither Mr. Kennedy nor myself ever mentioned it to any person. You say that Derrstown or Milton must be the place of meeting. Mention yourself either of the two places, and the time, and Mr. Kennedy and myself will be punctual in attending, provided you meet to-day.

SAM. STEWART.

JOHN BINNS.

So soon as the constable left Mr. Bonham's, Mr. Maclay went to Northumberland to make the necessary arrangements with Mr. Stewart's friend. On his return, he informed me that the meeting was to be at seven o'clock the next morning, at the end of a fence behind Laushees' house, opposite Derrstown, where we had agreed to sleep that night. We were on the ground at seven o'clock, just in the gray of the morning. In a few minutes, we saw Mr. Stewart and Mr. Kennedy coming down the lane. After mutual salutations, Mr. Maclay proposed that we should cross the swamp and retire to a more private place, where the ground was perfectly clear. Having arrived on the ground, Mr. Kennedy proposed that the parties should settle the distance, &c. To this I objected, that being the duty of the seconds, and not of the principals. Messrs. Maclay and Kennedy then retired, and after some conversation, stepped eight paces, and placed Mr. Stewart and myself at the extreme ends of the line. Mr. Maclay then said: "Gentlemen, you will understand that it is agreed, between Mr. Kennedy and myself, that if either of the parties shall leave his ground until the affair is finally settled, such party shall be regarded as disgraced." The seconds then retired to load the pistols and complete their arrangements. Mr. Maclay, as he subsequently told me, suggested to Mr. Kennedy the propriety of an effort, on their part, to effect a reconciliation. Mr. Kennedy said: "That is impossible, unless Mr. Binns will apologize for the language he used in his message to Mr. Stewart. For my own part, I think nothing should be attempted until the parties have at least interchanged a shot." The terms proposed by Mr. Maclay, Kennedy said, "were inadmissible." The seconds then drew near to their principals, when Mr. Maclay said: "Gentlemen, when the word 'fire' is given, you are to fire as soon as you conveniently can. If either of you shall delay while one of us shall count three, and say stop, that one shall, for that time, lose his fire; a snap to be considered a fire." The seconds then tossed up to determine which of them should give the word. It was won by my friend. The pistols, having been charged, were handed, one to each of the parties. The word being given, the pistols were presented, and discharged so simultaneously that but one report was heard. Neither of the balls took effect. The pistols were again handed to the seconds. They retired a few paces, and, while loading the pistols, Mr. Maclay used, as he assured me, every honorable argument to move Mr. Kennedy to present to the parties a proposition which might terminate the affair. This he did without effect; at length he raised his voice, and said to Kennedy: "You had better consult your principal, and I will do the same." He then came to me, and Mr. Kennedy went to Mr. Stewart. Maclay's first words to me were: "Kennedy is a scoundrel. He is determined, if he can, to have you shot." I said: "Very well; you know the terms we agreed upon, and we will carry them out." Each of the principals then had a loaded pistol handed to him by his friend. After a short pause, Mr. Maclay came nearer to, and rather between the parties, and said: " Gentlemen, I think this business has now gone far enough, and may be amicably and honorably adjusted. To effect this, I propose that Mr. Stewart shall apologize for the attack he made upon Mr. Binns, and that then Mr. Binns shall declare that the publication, which gave offence to Mr. Stewart, was not made from any wish to wound the feelings, or injuriously affect the character of Mr. Stewart, but because Mr. Binns believed it to be true, and that it was matter proper for public information." This proposition was followed by a short silence, when Mr. Stewart said: "If God has given me more strength than other men, I do not think I ought to abuse it. I never struck a man in my life that I was not sorry for it." This general declaration was, as an apology, declared to be wholly inadmissible. Again there was a short silence, after which Mr. Stewart made the required apology, and I made the declaration which my friend had proposed.

The matter being thus satisfactorily arranged, the parties stepped forward, shook hands, and, at a tavern in the neighborhood, they and their friends breakfasted together.

It is forty-nine years since that duel was fought; there has been no duel fought in Pennsylvania since that in 1805. The pistol is no longer acknowledged as a redresser of grievances, or an arbiter of right and wrong.

Mr. Stewart and myself continued friends to his death, which was many years after. As evidence of this good understanding, I may mention that, several years after, when Mr. Stewart was, by the Federal party, elected to represent the county of Lycoming in the General Assembly of Pennsylvania, he every year voted for John Binns, then the editor of the "Democratic Press," as a Director of the Pennsylvania Bank.

The affair being satisfactorily terminated, Major Maclay returned to Buffalo, and I to Northumberland. I soon found that no doubt was entertained there but a duel had been fought, and much anxiety felt as to the result. It was gratifying to be welcomed, as I was on my return, by my fellow-townsmen, and by none more cordially than by my friends Judge Cooper, Joseph Priestley, Esq., and his family. I ascertained that it was Mr. Priestley who had issued the warrant for my arrest; he had seen me leave his house with a small mahogany case, in which he knew Judge Cooper kept his pistols, and suspected what was about to take place. If I had been arrested, and the duel prevented by that warrant, it would have been said, ay, and by many believed and asserted, that it was I who had given the information to my friend, Squire Priestley, in order to prevent the meeting. Such a belief in the public mind would have branded me as a coward, and sunk me in public opinion where fathom line could never reach.

The termination of this business put an end to anything like personal rudeness by any member of the Federal party so long as I remained in Northumberland, and doubtless had its influence after my removal to Philadelphia.

In 1806, Simon Snyder was again returned to the House of Representatives of Pennsylvania, and again chosen speaker. The "Aurora," edited by Mr. Wm. Duane, was, at that time, the ablest and most influential Republican paper in Pennsylvania, and probably had as much, or more, influence with that party in the Union, than any other paper then published. Dr. Leib, an able, zealous, and influential Republican, was the fast and faithful friend of Wm. Duane and his newspaper. The "Aurora" and its editor were equally zealous and devoted to the political interests of Dr. Leib. The doctor, at this time, was a member of the House of Representatives of the United States. It was generally believed that he did not desire the election of Mr. Snyder as governor; there were other persons whose election to that office he much more desired. It was believed that he was anxious to have some person chosen governor who would appoint him Secretary of the Commonwealth, and thus place him on the direct road to fill the governor's chair, and he thought Snyder would prefer N. B. Boileau, of Montgomery County, as Secretary of the Commonwealth. In these political views of Dr. Leib, Mr. Duane was believed to coincide. The cool support which was given by the "Aurora," in 1805, to the election of Mr. Snyder, weakened the hold which that paper had upon many men of the Republican party throughout Pennsylvania. The party, however, had entire confidence in the principles, the qualifications, and the integrity of Mr. Snyder for the office of governor, and it was generally believed that he had, in 1805, polled as many votes as any man the party could have selected. These considerations led to the general wish that he should again be taken up as the candidate of the party. Governor McKean could not serve longer than the three years for which, in 1805, he had been elected, and the seceders from the Republican party, who had voted for Governor McKean, were said to be desirous of reuniting with their former political friends, and giving their votes to Mr. Snyder, rather than to the candidate of the Federal party, who, it was known, would be the Hon. James Ross, of Pittsburg. The Quids could not, however, be prevailed upon to fall into the support of Mr. Snyder, under the banner of the "Aurora," where they had been politically whipped most unmercifully, and their influential members, one by one, denounced and expelled from the Tammany and other political societies, and Republican gatherings.

Mr. McCorkle, who has been dead some years, was then the editor of the "Freeman's Journal," the Quid paper in Philadelphia, but was believed to be wholly unable to cope with the Federal press, and was also believed to be rather disposed to fall in with the Federal party and advocate Mr. Ross, than to support Mr. Snyder; he was, therefore, deserted by many of his most influential Quid friends, who would not vote for Ross, and could not be prevailed upon again to subscribe for the "Aurora." The Republicans of the city and county were also at that time divided, and it was suggested and recommended to me by many of the Democratic members of the legislature and some influential Democrats in Philadelphia, that I should leave Northumberland, and establish a Democratic paper in Philadelphia.

My first visit to Philadelphia was in 1802. I rode on horseback from Northumberland, and was, together with my horse, ferried in a scow over the river Schuylkill, where the permanent bridge now spans it. Market Street was then paved only as far west as Delaware Ninth Street, and Chestnut Street to Delaware Fifth. I had, by some of Alexander Moore's relatives in Northumberland, been recommended to put up at his hotel. I accordingly rode to where I had been directed, at the S. W. corner of Chestnut and Delaware Fourth Streets. It was a very large log building, weather-boarded. It was not less than four stories high. The entrance was on the outside of the house, on Fourth Street, and was by means of a flight of wooden stairs, with a wooden hand-rail, which reached to near the top of the building, where there was a room, and stairway by which you descended into the several rooms in that spacious hotel. I have been thus particular; that the then wooden building may be contrasted with the large white marble palace which for many years has occupied the space on which, fifty years ago, stood Moore's celebrated hotel. In that marble building the business of the Philadelphia and Western Banks, and other public offices, is now, and for many years has been, transacted. At that time picnic parties were made up to meet and spend the day in the Centre Square, which was then well shaded with trees. Numerous tea-parties were, every fine summer evening, to be seen enjoying themselves in what were called Markoe's woods, between Market and Chestnut Streets, above Ninth. What was then Joseph Parker Norris's, Esq., dwelling and gardens, is now occupied, in part, by the chaste and classic marble building in which is transacted the custom-house business of the port of Philadelphia. Opposite the State House, on Chestnut Street, there then remained a few of the large walnut-trees under which our red brethren, in the time of William Penn, used to refresh themselves, their squaws and papooses, after the fatigues of the chase.

Our now splendid public squares, enriched with fragrant

flowers, shrubs, and trees, the air purified with the sweetest grass, and occasionally by new-mown hay, which, but a few years back, were cow markets or uninclosed burying-grounds, are now inclosed by tasteful and expensive iron railings, and care taken that everything inclosed, seats and ornaments, shall be kept in good order, with a keeper whose duty it is to prevent injury to the public property, and to exclude all rude or noisy company. In the summer and fall, their gates are thrown open, "music stirs the glad ear," and their walks are crowded with the beloved little ones, their delighted mothers and nurses, and the gay and beautiful of our city. Such is now, and for many years has been, the condition of all our public squares, save only *Independence Square*, the only square which has ever yielded a revenue to the city, furnished court-rooms, Select and Common Council rooms, mayor's offices, and many other public offices. That square on which stands the *Hall of Independence*, which is visited by all strangers, is the only unimproved square in Philadelphia. It is not forgotten that, some thirty years ago, the floor, and the heavy, old-fashioned cornice of that sacred hall, to give a job to one of our commissioner's relatives, were torn up and torn down, and cut and sawed and broken to pieces, many of which were sold at high prices as relics, and not a pen was moved in reprobation of the sacrilegious outrage by any editor of any public journal, save only by him who is now committing his recollections to paper.

Where the large public tobacco warehouse now stands, was a large dock from which lumber, sand, and other building materials used to be landed from sloops and barges, which passed from the river Delaware through an opening by a drawbridge on Front Street. Those who look at the chaste and beautiful building on South Second Street, in which the business of the Pennsylvania Bank is transacted, may be somewhat surprised at being told that, in the title-deed for the lot on which that bank is erected, the grantor guarantees to the bank the right to a wharf on the rear or west end of the lot, at least three squares from the river Delaware.

About the time of which I am writing, there was a large Quaker meeting-house, inclosed by a brick wall and wood en gates, at the S. W. corner of Second and Market Streets. There was also a large place of worship and a burying-ground on the rear of it, on the S. E. corner of Market Street and Bank Alley, now Bank Street. On Market Street, in front of this place of worship, were several large buttonwood-trees. The meeting-house was designated "Old Buttonwood." *All* the places of worship in the city were then authorized to put up, and did put up, iron chains across the street to prevent the approach of horses or carriages within, I think, twenty feet of the church, for fear of disturbing the congregation. These chains have all been taken down many years.

At that time, and for many years after, the eastern, or Delaware, front of the city was irregularly wharfed; the houses and warehouses were small, and for the most part of wood. A few yards below Market Street the river washed the walls of the houses, and those who passed that way had to walk over this inlet of water on a rather narrow, loose board. The consequence was that many people fell into the river and were drowned. On the north side of Market Street, near Race, for many yards, the avenue was covered by river-water, and passengers walked over it on elevated boards.

Delaware Avenue is now a broad, well-paved, well-built street, for probably two miles, and Water Street is widened and improved. No wooden building of any kind could, for the last twenty years, be erected in Philadelphia. For those improvements the public are indebted to our late wealthy, enlightened, and patriotic citizen Stephen Girard. In his last will is the following passage: "I have sincerely at heart the welfare of the city of Philadelphia, and, as a part of it, am desirous to improve the neighborhood of the river Delaware, so that the health of the citizens may be promoted and preserved, and that the eastern part of the city may be made to correspond better with the interior." Mr. Girard not only bequeathed millions of dollars to the city of Philadelphia, and for the education of orphans, but he gave the strongest possible proof of his confidence in the good sense of the people, and in the stability of a republican form of government. I have no knowledge of any man, in any age or any country, who has given such conclusive evidence of his entire confidence in the prudent wisdom and good sense of the people as Mr. Girard has done in his last will and testament. In it he has made provision that the expenditure of the immense wealth he has left shall be in the care, and at the disposal, of men—the Select and Common Councils of the city of Philadelphia—who are to be *annually* elected by the votes of its citizens.

I had been introduced to Mr. Wm. Duane, in London, in 1795. On my arrival in this country, he was the editor and proprietor of the "Aurora." He expressed for me the most friendly regards, and made me advantageous pecuniary offers. He proposed, if I would remove to Washington City, I should be intrusted with the editorial department of a Republican newspaper, about to be established there; or, he said, if I would come to Philadelphia, I should have charge of the editorial department of the "Aurora." I had, however, so fully, at that time, committed myself in the party warfare, in Northumberland County, and had made so many friends and so many enemies there, that I deemed it advisable to establish a paper there, rather than remove to any other part of the country. I therefore came to Philadelphia in 1802, and in a friendly conversation explained my position to Mr. Duane. He, after full explanations, thought I had better remain where I was, and it was so determined. I returned to Northumberland, and there established the "Republican Argus." Mr. Duane and I continued, in our respective papers, to advocate the same principles and the same men, and were warm personal and political friends, when I came to Philadelphia, early in 1807, with intention to establish a newspaper. He and I had many conversations on the subject; he, however, and many other Republicans, expressed a fear that, if I did establish a paper in Philadelphia, it would tend to divide and enfeeble, rather than strengthen the party. At length Mr. Duane, with all zeal and friendship, embarked heartily in my support. He gave me information as to the societies and individuals who could most effectually serve me, and, for the purpose of recommending them to patronize my paper, accompanied me to them. All, however, was not sunshine. Dr. Leib, who was active, intelligent, and influential, and as a politician, ambitious, was the fast friend of Mr. Duane, and Mr. Duane and he would have preferred to have no Republican paper in Philadelphia but the "Aurora." My friend Duane, however, succeeded in weeding out the suspicions of the Doctor, and the Doctor and I walked arm in arm to Mrs. Saville's, at Spring Garden, where, on St. Tammany's day, 1807, I delivered the Long Talk before the Tammany Society. The Long Talk was ordered to be printed, and the thanks of the Society unanimously presented to the orator.

My proposal was to print an evening paper three times a week. Mr. Duane was of opinion that a tri-weekly paper would not be acceptable, that it should be daily; he also did not approve of the name I proposed for the paper, which he thought was impolitic, and dangerously in advance of public opinion. Parties, he said, were, in all the States, known as Republicans and Federalists; the name of Democrat was nowhere in use. He feared the title of "The Democratic Press" would prejudice the public against the paper.

"Recollect," said he, "that Mr. Jefferson, the able leader of the party, in his inaugural speech took occasion, in speaking of the political parties of the United States, to say, 'We are all Republicans; we are all Federalists.' The word *democrat* or *democratic* is not used indeed, or scarcely known, as applied to politics or parties."

I was, however, determined on that name, and, on the 27th of March, 1807, I published the first number of that paper, with the motto, "The Tyrant's Foe; the People's Friend." It was the *first* paper published in the Union, or anywhere else, under the title of DEMOCRATIC, and it was some years before the title was adopted by any other newspaper or by the party. It, however, in time, won its way into public favor, and the political parties in the Union recognized and adopted it. The name of Republican faded away, and that of Democratic was adopted in its place, and has continued to gain ground throughout the Union.

Soon after the establishment of the "Democratic Press," on the 22d of June, 1807, the British frigate, the Leopard, of fifty guns, gave chase to the American frigate Chesapeake, as she sailed down the Chesapeake Bay, overtook her, and demanded that four of her crew should be delivered up as British deserters; three of them, it was said, had deserted from the British frigate Melampus, and the fourth from a British merchant-ship. The American commander refused to deliver the men thus claimed, in consequence of which, the Leopard made an attack upon the Chesapeake, which ship was wholly unprepared. Three men were killed, and sixteen wounded, upon which the American commander, Barron, struck his flag, and surrendered his vessel. The British commander sent an officer on board the Chesapeake, who seized four of her crew as deserters. One of the prisoners thus seized was tried at Halifax, found guilty of desertion, and hanged. One died in confinement, and two were kept in bondage. This outrage excited general indignation. All parties united in clamoring for reparation for the insult, by public meetings, and declarations of devotion to the cause of their country. Never, perhaps, did a more unanimous desire for revenge or an ample apology animate the nation than at that period. From Vermont to Georgia, from the Atlantic to the Lakes, all hearts panted with a desire to " pluck up the drowning honor of their country."

Mr. Jefferson, our then President, was an ardent lover of peace, and manifested as anxious a desire to preserve it as the public did to cast it away. To effect this object, and calm the public mind, on the 2d of July, 1807, he issued a proclamation, excluding all British vessels from our waters. This non-intercourse was followed by an embargo.

The effects of the non-intercourse and embargo were to cut off a considerable market for our agricultural produce, nearly annihilate our commerce, and raise the price of all colonial produce, on which we were then depending for tea, sugar, and coffee. None of these articles, save only a small amount of maple sugar, were then raised at home; thousands of families were driven to the necessity of using roasted rye and vegetables, as a substitute for coffee. We had no manufactures for making our wearing apparel, save only of coarse homemade stuff, linsey woolsey, spun and woven by our females in farm-houses. Wool was very scarce, and consequently very dear. Fine goods, of all sorts, for wearing apparel, were extravagantly dear. There were then but two tailors' shops, the Watsons and M'Alpins, in Philadelphia, out of Water Street; now we have hundreds of ready-made clothing-stores, extending from the Delaware to the Schuylkill. The seat of the State Government was then, and for many years after, in Lancaster. The first turnpike road made in the Union was between Philadelphia and Lancaster, sixty miles. There was a line of four-horse stages between those two cities, and those stages in from twenty-four to twenty-six hours transported you from one city to the other. It is now travelled in two or three hours. Our stages, at that time, travelled between Philadelphia and Pittsburg in from two to four weeks; now our passenger and burthen cars perform it in thirteen hours.

What were the consequences of the non-intercourse? Our merchant ships were under British orders in council, and French decrees; the British had our crews mustered by English officers, and such portion of them as they declared deserters were taken on board their ships of war, and compelled, not only to fight their battles, but to assist in plundering the merchants' ships of the United States.

At length the patience and forbearance of the country were exhausted; Mr. Jefferson had retired from the Presidential chair, and Mr. Madison had been elected in his place. On the 19th of June, 1812, after a long and embittered opposition from the Federal members of Congress, war was declared between the United States and Great Britain. We were ill prepared for war. We had a small army and a small navy; we were ill provided with implements of war; had few and feeble fortifications, or other means of defending our country or assailing the enemy; but the patience of the democratic party was exhausted; they relied on the bravery and patriotism of their countrymen to "pluck up the drowning honor of their country." At that time we did not even talk of American manufactures. There were then no manufactories of any kind in the country; we depended upon foreign nations, not only for our clothing, but for nearly all the articles required to furnish our houses or work our farms. We were inexperienced, and nearly destitute of warlike instruments; even of gunpowder, we had but one manufactory.

Soon, however, we had many first-rate privateers afloat, and manned by as brave sailors as ever stepped from stem to stern. Our navy was, as the English papers said, but a few "fir-built" ships, but these frigates, with bravery, and patriotism in the officers and men, made up for the want of numbers, and they did indeed do honor to their country. Charles J. Ingersoll, Esq., in his "History of the Second War between the United States of America and Great Britain," *second series*, has done credit to himself, and justice to his country. Those who read it will not hesitate to affirm that the war of 1812 was the war which gave the nations of Europe to understand that the Star Spangled Banner was the flag of another great nation, to be seen, felt and respected on the lakes and on the ocean. Since that war, "Rule Britannia" has become obsolete, and "Hail Columbia" is cheerfully and fearlessly sung on every sea and every lake.

CHAPTER X.

A town meeting of both parties—A scene in the State Legislature—Pennsylvania politics—Pennsylvania in the war of 1812—The rights of citizens—The enemy and John O'Neill.

A TOWN MEETING OF BOTH PARTIES.

THE enforcement of the embargo and non-intercourse, in the administration of Mr. President Jefferson, gave great offence to the Federal party, and moved them to adopt all possible means to have them taken off. On the other hand, the Republican party regarded the measures taken by the Federalists as anti-American in principle, and zealously supported the measures adopted by the administration. Public meetings of each party were held in all the commercial towns, and resolutions in favor of their respective party opinions adopted. The Republicans of Philadelphia called a meeting in the N. W. square of the

State-House yard—chair to be taken at twelve o'clock. The Federalists and the American Republicans held private meetings; took measures and made arrangements for a meeting in the same square an hour earlier, with a determination to take possession of the rostrum, chairs, and other things provided by the Republicans. Accordingly, at or before 11 o'clock, a large number of the obtruders took possession of the platform, surrounded it by still greater numbers, and made arrangements to proceed to business by calling Commodore Truxton to the chair, and appointing secretaries, &c.

What was thus doing was soon noised abroad. The Republicans were upon the alert; some of them drew near the platform for the recovery of what they justly regarded as their property, and as necessary to the transaction of their business; not a few had sticks, and limbs and branches torn from the trees, with which, and loud voices, they proclaimed their determination. In the mean time, many of them who were swift of foot ran to the Northern Liberties and Southwark, where the Republicans were assembling to proceed to their town meeting. Before half the proceedings contemplated by the Federalists had been gone through, not less than fifteen hundred or two thousand of the Republicans entered with a quick step, from the Northern Liberties and Southwark, the gates of the State-House yard on the northeast and south sides; they ran at once to the rostrum, while those of the Republicans who were near it were not idle, but with their hands, fists, sticks, and voices announced their determination to take possession of the platform which they had erected. In the mean time, the Federalists bestirred themselves, leaping from the platform, and making their escape through the western and northwestern gates on Sixth and Chestnut Streets. The Republicans, loudly laughing and hooting, drove their opponents clear off the ground, called Captain Wm. Jones to the chair, appointed other officers, and with loud cheers and hearty acclamations adopted the proceedings which they had prepared.

A SCENE IN THE STATE LEGISLATURE.

During the session of the Legislature, 1804-5, I was in the House of Representatives of Pennsylvania, when a well-dressed young man of a respectable family from Northumberland County, about the dusk of the evening, threw open the inner doors and entered the body of the House of Representatives at Lancaster. In a loud, clear, and distinct voice, he said: "Mr. Speaker, I am charged by the Lord God with a message to this House: to direct them forthwith to pass a law for the removal of the seat of Government from Lancaster to the top of the Blue Hill." Many of the members loudly called, "Turn him out—turn him out." Instantly the doorkeeper and sergeant-at-arms, both elderly men, one at each side seized the intruder by the collar of his coat to eject him from the House; upon which he tripped up their heels and laid them both sprawling on the floor. A motion to adjourn was promptly made and adopted. That young man, who was laboring under insanity, remained about three days in Lancaster; he then started for home on horseback. It was said and believed that he never drew bit until he arrived at home, a distance of one hundred and fifteen miles. In a few minutes after he arrived, the horse dropped dead.

PENNSYLVANIA POLITICS.

Finding the wishes of the republican party, in and out of the Legislature, to have Mr. Snyder as their candidate for governor in 1808 too general and determined to be broken down, and that his election would in all probability follow his nomination, the "Aurora" and Dr. Leib took such measures as they deemed most likely to insure the appointment of the doctor as Secretary of the Commonwealth. To effect this, Dr. Leib induced his most influential democratic friends throughout the State to keep his appointment as Secretary of the Commonwealth constantly in view, as the one thing needful, in the event of Mr. Snyder's election. The "Aurora," to assist the Doctor, took all possible pains to break down the character of Nathaniel B. Boileau, who had frequently sat in the Assembly as one of the representatives of Montgomery County, and was not only known to be on the most friendly terms with Mr. Snyder, but suspected to be looked on as his choice for Secretary of the Commonwealth. Among the least defensible of the means resorted to in order to prevent his appointment as Secretary, were insinuations that Mr. Boileau was fond of liquor; these insinuations were followed by the broad assertion that he was a drunkard. These hints and assertions were repeatedly and unsparingly directed against Mr. Boileau, and credited, reiterated, and affirmed to be true by very many of the readers of the "Aurora." It is due to the memory of Mr. Boileau to state that, from early in 1808, I knew him intimately. It was the custom of Governor Snyder, during the session of the Legislature, to invite large parties of the members of Assembly twice a week to dine with him. Whenever I was at the seat of government, I was an invited guest at those dinners. Mr. Boileau, as Secretary of the Commonwealth, and the friend of the governor, always made one of the party. He usually was one of the last to take his seat at table, and one of the first to leave it. My opportunities to ascertain his general habits were of the first order; yet I never, at any time, at any place, or upon any occasion saw Mr. Boileau in the least intoxicated. He was in truth a very temperate and studious man. Governor Snyder, from his experience and opportunities of ascertaining the qualifications, political principles, and integrity of Mr. Boileau, would have been gratified if he had been nominated as the democratic candidate for governor when his own constitutional term was about to expire. Many times he expressed his regret at the reserved manners and habits of Mr. Boileau. "What can you do," he would say, "for a man who comes to dinner when the last dish is about to be set on the table, and retires with the first which is about to be carried away?" Mr. Snyder, in 1808, was, with great unanimity, nominated as the candidate of the Republican party for the office of governor.

There were other respectable and influential German families in the State, particularly in Berks County, who had done the country good service in the war of the Revolution, and who had always ranked, and ranked high, with the Republican party in Pennsylvania. I may, without offence, name the Muhlenbergs and the Hiesters. These families regarded Mr. Snyder as by no means entitled to a preference, and although they could not, and would not, be persuaded or provoked into the support of Mr. Ross, who was the candidate of the Federal party, they could not prevail upon themselves to vote for Mr. Snyder, whom they regarded as a new man about to be elevated to the platform which they had so long exclusively and respectably occupied. To avoid this dilemma, Mr. John Spayd, a son-in-law of General Joseph Hiester, was nominated as a candidate for governor. He got about 5,000 votes, principally in Berks County. The number of votes for the other candidates I cannot at this time recollect, but I remember that Mr. Snyder, in 1808, had a majority of 28,400 over Mr. Ross, and was declared governor of Pennsylvania. Soon after his election was ascertained, he wrote and expressed a wish that I should pay him a visit. I accordingly went to Selin's Grove, accompanied by my wife; at Selin's Grove we remained a few days, and paid a visit to some of our old and truest friends in Northumberland County. Early as that visit was, after the election of Mr. Snyder had been ascertained, he had received letters from several influential Democrats, urging the appointment of Dr. Leib as Secretary of the Commonwealth. It should be borne in mind that, for many years, Dr. Leib had been an active and distinguished Republican, and had filled many public stations; these gave him opportunities which, to do him justice, he never neglected of promoting the interests of the State and obtaining appointments for his political friends. During this visit, Mr. Snyder was, I may truly say, as unreservedly confidential with me as one friend can be with another. He has long since been committed to the silent grave. My recollections shall do justice to his memory; I shall, however, "nothing extenuate." Somewhere about the close of his administration, he prepared, at my request, and gave to me, a small manuscript-book, in which he had written an outline of his life. I regret to say, I have lost or mislaid it. I shall diligently look for it, and, if fortunate enough to find it, shall avail myself of anything interesting I may find in it. In that manuscript he stated that he was born in York County, Pa., and that it was there, at a night-school, he got his early education, and learned the business of a tanner. He advised with me touching the arrangements preparatory to, and immediately preceding his inauguration, and as to the persons most proper to be appointed to office, expressing the opinion that, although he was aware of the great number of applications already before him for offices from the country, his great difficulty would be in the city of Philadelphia, where there were so many offices to fill, and many of them so lucrative as to insure for each a number of applicants.

It should be borne in mind and not forgotten, that during the whole nine years of the administration of Governor Snyder, he was constitutionally bound to appoint, and did appoint, to all the offices in the commonwealth, from that of Chief Justice of the Supreme Court to the Justices of the Peace and County officers, Prothonotaries, Registers, &c. &c. To his honor, and that of his friends, be it called to mind and perpetuated, that neither he nor they were, at any time, suspected of being induced by any improper or corrupt means to do what they ought not to have done, nor on any account whatever charged, or, so far as I know or ever heard, suspected, of taking a bribe.

The first, most important, and confidential officer was that of Secretary of State. After much conversation as to the qualifications, political standing, and probable consequences, the governor authorized me, on my return to Philadelphia, to wait on Mr. Boileau, and, if he made no objection, to inform him that the governor would appoint him Secretary of the Commonwealth, but that it was thought advisable not to make known that determination, as it would, in all human probability, induce an active opposition to other appointments if not to the governor. To prevent this, I suggested that it might be well to have Mr. Boileau, who had been elected a member of the House of Representatives, chosen speaker, an appointment in which, without a doubt, the friends of the "Aurora" would willingly concur in order to take Mr. Boileau out of the way as Secretary of the Commonwealth, and Mr. Boileau's friends would willingly unite in the vote, as, by that means, those who had made against him the charge of inebriety would themselves extinguish the flame they had lighted. This suggestion was adopted.

When the House of Representatives met, Mr. Boileau was proposed, and had the vote of every Democratic member in the House, and was inaugurated as Speaker. Thus was he, by his accusers, purified of every foul imputation. A few days after, he resigned the Speaker's chair, and was appointed Secretary of the Commonwealth, which office he held, and with ability and integrity discharged all its duties, during the nine years which Mr. Snyder was governor.

When the governor had appointed the Secretary of the Commonwealth, he turned his attention to that of Attorney-General. The very large Democratic majority which Mr. Snyder had over the Federal candidate, made it, in his opinion, his duty to bestow all the offices in his disposal on the members of that party which had elected him. There was not, at that time, in Philadelphia a Democratic lawyer known to either the governor or to me, although I then resided, and for nearly two years had resided, in the city. The governor dwelt with much and entire satisfaction on the high character of Jared Ingersoll, Esq., and expressed a determination to appoint him, if that gentleman would accept. It was the constant practice of the governor never to send a commission without having first ascertained that it would be accepted by the person to whom it was addressed. Having ascertained that Mr. Ingersoll would accept the commission, it was forthwith forwarded to him.

While Mr. Snyder was governor, there was a general belief that I enjoyed a very large portion of his confidence, and greatly influenced his judgment and his appointments. This understanding was not altogether unfounded, and I may presume to say was consequent upon the governor's conviction that, in no instance, would I be so far blinded by personal considerations or predilections in favor of unworthy applicants, or moved, from selfish considerations, as to advise the adoption of measures or appointments which would be injurious to his good name, or prejudicial to the honor or interests of the commonwealth. If, at any time, I had been so mistaken as to give such advice, the sound sense and general knowledge of the governor would be sure to correct it, and do that which was lawful and right. Mr. Snyder was an industrious and conscientious public officer. His position as Speaker of the House of Representatives afforded him excellent opportunities of acquiring a knowledge of the wants of the State and the opinions of her representatives. Of these means, he failed not to avail himself. I doubt whether there were many men as competent as Mr. Snyder to discharge the duties of governor as he was when elected. During the nine years Mr. Snyder was governor, there were only four Federalists in the House of Representatives—two from Adams and two from Delaware County—and now, Pennsylvania has elected a Federal governor, and a Federal majority in the House of Representatives, and in Congress.

Governor Snyder was pleased to appoint me one of his aides-de-camp, and, in 1812, to intrust to my care the organization of some companies and regiments, and to muster them into the United States service; and also with the payment of some who had performed their tour of duty, and the forwarding of others to the seat of war; and also a large amount of ordnance, small arms, and ammunition, the property of the State, for the use of the United States. These several duties, I had the gratification to know, were performed not only to his satisfaction, but also to that of the officers of the General and State Governments, with whom I had business to transact. When called upon, after the peace, by the Register-General of Pennsylvania, to transmit to him the amount of my claim against the United States for pay, rations, &c. (for which two of the governor's aids received each $7,500), I made answer that I was amply paid in the happiness and gratification I enjoyed in having been honored by the services I was permitted to render to the country which had adopted me. I have had much experience since I forwarded that answer, and have ascertained that I could not then, nor for a long time after, command as much money as I thought I could, or as I was entitled to command. Those who keep me company through these recollections, will ascertain that, at several periods of my life, the amount of this claim would have greatly contributed to my happiness, and to that of those who were best entitled to look to me for that, which, although not in itself happiness, is not only the means of barring the door against evils and privations, but also of throwing wide every avenue through which the means of happiness may plentifully flow.

In 1817, previous to the expiration of Governor Snyder's term of office, Wm. Findlay, Esq., then State Treasurer, was nominated as the Democratic candidate for the office of governor. His election was opposed with more than usual personalities and bitterness of spirit. The "Democratic Press" steadily, and with its best ability, advocated his election. The opposition candidate was General Joseph Heister, of Reading. Mr. Findlay was elected by about seven thousand majority over General Heister.

On my first visit to Harrisburg, after the election of Governor Findlay, I waited on him, and had many conversations with him and his amiable lady. In one of them, talking of the bitterness of the opposition, Mrs. Findlay said: "You remember, governor, how glad we used to be when the 'Democratic Press' would come." She said many other kind things—among them: "Governor, mind what Mr. Binns says; he will always advise you for the best." I do not put to paper these remarks for any other purpose than to introduce to my readers a very estimable lady; one who commanded very general respect; nor will I, even at this late day, deny myself the pleasure, or Governor Findlay the justice, to say, that he was an honest, kind-hearted man, betrayed into the errors of which he was guilty by bad advisers and embarrassed circumstances, rather than a corrupt mind. I would, at all times, rather scatter flowers than bitter herbs, on the graves of the deceased.

In consequence of certain conduct in Governor Findlay soon after his inauguration, which the editor of the "Democratic Press" and many of his political friends regarded as unbecoming in the governor, a committee of inquiry was prayed for by a petition to the House of Representatives at Harrisburg. The petition for an inquiry into the conduct of the governor was presented December 8, 1819, to the House of Representatives by Josiah Randall, Esq., then one of the Representatives from the city of Philadelphia. The ability, integrity, and independence with which that gentleman presided over that committee, an arduous duty, were not only acceptable to his friends, but commanded the respect of the governor and his friends. Messrs. Dallas and Douglas acted as counsel for the governor. The petitioners were represented by A. S. Coxe, Esq., and John Binns. The inquiry was carried on in the hall of the House of Representatives. It commenced daily at three o'clock in the afternoon, and usually continued from three to four hours every business day, from January 8th to the 3d day of February, 1820. The committee reported in favor of Governor Findlay. In the mean time, while the inquiry was going on, a convention of Republican delegates assembled at Lewistown, and nominated Governor Findlay for a re-election as Governor of Pennsylvania. A convention of delegates, of what was called at that time the old school party, met at Carlisle, and proposed General Joseph Heister as their candidate for governor. A third convention of Democratic delegates was called, and, in December, 1820, met in the town of Northumberland. To that convention I was elected, and attended as a delegate. When this convention assembled, it was promptly ascertained that a majority of the delegates were in favor of taking up N. B. Boileau, Esq., as a candidate for governor. I spoke frequently, and with much earnestness, for part of two or three days, before I succeeded in convincing a majority of the delegates that "the taking up of Mr. Boileau would be the certain means to insure the re-election of Governor Findlay." This convention at length adjourned without taking up any candidate, leaving the election to rest between the same candidates that it had rested between in 1817, at which time Governor Findlay was elected, having 7,059 votes more than General Heister. In 1820, the "Democratic Press" advocated the election of General Joseph Heister as an event much more to be desired than the re-election of Governor Findlay. The result of the election was, that General Heister was elected governor by a majority of 1,605 votes over Governor Findlay.

In 1808, the Federal party regarded the running of Simon Snyder, a storekeeper and a farmer, in a small country town in the backwoods, as a candidate for governor in opposition to the Hon. James Ross, who had represented the State in the Senate of the United States, as an act little short of insanity. This was pre-eminently the opinion and feeling in Philadelphia, where Federalism held its head so high as neither to see nor to hear what was going on in the political world out of the city. Betting on elections was then permitted by law, and a rather high-toned Federalist was pleased to sneer and laugh outright at the presumptuous folly of the Democrats. The idea of a country storekeeper, who had learned to read and write at a country night-school, and who could only speak English and German, running against a gentleman who had had a collegiate education, and could speak Greek and Latin, was a theme for Federal orators, inexhaustible at their town meetings. It was one which never failed to excite the merriment of their hearers, who laughed to scorn the nomination of Mr. Snyder. As the election drew near, the Federal party began to entertain apprehensions that the election of Mr. Ross was not so certain as they had supposed, and that it was not altogether impossible Mr. Snyder might be elected. This fear became more and more manifest as the day of election drew near. Then it was that many of the Federalists discovered how foolish it was to bet on elections, and began to manifest their dislike for such practices by proposing to withdraw their bets. The party called Quids, who, from affection and respect for Governor McKean, had voted for him in 1805, now returned to their first love, and voted for Mr. Snyder. One consequence of the doubts and fears of the Federal party was their resort to measures unbecoming in any party, but to which factions sometimes resort. On the morning of the day of the general election, a letter, said to have come express from Selin's Grove, brought and widely circulated the news that some desperadoes had murdered Mr. Snyder, and that his dead body was found in a field, covered with limbs of trees and fence rails. This scheme had no effect upon the election.

Thomas Passmore, a most respectable citizen, who has

been dead many years, was so blinded by his wishes and his Democratic principles as not to think the chance of Simon Snyder altogether desperate, and probably with a view to keep up the spirits of his political associates, ventured, when bantered by a high-toned confident political opponent, to say: "Well, now, I tell you what it is; I will give you a hundred dollars if you will enter into a written agreement to pay me an eleven-pennybit for every vote majority Mr. Snyder shall have over Mr. Ross." "Agreed, my dear fellow, I would not wish for anything better." The writing was drawn and signed, and the $100 paid and receipted for. In a few months the election was held, and it was authoritatively and officially announced that Simon Snyder's majority over James Ross was 28,400. The gentleman who made the bet neither hesitated nor delayed. He called on Mr. Passmore and gave him a check for three thousand five hundred and fifty dollars, which was duly honored. This is not a bad illustration of "Hear both sides," and "Look before you leap." The whole vote of the State was: Simon Snyder, 67,975; James Ross, 30,433; John Spayd, 4006; whole vote in 1808 was 110,414.

PENNSYLVANIA IN THE WAR OF 1812.

Early in the session of Congress of 1811-12, I went to Washington to ascertain, as far as I was able, the probability of war being declared that session against Great Britain, and as well as in my power, by an honest representation of the public opinion of Pennsylvania, to encourage the declaration. I had an early introduction to Mr. President Madison, who had the honor done me of an invitation to one of his public dinners, where, as on all apposite occasions, I made known what I believed to be the desire of the Democratic party of the State of Pennsylvania, on the question of declaring war against Great Britain.

Every representative but two from Pennsylvania, and both the senators voted in favor of a declaration of war against England. Nobly did their constituents make known their approval of that vote. The two members who did not vote for the war were at the next election left at home, and men in favor of the war elected in their place. Throughout the whole of that war, no enemy ever set a hostile foot upon the soil of Pennsylvania; yet she was the State that furnished more men and more money to carry on the war than any State in the Union. The city of Philadelphia sent from her State-House yard more than a brigade of volunteers to Camp Dupont, of the flower of her population. When Federalism, from its pulpits and its presses, was denouncing as murderers and traitors those who loaned their money, or enlisted in the service of their country, and publishing the President of the United States, the pure and patriotic James Madison, as a pensioner of France—*then* was Pennsylvania doing all in her power to unite the men of America in defence of their country's rights.

The country has not forgotten, it will be long before it does forget, that when General Van Rensselaer, with a division of four thousand New York militia, arrived at Buffalo, on their march to invade Canada, they refused to cross the line on the traitorous pretext of the Federal party, that the United States militia were not, even when mustered into the service of the United States, obliged to cross the boundary line of their country to fight their country's enemies; nor can it be forgotten that soon after, when General Tannehill, with a brigade of two thousand Pennsylvanians, arrived at Buffalo, they did not hesitate, but promptly crossed the line, and crossed bayonets with their country's enemies; nor is it forgotten that the militia of New York thereupon turned a deaf ear to the persuasions of Federalism, and took up the line of march under "the Star-Spangled Banner," and bravely fought, and bravely conquered in the cause "of these United States;" nor is it, nor can it be forgotten, that it was the militia of Pennsylvania who volunteered and manned Perry's fleet on Lake Erie, and enabled him to announce, "We have met the enemy, and they are ours!" Pennsylvania also, with pride, remembers the skill, the courage, and the seamanship which were displayed by her Decatur, her Biddles, and her Stewart, and of which their State and the United States were justly proud. What a glorious theme for some warm-hearted Pennsylvanian would it be to write her history from the landing of William Penn! That historian would not forget to do justice to the defender and saviour of Sacket's Harbor, the gallant Major-General Brown, one of our Bucks County Friends. For many months after the declaration of war, there was a general complaint that the United States had an empty treasury, and was thus unable to do as she otherwise would have done. This want of money was mainly attributed to the want of talent and patriotism, or timidity, in those who were called to fill the office of Secretary of the Treasury. This charge was reasonably well founded; but when Pennsylvania was called upon, and her highly gifted and patriotic son, the Honorable Alexander J. Dallas, was called to the head of the Treasury, his heart knew no pulsation of fear when his country wanted his services. He went to Washington, and his first report, fearless of personal consequences, and relying on the patriotism of the country, levied taxes, a dollar on every barrel of flour, and soon filled the treasury. *The United States had then offers in abundance to loan her money, because ample provision had been made to insure the prompt payment of the interest. Mr. Dallas proved that it was timidity in the secretaries of the treasury, and not want of patriotism or an unwillingness to pay taxes which crippled the arms of Government.

THE RIGHTS OF CITIZENS.

During the war of 1812, the Prince Regent of the Kingdom of Great Britain and Ireland issued a proclamation declaring that every native of Great Britain or Ireland taken in the service of the United States of America, should be hung as a traitor. In pursuance of this proclamation, twenty-three Irish and English officers of the army of the United States, who had been taken prisoners, were, under this proclamation, sent to Quebec, with the intention of transporting them to England to be hung as traitors. The President of the United States, His Excellency James Madison, retaliatory of the conduct of the Prince Regent, ordered that the same number of officers in the British army, who had been taken prisoners, and of the same rank as those of the American officers, who had been ironed and imprisoned, should be forthwith in all respects treated as the officers of the American army had been treated. This was done forthwith, and the consequence was the American officers were liberated, and the Prince Regent's proclamation became a dead letter.

The following letters to the then acting Secretary of State and President of the United States, his answer, and the act of Congress, will give the reader a tolerably clear view of the opinions entertained by the Irish and English naturalized citizens, and the decided principle on which the American authorities, legislative and executive, acted. The letter of the President affirms, and the Government acted on the principle, that "the rights of naturalized citizens being under the same guarantee of the national faith and honor, with the rights of other citizens, the former may be assured that it is the determination, as it will be the duty, of the executive department of the Government to employ whatever just means may be within its competency for enforcing the respect which is due from the enemy to the rights and persons of those who combat under the banners and in defence of the rights and safety of their adopted country."

LETTER TO THE HONORABLE RICHARD RUSH.

SIR: At a very numerous and respectable meeting of citizens of the United States, natives of the United Kingdom of Great Britain and Ireland, held in the city of Philadelphia January 2, 1813, to consider the proclamation of the Prince Regent of the 26th October, 1812 (a copy of which is enclosed), it was resolved to communicate to you, sir, the sentiments of the meeting on this proclamation, and respectfully, yet very earnestly, solicit such information as you may think proper to communicate on this very important subject. We are instructed to give the most unequivocal assurances of the sincere confidence they repose in the justice of the present administration of the General Government, of a devoted attachment to the Constitution of the United States, and a determination, with heart and hand, life and property, to defend the rights, the honor, and interests of the nation. The meeting, sir, were duly sensible of the peculiar delicacy and embarrassment of their situation.

As citizens of the United States, they know that they are entitled to the protection of the Government, and they are not unmindful that you, sir, as Secretary of State, have informed the British minister that "it is *impossible* for the United States to discriminate between their native and naturalized citizens." These facts are impressive, and would, even under the proclamation of the Prince Regent, have been altogether conclusive, were it not that facts, apparently in contradiction, are busily circulated and too often misrepresented not to induce fears and opinions calculated to injure the public service. Many thousands are the hearts which beat with anxiety to know the result of this application; yet their feelings, their fears, or forebodings are, in our judgment, but of small account compared with the public interests which are involved in the inquiry. Our opportunities enable us to see, and hear, and know the extent to which this proclamation has carried apprehension and excited distrust—an extent scarcely credible to persons whose situations and stations concur to preclude such opportunities, and shut every avenue to such knowledge, except from formal representation.

May we not hope, sir, that these circumstances will by you be accepted as an apology for occupying so much of your time. Our motives, we trust, will excuse our errors, if our zeal should lead us into error. We affirm, not merely for ourselves, but for thousands, whose hearts are known to us, that we are desirous to be satisfied; we wish to be convinced; we are anxious that no loop be left on which skepticism or disaffection should hang a doubt to overshadow the minds of the timid or the wavering. Our feelings, our principles, our attachments are all embarked in the just and sacred cause of this our chosen, our adopted country.

Here are our families, here our fortunes, here all that is most dear and precious to us, and it would wound us sorely if any device of the enemy should scatter such suspicion as to thin our ranks, when they were to be mustered to fight the battles of the United States.

We arraign not the motives of those who go about and take pains to state that the hanging of a naturalized citizen at Halifax, taken from on board a national ship, in time of peace; the not seizing hostages for those of the crew of the Wasp, put in irons and threatened with execution, and this with a knowledge of the regent's proclamation, are regarded as symptoms of an indifference to the fate of naturalized citizens; certain, however, we are that such statements have excited, and continue to excite, fears which we believe to be groundless, but which we certainly know to be injurious to the public service.

Independent of all considerations connected with public or private armed ships, it is within the knowledge of this meeting that many persons who have enlisted in the army from the purest and most patriotic motives, men who enlisted determined to conquer or die, are now pausing and considering consequences, and some are actively employed in devising ways and means to procure their discharge, or otherwise to be permitted to leave the service.

Similar feelings and fears prevent many at this time from enlisting. It is also a fact that a volunteer company, in this city, one hundred strong, principally naturalized citizens, whose zeal had prompted a tender of their service to the United States, have become so alarmed, under the proclamation, that the company will rather disband than hazard being hung as traitors. No inconsiderable portion of the militia of this State and of the States of New York and Maryland are naturalized citizens, principally natives of the United Kingdom of Great Britain and Ireland, and we regret to state, but we know the fact, that this proclamation has caused much conversation, which has awakened apprehensions which cannot fail to strengthen and to be productive of evil, if some means be not taken to eradicate them, and restore that perfect confidence which existed previous to the proclamation.

We trust, sir, that the circumstances which have given rise to this letter, our apprehensions as to the probable magnitude of the evil, and the facts we have stated, will justify us to you for the length of this communication, and induce you to give such an answer as will dispel all fear, reanimate confidence, and make gratitude and patriotism burn with a still brighter and more vivid flame.

On behalf of the meeting, we have the honor to be, sir, with high consideration, and great personal respect, your fellow-citizens,

JOHN BINNS, *Chairman.*
WM. SMILEY,
JNO. W. THOMPSON,
FRANCIS MITCHELL, } *Committee.*
JOHN MAITLAND,
GEORGE PALMER,

The above letter was forwarded addressed to "The Hon. Richard Rush, acting Secretary of State," to be by him laid before the President of the United States, which duty he performed so entirely to their satisfaction as to command their unanimous and grateful public thanks.

TO JAMES MADISON, ESQ., PRESIDENT OF THE UNITED STATES OF AMERICA.

SIR: The naturalized citizens of the United States, residing in the city and vicinity of Philadelphia, natives of the United Kingdom of Great Britain and Ireland, have, at various meetings, had under their serious consideration the proclamation of the Prince Regent, under date of the 26th of October, 1812; upon which subject, with all the respect due to the Chief Magistrate of a free people, and with all the solicitudes and anxieties which so important a subject demands, we, a committee appointed for the purpose, address your Excellency. The inhuman threat, the barbarous policy which is manifested in the proclamation, are presumed to have issued from counsellors determined and desperate enough to dare to do that which they have dared to threaten. With the shield of the Constitution and laws between them and the vengeance of the Prince Regent, the naturalized citizens would have stilled the tumultuous throbbings of indignation and apprehension which this proclamation had caused, were not their bosoms, from time to time, agitated and distracted by statements of naturalized citizens having been taken from among the prisoners in the United States army and navy, and put in irons and sent to the United Kingdom to be tried for high treason, "for having taken up arms against their natural and lawful Sovereign, George III."

These statements do damp—indeed they cannot fail to

damp the warmth of patriotism, and check the ardor of devotion to the public service which otherwise would, and which previously did, glow in the hearts of naturalized citizens toward the country of their adoption; a country which is made dear to them by the most sacred principles of truth, by the most interesting associations and the tenderest ties of gratitude and affection.

On the justice of the constituted authorities of the United States, we repose with the most entire confidence, and their assurance that the rights and persons of the naturalized citizens, proscribed in the Prince Regent's proclamation, should be protected, would be entirely satisfactory, and would invigorate their arms in every contest against the enemies of the United States; that cruel enemy whose persecution and tyranny drove us from the land of our fathers, and would vindictively pursue us, even to death, in the only country whose hospitable arms are open to receive the persecuted and oppressed.

The committee feel assured that you, sir, have given this momentous subject a consideration commensurate with its extent of bearing and importance of effect; and we pray you to be assured that considerations connected with the public weal as intimately as they involve the rights and feelings of those whom we represent, could alone induce us to trespass upon your time, and very respectfully, yet not less earnestly, solicit from you some information as to the course which the executive of the United States are determined to pursue in the event of the Prince Regent carrying into effect the measures threatened in his proclamation.

We have the honor to be, sir, on behalf of the naturalized citizens of the United States, residing in the city and vicinity of Philadelphia, natives of the United Kingdom of Great Britain and Ireland, with sentiments of attachment, personal and political,

Your friends and fellow-citizens,

JOHN BINNS, *Chairman.*
WM. SMILEY,
JOHN W. THOMPSON,
FRANCIS MITCHELL, } *Committee.*
JOHN MAITLAND,
GEORGE PALMER,

PHILADELPHIA, *February* 6, 1813.

WASHINGTON, February 11, 1813.

GENTLEMEN: I have received your communication in behalf of the naturalized citizens in and near Philadelphia, who were born within the British dominions, occasioned by the proclamation of the Prince Regent of Great Britain, dated the 26th of October last, and by other indications of a purpose of subjecting to the penalties of British law such of that description of citizens as shall have been taken in arms against Great Britain.

As the British laws and practice confer all the rights and immunities of natural born subjects on aliens serving even a short period on board British vessels, it might have been concluded that an intention would have been neither formed nor proclaimed by the head of that nation, which is as inconsistent with its own examples as it is repugnant to reason and humanity.

The rights of naturalized citizens being under the same guaranty of the national faith and honor with the rights of other citizens, the former may be assured that it is the determination, as it will be the duty of the Executive Department of the Government, to employ whatever just means may be within its competency for enforcing the respect which is due from the enemy to the rights and persons of those who combat under the banners and in defence and maintenance of the rights and safety of their adopted country.

Accept my friendly respects.

JAMES MADISON.

To JOHN BINNS, *Chairman.*
WM. SMILEY, ESQ.
JOHN W. THOMPSON, ESQ.
FRANCIS MITCHELL, ESQ. } *Committee.*
JOHN MAITLAND, ESQ.
GEORGE PALMER, ESQ.

AN ACT VESTING IN THE PRESIDENT OF THE UNITED STATES THE POWER OF RETALIATION.

Be it enacted by the Senate and House of Representatives of the United States of America in Congress assembled: That in all and every case wherein, during the present war between the United States of America and the United Kingdom of Great Britain and Ireland, any violations of the laws and usages of war, among civilized nations, shall be, or have been done and perpetrated by those acting under authority of the British Government, on any of the citizens of the United States, or persons in the land, or naval service of the United States, the President of the United States is hereby authorized to cause full and ample retaliation to be made, according to the laws and usages of war among civilized nations for all and every such violation as aforesaid.

Approved March 3, 1813.

THE ENEMY AND JOHN O'NEILL.

In the war of 1812, in various parts of the United States, the English officers, particularly those of the navy, carried on a species of predatory warfare disgraceful to a civilized people. They were, in many cases, so shameless, while in the Chesapeake Bay, as to boast, in their letters to their relatives and friends, some of which were intercepted in prizes captured by our vessels of war and privateers, that they had purloined and carried off from the farm-houses on the bay, river, and creek-side, "tables, and chests of drawers, and other household and kitchen furniture."

A party of these marauders, under Admiral Cockburn, in 1813 burned the small town of Havre-de-Grace, situated on the west bank of the Susquehanna near the Chesapeake Bay. The inhabitants, scared by the known savage behavior and the pilfering conduct of these invaders, left the town, save only one man, John O'Neill, who mounted a small cannon on the brow of a hill, and as the invaders advanced up the road he fired upon them until he was shot down and made prisoner.

This patriotic conduct excited a kindly feeling toward O'Neill; a sword was bought and sent to him. A subscription was also set on foot in Philadelphia, and the sum of two hundred and fifteen dollars was subscribed and forwarded to him. The subscription list is now before me. There are thirty-seven subscribers' names to it; of these, two only, J. Randall and the writer, are now living. The letter of thanks received from John O'Neill I have just read; it is altogether characteristic, and claims a publication. If he has left any family, they will be proud of the sentiments and conduct of their relative, who has long since been consigned to the grave.

"HAVRE-DE-GRACE, June 8, 1813.

GENTLEMEN: This morning I received yours of the 2d inst., together with its inclosure (the money subscribed), which is accepted with sentiments of gratefulness. I am now upon parole of honor, and it grieves me to think, if the oppressors of the human race, and particularly of my native country, Ireland, should come within such a distance of me as that I could be of any service to my fellow-citizens, in repelling the merciless bloodhounds, that I could not have the pleasure to assist in protecting my adopted country and revenging their insults, while I am their prisoner on parole. I have been to Baltimore some time since, and General Miller promised to have me exchanged as soon as possible, which I hope will be shortly. Although my age exempts me from military duty, I am able and willing to take up arms in defence of our pure Republican Government, as soon as honor will permit, when there is necessity. To my Democratic fellow-citizens of Philadelphia I return my sincere thanks for their very liberal assistance, which will be held in grateful remembrance by their fellow-citizen. I am, gentlemen, with esteem, your friend and faithful fellow-citizen,

JOHN O'NEILL.

To THOMAS LEIPER, &c. &c.

N. B.—The gentlemen who addressed the letter to me I am sorry not to have a personal acquaintance of; but I hope, if either of them pass through this place, they will do me the honor of calling upon me.

J. O'NEILL.

CHAPTER XI.

The news, how did it come?—Honor to the brave—Fundamental difference between the Government of the United States and that of Great Britain—Some public services—The forty banks—The Declaration of Independence—Mr. Jefferson and Mr. Adams.

THE NEWS—HOW DID IT COME?

By the regular mail from Washington City, I received a letter early in the year 1815, informing me that advices had there been received that a Treaty of Peace between the United States and Great Britain had been signed at Ghent. I received the letter in the forenoon, on a week-day. I had no knowledge of the handwriting, and there was no name subscribed to the letter. I was aware of the importance of the information, and of the influence it would necessarily have upon the prices to be obtained for the immense amount of cotton, rice, and other home produce which was then in the United States, to say nothing of the consequent fall in price, which must take place in tea, sugar, coffee, and other colonial produce, a large amount of which had been laid away, and it was then extravagantly dear in the United States.

I was perplexed what to do, and unwilling to consult any one, lest they should take advantage of the news at the expense of others. I mixed with the persons I thought most likely to have received advices, such as I had received, but I was unable anywhere, or in any manner to hear even a whisper corroborative of the information in the letter I had received. I felt apprehensive that the news might not be true, and that thus I might lead persons into loss and difficulty. In this perplexed state of mind I remained until near the dusk of the evening; I then sent the letter I had received, just as I received it, by one of my clerks to the Merchant's Coffee House, with directions to place it, in my name, on the coffee-house books. He did so, and had scarcely returned to his desk when the sailors in port were all hard at work to send the ships in the river to the South for cotton and rice, and every fleet horse was on his way to order the sale of what teas, coffees, and sugars, and other colonial produce was stored away on speculation. Whatever doubt I may have entertained as to the truth of the statement in the letter, it was very clear it had implicit credit with our merchants and traders.

Governor Coles, who, during the administration of Mr. President Madison, was his private secretary, being at my office, some months ago, I mentioned to him the facts above stated, thinking it possible he might have written *the* letter, or that, if he had not written it, he might have some knowledge who had.

After he had heard my statement to the end without interruption, but evidently with much interest, he said: "Well, I declare, that is very extraordinary, sir. We got the first news of the signing of the treaty at Ghent very much in the same way at the seat of Government, and, I suspect, through the same channel that you obtained yours. A person, not known in Washington, arrived there about the time you received your letter, and, making inquiry for the President, was introduced to me as his private secretary. He communicated to me, in substance, what your letter had made known to you. I requested he would be seated while I made known to the President what he had communicated. Mr. Madison seemed very much surprised at what I told him, and said the stranger should be introduced, and if what he said should have the appearance of being founded in truth, he did not think he should be permitted to go at large to speculate at the expense of our fellow-citizens. Mr. Madison and the Postmaster-General closely examined the stranger, who evinced no disposition to withhold what information he had, and the means by which he had obtained it."

I never ascertained who this stranger was, nor what was the issue of his visit to Washington, or whether the authorities there laid any restraint on him. Official news of the treaty having been signed at Ghent arrived soon after these communications.

HONOR TO THE BRAVE.

In 1813-14, Governor Snyder sent orders that I should have made, and splendidly mounted, two first-rate swords, ordered, by the government of Pennsylvania, to be made and presented, one to Commodore Stephen Decatur, and one to Captain James Biddle, two Pennsylvanians, navy officers, who, by their courage and seamanship, had done honor to their native State and to the United States. When those splendid swords were finished and approved, the governor did Col. Binns the honor to appoint him to present them to the officers for whom they had been ordered.

At that time, the frigate Macedonian, Commodore Decatur, the frigate United States, Captain Jones, and the sloop-of-war Hornet, Captain James Biddle, were in the harbor of New London, blockaded by Commodore Hardy, with a British 74, three frigates, and some small craft. So soon as I arrived at New London, I communicated my arrival and my orders to Commodore Decatur, who informed me that he would the next day send a pinnace to take me on board; that we might make the necessary arrangements for the presentation. This was done accordingly, and the following day I went on board the Macedonian, her yards being manned, and the marines under arms. The commissioned officers from the other United States ships were invited and present, in full uniform, on the quarter-deck, at the presentation and at the dinner. There were several Pennsylvania officers on board the squadron, proud of their State and the cause of the visit. Those gentlemen vied with each other in doing honor to the representative of the State of Pennsylvania, and in making his time pass agreeably.

Previously to the presentation, the officers were arranged on the quarter-deck, Commodore Decatur in the centre, and a few steps in advance. Col. Binns then came forward, and addressed the commodore as follows:—

"As the representative of the constituted authorities of the State of Pennsylvania, I come, deputed by the governor, to announce to Commodore Decatur that they, in consideration of the courage and seamanship displayed in the capture of the enemy's frigate, the Macedonian, have ordered, and had prepared for his acceptance, a sword suitable to the occasion. The State of Pennsylvania is proud of her distinguished son, and to him I am ordered to present, and do now present, this sword in their name. Long, sir, may you live to do honor to your native State and country, and to receive the honors and distinctions to which you are, and are deemed to be, so richly entitled."

The air rang with loud and cheerful huzzas, and gave every nautical evidence of much joy. Music and great guns were given with a hearty good-will. Many were the proud and gladdened hearts on board the whole fleet on this joyous occasion.

After the presentation, I was taken through the frigate, and introduced to the officers. At dinner, Commodore Decatur said: "Stewart, have that double Cheshire cheese set on the table which Commodore Hardy sent me yesterday." This led to some conversation, from which I learned that Commodore Decatur frequently sent vegetables, and other acceptable presents, to the British commodore, which he, in the politest manner, reciprocated. One of the officers took occasion, in a ludicrous manner, to describe the alarm in which the enemy were kept from apprehension of the torpedoes floating around their vessels, which they feared, every night, would attach to their ships' bottoms and blow them up; to prevent which they constantly kept a good lookout, and had boats sailing round their ships after it was dark. The torpedoes proved to be a very innocent and harmless warlike instrument.

Walking the quarter-deck with the Commodore, he said: "While our ship, the United States (the ship in which he captured the Macedonian), was in the Chesapeake, Captain Carden, who, in the Macedonian, was lying near us, dined with me. After examining our ship, Carden said: 'She is a very fine ship; but if, unfortunately, our countries should go to war, and we should meet, I should be obliged to capture you.' It is a remarkable fact," said Decatur, "that I brought this prize—the Macedonian—two thousand miles over sea, and never met a British vessel." "What would you have done, Commodore, if, on your way home, you had met another British frigate?" "I'll tell you," said he, "what I would have done; I would have taken my crew out of the United States, put them on board the Macedonian, and would have whipped and captured the enemy with one of their own frigates. That's what I would have done." The next day similar arrangements, presentation, and public dinner took place on board the Hornet, Captain Biddle, to whom I had the honor and pleasure, in the name and on behalf of the State of Pennsylvania, to present the sword which the authorities of his native State had voted him. This was to me the most flattering and gratifying commission with which Governor Snyder ever honored me.

THE FUNDAMENTAL PRINCIPLE OF DIFFERENCE BETWEEN THE GOVERNMENT OF THE UNITED STATES AND THE GOVERNMENT OF GREAT BRITAIN.

Some years ago, a granite column was erected near London, over the grave of Thomas Hardy—of that same Thomas Hardy who, in 1794, was arraigned at the Old Bailey, for nine days, on his trial for high treason, for having acted as the Secretary of the London Corresponding Society. The erection of that granite column can be regarded in no other light than as an evidence of the favor in which certain political principles are now held, which, in 1794, were denounced and prosecuted as treasonable.

This tribute to the memory of a plain, fearless, honest man—one of that class which Edmund Burke was pleased to call "the swinish multitude"—demonstrates that the good cause of universal suffrage and annual parliaments is cherished and advocated by a larger portion of the people of England than heretofore. The aristocracy of that country—probably the best educated aristocracy in Europe, and the one which meets and mixes most with the people—feel that it is necessary to pay such attention to public opinion as will keep tranquil the public mind. Already, for this purpose, they have consented to give to some of their most valuable colonies nearly the whole of the law-making power. The lesson she was taught by "these United States" has not been lost upon her.

The aristocracy have continued to seize and keep in their possession an immense over-proportion of the landed property of England. The great advantage which resulted to France from the revolution of 1789—the greatest under which "thrones, principalities, and powers" ever tottered—was the immense increase of landholders. In M. Michel's lectures in Paris, in 1843, he stated that "there are in France twenty million of proprietors in a population of twenty-four millions; while in England there are but thirty-two thousand in fourteen millions." To this cause he attributes the attachment which the Frenchman bears to his country. "He is," says he, "wedded to the earth. We never see them leaving their country, like the English, or emigrating *en masse*, like the Germans."

The great stumbling-block appears to be that neither the people, nor the statesmen of Great Britain understand the proper and legitimate mode of making, or the binding force of a CONSTITUTION of government as it is understood in the United States. *Here* the *people* are sovereign. It is *they* who select and elect the men who make the Constitution of Government, upon which the people must pass approvingly before it becomes the acknowledged and fundamental law of the nation—equally binding upon the legislators and the people.

The legislators are elected for short periods, generally annually, by the people, by universal suffrage, and to the *people*, they are answerable. For this reason, they do but rarely venture to infringe the Constitution, under the provisions of which they were elected, and by the provisions of which they ought to be bound. Thus the people, by their representatives, make laws which, when made, are equally binding upon all. In the Constitution of the *United States*, and in those of *all the States*, provision is made not only for the election of our legislators, but for that of the governors of our States, and for that of the President of the United States. Thus our Constitution and our laws, our legislators, magistrates, and judges, *all* emanate from the people.

In England, *in* parliament and *out* of parliament, they *talk* of the Constitution, when in truth they have no such thing as a Constitution, as we use and understand the meaning of the word; *there* you are told of "Magna Charta," as a charter of certain privileges *granted* by their kings six hundred years ago; of the "Habeas Corpus" act, passed in 1679, which act parliament repeals whenever, and for so long a time, as the administration for the time being shall require; or, perhaps, you may be told of "The Bill of Rights," declaratory of the rights of British subjects, passed by William and Mary, February, 1689. These are the only written laws respecting the liberties of the people, except "Magna Charta." (*Viner's Statutes.*) *There* the *government* grants privileges to the people, not the *people* to the *government*. Having thus ascertained that the government is there the grantors of all privileges to the people, it may be well to state what that government is. It is said to be a government of king, lords, and commons. The king or queen, as it may happen, inherits the crown as their birthright. The lords are created by the crown, in the first instance. Their eldest son, on the death of his father, succeeds to the title, estate, and a seat in what is called the House of Lords. They are unlimited in number, and the peers are created *at pleasure* by the crown. This House, with the House of Commons and the king, constitutes the legislature or law-making power of the British Empire. The House of Lords is called the "Upper House;" the House of Commons is called the "Lower House." At this time, the number of members is six hundred and fifty-eight. Forty members, not one-sixteenth of the whole number of members, are a quorum to do business, and with such a quorum most of their laws are passed. The bishops sit and vote in the House of Lords, where the twelve judges also sit. In the Lower House, the members do not wear robes, as the Lords do, in the Upper House, but they sit with their hats on; when they address the house they must be removed. In the Upper House, the peers may vote by proxy; in the Lower House, no member can vote by proxy. When the king is in the Upper House, with his crown on his head, the lords are all uncovered, and the commons are invited to attend. The sons of peers, if elected, are eligible to a seat in the House of Commons. They were first admitted to such seats in 1550. The members are elected for seven years.

Some idea of the qualifications required to enable a man

to become a voter, in a county, for a member of the Lower House, may be formed when it is known that it was proved, before a committee of the House of Commons, by Mr. Wilson, that it may be acquired in no less than 1,276 different ways, viz:—

Varieties of freehold title	576
Varieties of copyhold	400
Leasehold qualifications	250
Occupying tenants	50
	1,276

"All of these," says the "Westminster Review," for January, 1852, "are open to inquiry and description before the registering barrister, and the consequent amount of vexation and inconvenience, the uncertainty and the influence of party organizations upon the registration, may easily be imagined." Parliament, at its pleasure, refuses and takes away the right of sending members to the House of Commons. By the reform act of 1832, they disfranchised fifty-six boroughs, and created forty-three new boroughs. Thus the people are granted or refused the right of voting, or it is taken from them by whole districts, as it pleases the king and the Houses of Lords and Commons, instead of the *people* vesting such rights and authorities as *they* should think proper in the king and Parliament. The king or queen, as the case may be, at their pleasure, may dismiss the House of Commons, and order the election of a new one. So soon as a new Parliament meets, the House of Commons elect a presiding officer, who is called a speaker. In the House of Lords, the Lord Chancellor presides. The session is opened by a speech from the throne, in the House of Lords, the speaker and the members of the House of Commons being present. On the return of the members to the House of Commons, the speaker informs the House that the sovereign has been graciously pleased to confirm their choice, and that he, on behalf of the House, had laid claim to their ancient and undoubted *privileges* of freedom from arrest for the members and their servants; the freedom of debate; free access to the sovereign at all reasonable times when they desire it, and that he would put the most favorable construction upon their words and actions; after which, the speaker and the members take the usual oaths. Thus, all right, all authority, all privileges, even that of speech, is *granted* by the king to the people's representatives. Mr. Stephen, in his elaborate "Book of the Constitution of Great Britain," says, page 5: "The trial by jury was the spontaneous and free *gift* of the crown. William the Conqueror planted this germ of English freedom."

SOME PUBLIC SERVICES.

Under orders from Governor Snyder in 1812, after the declaration of war, I rode to Chambersburg, Carlisle, and York, to forward and deliver cannon, small-arms, ammunition, and camp equipage, the property of the State of Pennsylvania, to Baltimore, where there was then a division of Pennsylvania militia and volunteers, to assist in the defence of that city, which, it was understood, the enemy, under Major-General Ross, was about to attack, and which he threatened to plunder, pillage, and destroy, as he had, a few days before, in a most shameless and disgraceful manner, burnt and destroyed, not only private houses, but the public buildings, even the public library, at the city of Washington. For this piratical conduct, the British Government, to their disgrace, erected to him a monument in Westminster Abbey. He was shot dead as he approached Baltimore at the head of his army. The army soon after retreated, embarked, and sailed for New Orleans, where it suffered a most signal defeat.

Some weeks after their arrival in Baltimore, the Pennsylvania volunteers and militia forwarded, through their commanding officer, complaints that they were, in all respects, miserably provided. The governor put me in possession of five thousand dollars of the public money, with orders to proceed to Baltimore, and do whatever could be done for the comfort of the troops. I went to Baltimore, where I had a conversation with General Samuel Smith, who was there as United States Commander-in-Chief. He complained bitterly of a want of attention by the General Government, and that he had received orders that a portion of his command should be sent to the city of Washington. I then went to Major-General Watson, who was in command of the Pennsylvania volunteers and militia. He reiterated the complaints I had just heard from General Smith. I next went through the camp where the Pennsylvanians were encamped. I find, on a slip of paper, that I wrote a letter to Governor Snyder (dated Baltimore, September 24, 1814, 1½ o'clock P. M.), informing him of the miserable condition in which I found the troops, without even straw to sleep on, and compelled to rest, as well as they could, on stones and hard gravel. In consequence of this state of affairs, I was, by the governor, ordered to proceed to Washington City, which I did. At Washington, I saw the Secretary of War and the President, to whom I succeeded in making such representations as induced arrangements to be made for the better accommodation of the troops. On my arrival at Bladensburg, six miles northeast of Washington, I had an interview with Commodore Barney, who complained that he had had no advice whatever of the advance of the enemy through Maryland, until they were about to wheel into the town of Bladensburg, on their way to the capital. "I tell you, Colonel Binns, we were in an enemy's country. I had planted a piece of cannon on the other side of the creek, and manned and took command, and did what I could until I was shot in the leg and dropped. The enemy came on; one of their officers raised me up and said: 'Commodore Barney?' I answered: 'Yes; may I ask whom have I the honor to address?' 'Admiral Coburn,' said he. I said: 'We call you Cockburn; but you may call yourself what you please.' He liberated me on parole, and the army and sailors pushed on to Washington." After I took leave of the commodore, on my way to Washington, I saw a number of new-made graves; the dead soldiers and sailors had been carelessly covered; their red coats and blue jackets, and white buttons and shirts, were in many places to be seen protruding from their graves. Such are the sad effects of war, even among civilized nations! General Watson represented dissatisfaction as prevailing among the Pennsylvanians in camp in relation to the cockade they wore; some of them wearing that of the United States, and others that of the State. Soon after, Governor Snyder issued a general order that the Pennsylvania troops should all wear the State cockade.

Not thinking it necessary, under the circumstances, that any part of the money committed to my care should be expended, I remitted the five thousand dollars I had received to the State treasury, and returned to Philadelphia. It was for these, and other like services under orders, that I declined, when called upon by the Register-General, to make a claim against the Government.

I paid out of my own moneys *all* the expenses attending my commission, including my servant and travelling expenses. I presumed I could afford it, which presumption, I subsequently ascertained, was not so well founded as I had supposed. I afterwards discovered that debts due to me were in no respect equal to debts collected and the money under my own control.

THE FORTY BANKS.

During the administration of Governor Snyder, there was, at one time, throughout Pennsylvania, a general desire to obtain acts of incorporation for "the establishment of banks." The tables of both houses were covered with petitions praying for charters. A large number of the members were urged and instructed by their constituents to vote for, and, by all means, to urge the passage of charters for the establishment of banks. In a few years, the number thus instructed were so numerous as to constitute a majority of the legislature, and a bill passed both houses to incorporate forty banks, to be located in the principal country towns. It was confidently asserted that Governor Snyder would not approve the bill, and that thus the measure would be defeated. While the bill was before the governor, all possible means were taken to induce him to approve of it. Such was the rage for its passage, that the governor was beset with people from all parts of the State, who assured him if he did not approve it, he would not, nor could not, be re-elected on the expiration of the term for which he had been chosen. The governor would not surrender his judgment, nor be overawed. He returned the bill, with his objections. This, however, did not prevent its passage; two-thirds of both houses voted for and passed the bill, after the governor had returned it, and it became a law. The governor, however, notwithstanding his veto, was re-elected.

Most of the banks thus authorized were incorporated and established. The consequence was a necessity for the issue of an unprecedented amount of bank notes. The presidents, directors, and cashiers of the several banks thus incorporated, well knew that, without they could get a certain amount of their bank-notes into circulation, they could not pay their expenses and make a dividend, without doing which their charters would soon become a burden instead of a benefit. In consequence of these fears, pains were taken to represent to the farmers throughout the State the facility with which they could get money, and thus be enabled to improve their farms. "You have nothing to do," a director would say, "but to get your neighbor to indorse your note, and the next discount day, the directors, who know you are very snug, will pass the note, and you will get the money for it next day." This seemed to Mr. Jones an easy way to get money and improve his farm; accordingly, he spoke to his neighbor Brown, and they mutually agreed to indorse each other's notes, and get the money they required out of bank; with which money Brown determined to raise a barn, and Jones to put good gates, and post-and-rail fences round his meadows. They got the money and went to work. The barn was built, and the gates and fences were put up, and the neighbors rubbed their hands with joy, and looked forward full of hope. Before their hopes, however, were realized, they were called upon by the banks for payment of their notes. This they were not able to make; their notes were protested, judgment obtained, and the sheriff came, levied, and sold. Jones and Brown were both ousted, but the purchasers of the property at sheriff's sales got bargains of the farms, which they rapidly improved. Such or similar doings took place all over the State. Is it not then reasonably clear that, although individuals were thus made bankrupt, the State became benefited and improved? The next inquiry is, did the passage of the law chartering the forty banks injure or benefit the State? I have always entertained the opinion that the passage of the act was a benefit to the State. The titles to land became more clear, settled, and certain; strangers were induced to purchase, and come to Pennsylvania and settle. Thus it is that the late census has exhibited in Pennsylvania a greater increase of wealth and population than in any other of the old States.

THE DECLARATION OF INDEPENDENCE.

Early in 1816, I issued proposals to publish a *splendid* and *correct* copy of the Declaration of Independence, with fac-similes of all the signatures, the whole to be encircled with the arms of the thirteen States and of the United States. For the correct preparation of the arms, I addressed letters to the Secretary of State of the United States, and the secretaries of the several States, respectfully requesting from each an impression and description of their several arms. Some of those impressions were mere pieces of wax, the impression upon which was unintelligible. These impressions and descriptions I was favored with from all the officers to whom I had written. As soon as received, I placed them in the hands of our distinguished artist Mr. Sully. From these materials, he painted, and I had engraved, arms for the several States, all of which are now the recognized arms of those States.

The arms thus painted were put into the hands of Murray, Draper, Fairman, & Co., to be executed under their inspection; and for their execution, they were unlimited as to expense, as was the case not only with them, but with all, and every artist, I employed in the publication.

I have now before me the second volume of the Journals of Congress, "published by order of Congress;" on page 741 of this volume, we are informed that "Mr. Harrison reported that the committee have agreed to a Declaration, which they desired him to report; the Declaration being read, was agreed to as follows: 'A DECLARATION by the Representatives of the UNITED STATES OF AMERICA, in Congress assembled,'"

Being pledged to publish a CORRECT copy of this important State paper, I obtained permission from the United States Secretary of State, J. Q. Adams, and sent an engraver to Washington City, who made a copy which is certified in the words following:—

"Department of State, 19th April, 1819. I certify that this is a *correct* copy of the original Declaration of Independence deposited at this department, and that I have compared all the signatures with those of the original, and have found them correct."

The reader will be surprised, on comparing the heading which is published *by order of Congress* on their journal, with the one which is certified to be correct, that the correct heading in the original Declaration is: "The UNANIMOUS Declaration of the Thirteen United States of America."

Thus it was forty-four years before the world was ever gratified and encouraged by a correct copy of this never-enough-to-be-admired declaration of the determination of the representatives of the people of the United States to establish "another great nation."

The copperplate was four years under the hands of the first painters and engravers in the United States. For the paper on which it was printed, I paid two hundred dollars a ream. I obtained what were regarded the best impressions of the best likenesses of George Washington, Thomas Jefferson, and John Hancock, deeming them the persons whose portraits were best entitled to accompany the Declaration of Independence. I then, in order to insure entire accuracy in the copy I was about to publish, sent Mr. Vallance, a letter engraver, to the city of Washington, to engrave this State paper from the original, and also to engrave fac-similes of all the names thereto subscribed, having previously, from the Secretary of State, John Quincy Adams, obtained leave for Mr. Vallance to engrave from the original, being then in his office. Mr. Adams subsequently gave, for publication, the above certificate. This publication was nearly four years in the hands of the artists before it was ready for publication, at an expense of nine thousand dollars. It is believed that no State paper has ever been published with more care as to its accuracy, or on which more expense has been lavished.

A few copies I sent to London, some as presents to old friends, and some for sale in England. These copies made in Europe a highly favorable impression as to the state of the arts of painting and engraving in the United States, to which arts in this country it gave no common impetus. It was the cause of several works of art being published; one of the earliest of them represented the interior of the hall of Congress, with the chairman, Thomas Jefferson, presenting the result of their labors, the Declaration of Independence.

I have had no cause to complain of the encouragement and patronage afforded by the people of the United States. If my agents, particularly those in the Southern States, where the subscription was large, had been honest, which they were not, the general subscriptions would not only have repaid, but enriched the publisher. I had no common pleasure and pride in not only having given to the world this splendid work, but in having, in addition to the merit of this first publication, given the first *correct* copy ever printed or published of this masterly assertion of the rights of men and of nations to the right of self-government, round which a mighty nation has gathered, and to which the friends of human rights, religious and civil, look with reverence and hope, only inferior to that with which the Christian world bends the knee and bows the head to the symbols of their holy religion.

This statement of facts is, with no little pride, submitted by the writer. In so doing, he is induced to add that, with all its claims on the governments of the United States and of the State governments, not a copy of this splendid and correct edition has ever been subscribed for to hang in their legislative halls, or in the offices of their foreign ministers, save only by the State of Texas.

Before and while this edition of the Declaration of Independence was in preparation, I made all possible inquiry of men of the Revolution, and all my aged acquaintances, to ascertain *when* and *where* the Declaration of Independence was *first read* to any portion of the *people* of the United States. All the world knows, and the city of Philadelphia is justly proud that it was *adopted* in the Hall of Independence, in the heart of that city. In the

Diary of Christopher Marshall, for which we are indebted to Mr. William Duane, Jr., for some extracts, we find the following: "July 6, 1776.—At eleven, went and met the Committee of Inspection, at the Philosophical Hall; went from thence in a body to the lodge, joined the Committee of Safety (so-called), and went in a body to the State House yard, where, in the presence of a great concourse of people, the Declaration of Independence was read, by John Nixon; the people declaring their approbation by three huzzas. The king's arms were taken down in the court-rooms, State House, at the same time." Such is the statement of a man of acknowledged veracity. The persons of whom I made inquiry assured me that the Declaration, on the day it was adopted, was read to the people in the State House yard, from the window over the door of the State House, from the door on Chestnut Street, and from the second story window of the market house, in Market Street, on Second Street. It may have been read from all those places. It, however, does not seem probable that it was withheld from the people *four* days after its adoption. May not the respectable Mr. Marshall have made a mistake as to the day?

MR. JEFFERSON AND MR. ADAMS.

In a letter from Mr. Jefferson, dated Poplar Forest, near Lynchburg, August 31, 1819, in answer to one I had written, inclosing a copy of the proposals for publishing an accurate and splendid copy of the Declaration of Independence, is the following passage: "The dedication of the Declaration to the People is peculiarly appropriate, for it was their work, and is particularly entitled to my approbation, with whom it has ever been a principle to consider individuals as nothing in the scale of the nation." In another letter I had from this distinguished Democratic statesman, he says: "John Adams was the *ablest* advocate of the Declaration of Independence on the floor of Congress."

It is a fact, not unworthy of notice, that the *author* of the Declaration of Independence and its *ablest advocate* should so widely differ, as these gentlemen certainly did, in their administration of the government, which was founded on that Declaration of which one was the *author* and the other its *ablest advocate* in the convention in which it was adopted. In 1797, when General Washington resigned as President of the United States, Mr. Jefferson and Mr. Adams were both candidates for the Presidency of the United States. Mr. Adams was the candidate of the Federal party, and Mr. Jefferson the candidate of the Republican party. The votes for President were, for John Adams 71, and for Thomas Jefferson 69; consequently Mr. Adams became the President and Mr. Jefferson the Vice President of the United States for four years. In 1801, the same gentlemen being again candidates for the same office, Mr. Jefferson had 72 votes and Mr. Adams 65 votes. At that time the electors voted for two persons; the one who had the greatest number of votes was declared President, and the one having the next highest number of votes was declared Vice President of the United States for four years. Thomas Jefferson and Aaron Burr were the candidates of the Democratic party, and having each the same number of electoral votes, it became the duty of the United States House of Representatives to determine which of the two should be the President, and which the Vice President of the United States for four years; each State, by their representatives, being entitled to one vote. It was known generally to be the intention and the wish of the Democratic party that Mr. Jefferson should be the President and Mr. Burr the Vice President, yet the House of Representatives balloted thirty-six times, giving an equal number of votes for Mr. Jefferson and for Mr. Burr; at length, a majority of one vote was obtained for Mr. Jefferson, and he was declared President and Mr. Burr Vice President of the United States. It was feared and believed that a contrary decision would have endangered the peace of the Union. An amendment was soon after proposed to the United States Constitution, making it the duty of the electors to vote for one person as President and another person as Vice President, which amendment was adopted by the States, and is now a part of the Constitution of the United States.

The Constitution of the United States, which has, in peace and in war, at all times, worked wonderfully well, and has had so very few amendments, has yet been so variously construed and administered, that the executive department has felt itself at liberty so to influence or concur with the legislature, as to give to the citizens general satisfaction, and at other times so as to excite general discontent. It is not to be doubted but Mr. Adams was as desirous to promote the prosperity and happiness of the country as was Mr. Jefferson, yet the means they adopted were of the most opposite character. Mr. Adams's *alien and sedition* laws were so hateful to the people that they embraced the first opportunity to eject him from the Presidential chair; while the conduct of Mr. Jefferson as President was so generally approved that a large majority of the State legislatures, and many public assemblies, besought him to consent to serve a second time, which he, in obedience to public opinion, consented if elected. He was elected, and served a second term. Ought not the example which the people made of Mr. Adams, be a warning to that portion of our public men and public officers who seem disposed to walk in his footsteps. It is worthy of remark that near the close of the lives of these two distinguished citizens, they renewed their early friendship and correspondence. That they died, the one in Virginia and the other in Massachusetts, on the same nautical day, and that the bell which hung over the Hall of Independence in Philadelphia was at the same time tolling for the death of these two eminent public men.

Thomas Jefferson was born in Virginia, in the year 1743, and died in 1826, aged 83 years.

John Adams was born in Massachusetts, in the year 1735, and died in the year 1826, aged 91 years.

CHAPTER XII.

John Randolph—A first interview—Mr. Boileau—Gen. Andrew Jackson.

JOHN RANDOLPH.

ONE of the first objects which arrested my attention in the United States House of Representatives, at Washington, in 1811, was the Hon. John Randolph. He sat on the end of one of the benches, near the speaker, enveloped in sundry greatcoats and silk neckerchiefs. On his right hand, stretched at their full length on the floor, were three very large dark brown hounds. After a short time, it was evident that Mr. Randolph was preparing to address the House. First he untwisted a long silk handkerchief which was carelessly thrown round his neck, over one of his loose light cloth greatcoats, and stretched the kerchief on the floor on his right; he then, in the same manner, took off and stretched another of his silk kerchiefs on the floor, and did the same with a third; he then took off and spread on the floor another of his light loose overcoats and handkerchiefs, which in due time he covered in the same manner with two other coats of the same description. The gentleman who had been addressing the House, having taken his seat, the words "Mis-ter Speak-er" reached your ear in a sharp, but not unharmonious tone of voice.

Mr. Randolph, with all his peculiarities, had many generous and amiable qualities and personal friends, and was in nowise devoid of ambition. Early in the administration of Mr. President Jefferson, Mr. Randolph became the opponent of that gentleman, because he would not appoint him United States Ambassador to the Court of London. At a much later period of life, Mr. Randolph was, by Mr. President Jackson, for whom he voted and electioneered, appointed Minister to the Court of St. Petersburg, with permission, after a visit to that capital, to spend the remainder of his time in London or elsewhere.

One of this gentleman's peculiarities was the pleasure he took in proclaiming, as I have often heard him, "I am not an American—I am a Virginian—it makes my blood boil, when I see these d—d Yankees come here to legislate over the sacred soil of Virginia.

"When I leave home for Congress," he would say, "I direct my overseer, if any of those Yankee tin peddlers come to the plantation, to have them hoisted up, and to give them forty lashes save one, well laid on." On one occasion, I heard him strenuously recommend to Mrs. General Mason, to have one or two black snakes set at liberty in her house, as the best rat-catchers in the world. "But," said Mrs. Mason, "would not the remedy be as bad as the disease?" "Not at all, madam; when you have obtained the snake, let your servant take him sharply by the back of the neck, and, taking Mr. Jefferson's advice, pinch him, to convince him he can do him the most harm, and he will go to work and clear your premises of every rat in it."

Among Mr. Randolph's peculiarities was his minute and accurate knowledge of the topography of England, and of her breed of race-horses and hunters. Drawings of noblemen and gentlemen's houses and out-houses, and topographic sketches of their woods and meadows, filled many of Mr. Randolph's portfolios. Others of them were filled with engravings of their thorough-bred horses, and genealogical trees of their sires and grandsires, their dams and grand-dams. It may well be doubted whether any gentleman in England was more thoroughly familiar with those subjects than Mr. Randolph. He was an able debater in Congress, but it is believed no act or resolution of his can be found, adopted, on the journals or among the acts of Congress.

A FIRST INTERVIEW.

While the Hon. Benjamin Crowninshield, of Massachusetts, then Secretary of the Navy, on his way to visit his family in 1812–13, was taken sick at the United States Hotel in Philadelphia, I usually went every afternoon and sat some time by his bedside. One afternoon, on entering his chamber, which was, as usual, darkened by the window-curtains, I saw a gentleman on a chair near the Secretary's bedside. The instant my eye rested on his broad expansive forehead and rich dark brown intellectual eye, I was so much impressed that, although it was but a few steps from the door at which I had entered to the chair on which the stranger sat, yet I was involuntarily arrested, and paused on my way. Mr. Crowninshield leaning forward said, "Mr. Binns, Mr. Webster." In America and in Europe I had had the honor of an introduction to some of the most distinguished men, yet I never had been so impressed by any man as I was by this introduction to the Hon. Daniel Webster.

MR. BOILEAU.

From my opposition at the Northumberland Convention in 1820, to the taking up of Mr. Boileau as a candidate for governor, he became very wroth, and published some angry attacks upon me, of which I took no notice. Some years after, when I was sitting behind the desk, in my office in Sixth Street, one afternoon, a short fat man stretched his arms so as to extend one hand to each end of the desk, at which I was sitting, and looking me full in the face, said: "Do you know me, sir?" I answered, "I do not." "Nathaniel B. Boileau—come to make an apology for having made a fool of himself and abused an old friend for having done what he is now satisfied it was that friend's duty to do. Fare you well!" He walked out of the office; not another word was spoken. I never saw him after. He has been dead many years.

GENERAL ANDREW JACKSON.

It will not, it cannot with truth be denied that the war of 1812, the war of the Democracy, was *the* war which first made "the United States of America" known and respected by the world *as a nation*; one, whose stars and stripes should not only be seen and felt, but found able to protect all who fought or sailed under them. To crown all our naval victories, that war was closed by the great and glorious victory achieved by the military genius, as much as by the daring courage, of General Andrew Jackson. I have heard, from undoubted authority, that, immediately after the signing of the treaty of peace at Ghent, Lord Goulburn, one of the British commissioners, turning to the American commissioners, said: "By that act, gentlemen, you have saved New Orleans from capture." "No danger of that," said Henry Clay; "Jackson is there."

This declaration was not the offspring of any personal affection which Mr. Clay had for General Jackson; it was a volcanic eruption from the love of country which ever burned bright in the bosom of that distinguished American.

A general illumination for the victory was ordered in Philadelphia. Few indeed there were, yet there were a few, who on that night closed their window-shutters, and mourned over the defeat of the enemies of their country. I had early intelligence of this joyous news, and gladly, by an extra, spread it abroad. I put the scene-painters to work, and had a transparency painted which covered nearly the whole front of my house. There had been a heavy fall of snow, and there was that evening from nine to twelve inches depth of snow on the ground. That, however, did not prevent men, women, and children from parading the streets, and delighting their eyes by looking at the illuminations and illuminated transparencies which made the principal streets of our city as light as day. My transparency represented General Jackson on horseback at the head of his staff, in pursuit of the enemy, with the motto: "This day shall ne'er go by, from this day to the ending of the world, but He, in it, shall be remembered."

About ten years after this victory, in the session of Congress which ended in 1822-3, the Hon. William H. Crawford was nominated, at a numerous meeting of the Democratic members of Congress, as their candidate for President of the United States; that being the manner in which, at that time, the party candidates for President and Vice-President were selected and nominated. Mr. Crawford was then Secretary of the United States Treasury, and had, as may be inferred from his station and his nomination, a very high character for principle, integrity, and talents.

It may not be improper to state that, although the nomination of this gentleman, and my support of that nomination and its consequences, had such influence on my political standing and pecuniary affairs, I never had the honor of a personal introduction. My support of him was on the principle of obedience to the regularly nominated candidate of the party. In an edition, published by the late Mathew Carey, Esq., of the "Olive Branch," it was suggested that a more acceptable way than that heretofore adopted for the party to select candidates for the Presidency and Vice-Presidency of the United States, would be for each party to elect delegates for that express purpose, to meet at some appointed place, from each State as many delegates as the State was entitled to send members to Congress; the delegates thus elected, when assembled, to select, nominate, and recommend a candidate for President and a candidate for Vice-President, as the candidates of the party who had elected the delegates. This plan, Mr. Carey stated, had been suggested to him by the editor of the "Democratic Press," who said it was founded on the then Pennsylvania mode of selecting their candidate for governor. The only difference being that, when a governor was to be nominated, the party held a convention, composed of as many members as constituted their State legislature; and that, when candidates for President and Vice-President were to be selected, the States were each entitled to send as many delegates to the convention as they were entitled to send members to Congress. Although the plan above stated was suggested by the writer, and seems to be approved, acted upon, and thought the best by both parties which has yet been suggested, yet it is open to serious objections. For example, in the one case, counties and cities, and, in the other, States, who have, in their elections under the laws of the State and of the United States, always given a majority of Federal votes, yet send delegates to their respective Democratic conventions, to assist in selecting candidates against whom the districts they represent are certain to give large majorities. How can this evil be properly remedied?

Besides Mr. Crawford, there were three other candidates before the Union for the Presidency: General Jackson, John Quincy Adams, and Henry Clay. The "Democratic Press" advocated Mr. Crawford, who was in a delicate state of health, and died soon after. Other papers advocated General Andrew Jackson, John Quincy Adams, and Henry Clay. The "Columbian Observer" intemperately advocated General Jackson.* A public meeting of the Democratic friends of General Jackson was called in the "Columbian Observer," to be held in the court-room, opposite the Hall of Independence, or in the Mayor's court-room, I do not recollect which. I attended that meeting; it was numerously attended. Mr. Stephen Simpson offered some resolutions pledging the meeting to support General Jackson. I took occasion to address the chair, at some length, in favor of William H. Crawford, as the regular candidate of the Democratic party. I was heard patiently, but I cannot say I succeeded in making many converts. I had, before that time, taken ground against the general. It so happened that, in the spring of that year, there were some merchants in Philadelphia from Tennessee, his near neighbors, who were his bitter enemies. These gentlemen took the trouble to furnish me with many serious charges against General Jackson, and with evidence to prove their truth. With the exception of the shooting of the six militia men, which caused the issue of the coffin handbills, and the letter of the general to President Monroe, recommending him to appoint one-half of his cabinet Democrats and the other half Federalists, the charges against the general were against his moral, or rather his domestic, than his political, character.

The statement in respect to the shooting of the six militia men was mainly supported by official documents. It was substantially proved that some militia men, having served out their legal term of service, and been, by their immediate commanding officer, under whom they had served, dismissed the service, and permitted to return home, were, by General Jackson, ordered to continue in the service until he (Jackson) should think himself warranted in discharging them. This the discharged militia men declined to do, and set out on their return home; when crossing a bridge on their way, they were, by order of General Jackson, fired at, and six of them shot dead. This act was defended on the ground that the service required these militia men, and that they were not warranted in leaving the service without permission of General Jackson, even though their term of service had expired. I was among the number of those who believed they were not bound to remain after they had served their legal term, and been by their own proper officer discharged. This ground I defended with all the zeal and ability which a conviction of its justice inspired.

In order to arrest public attention and impress the public mind with the injustice and the enormity of the crime of General Jackson, in respect to the shooting of these militia men, I had six coffins cast in type metal, and on each of them the name of one of the men who had been shot. I had supplements to the "Democratic Press" printed, with the coffins printed on them, together with the history of the whole transaction, and had one of those supplements sent with every copy of the daily, tri-weekly, and weekly "Democratic Press." Thus several thousand coffin handbills were circulated through the United States. It may well be doubted whether there ever was a publication which brought upon the publisher such active, general, and intense odium as those coffin handbills brought upon the writer of these recollections.

The only letter on the subject of General Jackson's letter to President Monroe, that I am at this time able to lay my hands on, is one from George Kremer, who was at the time a member of Congress from Pennsylvania, known to be the general's friend, and in his confidence. I know not whether my old friend is yet alive, but I do know that if alive he would forgive me for correcting the spelling of his letter before I send it to the printer. With those corrections, I shall publish the letter word for word, as it now lies before me. At the time this letter was written, Mr. Kremer had known me personally at least twenty years; at that time he was storekeeper to Mr. Snyder, in Selin's Grove. He was then generally regarded as one of the most efficient electioneerers in Northumberland County, particularly among the Germans; he spoke their language fluently, and spared no trouble in canvassing the county. He was there usually called "the white headed boy." I have not heard of him for some years; he was then living at or near Derrstown.*

"WASHINGTON, January 26, 1823.

"DEAR SIR: On the receipt of your paper (the "Democratic Press") of the 20th inst., I called on General Jackson, and handed him the paper. After he had read your remarks on his letter, he said that I was at liberty to inform you that he never had written any such letter to President Monroe, or any other man; that he had no hesitation in permitting me to inform you that he had, as soon as he had heard of the *charge* contained in your paper, written to the President (Mr. Monroe) for a copy of his letter; that he had received a letter from the President, informing him that it could not be found; that he had since written to Nashville for a copy of it, and that, on the receipt, he would furnish me with a copy. The general appeared perfectly satisfied with your conduct; as for myself, I never had a doubt but that you had been led into error by men in whom you reposed confidence. It may be proper to inform you that I did not consult General Jackson, nor any of his friends, when I wrote to you,† nor had the general any knowledge of my intention to write to you. After I had written, I showed a copy to Mr. Findlay, who had heard the President say the same that he told me. Since I received your paper, mentioning his (Mr. Findlay's) name as authority, I called on him, and he assured me that he never had heard the President read such a letter. You may rest assured that there is not this day a more worthy man, nor one who has been more wickedly persecuted. The intrigues at this day baffle all

---

* It is out of place here to state some facts touching a much respected German, who, forty-five years ago, was a justice of peace in that town. He was not tall, but what he wanted in height he made up in rotundity. To his obesity he owes his introduction to the reader. He was always in attendance, on official business, the first week of the Quarter Sessions, and put up at Henry Shaffer's hotel, in Sunbury. When he slept, he snored so loud that the cot on which he was to sleep was never admitted into a room, but was always made up on some one of the lobbies, or landing-places, where he slept and snored as little to the annoyance of the household, and as entirely to his own satisfaction, as any other good-natured man under the same roof.

† This refers to some former letter, which I have been unable to find.

description; every effort to prop up J. C. Calhoun,* that hungry, needy, and corrupt man can employ is done; but his sun is set, and I believe that he will be compelled to withdraw his name as a candidate (for Vice-President). You may rest assured that the general's friends have a perfect knowledge of the cabal from Pennsylvania.

"I regret to see the violence and abuse of the 'Columbian Observer;' it is not approved of by any of the general's friends. The Greek mania has occupied Congress during the whole of last week, and perhaps will not be closed to-day, but it will generally be rejected. Accept my good wishes.

"Respectfully, your friend, &c.,
"GEO. KREMER.

"COL. JOHN BINNS.

"I shall, perhaps, find it necessary to inform you of an intrigue going on for the purpose of cheating Jackson out of the electoral vote of Pennsylvania; but it won't do at this time to disclose it."†

It will be observed that, in this letter, Mr. Kremer does not, in his own name, nor in that of General Jackson, deny that the general wrote a letter of the kind alluded to in the "Democratic Press;" yet, in his own name, and in that of the general, Mr. Kremer wished to persuade me to believe that no such letter had ever been written. If it had not been written, why express doubts? Why send to President Monroe for a copy? Why write to the general's residence at Nashville for a copy? I have no more doubt that General Jackson wrote a letter to Mr. Monroe to take two of his cabinet from the Democratic, and two from the Federal party, than I have of another fact; that is, that a belief in its truth, and the hope that it would, in some measure, be acted upon by General Jackson if elected, had no inconsiderable effect upon the vote of the Federal party, at least in Pennsylvania. For ex-

---

* Mr. Calhoun was the gentleman nominated as the candidate for Vice-President on the same ticket that General Jackson was for President.

† I have, since copying the above letter, heard of the death of Mr. Kremer, in the 80th year of his age. He died at Derrstown, September 18, 1854.

ample, some weeks before the popular vote for President was taken in Pennsylvania, Mr. Ross, of Pittsburg, and Mr. Coleman of Lancaster, two of the most influential Federalists in Pennsylvania, came to Philadelphia, and at the house of Judge Hemphill, the son-in-law of Mr. Coleman, had interviews with many influential Federalists of this city, in which they represented how long and how generally their party had been excluded from office under the United States Government; and that now, according to General Jackson's letter to President Monroe, they, the Federalists, if he (Jackson) were elected, would have a chance of being appointed. The effect of these representations was evident in this Federal city, where General Jackson had a large majority.

In 1824, the electoral vote of the United States for President, as returned to Congress, was as follows: Andrew Jackson, 99 votes; John Quincy Adams, 84; William H. Crawford, 41; Henry Clay, 37. None of the candidates having a majority of votes, the election of President constitutionally devolved on the House of Representatives, who were bound to choose one of the three first named. They elected John Quincy Adams. The Democratic party were disappointed and mortified, not only at the rejection of General Jackson, but at the election of John Quincy Adams; yet the talents, integrity, and American principles of Mr. Adams were unquestioned and unquestionable.

It was very generally believed that several of the Democratic members of both houses used their influence to effect the exclusion of General Jackson, and not a few of them published explanations of their conduct; among them one of the senators from Pennsylvania. Henry Clay, however, not only openly and actively used his influence against General Jackson, but accepted, under Mr. Adams, the appointment of Secretary of State. This conduct of Mr. Clay blighted forever his prospects of preferment from the Democratic party. If Mr. Clay had at that time given his influence to General Jackson, there is no doubt but the general, and not Mr. Adams, would have been chosen President by the House of Representatives; and that Mr. Clay would, under the general, have been

Secretary of State, and thus insured his election as President on the expiration of the general's eight years.

Mr. Clay, from an early period of life, was, and continued to be up to this period, a very popular man; perhaps, at various times, the most popular in the Union. This popularity was founded, in an eminent degree, on his suavity of manners, his eloquence, his statesmanship, his acquirements, and public services. Few men have rendered their country more effective services than Mr. Clay. Few men have so happily proposed and carried through Congress so many valuable public laws; and no man has so frequently been the favorite of all parties. No man more ardently sought to obtain the Presidential chair, or would have filled it with more ability or patriotism, than Mr. Clay; yet he never could attain it. Was it not his extreme desire, his feverish anxiety to obtain it, which put it beyond his reach? The study of his life will richly repay the time which our statesmen may bestow upon it.

Soon after his election as President, Mr. Adams came to Philadelphia, having previously appointed his cabinet. My hostility and opposition to General Jackson as President was so steady, determined, and bitter, that it made the election of Mr. Adams to me a matter of personal gratification, and I so expressed myself in the "Democratic Press." Thus was it that I was thrown, head and heels, newspaper and all, into the Federal ranks, which about that time adopted, and, for a short time, kept and used the name of the *Democratic* Whig party, and then became the Whig party, omitting the word *Democratic*.

On the arrival in Philadelphia of President Adams, he did me the honor of an invitation; I waited on him at the Mansion House Hotel, and took an opportunity to introduce the subject of his appointments. I was promptly told that Mr. President Adams did not intend to make any removals. I bowed respectfully, assuring the President that I had no doubt the consequence would be that he would himself be removed so soon as the term for which he had been elected had expired. This intimation gave the President no concern, and assuredly did in nowise affect his previous determination. My opposition to General Jackson had great influence, not only upon my editorial and political position in the United States, but it and my opposition to Governor Findlay in Pennsylvania in 1819-20, sadly affected my pecuniary affairs. This will be more apparent and distinctly understood hereafter.

The *Democratic* arrangements to meet the expenses of elections were, by the Democrats, collected, for the most part, before the election. The most of their printing was done at my office and paid for; the balance, there was little, if any, difficulty in obtaining. My paper, however, had gradually assumed a new character; it was no longer, in public opinion, the "*Democratic* Press." Many of the daily subscribers gave it up, and my country agents and collectors no longer took pains to collect and remit their collections with the punctuality they had heretofore done, the money which was paid into their hands on my account. I will state a case, a matter of fact. One of my most regular agents, who had obtained many subscribers, and always remitted punctually, early in 1820 wrote me a letter, stating that he had received, on my account, one hundred dollars; but that, having a barn to build, he had appropriated that hundred dollars, with his own money, to the building the barn; assuring me that I might depend on his remitting the one hundred dollars in the fall. I waited, and the fall passing away without hearing from my agent, I wrote to remind him of my expectations. I waited some months, but no answer came. I wrote again, but with no better success. I then determined to bring suit for the one hundred dollars. I sent *his* letter to me, in which he stated the receipt of the one hundred dollars, the use he had made of it, and his promise to remit it in a few months, to a respectable lawyer, with instructions to bring suit. He did so, and, in a few months, wrote me that the case had been tried, a verdict given for defendant, and that I had fifteen dollars costs to pay. I paid the costs; but as that was the first, so it was the last suit I brought for the recovery of outstanding debts.

The members of the party with whom I had now to act were, in a great measure, strangers to me and my affairs. They desired the influence of my paper, and did not feel under any obligation to give me pecuniary assistance. I had been almost imperceptibly taking my place among them without having any desire to find myself there. I am quite sensible of the delicacy of the subject upon which I am writing; but, delicate as it may be, it must not be avoided nor slurred over. I do not, when I can honestly avoid it, give *names;* and thus I am, in a great measure, relieved. The exposition here called for will expose no one so entirely as myself. I have, however, undertaken to be candid, and to give the portrait I have promised as faithfully and as like the original as my recollections will enable me. When I obtained courage, from the urgency of the case, to intimate to my new political associates that my resources were nearly exhausted, instead of subscriptions being set on foot, and funds raised to assist me, it was hinted, and, after a short time, I was told, that what money I wanted I could have on mortgage on my house in Chestnut Street; and, in that way, I obtained between three and four thousand dollars, nearly every dollar of which I expended on the election; a very few dollars of which were refunded by Mr. Adams's friends, but every dollar of which I had to pay, and did pay. Thus, my support of Mr. Adams threw me and my paper into the Federal ranks, caused my heretofore Democratic friends to look coldly on me, and withhold their aid and subscription, while I, from the peculiarity of my situation, tempted by my new political allies, did not only do their work, but found the money required to enable me to do it.

My readers will be the more surprised at this lukewarmness, this penurious holding back of the Whig party, when I assure them that the Fourth of July public dinner of the friends of President Adams, at the Masonic Hall, was one of the most numerous, wealthy, influential, and apparently zealous political gatherings I have on any occasion sat down with. I do not remember the names of any of the officers of the day save only that of the president, who was a Democrat, Samuel Wetherill, Jr.

While I write these pages, I cannot but smile at the awkwardness of my political position. I could laugh outright at my folly, and would not withhold the outburst, did I not feel assured that the picture I am bound to draw and exhibit will cause some to pity, and many to think I deserved the punishment inflicted, and which my editorial experience should have enabled me to guard against. Every reader of reflection will, for himself, place the proper construction on the result. Some, perhaps, may receive instruction for their guidance, should they venture on the slippery paths of politics; a career in which they will surely have many companions and competitors, yet but few friends; and on which I honestly believe, that where one ambitious aspirant is able to keep his feet, many become weary, from the troubles to which they are necessarily and unexpectedly exposed; while hundreds will slip through the treacherous trap-doors so thickly set on the political bridges over which they have to pass.

At the next presidential election, General Jackson was the candidate of the Democratic party. If I had not so entirely committed myself by what I had previously published against General Jackson, and could have felt, as in the case of Mr. Crawford, bound to advocate the nominee of the party, *now* was the time for me to return to my first love, and again to publish the "Democratic Press." I have sometimes thought that if my aid had not been so anxiously sought and myself thought purchasable, it is not altogether improbable that I should have fallen into the ranks with my old friends, and again become the editor of the "Democratic Press;" of that press which had given its name to the party.

Soon after General Jackson's nomination by the party, General Eaton, then the special confidant and political friend of General Jackson, and one with whom I had had some previous personal intercourse, called on me, with the declaration that he was authorized by General Jackson to assure me that, "if I would advocate the election of the general, when he was elected President, I should, if I thought well of it, remove to Washington City, become the editor and proprietor of the government newspaper, and do as much as I chose of the public printing; or, if I did not wish to leave Philadelphia, as much of the public printing as I desired should be forwarded to Philadelphia for me to do, at the government prices." I assured General Eaton that "I was as grateful as any man could be for the distinguished services which General Jackson had rendered the United States, but that, after what I had written and published in relation to the general, I could not, from self-respect, give myself the lie direct, as I must do, if I were now to advocate his election." Two or three weeks after this interview with General Eaton, I was called upon by three gentlemen, of high standing in the Democratic party: Thomas Leiper, James Ronaldson, and Samuel Carswell. To all these gentlemen I had, for many years, had the honor to be personally known, and had frequently served on Democratic committees with them; I was sensible of their zeal and influence, of their liberality and their services, as members of the party, and of their personal good-will toward myself. Their business was in substance, and opened in language very much the same as that which had been used by General Eaton. I listened with attention and respect, expressed my thanks for their visit, was sure it was consequent upon their desire to serve me, and regretted that I was unable to see any honorable way in which I could follow their advice and advocate the election of General Jackson. I represented how impossible it was, with a proper sense of self-respect, to act as they were desirous I should act. I believed that the objections I had alleged against General Jackson were founded on fact, and for me to turn such a somerset as they proposed, must inevitably disgrace myself, without reflecting honor or doing service to the general.

I have never doubted but General Jackson would have fulfilled all the promises made by his friends. He was so much a man of impulse, so anxious to succeed, and so grateful to his partisans, that he would have labored hard to serve them, even beyond his promises. All the world are aware how much the general labored to overpay his friends and partisans at the public expense. This he did without suffering his own political opinions or their political opinions to hamper his conduct or appointments. It is a well-known fact that some of the highest and most important offices were by him bestowed upon Federalists, whose only recommendation was that they had voted for him for President. I have, however, never regretted that I adhered to what I believed to be the truth, even though my determination not only shut me out from all approach to the public crib, but was the cause of my never recovering thousands of dollars which I had honestly earned.

On the night the vote for electors was taken in this city (1824), so soon as it was ascertained that there was a majority, in this anti-democratic city, for Jackson electors, than a rumor ran through the multitude that it would be well if they were to go down the street, and mob the office of the "Democratic Press." This proposition was soon improved upon by another, to wit: that to punish the editor appropriately for his coffin handbills, an empty coffin should be forthwith procured, and taken with them, in order to put the editor of the "Press" into it and carry him round the town. What further was to be done with him, was left for future consideration. I was, by some friends, soon made acquainted with these suggestions and arrangements. It so happened that my apprentices were all out, and I was the only man in the house or office. My three daughters and the servant girls were in their beds. My house, in the rear of which was the printing-office, was in Chestnut St., No. 70, within one door of a narrow passage called Goforth Alley, now Exchange St. I owned the lot at the back of the next door house, which lot was separated from the alley by a high brick wall.

The first thing I did on receiving the above very unwelcome information, was to lock and put the wooden bar across the publishing office door, on Chestnut Street, and bolt it. The office window on Chestnut Street had been previously fastened. It had outside window-shutters. I then made fast the front door, the outside window-shutters on the second floor, and the back door, and a door which opened into the alley. All this had not been long accomplished before "the stormy wave of the multitude" was heard approaching. My faithful wife accompanied me, carrying the light, and giving what aid she could. We went quietly up stairs into the front garret, taking our children and the girls with us. The mob, the night being dark, had many lights of various kinds and colors, and shouted vociferously. We were as still as mice. My wife and I then went on the roof of the house, and peeping over the edge of the coping-stone, I saw at the front door the coffin, without a lid, in which it was proposed to carry me round the city, and land me, or water me, I knew not where. The next door below me was Russel's oil store; an aged infirm man, a Quaker, one who required two stout sticks to enable him to walk; his name was Isaac Billings; he had the care of the store, and slept in the room over it. So soon as he heard the uproar in the street, he threw up the sash of his window, and, in a loud voice, and in plain language, reproached the mob with their cowardice and their violence.

Thirty years after this disgraceful uproar, Isaac Billings, feeble as he was, came on his two sticks, from Green St., to the funeral of my wife, in Sixth Street near Chestnut Street. Since then, he has descended to "the house appointed for all living," thence, I humbly trust and pray, to rise and receive the reward of the righteous and the single-hearted.

Having ascertained that they could not force the doors, the more violent among the mob threw stones at them and at the window-shutters, many of which they split. Some idea of the yelling of this mob may be imagined when I inform the reader that Chestnut Street, from Second to Third Streets, with all its alleys, was crowded with angry noisy people. After two or three hours screaming and screeching, the rioters slunk away in squads, taking with them the coffin and whatsoever else they had brought.

There was a meeting of some of my personal friends the next morning, and it was determined that myself and family should for a night or two leave the house, and sleep in the houses of some friends. The next night, some thirty or more friends took possession of my house, which was supplied with food and all things necessary for their comfort, and for the defence of the house and office. The street, at night, was again filled with a noisy mob for several hours, after which they slunk away. The family returned, after three nights' absence, and we heard no more of the baffled besiegers. I have never heard that the constituted authorities took any measures to protect the house or office. I am very sure I never called upon them to indemnify me for the damages done, the expenses incurred, or the injuries inflicted.

When General Jackson was inaugurated as President of the United States, he was, to a greater extent than any former President ever had been, besieged by office-hunters; those who had advocated his election, and those who had voted for him. It had, up to that period, never been the custom of the President of the United States to remove more than a few of the principal officers of the Government; and when vacancies occurred, from death or resignation, to fill them by appointing their successors from the party by which the President had been elected. Neither the triumphant and thankful feelings of Mr. President Jackson, nor the clamorous claims of those who had voted or claimed to have voted for him, would admit of his following the usual mode of removing and appointing. *For the first time*, not only principals, but subordinates—not only heads of departments, but deputies, their book-keepers, clerks, and door-keepers must all be ejected, to the end that their places might be filled with the friends and partisans of the newly-elected chief magistrate. This was a sad precedent; it was calculated injuriously to affect all classes of society. A similar course of conduct has ever since been expected; no matter what party, or union of parties have succeeded, the President has been called upon to turn out his political opponents and to turn in his political partisans. "*The spoils belong to the victors*" has been broadly inscribed on the flag under which subsequent Presidents have been elected. Thus the voters on both sides are subject to the vulgar imputation of contending for the spoils, rather than to elevate a man of worth, of principle, and patriotism to the chief magistracy of the country. This is a state of things greatly to be regretted.

The conduct of General Jackson in his southern campaign, on the petition of a large number of citizens to the Senate of the United States, was referred to a committee, of which committee, Abner Lacock, a senator from Pennsylvania, was chairman. How the report of that committee was received by the general and his staff, may be learned from the following letter of Mr. Lacock, which I have by accident laid my hand on. It is probable I have many other letters from members of Congress, received about the same time, who spoke no higher of General Jackson's qualifications for being President than my friends Lacock and Roberts did:—

"WASHINGTON, February 8, 1818.

"DEAR SIR: I expect to stay here until about the 15th instant; in the mean time, I should be glad to hear from you. Mr. Roberts [the colleague of Mr. Lacock] promised me to call and tell you to send me your paper while I staid here, but I have not seen it since the 3d instant.

"General Jackson is still here, and by times raves like a madman. He has sworn most bitterly he would cut off the ears of every member of the committee who reported against his conduct. This bullying is done in public, and yet I have passed his lodgings every day, and still retain my ears. Thus far I consider myself fortunate. How long I shall be spared without mutilation, I know not; but one thing I can promise you, that I shall never avoid him *a single inch;* and, as the civil authority here seems to be put down by the military, I shall be ready and willing to defend myself, and not die soft. I will remain here as long as he does, and take the consequences. I have most conscientiously discharged my duty to the nation, and shall take with me to private life what will console me much, the approbation of a good conscience; of this the world cannot deprive me.

"The officers of Jackson's staff have drawn up what is called strictures on the report and conduct of the Committee of the Senate. This will appear to-morrow in the 'Intelligencer.' It is said to be personal and abusive. They will leave their names with the printer, with a view of giving all concerned an opportunity of having personal satisfaction if they want it. Jackson will of course keep himself out of view, and these young men will be put forward by way of defence. They are safe enough, as men of family and standing would not contend with such small game.

"Yours, faithfully,
"A. LACOCK.

"COL. BINNS."

It was the established rule in my office for the chief clerk every year to take an account of stock, to note the several sums of money which I was indebted, and those which were due to me. I was myself by no means a man of business, nor had I a correct idea of the proper manner of collecting debts and having the money due to me under my own control. I was, however, at all times attentive to the payment of debts. One of the results of this want of tact was, that I regarded the money which was due to me as my own, as much as if it were in my desk or to my credit in bank. This was a ruinous error; dearly and sorely have I paid for it. The knowledge that I was indebted and ought to pay a certain sum of money at a certain time, accompanied by the fear that I should be unable to pay it, not only distressed me by day, but afflicted me with the most distressing nightmares. So frequently was I thus afflicted that, as I lay in bed a victim of nightmare, I had so much consciousness of my situation in some instances, as I lay on my back, I felt that if I could but move any part of my body, my fingers or toes, the incubus would depart. One night, when under this influence, an elephant, nothing less, I thought, was lying by my side in the bed on his back, his feet and proboscis straight up in the air. I was trembling lest he should fall on me and crush me to death; yet I had a consciousness that if I could but move a finger or a toe, I should forthwith awake and be relieved. So long did I thus lie that, when I did awake, it was some minutes before my blood flowed in its natural channels, or my mind was cleared of the frightful and alarming picture with which it had been filled and distressed.

For many years I have been able to ascertain with tolerable accuracy my probable income; because I give no credit, my receipts are in cash; and, as I can easily ascertain my income, all I have to do is to live within it. I have no debts to pay, and take care not to incur any. I have for years had no nightmare; a conclusive proof that it was my indebtedness, and consequent fears of not being able to meet my engagements, which caused those oppressive feelings.

CHAPTER XIII.

The Bank of Pennsylvania—Nullification in South Carolina—Pennsylvania coal—Fire buckets—The watch-box—A somnambulist—London amusements—Country hospitality—The barber bleeder—Ann Carson and her schemes—An insurrection in prison—Public executions—Behavior of convicts.

THE BANK OF PENNSYLVANIA.

ELI K. PRICE, ESQ., a gentleman too generally known and too highly respected to warrant me in introducing him, called upon me, I think for the first time, near the end of December, 1852. "I have just received," said he, "'The Village Record,' of West Chester, of the 20th inst. In it is published an obituary notice of General Anthony Wayne, and of his son, General Isaac Wayne, whom you must have known in the Senate of Pennsylvania. Between the two notices is a paragraph, from the same pen, which I think cannot but be gratifying to you. I will leave you the paper."

The following extract is the passage to which Mr. Price called my attention. I may be permitted to add that at the foot of the obituary notices was the letter M., which gave additional interest to the compliment, as, from it, I concluded that the publication was from the pen of Mr. Miner, a gentleman who was the editor of the Federal newspaper published in Luzerne County, at the time I was publishing the "Republican Argus" in Northumberland—but now a citizen of West Chester.

From the Village Record (Tuesday, December 20, 1852).

"And here I cannot deny myself the pleasure of paying a compliment (on the authority of Colonel Wayne) to an old political enemy, 'The *notorious* John Binns,' as the double distilled verjuice from our ancient Federal pens used to designate him, but, in the main, as the able and sagacious friend and adviser of Governor Snyder, as historical truth should speak of him. At the moment of his highest prosperity with his own party, of his dreaded, feared, and hated influence by the Federal party, the legislature chose Mr. Binns one of the Directors of the Bank of Pennsylvania. 'I looked out for trouble,' said Colonel Wayne, who was a director. 'We all expected a scene, and were prepared for it.' Mr. Binns took his seat at the Board like any other independent gentleman, neither abject, as if he felt he had gotten into company of his superiors (for the reader should be apprised that if there ever was a moneyed aristocracy in the State, it was comprised in the Stockholders and Directors of the Pennsylvania Bank, forty years ago), nor *assuming*, as if he felt that he bore the *fasces* of the commonwealth as his warrant, but deported himself with such strict propriety, that the terror of his advent was soon merged in confidence and respect."

NULLIFICATION IN SOUTH CAROLINA.

About the years 1832-3, some of the constituted authorities, and, through their influence, large masses of the people of the State of South Carolina, expressed toward the Congress of the United States and its laws a discontent of so violent a nature as very nearly to amount to high treason, by declaring their determination to resist certain laws which had received the sanction of the constituted authorities of the United States. From a sincere desire to conciliate the authorities and people of South Carolina, a public meeting was called in Philadelphia at the Musical Fund Hall. I do not know who the gentlemen were who called that meeting, but from the character of the officers of the meeting, and of the gentlemen who from the platform addressed the meeting, it was not a party meeting, but a town meeting of all parties. I went to the meeting, as I have usually gone to public meetings, by myself, and occupied a place on the floor, having drafted a preamble and resolutions to submit to the meeting, if I should deem it proper so to do, after the prepared proceedings had been submitted. The meeting was very large, the hall was crowded. The prepared proceedings having been submitted, and the question on their adoption being about to be put, I from the floor addressed the chair, and read for the consideration of the meeting what I had prepared, and which I deemed in nowise incompatible with what was already before the meeting. What I did read I shall subjoin to these introductory remarks. It was received with loud and very general shouts of approbation; so general that, no doubt if submitted, it would have been adopted by a nearly unanimous vote. The gentlemen on the platform gave unmistakable evidence of their desire that nothing should receive the sanction of the meeting but what they had prepared. They rather expressed their approbation of what Mr. Binns had offered, but thought it would be better to call another town meeting for the adoption of the propositions so unexpectedly offered, and which, if carefully examined, might be found to contain matter which would clash with what had already been submitted. The issue was, that Mr. Binns was prevailed upon to withdraw what he had submitted, with the understanding that a town meeting to consider his proposition should be called. No such meeting has ever been called. The propositions I then submitted have from that time to this been unpublished, and have been unacted upon in the desk of the writer. He is now induced to publish them as a matter of self-defence, believing that they have been greatly misrepresented. He is induced so to believe, from a knowledge that two grand juries in South Carolina, and two in Georgia, presented the writer of them as not only a public nuisance, but as deserving of death as a traitor. I beg to state that the copy I am going to send to the printer is the very paper from which I read at the Musical Fund Hall, without the alteration of a word, a letter, or a point:—

"*Whereas*, Some of the constituted authorities and citizens of the State of South Carolina have manifested strong feelings of hostility to any protection which may be given by the laws of the United States to American manufactures, and have denounced them in language the most intemperate, not only as unconstitutional, but so clearly a dissolution of the Union as to warrant not only an appeal to the citizens of other States, but to justify the last resort among men, a resort to arms, against their brethren and fellow-citizens who may entertain different opinions, or resist their secession from the other States of the Union: And whereas, the promulgation of such doctrines, from men high in authority and from public meetings, is calculated to sow discord and engender treason, and ought to be wholly discountenanced, unless the evils complained of could be demonstrated to be well founded, which, in this case, we are persuaded cannot be done; because, notwithstanding the zeal and talents of the nullifiers, their quick-sightedness to discover, and their readiness to publish whatever may give a tint of truth to their representations, no attempt has been made, by reference to their imports and exports, or to the prices at which they sell and buy; or by any statement of the comparative prices now paid by the complainants for the necessaries, comforts, or luxuries of life, to what they paid for the same articles before protection was afforded; or by any well-established facts, and fair conclusions, and arguments; or by anything, but declamation; to show that injury or injustice has been done by the laws for protecting American industry to any State, or the citizens of any State, in the Union: And whereas, however the friends of American industry may regret or reprobate the idle, seditious, and treasonable language held by a section of the South—that section most endangered by an over-proportioned slave population—yet would this meeting assure their southern fellow-citizens that the language held, and the threats uttered, have so little alienated the affections of the manufacturing States, that, while unfounded complaints and bitter denunciations are poured forth from the South, these States, this meeting is persuaded, would cheerfully give substantial proof of their entire willingness to be taxed for the common good of their common country, by yielding a ready assent and prompt obedience to any law which may be passed by the national legislature, not for dividing the surplus revenue of the Union among the States, after the payment of the national debt, but for appropriating the millions of dollars now annually appropriated to the payment of that debt, on its extinguishment, to the purchase and transportation to Africa of all the slaves in the United States; thus conferring incalculable blessings on both countries; on the one, by clearing a country of free institutions from the foul pollution of slavery; and, on the other, by pouring into Africa's benighted regions a regenerating mass of knowledge and skill, of various kinds, which would hold forth higher prospects, and afford more certain promise of the civilization of that immense continent, than have been given from the earliest ages; thus, also, making, to the injured sons of Africa, all the atonement in our power as a people for the countless evils inflicted upon them, to which we have been made accessories. In return for which act of national justice, even the present generation would not pass away without having seen the ivory and gold, and other rich productions of Africa, flowing into these United States, and a ready market opened with her for the annual reception of millions of dollars' worth of our manufactures and produce: Wherefore, for these, and many other reasons founded in substantial justice and sound policy, be it, and it hereby is,

"*Resolved*, That it be very earnestly recommended to the Legislature of the Commonwealth of Pennsylvania to instruct her senators, and recommend to her representatives in Congress, to take the earliest occasion to call the attention of that body to the number and condition of the slave population of the United States, and to raise a committee to devise ways and means to cause all the slaves in the United States to be promptly transported to Africa; making to their owners such compensation as shall be deemed just and equitable."

PENNSYLVANIA COAL.

When this coal was first discovered, about the year 1805, there was much speculation, and not a little anxiety, as to its quality and quantity. In the legislative session of 1810-11, an application was made for an act of Assembly to incorporate a company to work the Lehigh coal mines. To assist in obtaining this charter, the persons most interested induced a German mineralogist to explain to the members of the legislature the nature of the coal, the probable extent of the mines, and the facility with which, at a moderate expense, the coal could be brought to market. This man was dressed in leather. He wore a tight close-bodied calfskin jacket, and trowsers of the same material; both of a darkish brown color. The object of this singular dress was, doubtless, to arrest attention. The man could make himself very well understood in English, and was very successful in his efforts to represent the mines favorably. The charter was obtained, and the mineralogist succeeded in making an arrangement with the Company, by which they were to pay him so much money, a small sum, I cannot remember the amount, say a cent for every ton they mined. This contract was afterwards annulled by compromise, for a certain sum paid at the time, and the mineralogist returned to Germany.

Before he left the mines, he sent to me to Philadelphia a wagon load of the coal, the best he had, in the hope that I would, in my newspaper, give it some celebrity; which, in truth, I was well disposed to do. To enable me so to do, I paid a stovemaker fifty dollars for a semicircular sheet-iron stove, and had it put up in my private office, in order to burn that coal. A sufficiency of charcoal, it was thought, was put into the stove, and the coal, which was in pretty large lumps, laid on the redhot charcoal. To assist ignition, we drew and kept together the circular sheet-iron stove doors. It was a cold morning; there were some half-dozen friends watching the experiment; but, alas and alackaday! after some hours, and the consumption of much charcoal, the stonecoal would not burn; all it would do was to look red, like stones in a well-heated lime-kiln. When taken out at night, the coals were, to all appearance, as large as when first cast into the stove. The coal thus sent was, probably, taken from the surface of the mine, where it had long been exposed to the weather in all seasons. The size of the coal sent was also much against its consumption, as was subsequently ascertained by experience. Whatever was the cause, such was the result of the *first* attempt to burn Lehigh coal in Philadelphia, where, since that time, millions of tons of it have been welcomed and consumed. At the time of the discovery of this coal, of such a quality and size as to burn freely, wood and other fuel had advanced to a high price. If the city had been left dependent on wood for its fuel, it would at this time have been exorbitantly dear, and our woods nearly all cut down.

It is to the facility with which abundance of good coal is brought to our market that Philadelphia is mainly indebted for its extent and prosperity. It is to the abundant supply of coal and iron which this city is indebted for being the first manufacturing city in the Union, and that it entertains no apprehension of a successful competitor. Steam navigation, which is of such immense importance to inland cities, will also do much to increase the population and prosperity of Philadelphia, by largely increasing its exports and imports. The flourishing city of Pittsburg is the next great manufacturing city. Her supply of iron and coal is inexhaustible, and her citizens are industrious and skilful. Long may they continue so.

A short time after the discovery of the Lehigh coal, a law was passed separating a portion of Berks County and incorporating it as a new county, under the name of Schuylkill County. The only objection made to the incorporation of the proposed county was its poverty. It was represented to be so rocky, stony, and hilly, that it was feared money enough to erect the court-house, and necessary county buildings could not easily be collected. The bill, however, passed, and in a short time the necessary buildings, a court-house and public offices, were erected, taxes were levied and collected, and men were found patriotic enough to accept the county offices.

After a few years, it was discovered that, although the surface of the county was uninviting, there was that beneath which it was hoped would invite a population able and willing to build not only a court-house but large towns. The county was found to abound in coal of an excellent quality. The mines were worked, and Schuylkill County is now one of our most prosperous and wealthy counties; not only able to take care of her own territory and population, but to keep the people of the neighboring counties and distant States warm and comfortable.

The quantity of coal produced in 1853, in the various parts of the world, is set down at seventy-five millions of tons, of which Great Britain produces forty-two millions, and the United States, the next highest, over nine millions of tons.

The London and Liverpool papers, of a recent date, give us assurance that arrangements are making to introduce into England our *anthracite* coal as an article of consumption. The amount of coal of that description in England and Ireland is found to be inconsiderable. It is probable, however, that under some late arrangements for a free intercourse with Nova Scotia and other English colonies, they will supply some of our Eastern States with bituminous coal in return for our anthracite.

FIRE-BUCKETS.

At the time of the great fire in Dock Street, about 1817-18, I lived at No. 70 Chestnut Street; we then had no hose to supply our fire-engines with water. At that time, and before and after, that service was performed by fire-buckets. By one of the city ordinances, in force at that period, every housekeeper was obliged, under a penalty, to keep four fire-buckets, each of which held more than half a gallon of water, hanging in his hall, or other convenient place. On each bucket were painted the name and residence of the owner. So soon as the cry of fire was heard, the housekeeper, with whatever hands he had, ran with his buckets, in the direction in which the fire was said to be. There the people ranged at convenient distances from the pumps—before we had hydrants—to the fire-engines. Thus it was the engines were supplied with water. Our city is indebted to one of the Messrs. Peales for the present improved method of ringing the State House bell so as to indicate the direction where the fire is to be extinguished; an improvement of no little value. Before that improvement, the cry of fire used to be heard, and the people ran hither and thither, not knowing where or in what direction the fire was, or whether there was any fire.

THE WATCHBOX.

Several years ago, say ten, we had what were called "watchboxes," for the comfort and repose of the city watchmen. We had not then such an army of men paid to guard and watch over us as we have now. Each of the watchmen had a particular beat, was armed with a long pole, carried a lantern, with horn and tin sides, perforated with many holes, in which was a lighted candle, so that all persons should have warning of his approach. One of these comfortable watchboxes was at the southeast corner of Ninth and Walnut Streets. Its inhabitant was one of your quiet, inoffensive watchmen, who, for his ease, passed most of the night, with his long pole and lantern, in his box. Returning from crying the hour, walking round his beat, and overcome with fatigue and sleep, he was rather in a hurry to enter his place of repose, the door of which he was about to open, when, casting his eyes down Walnut Street, he saw an immensely large body moving up the street. What it was he could not tell, no, not for his life; but to him it was some living thing, and there was danger in its approach. He therefore, like a careful and prudent watchman, made preparation to seek safety, where he had always found it, in his wooden watchbox. No time was to be lost, for the enemy was near at hand. To increase his alarm, the moving substance made a hideous noise. The watchman made haste, and, the better to conceal himself, put out the candle in his lantern, and retired to where he had often had a comfortable nap. He got into his box and made fast the door. This was scarcely accomplished when he heard a loud snorting, and the box itself gave evidence of a disposition to prostrate itself before the monster which was at the door. By this time the watchman had come to the conclusion that the enemy at the entrance to his wooden house was neither more nor less than an elephant, which had made its escape from the menagerie. In the mean time, the elephant, instead of opening the door, overset the box, and began rolling it down the street, turning it over and over with his proboscis. He had not made much progress, when his keepers came up, put a halter round his neck, and led him back to his old quarters, to the inexpressible joy of the watchman, who lost no time in setting up his box, ensconcing himself in its wooden walls, and getting fast asleep.

A SOMNAMBULIST.

When I resided in Chestnut Street, among other apprentices I had to learn the printing business, was Doyle Sweeny. After he had been with me some years, he took to walking in his sleep. He slept in the same room with the other apprentices. Their bedroom was on the third story. He used to get out of bed generally about midnight, and, without disturbing the other boys, quietly come down stairs, unlock the door which opened into the yard, and, taking the key of the printing-office door off the hook, open it, walk up three flights of stairs, and go into the composing-room. Thus far he quietly made his way in the dark, at least without any artificial light. He would there light one of the office lamps, walk to his case, and set up whatever copy he had before him or took with him; sometimes as much as five or six stickfuls of matter. He would empty them, from his composing-stick, in regular order on his galley. He would then put out his lamp, and return the same way quietly to bed without any light. In the morning he would get up with the other boys, by whom through the night he had not been missed. At the usual hour he would dress himself and go to the office, altogether unconscious of what he had been doing through the night, until he found the matter he had set up in his sleep laid in order on his galley. I have no knowledge how frequently those sleep-walkings took place. One night, Mrs. Binns, after the apprentices were all in bed, caused the girls to place a large wash-tub, about two-thirds full of hydrant water, at the foot of the stairs; into which, that night, Doyle stepped with both legs into the cold water. He awoke instantly, made no noise, but turned about, walked up stairs, went to bed, and never again played the somnambulist. If I had been consulted, I should have protested against so desperate, and, as I should have supposed, dangerous an experiment. It was, however, fortunate for the young man. He got a commission in the United States Army in 1813, when he was out of his time; served with credit until the peace of Ghent, and then went on a whaling voyage. He afterwards established a Democratic paper in South Carolina, married, and died in a few years, leaving his family in easy circumstances.

COUNTRY HOSPITALITY.

When I resided in Northumberland, the mill at which the paper was made, on which I printed the "Republican Argus," was made near the Beaver Dam, which was not less than sixty miles from the town where I lived. Being nearly out of paper, I mounted my horse and rode until night overtook me, about ten miles from the mill. While I was sitting in a tavern, undetermined what to do, one of my Republican friends, a justice of the peace, came in and insisted I should go to his house, which was only half a mile distant, and there sup and spend the night. I complied with his request. The room into which we were shown was a very large one, in the shape of an L. The supper was set on the table; bacon and eggs, and whiskey and water in abundance. The squire had three or four grown-up young men, sons, who took charge of our horses. In a word, everything was said and done to assure me of a hearty welcome. After we had supped and smoked a pipe, and drank some Monongahela whiskey and water, we prepared for bed, in which I had a very warm if not a very comfortable, reception. Nothing would satisfy the squire but my being his bedfellow. The bed was large, and my host was more than two hundred and fifty weight. I submitted myself to the authority of the squire, got into bed, and lay as directed, on the far side. My host having got under the bedclothes, of which there was great abundance, deliberately proceeded to buckle to the bedstead, on his side, two leather straps about four inches wide; both the straps being before fast to the bedstead, next the wall. One of the straps passed over the bed about our mid-leg, and the other strap passed over the bed across our arms. Thus were we both tightly buckled under a large number of blankets. These, however, were by no means all the comforts provided. There was a large ten-plate stove in the room, which the sons of my host, who slept in the same room with us, got up several times in the night to feed, with large sticks of good dry hickory wood, so that the sides of the stove were kept constantly red. Imagine how we must have perspired!

The weather was cold, and several inches of snow on the ground; yet, long before day, the sons of my host, who put the wood on the fire through the night, were up and out, in their smock frocks, to feed the cattle, to be ready to put them to work so soon as there was daylight, at which time the squire's wife had the table spread, and soon after well covered with rashers of bacon, eggs, milk, and other human comforts. My bedfellow being informed that all these things were in readiness, communicated the information to me; the straps being unbuckled, and my bedfellow turned out, I was soon on the floor, and we were both, ere long, at table, enjoying the refreshments provided. After which my horse, well fed, curried, and ready for the road, was brought to the door, and I was mounted, and failed not to make acknowledgments to my hospitable host and hostess.

Near the paper-mill I saw a beaver dam, which had long since been abandoned by the beavers, on account of the increase of population. The dam appeared to be from fifty to sixty feet wide, and twenty-five feet high. The water flowed over the top of this dam, and some through breaches in the front of it. It appeared a mighty architectural work to have been built by so small an animal. I presume there are at this time but few beaver dams in Pennsylvania.

LONDON AMUSEMENTS.

When I was in London, say from 1794 to 1800, the Opera-house in the Haymarket, Drury Lane, and Covent Garden, were all the regular winter theatres in London. They were all constructed on a very large scale. I remember the first night I went to London; my brother and I went to the middle gallery of Drury Lane Theatre. We went early, and got seated on the front seats. On casting our eyes to the stage, it seemed at so great a distance that we came to the conclusion that if we remained where we were, we should neither see nor hear distinctly, and that it would be better to pay the difference in price, and go into the pit. The gallery was two shillings (50 cents), and the pit three shillings and sixpence (87½ cents).

We ascertained subsequently that in the middle gallery you could see and hear very well, and there we very often sat and saw, and heard, distinctly the best performers of whom England could ever boast.

All those theatres were burned down in less than four years. None of the theatres erected on the same sites were constructed on anything like so large a scale as those burned had been built.

There was also a minor theatre, called Saddler's Wells, at which the dancing, singing, and harlequinades were admirable. Astley's Circus was on the south of Blackfriar's Bridge, and drew large audiences. There was also Bermondsey Spa, for fireworks and singing. But the most brilliant and numerously attended of all the places of amusement, on a gala night, was Vauxhall. Dibdin had a small theatre on the Strand, to which the admittance was one shilling and sixpence (33 cents). At this theatre Mr. Dibdin was the *only* performer. He wrote all the songs, set them to music, played the piano, and sung the songs, all himself. All those places of amusement opened about six o'clock in the evening, and the performance commenced about half past seven. In the reign of Queen Elizabeth, the prices of admission were, gallery, twopence (3½ cents); lord's room, one shilling (25 cents). In 1663, it was stated "the play will begin at three o'clock."

A London paper, of 1854, informs us that there are at this time twenty-five theatres and saloons for dramatic representations open in London, from October to August. The audiences nightly resorting to these twenty-five houses, amount to about 5,000 on the average. Equal to 200 persons as the audience of each theatre.

In Covent Garden, a large inclosed square, about equidistant, from the Theatre Royal, Covent Garden, and Drury Lane, say two hundred and fifty yards from each of them, was a frame building, about eighty feet long, and twenty feet wide, called the "Finish." It was, properly speaking, a genteel tavern, which was the general resort of the performers of both the theatres, and the wits and songsters among the audiences. There were, every evening the theatres were open, to be seen and heard the Bannisters, Munden, Fawcett, Incledon, and others. It was one of those taverns which was privileged to be open until midnight, and often later. I was often, to my great delight, "a looker on in Venice," when wit and song "delighted the glad ear."

In summer, there was a theatre in the Haymarket, in which the performers were excellent, and the house usually well filled.

THE BARBER BLEEDER.

From the year 1810 to 1814, I was daily shaved by a barber, whose name it is not necessary to mention. He was a bleeder and leecher of much celebrity, and in extensive practice. He had a large pond at the back of his house, in this city, in which he reared all the leeches which his business required. I went more than once to look at this curious nursery. The leeches swam in great numbers on the surface of the water, where was to be seen, floating, a light-colored frothy substance, in small parcels; these light substances, in a few days, assumed a circular form, about the size of a large marble. On taking one of these globular substances out of the water, and opening it, you would find a number of small, active, thin, worm-like, living creatures, who, on the breaking of the membranous substance in which they had been inclosed, would swim about with great activity, and in good time become leeches of the usual size, and with the usual properties appertaining to that aquatic worm. This barber was married, was a good provider for his family, an excellent bleeder and leecher, and was generally respected; mild, attentive, and obliging in his intercourse with the world; his honesty unquestioned.

I was favored with some curious presents from the barber; such as a wooden chain of many links, and more than a yard long, made in the Walnut Street prison; and also some animals, cut in wood and painted the color of the living animals they were made to represent.

In 1814, I was requested to go to the old Masonic Hall, in Zane Street, to ascertain if some books and other things there were not my property, which, it was believed, had been stolen by my barber. I went, and found several articles which the barber had taken; many books, a patent lamp, patent snuffers, and other articles which, from time to time, he had carried away from my house. The things supposed to be stolen were arranged on a wide table, the whole length of the hall. On the floor was a ten-plate stove, an oil-cloth carriage cover, and many other heavy and cumbersome articles, all of which the barber acknowledged he had, by night and by day, stolen and concealed, and for all which articles claimants were expected and did come.

It did not appear that he had, at any time, appropriated a single article to his own use, or that of his family; all the articles which had been missed from the houses to which he had access, were found in this large hall, and were restored to their respective owners. The barber, however, was prosecuted, convicted, and, for a time, imprisoned. His pilfering was the ruin of him and his family; I am sure it reduced them to indigence.

This is a remarkable instance of stealing, and carrying away, and laying up, of a large amount of property of others, by a man generally respected, and who, it seems, stole all the articles he did steal without any benefit to himself or to his family; considering how much, and how long, he labored in his vocation, by night and by day, constantly exposing himself to detection and punishment, it is remarkable he was able so long to conceal his pilferings; such a thing as his being dishonest had never passed across my mind, nor that of any of my family, nor that of any one else, to my knowledge.

ANN CARSON AND HER SCHEMES.

Early in the year 1816, Richard Smith, as principal in the first degree, and Ann Carson, in the second degree, were tried in Philadelphia, before the Hon. Jacob Rush and his associates, for the murder of John Carson, her husband. This trial issued in the conviction of Smith for murder in the first degree, and in the acquittal of Ann Carson. It is now nearly forty years since that trial; in all that time no criminal trial has excited so much interest as the one I have just named. Richard Smith was the nephew of Daniel Clarke, of New Orleans, and heir to his large estates. Never has there been so much feeling manifested, in the desire to obtain a pardon for murder, as on this occasion. Smith was young and inexperienced, and was believed to have fallen a victim to the lurements of a woman much older than himself, and who had been the wife of another man for many years before she ever saw Smith. Her passionate attachment to Smith induced her, fearless of all consequences, to run all hazards to preserve his life; no means, which she thought likely to attain that end, were in her eyes too daring or too dangerous; to effect that darling object, she devoted soul and body. She and her mother, and other relations, called on me more than once, and labored, with singular earnestness, to enlist my feelings and induce me to use whatever influence I had with the governor, to step between Smith and death. As I could not be prevailed upon to give any satisfactory promise to that effect, it was resolved, by this desperate and devoted woman, to coerce me into her measures. I had, at that time, a son, who had been christened Snyder, after the then governor. This boy was about five years old, and went daily to school. Mrs. Carson had at her command a few desperate men, who never hesitated to execute any command which she thought proper to issue. She determined to order those men to seize and secrete the above child, in the expectation that the governor would, from his attachment to me, grant a pardon for Smith, in order to insure the liberation of my child. This scheme, and others of the same kind, were promptly communicated to me by a lady-cousin of Mr. Smith's, who came from one of the western States to render him all the service, and give him all the comfort and consolation in her power. The child was not allowed to leave the house; and this scheme not succeeding, and the conclusion came to that it had, by some inscrutable means, been discovered, a new and yet more daring one was devised. The men, who had undertaken to carry off my child, were induced by Mrs. Carson to go to the seat of government and carry off, and keep in custody, the governor himself, under a threat of being put to death if he did not grant a pardon and discharge for Smith.

The night this scheme was determined on, it was, through the same unsuspected channel, communicated to me, and I forthwith wrote an account of the whole plan to the governor. The conspirators went to Harrisburg, where they were observed lurking about the governor's dwelling, and were arrested, and bound to attend court and be tried; a bill of indictment was found against them, and they were tried; but party prejudice overcame justice, and they were acquitted. Smith being executed, no more schemes connected with him were set on foot.

Some time after the death of that unfortunate young man, Mrs. Carson was concerned in feloniously assisting to secrete and carry off some kegs of dollars. I think it was for this offence she was sentenced to be confined for some years in the Walnut St. prison, where she died. While in prison, she was a kind and most attentive nurse.

AN INSURRECTION IN THE PRISON.

Walnut Street prison was on the S. E. corner of Sixth and Walnut Sts. The front, on Walnut St., was principally of cut stone; it extended on Walnut St., easterly, about 150 feet; the prison yard was inclosed by a lofty stone wall, extending along Sixth St. from Walnut to Prune St., at the N. W. corner of which street was a large building called "the Debtor's apartment." From the east end of that "apartment," to Walnut St., there was also a stone wall, from the corner of Prune to Walnut St., along Sixth St. The square thus inclosed by those walls was called the Prison Yard. To this prison the magistrates committed those who were to be tried before a criminal court, and the criminal courts sent thither convicts sentenced for a term of years.

On the east side of the western wall of the prison yard, which ran from Walnut to Prune St., about midway, was a place of worship for the prisoners, keepers, turnkeys, &c. This church, during service, including the whole auditory, generally inclosed a large congregation. The idea of insubordination, or insurrection, does not seem to have passed across the mind of any one interested in the maintenance of the discipline of the prison. The ready obedience and good order which, for many years, had been observed, appears to have been considered as so many bonds and sureties for its future quiet. The idea that the prisoners, or any portion of them, should talk of resistance, or attempt an outbreak, if suggested, would have been treated as an idle dream.

That prison, during a portion of the Revolutionary War, was in possession of the English, and in it they confined suspected persons. The keeper, at that time, was a Capt. Conyngham, of the British army; that same Capt. Conyngham who, twenty-five years after, was the Governor of Gloucester prison, in England, where the writer was confined nearly two years for treasonable practices, under a suspension of the habeas corpus act. I have always understood that Capt. Conyngham was very much hated while acting as keeper of Walnut St. prison. I do him but justice when I assure the readers that, during nearly two years, while I was under his charge, I never had cause to complain of his deportment, nor did I, from prisoners or keepers, at any time, hear any act of misconduct or harshness laid to his charge.

One Sunday forenoon, about thirty years ago, when our streets were thronged with orderly, well-dressed men and women, on their way to their respective places of worship, their steps, in some cases, quickened by the ringing of their church bells; on such a day and at such a time, an alarm-bell was heard to ring; the passengers' feet were arrested; they stood still, listened and asked: "What is that?" in an accent of fear which was uttered by many with trembling looks. Few minutes passed before hundreds of voices were heard crying aloud: "There's an insurrection in the prison!" Thousands of feet were forthwith directed on their way to the scene of action; men with fire-arms and other weapons in their hands, while the women quickly returned to their homes and their little ones. I was then an alderman, and felt it my duty to hasten to the prison. I soon ascertained that the prisoners, in their place of worship, had, on signal given by the clapping of hands, seized and gagged the clergyman and every person in the church, save only the prisoners, many of whom in the conspiracy had come prepared with hammers, hatchets, pickaxes, &c., to break out the wall of the church, on Sixth Street. They were aware of the danger of delay, and therefore, as soon as a few stones were knocked out of the wall, some of the prisoners squeezed their way out, and a few, I think not more than three or four, made their escape.

In the mean time, the Mayor, Robert Wharton, Esq., sent an express to the Navy Yard, and in less than an hour a company of marines, with arms and ammunition, arrived at the prison and entered at the principal entrance. There they were ordered to prime and load with ball and cartridges, which, having done, the inner gates of the prison were thrown open, and the civil and military authorities entered the prison yard; a small force having been previously stationed to prevent any escape at the breach in the wall. I have a clear recollection of the whole scene in the yard, when the marines marched into it. Some persons had previously, from the top of the prison, fired down upon the most riotous of the prisoners, some of whom were wounded. All the prisoners saw that they could offer no resistance against the military; yet nothing could be more sullen and dogged than their submission. There has not been any attempt of a serious nature at riot or insurrection in the prison for many years. There is reason to believe that more attention is now paid to their wants than heretofore, and justice is more certainly and promptly administered. The appointment of Mr. Wm. J. Mullen to watch over the manner in which justice is administered to the prisoners, will greatly assist in securing a due administration of justice, than which nothing will more assuredly tend to the reformation of prisoners.

Among the accused of crime, yea, even among those who are guilty of crime, there are many duly sensible of the portion of justice and humanity administered to them, and fully as sensible when they are treated unjustly or punished severely, disproportioned to the offence and unwarranted by law. In the discharge of the duties devolved upon me as an alderman and a judge of a criminal court, for more than twenty years in this city, I was afforded abundant opportunities of observing and speculating upon the characters of persons charged and guilty of crime. I am clearly of opinion that the people and the lawmakers, and the administrators of the law, who make and administer them in a spirit of mildness, humanity, and a sense of justice, are the people, the legislators, and the judges who will most certainly command the largest portion of respect, not only from the public, but from those most exposed to, and most deserving of, punishment. Legislators should ever bear in mind that the mass of what is called criminal law is concocted and enacted to protect the property of the wealthy against the wants as much as the vices of the poor, the suffering, and the ignorant. This consideration should strengthen and invigorate the growing desire to protect our system of general education, and greatly tend to the reformation of offenders. If those appointed to administer justice have the baseness to do wrong in order to extort fees from those charged with crime, how can they, the magistrates, hope for reformation in those whom their example teaches injustice? Magistrates should not only do justice, but, so far as in their power, should temper justice with mercy. Thus they would become blessings, not curses, to the country.

PUBLIC EXECUTIONS.

The punishment of death by hanging was, in 1798, and long after in Great Britain and Ireland, inflicted not only for murder in the first degree, but for highway robbery, house-breaking, arson, horse-stealing, forgery, sheep-stealing, and several other offences. Before that time, to wit: on the 22d of April, 1794, an act was passed in Pennsylvania, in the following words: "No crime whatever hereafter committed (except murder in the first degree) shall be punished with death in the State of Pennsylvania." This humane provision has long since been enacted into a law in Great Britain and other States. Is it not honorable? Is it not a matter of which to be justly proud, to lead the way in humanizing the bloody code which so long disgraced the statute books of what is called the civilized world? Is it not also a rich reward to know that even the basest, the very dregs of mankind, were, by this regard for human life, taught to feel that they are considered and regarded as members of the great family, to acknowledge their obligations, and to bow down with gratitude to the legislators, and to the people who elect those who manifest kindly feelings even for the wicked, and will not for slight causes take away their lives, and thus cut off all opportunity of repentance and reform?

In 1794, in London, all executions for crime were in front of Newgate prison, on a gallows erected over the entrance to the jail. On all such occasions, an immense crowd assembled on the broad space of the Old Bailey. It was a curious sight to observe, out of every window, through the iron bars, was a stick, on the end of which was a piece of looking-glass, which the persons inside endeavored so to turn toward the prison door as to give those who held the glass a view of those who were hanging. I was in the Old Bailey on two execution days. On one day I saw the stand on which was the gallows, and on the stand there were twenty-three men and women, with ropes round their necks, all their arms being tightly bound with cords. They were all apparently in full health, praying, trembling, and expecting death. At an unexpected moment, the drop suddenly fell from under their feet, and their lifeless bodies in a few minutes were the sport of the wind, moving hither and thither, more like empty garments in front of a tailor's ready-made clothing store, than the remains of what, but an instant before, were human beings animated by the breath of life. "And the Lord God made man of the dust of the ground, and breathed into his nostrils the breath of life, and man became a living soul." Such crowds do not now gather together for such purposes; the convicts are there now hung, as they are in Pennsylvania, in the prison-yard, and by law not more than a small number of persons, with the required officers, are permitted to be present at an execution.

THE BEHAVIOR OF CONVICTS.

Is it not strange what a general desire there is in men and women to witness the execution of criminals? The greater the crime committed, the greater the desire, in all ranks and conditions, to witness the punishment. This, probably, arises from an expectation that the punishment will, in some measure, be proportioned to the crime. It is yet more strange to witness, as I have witnessed, a disposition manifested to regard a criminal, on his way to the place of execution, accompanied as though he were a martyr, about to suffer for some glorious truth he had promulgated for the benefit of his fellow-men. We had an instance of this kind, some twenty-five years ago, in Philadelphia. A man of the name of —— —— was, upon the clearest evidence, convicted of murder in the first degree, and sentenced to be hung. When the day arrived on which he was to be executed, he was seen descending the steps of Walnut Street prison, on his way to the place of execution. He was dressed in white linen trowsers and shirt, which were tied, fastened, and ornamented, here and there, with blue ribbons. Some officers surrounded him, and a procession was formed; many of those in it having on white shirts and trowsers, carrying garlands of flowers and many-colored ribbons. He was also accompanied by some clergymen, and hundreds of zealous, warm-hearted Christians, who united with him in shouting and singing "Glory! glory! Praise ye the Lord," &c. &c. Thus accompanied, he was conducted to the gallows and there executed. I saw him hung. I have no recollection that anything was said or done at the place of execution other than what is usually said and done on such occasions.

Before I left Dublin, in the 22d year of my age, I was intimate with a gentleman named Rossborough, some five or seven years older than I was. He was in very easy circumstances, and of a benevolent disposition. He took pleasure in contributing largely to relieve the poor, and, in all ways in his power, endeavored to comfort those who were in distress. He visited, for these purposes, not only the apartments of the debtor, but the cell of him who was under sentence of death. In all these cases he gave his time, his advice, and his money freely. In talking with me on these subjects, he remarked upon the singular desires of some men whose days were numbered. He told me of a young man under sentence to die for highway robbery. "I had," said my friend, "done all in my power to tranquillize his mind, and reconcile him to his fate; it was, however, evident to me that there was something on his mind which he wished to communicate, but which he wanted courage to mention. At length, after much persuasion, he said: 'God bless you, sir, you are too kind to me; yet, if I dare, I would ask one more favor. Will you, for the love of God, grant my last wish on earth?' I assured him I would, if in my power. 'Will your honor,' said he, 'give me a ruffled shirt to be hung in?' I said: 'Certainly; I will have it brought to you as soon as I go home.' This poor, unfortunate, uneducated wretch (said he), who had wantonly dared death many times, was so overcome that he wept profusely, not tears of sorrow, but of thanks."

CHAPTER XIV.

Debased humanity—The yellow fever—Sagacity of animals—Ants at work—Bengal tiger—The paddle-wheel—Where I have lived—Troops of friends—An accident—The club—John Binns is made an alderman —A scene in an alderman's office.

DEBASED HUMANITY.

About forty years ago, on my way to Lancaster, I stopped all night at the tavern called "Big Chickeey's," which was regarded as a half-way house. Coming down stairs, early in the morning, I saw some people gathering round and intently gazing at some object which appeared deeply to engage their attention. I immediately directed my steps to the place round which the people were assembling; I looked and saw what, some hours before, had been a sturdy man, but was now a most deplorable and revolting object. The cause of the change was obvious;

he had been drinking spirituous liquor until he had become so beastly drunk as to be unable to take any care whatever of himself, and had fallen or sat down on the roadside. The weather was piercing cold; it had frozen very hard the night before. When I drew near, I saw that his legs were stretched before him on the ground; his arms and his hands, without any covering, rested on his thighs; his fingers and thighs were so frozen that they were as hard and insensible as glass, and could probably be as easily broken. He had no command whatever of any part of his body; his tongue, in his half open mouth, lay as hard and immovable as a stone. He was utterly incapable of moving any part of him; there was no joint in his body. His eyes were set in his head; and so gaseous was his breath that it could hardly be said he breathed enough when frozen as would form a slender icicle. A spectator could come to no other conclusion than that his heart was frozen in his body. Such was probably the fact, for the last pulsation in any part of his frame took place soon after I left him.

What a theme would the miserable fate of this drunkard be for a temperance lecture!

I had seen the bodies of men who had been drowned, who had been murdered, and who had been blown up and killed by gunpowder; but none of them, no, not all of them, if thrown together in a heap, would have exhibited so shocking a picture of fallen humanity as was this wretched dead-drunk suicide.

It may be that as many die of over-eating as of over-drinking, but if there does, they do not present to our view such stupid, foolish, staggering exhibitions of fallen human nature as the drunkard. It is certain that many of the human family, particularly men, die of over-eating. One of Mr. Jefferson's wise maxims was: " Do not be afraid of eating too little." Attention to this maxim would assuredly prolong the lives of thousands, and give health, strength, and the use of all their faculties to millions.

The writer has all his life been regarded as a small eater and a moderate drinker. If he lives, he will be eighty-two years of age the 22d of December, 1854. He is at his desk six days in the week, on an average eight hours a day, reading or writing without spectacles, which he never did wear, reading or writing; he is in the enjoyment of excellent health, for which he is truly thankful to the Bestower of every good and every perfect gift.

THE YELLOW FEVER.

In 1820, Philadelphia was visited by the yellow fever. Dr. Jackson was at that time one of the five members which composed the Board of Health. The fever first manifested itself along the wharves and Water Street, to the south of Market Street. It was most violent in the vicinity of Water and Chestnut and Walnut Streets. Dr. Jackson was daily among the poor who were prostrated by the fever, and who were most in want, not only of medical aid, but of care and attention of all sorts. In the hope of preventing the spread of the fever, the doctor had a high board fence erected on Water and Front Streets, which he presumed would, and which it was believed did, arrest the spread of the fever, by cutting off the communication between the healthy and the sick. Dr. Jackson had so much interested and exerted himself in taking care of the poor, and to insure the erection of a proper fence, and had so often and so long visited the infected district, that he was himself at length prostrated by the fever. As it was known that his life was thus endangered from his extreme anxiety to protect the public, by staying the spread of the fever, the public universally felt a deep interest in his recovery, and the inquiries as to the state of his health were as general and anxious as we recollect them to have been in the case of any individual. Happily, he recovered!

At that time I was publishing the "Democratic Press," and my house and office were in Chestnut Street, midway between Second and Third Streets. Notwithstanding the precautionary measures which had been taken, many of our neighbors became alarmed at some deaths from the fever, which had taken place in Strawberry Alley, Bank Alley, and Carter's Alley, and they moved, with their families, into the country. My family, including children and apprentices, was large. I took a *country* house, on the west side of Broad Street, between Chestnut and Market Streets, *now about the centre of the city of Philadelphia*, and moved my whole family there. The paper continued to be printed at the usual place, and served to the subscribers by the carriers. I went down with the apprentices to the office every morning, taking our dinner with us, and returning before dark. The youngest apprentice, who took the packages to the ferry-houses, caught a fever. He was brought home, and in all respects carefully prescribed for and attended, and after a long confinement he recovered. We remained at our country house in Broad Street several weeks. I was induced to move back to Chestnut Street in somewhat of a hurry, from the following circumstances: On the evening of one day in the fall, one of the servant girls was seized with a vomiting, which so alarmed the other females, that early the next morning, when I came down stairs, I found every female in the family as actively engaged as if they had each taken an emetic. The whole establishment was that day returned to Chestnut Street. There has been no visitation of yellow fever in this city since 1820, save only a slight local epidemic of that character, caused, it was said, by the carelessness of the officers at the Lazaretto, for which they ought to have been turned out of office.

SAGACITY OF ANIMALS.

At the head-waters of the Delaware River, in Bucks County, runs Neshaminy Creek. It is occasionally a rapid stream, and its breadth, near Bristol, some hundred yards. Forty years ago, this creek being frozen over, a pig, of rather a large size, with some care, and not without fear, walked some distance on the ice, and feeling it strong under his tread, he went on his way, evidently with intention to go to the other side of the creek. Having reached about half way across, the ice gave way, and the pig went down, his hind legs and the lower part of his body being in the water.

A friend of mine, who was watching the progress of the pig, saw him cautiously feel the strength of the ice all round the hole into which he had sunk, in order to ascertain the strongest place to make an effort to get on the ice, and travel to the other side. The ice at all points gave way, and the pig sank into the stream. Not doubting but the undertide would sweep the pig away under the ice, my friend was about to walk away, when extending his vision over the creek, he saw that the pig had, under the ice, swam toward the shore, until he felt the bottom under him, then pushing up its back, broke through the ice, and, with all due deliberation, walked ashore, and went about his business. This is one of those instances of animal sagacity, of which the pig furnishes more than any other four-footed animal, except the elephant.

If the pig were, as Pliny accounted him, only one degree below the scale of human beings, the almost reasoning animal could hardly have conducted itself with more skill and judgment than did the above pig.

The large elephant, at Exeter Change, London, used occasionally to have small pieces of money thrown into its show cage, which the animal picked up with its proboscis, and handed to his keeper, who, in return, gave the elephant fruit or other acceptable presents. On one occasion, a silver sixpence was thrown into the cage, but beyond the reach of the elephant's proboscis. Having, after many efforts, ascertained that he could not reach it, he very ingeniously blew the wind from his proboscis against that side of his cage which was opposite where the sixpence lay, until he ascertained exactly that part of the cage from the return of which the wind came to the edge of the sixpence. He then blew in that direction with such violence as to turn over the sixpence. A few turns brought it within reach of his proboscis, when he picked it up, gave it to his keeper, and was duly rewarded. I saw this display of sagacity, being in the exhibition room at the time.

The eye is believed to be the most expressive, if not the most valuable of the senses. There is more similarity in shape and in expression between the eye of the elephant and that of the pig than between the eyes of any other animals. It is differently set in the head of the elephant and the pig than in the head of any other animal. It has been frequently remarked that men whose eyes are somewhat angularly set in their head, are men of more shrewdness, not to say cunning, than most other men. Has Lavator said anything, and if he has, *what* on this distinctive kind of eye?

I take leave to introduce a very different animal from a pig or an elephant; indeed, one of the most hated of those which infest our houses—a rat. When in Ireland, in 1797, standing at a back room window, which was about ten yards from the end of the forge of my uncle, Ambrose Binns, the workmen had gone to dinner, and the door of the smith's shop was partly open. There was no noise whatever, when I observed two rats, nearly side by side, slowly walk from the door into the yard. On looking more closely, I saw that one of the rats was gray, and that they were connected by a straw or a bit of light wood; each of them having one end of it in his mouth. In this manner, the two rats walked to a small run of water from the hydrant, in the yard. When there, the gray rat let go the straw or stick from his mouth, and drank of the water. He then took the straw or stick again into his mouth, and they both went back to the shop in the same order in which they had left it. It was clear that the gray rat was blind, and that he was led to the water to drink by the other rat, probably one of its young, who was at the other end of the straw.

ANTS AT WORK.

Oliver Goldsmith informs us that ants are "a species of four-winged insects, that are famous, from all antiquity, for their social and *industrious habits;* that are marked for their *spirit of subordination;* that are offered as a pattern of parsimony to the profuse, and of *unremitting diligence* to the sluggard."

When I resided at No. 70 Chestnut Street, Messrs. Pratt & Davis kept a lottery office a few doors lower down. About the year 1820, one of those gentlemen invited me into their office to witness the movements of some ants. I went with him. Their room was about fourteen or sixteen feet square. There was a fireplace on one side of the room, in which there was no fire. About ten feet from the fireplace, on the floor, was a large spider; about him were a great number of ants; some of them were busily employed in endeavoring to disable him, in order to enable them to roll him into a hole near the fireplace, for food at some future time. They had succeeded in breaking and cutting off some of the spider's legs. He resisted as much as he was able, encumbered and surrounded as he was by assailants, sometimes, by a violent effort scattering the ants from about him. When this was done, one or more of the ants, under orders, it would seem, and acting as aides-de-camp, would run with all speed to the fireplace, go down into the hole near it, and soon return with a reinforcement of some fifteen or twenty ants, who lost no time in making their way, in regular order, to the battle-ground, where they joined in the attack upon the common enemy, the spider. I am within bounds when I say that I saw these reinforcements sent for and return six or eight different times. At length, in defiance of all the resistance the spider was able to make, he was, by the ants, rolled into the hole near the fireplace, into which all the ants speedily followed him. Nothing could be more methodical and regular than the proceedings of these ants. They acted with as much judgment, labored as hard, and were apparently as well disciplined as so many companies of regular soldiers.

A BENGAL TIGER.

About the years 1797-8, I was walking up Holborn, London, on the south side of the way, in the forenoon, when my eyes were arrested by seeing a royal Bengal tiger walk out of a house, in which there was an exhibition of wild beasts, on the north side of the street. The street, at the place of which I am writing, was not less than eighty feet wide. The tiger took very long, but not hasty steps, and did not exhibit any evidence, by his manner, of being under any apprehension of ill-treatment; nor did he exhibit any disposition to do harm. He walked in an oblique direction across the street, and walked into Thavies Inn, a twenty feet wide street. About the time he entered this street, I saw two men, each with a small-rope in his hand, come out of the exhibition-house, in pursuit of the tiger. Neither of the men carried a weapon of any kind. They followed the tiger into the street into which he had retreated. I was curious enough to follow them to see the issue. On entering the street, there was no tiger to be seen. The keepers, one on each side of the way, were looking after the tiger. He was at length discovered quietly ensconced under the marble steps of one of the front doors. The men went under the steps, threw a cord, not thicker than a bedcord, round his neck, and gave him to understand he must return home, which he did without any apparent reluctance. He followed the keeper, led by the bedcord, across the street as quietly as a pet animal of any kind could have been led.

THE PADDLE-WHEEL.

In the year 1790, when I was 18 years of age, and my uncle, William Binns, about two years older, I remember to have gone out frequently with him to the canal, near Dublin, and other watercourses, for the purpose of swimming a neat little boat, which he had made, and which he caused to be propelled by a large rat. In the centre of the boat was a wire cylinder, such as are frequently put in motion by a squirrel; in it was a sturdy rat, and at each end of the axletree was a paddle-wheel, which was put in motion by the rat turning the cylindrical wheel, and thus the boat was driven through the water. Numberless ships and boats now traverse the ocean by similar paddle-wheels put in motion by steam. Was not the principle the same?

WHERE I HAVE LIVED.

In 1807, when I came to Philadelphia, my family was small. I had my wife, one daughter, and two apprentices. It was but five weeks after I had published the last number of the "Republican Argus," in Northumberland, when, in Philadelphia, I published the first number of the "Democratic Press," having, in the meantime, obtained the subscribers, taken a house and office, purchased the necessary printing materials, paper, &c., and hired hands.

The first house and office were on the east side of Front St., below Walnut—rent $400 per year; it was very much out of the walks of business. So soon as my first quarter was up, I left it. I then took, as a printing office, the first house in Church Alley, on the north side, at $600 a year. At that time there was very little business done in that alley, and there were but few dwelling-houses, and those but small and inconvenient.

At the time I took the office in Church Alley, I took a dwelling in Vine St., on the north side, above Fifth St. There were, at that time, but few houses west of Sixth St., in Vine. The house was a rather small three-story house; I paid for it $500 a year. From Vine St. I moved my family into a small house on the south side of Church Alley; the rent $160 a year. It was but two stories high, with back buildings. In this house we lived until 1810, when we removed house and office to No. 108 Market St. In the rear of this house was a large office, which had been occupied as a dwelling by the late Dr. Franklin. I rented the store on Market St. This house and office had, before I moved into it, been occupied by Col. Duane. It was in that house he lived and kept a bookstore, and had the printing office of the "Aurora" in the large back building. I have no distinct recollection of the rent I paid for those premises, but I know they were all offered to be sold to me for eighteen thousand dollars. Since that time that property has been worth more than five times that sum. I have given the rent I have paid for the houses I occupied that it may be compared with the rents now paid for the same premises. From these premises, in 1815, I removed to the house and office, No. 70 Chestnut, between Second and Third. I have no hesitancy in saying that there is now more business done in that square than, in 1815, there was done in all Chestnut Street, from the Delaware to the Schuylkill. From the time we came to Philadelphia until some time after we moved into Market St., we kept a cow, and had her milked morning and evening. While in Market St., our cow was stolen, and we "ne'er saw her more."

I remained fourteen years at No. 70 Chestnut St. During those years, my exposition of the abuses of Gov. Findlay's administration; my exposition of the character and conduct of Gen'l Jackson and their consequences, had the effect of changing the character of my paper, reducing its circulation, abridging my means of collecting my very large amount of outstanding debts, and throwing me and my newspaper into the ranks of the Federal party, who had heretofore hated me and my paper. While there, I received an alderman's commission from Governor Heister; at the time it arrived, I was fully sensible of my declining fortune, and made haste to open an alderman's office, in the hope that its receipts would prop my falling political fortunes. I opened an alderman's office where I had heretofore had my publishing office, which was removed into the back room. The receipts of my office were not sufficient to sustain the printing office. Many of my political friends seemed determined to adhere to me, and do all in their power to assist me; they were aware I was sinking deeper and deeper, and they at length induced me to consent to sell out the paper and the printing office. Thus I was enabled to reduce my outstanding debts, and to reduce my expenses by removing to S. Sixth St., where I opened an alderman's office, opposite to the entrance of the court-house. I had, in Chestnut St., a large and valuable library, all of which I had put into furniture cars, taken to the auction store, and sold for very little money. These arrangements so far relieved my mind and circumstances, as to enable me diligently to devote my time to the dispatch of the very large business which was done in my alderman's office, and greatly reduce my debts. In that office, as an alderman, I continued until 1844, when I was, by the Native party, ejected from office, and I was, for a time, left without any employment, and moved into some upper rooms in a house in Market above Ninth St., where I remained, most uncomfortably situated, for about a year. My means were very slender, and derived from the sale of books, paper, and other things which I could best spare. From those gloomy rooms in Market St., in which we had not even the cheerfulness afforded by gas, at the end of a year, I moved to Walnut St., below Fifth. I remained in that neighborhood from 1845 until 1850. I then removed to No. 46 S. Sixth St., nearly opposite to the court-house, where I calculated, from my increased nearness to the courthouses, an increase of business. In this I was much mistaken, and found that my nearness to the court-houses did not compensate for my removal from scriveners and conveyancers, and instead of an increase in my business, it decreased about one-third. Here, however, I earn enough to keep the wolf from the door, and live reasonably comfortable, and in the enjoyment of good health, able to take as many acknowledgments as are required of me, as a Commissioner of the United States, and Commissioner for twenty-seven States.

TROOPS OF FRIENDS.

In the years 1814 and '15, I had a summer residence, a very neat establishment, distant about three miles from the city, on Upper Harrowgate Lane. I generally went out every afternoon, and came to the city every morning. I was in the country all day on Sunday. I had about five acres of land. It was a very handsome house, with balconies all round it. I had no conception of the many friends, ladies and gentlemen, which I had, until I purchased that place. We pass over week-days, and come to Sunday, which, if it did not pour rain, was always with us a gala day. There were tea and coffee, and wine and other liquors, suitable for the palates of ladies and gentlemen who had taken the trouble to go so far to taste their flavor, and do honor to the host and hostess, and their amiable family. In a word, the house and garden were so well frequented, and the fare so highly relished, that the host and hostess, after a trial of two seasons, sold their country-seat for $500 less than they gave for it, and were ever after content to live in the city, and give their visiting friends no further trouble.

AN ACCIDENT.

The following narrative will show that independent of the untiring attentions of our visiting friends, and our pecuniary expenditures and losses, I had the misfortune of a broken leg, all of which, combined, did not satisfy me that I was incurring expenses and wasting time, which ought to be devoted to establishing my own character and that of my paper; all was dazzling light before me. I saw no dark clouds—no hidden rocks—and was wholly unprepared for the shipwreck which was not far distant, but of which I had no conception. I have before said, or ought to have said, I was not a man for business.

In the fall of 1814, I was in a light carriage, driving my wife, her sister, and two of my children to our country-house on Upper Harrowgate Lane. On the road Mr. Poyntell had a handsome house, on the brow of a steep hill; at the foot of that hill was a stream of water which ran across the road; over that stream was a narrow bridge of considerable height; on each side of the bridge the bed of the water was deep and narrow. From the brow of the hill to the bridge the distance was not less than forty yards, and very steep. The horse I was driving was not my own; he was a hired horse. Just as we arrived at the brow of the hill, a portion of his harness, the back-band, gave way, and fell about the horse's hind legs. I was sitting on the right-hand side of the front seat of the carriage, my right foot resting on a crosspiece. The moment the harness fell about the horse's feet he kicked up his heels, and broke my right leg just below the knee. I was conscious of the danger to my family if I dropped the reins, and therefore crept on the left-hand shaft of the carriage until I hopped down, and seized and held the horse by the head while my family all got out. I then lay exhausted on the roadside.

In the meantime a lady in a private carriage, a stranger, was kind enough to loan us her carriage and horses to take us home to Market Street. With many thanks my wife stepped into the carriage, and I was helped into it, and laid my leg across her lap. In the meantime a friend rode in to town to order the room, &c., to be prepared, and to have Dr. Physick there. On our arrival, all things were in readiness. We found everything was in good order. Friends were there who carried me up stairs and laid me on the mattress on my bedstead. My clothes were taken off, and my wounded leg, from the wound to the toe-nails, was reported to be as black as an African's. The doctor made the necessary examinations, poulticed, bandaged, laid in a wooden case my broken leg, gave such orders as he thought proper, and said very little more than that he would come early, and took his leave.

He did come early, bringing with him two of his students and the instruments necessary to perform an amputation. Having felt my pulse, he said: "This is extraordinary and unexpected. Why, Mr. Binns, you have not a beat of fever!" He then had a quantity of linen rags, some boiled milk and bread laid on the toilet table. My ever affectionate wife was waiting on the doctor, and I heard him say—"Now, Mrs. Binns, I beg your attention while I give some instruction as to what I expect you to do." He then gave her what instructions he deemed necessary, to which she paid so much attention that he never had to repeat them while he attended. The first nine weeks I lay altogether on my back; my friend, Dr. Hudson, coming every day to rub it with oil to prevent the skin from abrading. During the attendance of Dr. Physick for ten or more weeks, his gentleness of manner and politeness of deportment won all our regards, and induced the belief that he felt a more than common interest in my recovery. The first six weeks the doctor attended me, I had no food but a sort of broth made of half-boiled sliced raw potatoes; for the next eight weeks I lived on celery and salt. I had very many encomiums from Dr. Physick for the contented exactitude with which I confined myself to his prescriptions for food. I do not recollect to have taken any medicine; if I did take any, it must have been very little. I have the gratification to say, that for the last forty years I have had much good service from that broken leg, for which I feel very thankful to the skill and watchful care of Dr. Physick.

THE CLUB.

In 1820, the following named persons, in Philadelphia, associated as a club: Thomas Cooper, Abraham Small, Wm. Y. Birch, Edward Hudson, Matthew Randall, and John Binns. They agreed to meet every Monday, alternately, at each other's houses, at 6 o'clock in the evening, to have supper at 8, and to adjourn at 10 o'clock. If any stranger, known to any of the members, was in town, the member to whom he was known was expected to bring him to the meeting of the club, where he was cordially welcomed. The club met at the appointed hour very punctually, and supped and separated with the same punctuality.

At the earlier meetings of the club, the supper was bread, crackers and cheese. After some time, they had roast potatoes and butter; next, they had cold roast beef and trimmings; the cold beef in a short time gave way to hot beef, beef-steaks, or mutton-chops; these, in a few months, gave way to lobsters, terrapins, roast ducks, or whatever it was the pleasure of the member where we supped to set before us. The members generally were cheerful; abounded in anecdote; were not deficient in general information, and appeared, at all times, disposed to contribute to the general information and good humor. For some years our social meetings were unimpaired.

The first breach was the removal of Dr. Cooper to South Carolina, as President of the State College. His extensive knowledge, wit, and good-humor were sufficient to instruct and enliven any society. His literary and scientific knowledge were of world-wide fame. I will venture a single fact illustrative of his singular literary ability. When Burke published his "Reflections on the French Revolution," among those who undertook to answer him was Thomas Cooper, then a resident of Manchester. His "Reply to Burke's Invective," was inferior to no answer which was published. It took rank with those of Paine and Mackintosh. At the time he was printing that book, Wm. Y. Birch was apprentice to the publisher. I have heard him say that on more occasions than one, when Mr. Cooper would step in to correct the proofs, the printer would say: "We want copy, sir." "Give me some paper," and he would write two or three sheets, and hand it to the printer—without reading, much less correcting it. He was a man of powerful intellect highly cultivated. He had a heart as warm and capacious as his mind was richly stored. He was my ardent and faithful friend from my first introduction to his death, a period of nearly half a century. His portrait, taken when he was about 90 years of age, and the portrait of my friend, Dr. Edw. Hudson, are within two yards of the desk at which I sit, and for years have sat, about eight hours a day. Judge Cooper was a chemist of no common calibre. He was admirable in compounding sauces and gravies, and enjoyed them very much. He was somewhat of a gourmand, yet he was never idle, and lived to the very advanced age of 98 or 99; cheerful and polite to his last days.

My friend, Dr. Hudson, was carried off, in 1830, by a miliary fever, at the age of about 58 years. I left his bedside when he was expiring. As I came to the lower gate of the State House yard, on my way home, I met the Hon. John Sergeant: "How is Dr. Hudson?" said he. "He is dying," said I. "Then you," said he, "will lose as fast and faithful a friend as ever man had."

Dr. Hudson was so severely attacked by the fever which caused his death, that he had neither time nor ability to make any disposition of his property; and thus to Mrs. Hudson fell the entire care of their large family and estate. I was aware that I was indebted to the doctor, not only for professional services, but for borrowed money. When I called upon Mrs. Hudson to examine the books of the doctor, to ascertain the amount of my indebtedness, I received for answer that there was no claim whatever on his books against me. I then examined my own memoranda book, estimated the services rendered, and came to the conclusion that I was indebted to the doctor's estate sixteen hundred dollars. For this amount I gave to Mrs. Hudson my note, which, in good time and with some difficulty, I paid.

This notice of dear friends has carried me away from the club where I passed for years so many happy Monday evenings. Mr. Small, who died in 1829, was a gentleman of ready wit, and had a well-stored memory. He suffered much for many years with gout. He was, so long as I knew him, corpulent. When he was dead, a child could have lifted his remains. His partner for many years, and his affectionate friend to his death, Mr. Birch, told me "that Mr. Small, to relieve himself of gout, took colchicum so freely that he entirely destroyed the coats of his stomach."

Mr. Matthew Randall was, perhaps, as generally known,

and, may I not add, as generally regarded, as any gentleman on 'Change? He was rich and abundant in anecdote, timed their introduction well, and told them with grace and vivacity. He was of a generous nature, and a choice companion. He died, I think, of colic. The general attendance at his funeral of the members of the bar and others showed how much he was respected.

There then remained of the club but Wm. Young Birch and the writer; and we, for some years after the death of our fellow-members, continued every Monday evening to meet as we had been accustomed. When he died, many years ago, he left his considerable property to the support of the Asylum for the Blind.

John Binns, the surviving member of the club, is left to write this brief notice of its existence and the departure of its members. Boswell, if he had been a member, would have found materials for a volume worth reading.

JOHN BINNS IS MADE AN ALDERMAN.

December 26, 1822, I was, by Governor Joseph Heister, appointed an alderman of the city of Philadelphia. At that time there was a Mayor's Court, for the trial of all criminal cases, save only murder, in the city of Philadelphia. This court had also the exclusive power of granting tavern licenses for the city of Philadelphia. I was especially attentive to my duty as a judge of that court; took some pains and gave some time to qualify myself to discharge my duty in such a manner as should reflect no discredit on myself, and should render some benefit to the community. On many occasions, I thought it my duty to charge the grand juries. Many of those charges, not less than six of them, was to call their attention, and their authority and influence to the enforcement of the law which makes it the duty of clerks of the market to take care that the bakers shall obey the law which makes it imperative upon them to sell their bread by the pound, avoirdupois, under severe penalties.

To enforce the observance of this law, by exposing the frauds of bakers, and the consequent loss to the public, I had bread bought, generally every session of the court, at five or six bakers' shops, and weighed at drug stores, to show the difference in their weight and the loss to purchasers. Every time I charged the grand jury on this subject, they returned thanks, and unanimously called for a copy of the charge for publication. In one of these charges, shortly before the court was abolished, I satisfied the grand jury, by the facts I submitted, that the best wheaten bread, made of *American* superfine flour, was at that time selling in Belfast, and that one-fourth more superfine bread was there sold for the same amount of money than it could be purchased for in Philadelphia.

I have also called the attention of several mayors of the city to induce them to make the clerks of the market, whose especial duty it is made by law, to make the bakers obey the law, sell their bread by weight, and do justice to the public. But it seemed all labor in vain, and I was given to understand, both by the bakers and the public authorities, that the bakers always voted the *right* ticket. I labored earnestly, and expended many small sums of money, in the hope of being able, at one time or another, to succeed, and get the law carried into effect, but I have been wholly unable. It is only a few days ago I had the law on this subject published in our newspapers, with a short heading, asking the attention of the present mayor and councilmen to the subject. I fear, however, that, after working at it for more than twenty years, I am as far from attaining my object as I was when I began. This is provoking and disheartening, but I will not give up what I know to be right, and get no other or better reason than that the bakers all take care to vote the right ticket, and to have it known at head-quarters that they do so vote.

If some of our merchants who do not meddle much with politics, would take the trouble to institute the necessary inquiries to ascertain the facts, I would lay a wager—yes, I am so confident of winning, that I would wager ten dollars or more—that bread, made of *American* superfine flour, is at this time selling cheaper in Liverpool than in Philadelphia; that is to say, that you can in Liverpool for the same money buy a greater quantity of the best bread, made of superfine *American* flour, than you can buy it for in Philadelphia. You can even get twenty per cent. more good bread for a certain sum, made of American superfine flour, than you can get bread for in Philadelphia.

I will here republish the law in relation to bread, in the hope that it may meet the eye and command the good offices of some of our public functionaries:—

"*All* loaf-bread, made for sale within this Commonwealth, shall be sold by the pound avoirdupois; and every baker or other person offering the same for sale, shall keep at his or her house, or at such other place at which he or she shall at any time offer or expose for sale any such bread, sufficient scales and weights, lawfully registered, for the purpose of weighing the same; and if any baker or other person shall sell, or offer for sale, any loaf-bread in any other manner, the contract respecting the same shall be void; and the person offending against this act shall, on conviction, forfeit and pay the sum of ten dollars for every such offence; one-half to the use of the informer, and the other half to the use of the Commonwealth; and it shall be the especial duty of the clerk of the market, in any place where such officer is appointed, to discover and prosecute all persons offending against this act."—3 *Smith*, 295.

"CLERK OF THE MARKET.—The clerks of the market, before they enter upon the execution of their office, shall take the following *oath or affirmation* before some magistrate or justice of the city, borough, or county, wherein they shall reside, viz: 'That he will, well and truly, to the best of his skill and judgment, do and perform all things enjoined and required of him as clerk of the market by the laws.'"—5 *Smith*, 397.

I continued an alderman by appointment and election, in Walnut Ward, until 1844.

While I was an alderman, I never saw a fight, or disturbance of any kind, by daylight, without rushing in and separating those who were fighting, putting an end to the fight, and restoring the public peace. I was emboldened thus to act in consequence of having ascertained that whenever there was a breach of the peace, which I interfered to quell, so soon as, in a loud voice, I commanded the peace, and pushed into the fray, the great body of the citizens would come to my assistance, crying: "Support the alderman." I never went into one of those affrays at night. At that time none of our officers were intrusted with blunderbusses, pistols, or bowie-knives; a good stick was found sufficient. Neither firemen, nor hose-men, nor any other men, who associated for the good of the public, carried weapons, the use of which endangered life or limb. If one party will carry deadly weapons, other parties, in self-defence, feel called upon to do the same. The strict enforcement of a law against carrying dangerous or deadly weapons, would do much to preserve the public peace. In London, where they have the best police in the world, by day and by night, policemen only carry a stick.

One consequence of my being an alderman gave me much pleasure. From party or personal considerations, my old and esteemed friend, Col. Duane, and I had, in our respective papers, charged each other with offences of no common magnitude. The colonel had been appointed an alderman some months before I was; thus we became associates on the bench, and restored our former friendly relations.

A SCENE IN AN ALDERMAN'S OFFICE.

About the year 1836, a well-dressed, middle-aged man came into my office, No. 36 S. Sixth St., and lodged a complaint, as near as can now be recollected, in the words following: "I am a peace officer of Boston; I was there employed, several weeks ago, to take care of, and travel with, a man deranged in mind; we have been as far south as Virginia, and I thought the man was much better until this morning; last afternoon we arrived in this city and put up at Jones's hotel; we were shown, at my request, into a two-bedded room; we went to bed, each of us in a separate bed, the bedsteads being ranged one by the side of the other; about an hour ago this man leaped on my bed, and was about to smother me, when my cries brought some of the servants to my assistance; they took hold of him, and now have him in custody, while I come to you, sir, for officers and a warrant to have him brought before you, and have authority given me to have him tied or handcuffed, so that I may be able to take him home to Boston." I swore the complainant to the truth of the statement he had made, and gave a warrant to a constable to execute. He took another officer with him; they went to the hotel, and in a few minutes one of them returned, accompanied by a person belonging to the hotel, who assured me that the man on whose oath I had granted the warrant, was himself the maniac, and the man against whom I had issued the warrant was his keeper. He then showed me the necessary papers, to convince me of the truth of the statement he had just made. The constable left in the hotel soon came to the office, attended by the complainant and his keeper. I heard the statement of the deranged man, not giving any indication of the information I had just received, and so conducted the hearing as not to excite, in the mind of the complainant, any doubt that I disbelieved any part of his statement. I then gave to a constable the papers I thought necessary. They all returned to the hotel, whence, in a short time, the keeper, his assistant, and the deranged man, set out for Boston. In a few days I had the gratification to learn they had all arrived in safety.

CHAPTER XV.

A deep affliction—Another accident—A compliment—Farewell to "Democratic Press"—Opinion of my capacity as a public speaker—A libel refuted—Daniel O'Connell.

A DEEP AFFLICTION.

ALL my children who died, but one, died in my house, under the watchful care of their mother and family. They had all attained a mature age, and died in the humble, yet reasonably confident hope that, through the mercy of the Creator, and the blood of the Redeemer, they would ascend to the enjoyment of a blissful eternity. The one who did not die at home, was called hence, to be no more seen of men, in a manner the most afflicting.

John, my eldest son, and Pemberton, my next eldest son, the one fifteen and the other fourteen years of age, on the afternoon of the 5th of February, 1828, with leave of their parents, went to skate on the Delaware River; they had not been gone an hour when John returned, bathed in tears, and said: "Pemberton is drowned!"

There was a sweetness of disposition, a desire to serve and oblige every creature, manifest in everything that boy said or done. He seemed to live but to be useful and to do good. The consequence was, he was generally beloved. All who knew him, even those who knew him but slightly, grieved at his loss. Many who were to me strangers, and some who had interchanged but a few words with him, wept over his early grave. Neighbors, upon whose sympathies I had no special lien, yea, strangers whom I knew not, came to mourn and to weep with the bereaved parents; at length night came, and, their doors being shut, they sat down together and wept bitter tears for the loss of their promising and beloved boy.

Promptly we offered a reward for the recovery of his lost remains. We were a hundred and six days—what an age!—before we heard one syllable in relation to them; at length, on the 27th of May, two boatmen came and claimed the reward, saying they had found and towed the body into one of the wharves. Our hearts warmed with thankfulness when we heard that the Lord had been graciously pleased to afford us the privilege of weeping over the remains of our lost one, and of laying them where, in good time, his remains and ours should hereafter rest together.

Accompanied by my eldest son, we went to the wharf, and the men said: "There it is," pointing to a mass so swollen, discolored and misshapen, that it was not until after many assurances from my son, that I could recognize it as what had been one of the most active, intelligent, and beloved of human beings. I sent for the undertaker to take them in charge. He had them taken and scoured and cleaned and tarred, and wound round and bound up, so as to be no longer unbearably offensive. At length it was brought home, and arrangements made for the funeral. It is now more than thirty years since those distressing dispensations; yet the eyes of the aged father of that boy are dimmed with tears. Prayers, and hymns, and spiritual songs, and the sobbings and groans of many an aching heart were heard when his remains were committed to the house appointed for all living.

There was an immense crowd at the funeral. It seemed as though everybody sympathized and mourned. My neighbor, the editor of the "Daily Advertiser," with whom I had never had any personal intercourse, and of whom I had too often spoken slightingly in my paper, when the undertaker was about to form the crowd, who were to walk in the procession, Mr. Poulson drew near to me, and, in the kindest manner, said: "Will my neighbor allow me to take his arm and walk with him on this melancholy occasion?" I did not speak, I could not say a word; I was overcome by his attention and his kindness. I drew close to him and bent my arm; he passed his arm through mine, and thus we walked to and from the burying-ground. We did not interchange a word, but while he lived, our intercourse was of the most friendly nature.

ANOTHER ACCIDENT.

The first floor in No. 70, Chestnut Street house, was the usual distance from the second floor, to which you ascended by one flight of stairs. I was at the head of that flight of stairs, talking with my wife about going to the theatre, when I picked up my youngest boy in my arms, who was then about three years old, and I, running in playful mood from the chamber to the head of the stairs, one of my feet caught in the carpet, and I fell from the top to the bottom of the stairs without touching anything. On the way, for the purpose of saving the child, I turned my body so that I should be undermost, and receive the greatest violence and most injury from the fall. The wall, which separated the stairs from the parlor was of brick, and against this brick wall, at the foot of the stairs, over which I was, with the child, rapidly descending, was a stout Windsor chair. My head, after striking all the feet from under the chair, went plump against the wall. It was on occasions like this that my wife was wonderfully collected. She neither fainted nor screamed, but came down stairs, and, having called a servant girl, she lifted up the child and set him on his feet. She said he spun round like a top. In the meantime she had me drawn into the hall, and let me lie there on my back until the doctor came to take charge of me. She then, as was her custom on all occasions of trouble, sent for my ever-ready and attentive friend, Dr. Hudson. I was laid on my bed, and was several hours before I became sensible. My recovering was a matter of several days; Dr. Physick, with his accustomed skill and attention, keeping watch over me. He was tender and watchful as a female.

A COMPLIMENT.

About the year 1824-25, I was honored by a visit from *Piero Monicelli*, an Italian patriot, the friend of *Silvio Pellico*, with whom he had been imprisoned for ten years, treated with great severity, and subjected to painful privations by the tyrants of Italy. He had had a painful attack of inflammatory rheumatism of long duration while in prison. His lower limbs were wrapped in flannel when he came to visit me, insomuch that he had much difficulty in descending from his carriage and entering my office. "I have come," said he, "to pay you, sir, my respects, having many times heard of you as a zealous and able advocate of the rights of man." As he uttered these words, he pressed my hand affectionately between both of his. Before leaving the office, he handed me his card, on which he had written his name. I am proud of this mark of respect from so distinguished a martyr of freedom. He assured me that the small room in which they had been confined was very hot; that the gnats were numerous, and their bites distressingly painful; at one time he said he was so miserable as to be driven to contemplate suicide.

FAREWELL TO "DEMOCRATIC PRESS."

When I was about to lay down my pen, forever, as the editor of a newspaper, I published a short address "to the public." I have just read the last paragraph of that address. Believing it to be strictly true, I feel at liberty to republish it:—

"Will not the subscriber be excused, if, at the moment

when his editorial existence is about to cease, and with it the political relations he has maintained with the public to be terminated, forever, he shall so far indulge his personal feelings as to assert, as he can with truth, that in all his long political career he never gave up a Correspondent or abandoned a Friend? Permit the writer to indulge so far as to call to public recollection that, amidst all the bitterness of political strife; amidst all the breakings up of old associations; the burstings asunder of long-cherished intimacies, and the fierceness of the contests which arose out of them, no man has been found so regardless of the obligations of truth, as to charge the subscriber with a disposition to make his political influence a source of personal gain, or with having corruptly received one cent for any political services he may have rendered. At this moment, these are proud and grateful recollections.

"JOHN BINNS.

"PHILADELPHIA, Nov. 14, 1829."

JOHN BINNS AS A PUBLIC SPEAKER.
(From the Pittsburg Statesman.)

We have seen a gentleman who heard the speech of Mr. Binns, delivered before the "Catholic Association of the Friends of Ireland" in Philadelphia. He was extravagant, as we then supposed, in his commendations of the style and matter of the address, as also in his description of the effects produced by the manner of Mr. Binns, who was represented as being very animated, as possessing a fine person, and a graceful figure, and a good voice, under perfect command, and disciplined after the best rules of eloquence and elocution. With these advantages, it is not surprising that Mr. Binns should animate and excite his hearers in the manner represented by those who have heard him, and *especially* when engaged on so engrossing and interesting a topic as the emancipation of a large portion of his countrymen, the people of Ireland.

We remember hearing it stated by a gentleman who was a member of the Legislative Committee that tried Governor Findlay, and who bore a conspicuous part in the proceedings of that trial, that he had never known what was meant by "Irish eloquence," until he heard the address of Mr. Binns before that Committee; and that every person engaged, and all who heard him on that occasion, acknowledged the force and power of his reasoning, and the influence of his energetic and fervid eloquence. The opinion of Judge Wilkins must have been an impartial one, for he was opposed to Mr. Binns during all the examinations and excitements that attended that trial; Judge Wilkins, in fact, took the lead in defending Governor Findlay against Mr. Binns, who was the principal on the side of the prosecution.

We have extracted into our paper, of this week, a part of the address delivered by Mr. Binns at a late meeting of the "Friends of Ireland" in Philadelphia. It was the perusal of this address that called to mind the remarks that we have often heard in relation to the effective eloquence of that gentleman. We are certain that these extracts from his address will be read with satisfaction and interest.

(To the Editor of the Cork Chronicle.)

Sir: I beg leave to send you a copy of the speech of Mr. Alderman Binns, of Philadelphia, alluded to in the report given in your paper of the 7th instant, of the proceedings of the Emancipation Dinner given in that city on the 14th of July last. I think the intrinsic merits of the speech would warrant its insertion, under any circumstances, in our journals at this side of the great waters. But there is a peculiar circumstance appertaining to it, and derived from the history of its author, which, in my opinion, entitles this piece to more than common notice.

Mr. Binns was once an active opponent of the Government of Great Britain, as a member of the Corresponding Society; and so formidable, from his talents and activity, that, after various unsuccessful attempts to convict him of treason, the ministers of the day were obliged to leave him to his own courses. When no longer persecuted, he determined to fix his residence in the United States, where his uprightness of character, and uncommon endowments of mind, have procured him independence and honors. There cannot be a more decisive proof of the wisdom of the Relief Bill than the warmth towards Great Britain, perceptible in the language called forth by that measure, from men long exiled from our shores, and whose previous feelings in regard to these countries had been decidedly hostile.

Mr. Binns is a native of Ireland, and Ireland has no reason to be ashamed of such a son.

T. M.

Cork, Sept. 8, 1829.

JOHN BINNS'S SPEECH.

Mr. Chairman: I rise, sir, for the purpose of submitting a volunteer toast to this company; I wish to be permitted to preface it by some remarks which so entirely enlist my faculties and absorb my feelings, that, for the *first time* in my life, I have committed what I intend to say to paper.

This is a theme and a place on which I should fear to trust even my own heart, lest it should carry my tongue beyond the bounds of prudence, or betray it into expressions which might wound the feelings of some who hear me.

In what an age of revolutions have we lived! In what a place, on what a day, and on what an occasion have we assembled! Centuries may pass away, yet such an extraordinary concurrence of circumstances may never again unite. The place in which we are is most apt to the time and to the occasion. In this hall, sir, the blessed air of independence was first breathed in the United States; here, indeed, the United States was first called into existence. It was under this roof, within these walls, that the imprescriptible rights of man—the whole volume, title-page and all—were first acknowledged. Everything around us is pregnant with associations and recollections the most sacred and holy! In the places which we now occupy sat John Hancock and Benjamin Franklin, John Adams and Samuel Adams, and Thomas Jefferson, and the host of worthies, the fathers of the Revolution, who declared and maintained independence. A mighty struggle followed that declaration, and mighty was the stake depending on the issue of that contest. Patriotism was victorious, independence acknowledged; and freedom, civil, political, and religious, was established in the land, and proclaimed to the uttermost ends of the earth. The necessity for brevity compels us to pass from this delightful theme to others but little less important, which have followed as its consequences. There is, however, a name, and associations with that name which will cause us to linger yet a little longer in the Hall of Independence, on the celebration of the triumph of the principles of religious toleration. Here, on this happy occasion, every heart cherishes with peculiar ardor the memory of that great man, who, after a long life, eminently useful to his country and to mankind, narrowed down the inscription for his tomb to these few words: "Here lie the mortal remains of Thomas Jefferson, author of the Declaration of Independence and the act of Religious Freedom." (*Loud cheers.*)

Passing from the *place* where we are to the *day* on which we have assembled, what an important and peculiarly appropriate anniversary presents itself on which to pour out our joys and our thanksgivings! It is forty years this day since the frowning towers of the Bastile were levelled with its ditch. (*Long and continued cheering.*)

It is forty years this day since humanity, invigorated by the enthusiasm of new-born freedom, carried up from "dungeons of darkness" the sick, the aged, and the infirm, to cower under and rejoice beneath the newly-restored light of heaven; to hear the transporting shouts of their emancipated countrymen, and, in the fulness of time, to see the sun of liberty in meridian splendor enlightening and invigorating the country of Lafayette. (*Loud cheers.*)

It is good for man that grass grows where the bastile stood. It is an honor, well earned by this country and its most distinguished citizen, that the massive key of that great state prison is now cankering, under the rust of time, in the halls of Washington, the pure and the brave. (*Cheers.*)

In such a place, and on such a day, have we assembled to indulge in some of the kindest feelings of our nature, and to rejoice that our beloved Ireland is emancipated. (*Loud cheers.*) What an assemblage has this happy occasion, common principles, and common feelings, brought together.

Here are the natives of the soil, some of whom in their youth cast off the yoke of slavery, and some of whom have never drunk of its "feculent flood;" here are men, who know, only by report, of "the wrongs and outrage with which the world is filled," and know no touch of persecution for conscience sake; with such men this company is thickly studded. Here are those who, when "there came to the beach a poor exile of Erin," would take him to their homes and raise him, who had no country, to the rank of their fellow-citizen. It is gratifying, and it is right and proper that such men should come among us, rejoicing on this day of our jubilee and their jubilee. (*Cheers.*)

The great mass, however, of this company are natives of the sweetest isle of the ocean; men whose country has been ground between the upper and the nether millstones of oppression; men who left the green fields and companions of their youth, and the hearths and homes of their fathers, to pass a mighty waste of waters in search of that peace, freedom, and happiness which seemed forever to have abandoned their native land.

They found here all that they sought, and they have been grateful for all that they have found. It does not become the brave to sound a trumpet before them, nor the grateful to make known what they have done to show forth their gratitude! The Irish emigrants have married and intermarried with the native Americans, until they have become as one people; a people proudly emulous to uphold and to advance the star-spangled banner:

"O! long may it wave,
O'er the land of the free and the home of the brave."

(*Loud and long-continued cheers.*)

But dear and precious as is that star-spangled banner, and fervent as is our devotion to our adopted country, yet are our hearts capacious enough to embrace within their warm folds the harp of Erin, the homes of our infancy, and the altars before which we bowed down in our riper years.

Persecuted and banished as we have been, and separated by an almost boundless ocean from her shores, yet I appeal to you, my countrymen, have not your hearts yearned towards Ireland, and your eyes everflowed because she was in thraldom? And shall we not rejoice because of her joy; "yea, shout for very gladness, because there is joy in Israel, and much rejoicing in Jerusalem?" (*Much cheering.*)

Irishmen no longer avert their eyes from the glowing west because the great luminary of heaven no longer goes down on their country in chains. That "gem of the ocean" is now, by the setting sun, resplendently decked in all the gay and rich colors of the rainbow, while its beauteous beams stream over the graves of our Tones and our Orrs, our Byrnes and our Emmetts. To their exalted worth, to their many virtues, and their chivalric patriotism, every tongue now does homage. *Now* shall their mausoleums arise, and their epitaphs be written! The people and statesmen of Great Britain—of her who was the oppressor—her king and her Parliament, unite to do justice to our country, and to our patriotic countrymen, and say, with a voice of authority, "thou hast done well, thy country shall be emancipated, and thy countrymen shall worship the living God, after the manner of their fathers; every shackle and every disqualification shall be stricken off; thy people shall be delivered; and thy people and our people shall be as one;" and the people said, "Amen;" and an angel from on high cried, with a loud voice, "Clap your hands, all ye people; shout unto God with the voice of triumph." (*Loud and long-continued cheering and clapping.*) After the applause had in some measure subsided, Mr. Binns gave as a toast, "The 4th of July, 1776; the 14th of July, 1789; and the 13th of April, 1829—the anniversaries of the emancipation of the United States, of France, and of Ireland."

A LIBEL REFUTED.

The following letter requires some introduction. I had published the "Democratic Press" some months, when it was denounced by the leaders of that portion of the party which was known as the "old school;" they generally resided in the Northern Liberties. Among the desperate and indefensible measures resorted to for the destruction of the paper was the adoption of every possible scheme to ruin the fair fame of its editor, by his expulsion from all the political societies where they, from long standing, could command the votes of a majority of the members; taking care to publish his expulsion in every newspaper which they could command.

The most dishonorable, might I not say diabolical measure to which they resorted, was charging him with having betrayed, and caused to be hung as a traitor, his esteemed and confiding friend, the Rev. James Coigley. This wicked lie was by many believed, and I was consequently by them looked upon with loathing. I perhaps unwisely scorned to call upon those who had it in their power to justify me. Some years elapsed, when a letter from my friend Arthur O'Connor arrived, which put the calumny to flight.

The following letter from Lewis P. Frank, which was written at its date, gives a minute history of the manner in which the base calumny was manufactured and put in circulation. To my knowledge I never saw L. P. Franks. I have reason to know that I am indebted to the interference of my good friend, Ald. Badger, that Mr. Franks was induced to write the following statement:—

"Philadelphia, September 6, 1823.
"J. Binns, Esq.

"Sir: I feel no manner of hesitation in complying with the request contained in your note of the 2d inst. Indeed it was my intention some time back to have disclosed the circumstances relative to the imposture which was practised upon the public, respecting you, in 1809. This was, however, principally prevented by my going about that time to the State of South Carolina. In the interim most of the more distinguished parties passed from this to the next world; and my own tenure of existence being perhaps not less fragile than that of others, I consider it no more than an act of justice to you to disclose the fact, and to prevent any further attempts to revive the matter, to do which, a disposition has of late several times manifested itself.

"The letter was manufactured in the fall of 1809 (I

think about the middle of November). I had obtained a pamphlet edition of the Maidstone Trials of 1798, to which you were a party. In the appendix to this edition, there was a letter from Dr. Coigley to a friend, stating the circumstances of his trial and condemnation, making several calls upon the generosity of that friend (whose name is not given), in regard to the unfortunate doctor's kindred. To the pamphlet was also appended an account of the execution, with a brief report of his words on the scaffold. The pamphlet was shown to a gentleman who then bore a prominent part in the management of parties, and who was conspicuous for his hostility to you. Having looked over it with some attention, he remarked that if there was no danger of being confronted by another copy of the pamphlet, it might be made very useful. The late Joseph Lloyd was then publishing the "Pennsylvania Democrat," and it was suggested that it might be played off upon him, and some idea might be formed from the impression likely to be effected, and other measures could be taken afterwards. Being myself devoted, body and soul as it were, to the individual alluded to, the idea was seized at the instant (being aware that it would be difficult to obtain in this city a copy of the same edition of the trial), to make it subservient to the cause of the Old School party. Hints were accordingly put into Lloyd's paper, glancing with some *mystery* at the Maidstone Trial, and darker innuendoes were occasionally dropped in conversation, and at public and private meetings, as a sort of preparation for the Monster in Embryo. Lloyd, who was not enlightened on the subject, more than was considered expedient, endeavored, at Mr. Byrne's and several other law bookstores, to obtain a copy of the trial, but without effect. This, with his accustomed love of communicating his pursuits, he occasionally detailed, to the no small satisfaction of those who were now only waiting an opportunity to gratify his curiosity. Things being thus ripened, and feeling perfectly well assured that nothing could be immediately had recourse to, which would defeat the fabrication, the doctor's letter, before mentioned, and a part of his address to the spectators from the scaffold, were taken and patched together, with occasional *interpolations* to excite suspicion and distrust (*of which not a syllable is in the original*), and occasionally throwing out innuendoes against you; and to give its genuineness the better appearance, the classical allusions and quotations in Dr. Coigley's own letter, were carefully transferred to the new version. When all was completed, the letter was shown in confidence to Peter Hay, now one of the editors of the 'Sentinel,' and who had been before shown the book containing the original: the new version being described to him as an experiment to see how far Lloyd and his Old School friends could be gulled, and with no other view did he consider it. Being afterwards submitted for the inspection of several active leaders, it was thought sufficient to answer the object in view, and next day sent to Lloyd in a circuitous manner, in order to keep from him all knowledge of the sources of the communication. A lad was employed to leave it for Lloyd at Miller's, where the same evening he received it, and read it aloud, to the amazement of the company; and in his next following publication, the fabricated letter appeared, suitably garnished with introductory remarks, notes, &c. &c. And an extra number of the paper was printed on the occasion, which was circulated by the individuals concerned, particularly in the southern part of the county; and among many people it was received as a *Gospel*. Lloyd, however, was still anxious to obtain a sight of the book, and in a second call at Mr. Byrne's, he had some conversation on the subject, and received from him every reason to doubt the authenticity of the letter; and to stop his further researches, the volume containing the trials was lent him, the whole of the appendix being previously *cut out*. In the meanwhile, those concerned having succeeded in scattering suspicion, took no further measures for the circulation of the letter, and induced Lloyd (who began to suspect that a trick had been played him) to drop boring the public on the subject, lest it should become threadbare. But to keep suspicion and hatred alive, it was frequently alluded to in the publications of the time, and its genuineness was by these means left as it were unquestioned. Though a separation between the parties afterwards took place, this transaction was never called upon the tapis in all their subsequent contentions; and whether they ever had any more printed is not known to me: though I believe they did not, as it had been intimated, if they did, the truth should be made public.

"During the heat of an electioneering campaign in 1814, Stiles, who then published the 'True American,' had obtained a copy of the 'Democrat,' containing the letter, and though he was assured of its *real* character, he never ceased for a succession of weeks to publish it in his paper as genuine; and, if my recollection is aright, he did the same pending the election which eventuated in the elevation of Mr. Findlay to the chief magistracy. From that period till within a few weeks past, I heard no more of the affair, when, having understood it was probable that it might be again brought forward, I determined to expose its real character. The principal persons concerned having passed from this to another world, their names can be of no moment to the present purpose, and with the exception of myself, I believe there is no one living of those concerned in the business. To Mr. Hay it was communicated in the manner already stated, and he saw both the original and the new version, and will no doubt confirm my declaration, that the letter published in the late Mr. Lloyd's paper, and afterwards in that of Mr. Stiles', as the Rev. Dr. Coigley's, *was a fabrication*—and that in the original there is nothing to warrant *any of the insinuations introduced in the spurious letter, which was manufactured* BY MYSELF, and conveyed into the world as above stated.

"Should this statement meet the scope of your note, I shall feel satisfied in contributing to check any attempt to revive an article, my participation in the origin of which has often been a matter of deep regret. In justice to myself, as well as to do you the act of justice requested, I have stated the facts relative to the origin of the letter in question, without any prejudice or resentment against former associates, and remain,

"Respectfully yours,
"L. P. FRANKS."

"CITY OF PHILADELPHIA, ss:

"Lewis P. Franks personally appeared, and being duly sworn according to law, did depose and say that the statement made by him in the above letter is in every particular just and correct, and that he wrote it, uninfluenced by the hope of gain or of reward, solely from a desire to do justice and reveal the truth. The deponent further declares that he has never had any conversation with Mr. John Binns on the subject of the above statement, or any other subject, nor did he ever receive any letter from him, save the one dated September 2d, 1823, to which the above statement is an answer.

"L. P. FRANKS.

"Sworn and subscribed before me this 14th day of November, 1823.

"S. BADGER, *Alderman.*"

LETTER FROM ARTHUR O'CONNOR.

MY DEAR BINNS: When your letter of the 25th of August arrived, I was absent from Paris. On my return, I was seized with a violent rheumatism, which has confined me to my bed. I take the first moment to answer your most kind letter. Never in my life did I see a more atrocious or a more completely unfounded calumny than that which has been so diabolically fabricated against you, and which has been so completely unmasked. I remember most perfectly well the circumstance you mention of Coigley's having told us of the paper that was in his greatcoat pocket, and of its dangerous nature. We had been kept separate from the moment of our arrestation until we arrived at the Bow Street office; there a rumor was spread that the Bow Street officer had lost the pocket-book that was found on one of the prisoners, and when this report reached us, Coigley said: "*I hope in God it is lost, for the paper it contained is of a nature to hang us all,*" and this was the first intimation any of us had of the existence of this paper, a paper which he got Dr. Crossfield to write, and, as I since learned, to give him the means of supporting an intrigue he was engaged in at Paris, on his former visit to France. Never had man less to upbraid his fellow-sufferers with than Coigley, never had sufferers more to upbraid another with than we had this man, for never did a man expose the lives of others more wantonly, or more foolishly, or more unprofitably, than he did ours. You remember when it was known that the priest Griffiths was making Coigley his numerous visits in the prison of Maidstone, you sent to him to know what they could mean, and that he returned you for answer, that was it not for his religious opinions, he would have put an end to his life. It is a justice I owe you to declare, that though you were the victim of Coigley's inconceivable folly, not an act, nor a word of yours, from the beginning to the end of this deplorable affair, that did not bear the character of the most generous loyalty towards that unfortunate man; and such was the firm and manly conduct you maintained, throughout the whole affair, that it was remarked to me by Fox, Sheridan, Grey, and all those who came to visit me in my prison after the trial.

In your letter of August, 1807, you did not say anything of this calumny, which I suppose had no existence until 1809. The letter (Franks's) says it was fabricated in the fall of 1809. On getting your letter, dated from Philadelphia, on the 31st of May, 1811, I instantly answered it in the fullest manner, but I must observe to you, that during the despotism of Bonaparte, the despot had so many thousands employed to prevent a line's leaving hence that could give an idea of the infernal despotism he was exercising in Europe, that it was universally practised to throw the foreign letters into the sea, for fear of the penalties the bearers were exposed to. It is to this I attribute that so many of my letters to my friends in America failed to arrive at their destination.

I am most happy that your fellow-citizens have so well appreciated your merit, and that they have placed their confidence where the most trying proofs have shown that your principles were not to be shaken.

I request you will accept my thanks for the splendid copy you sent me of the Declaration of American Independence. It is the most precious gift a *stanch Republican* can make to his *fellow*. The instant I can get into a carriage, I will carry the other copy, with your letter, to my friend Lafayette.

I am not astonished you should have been basely calumniated by some of our unworthy, intriguing countrymen. I do assure you, I have experienced more treachery, calumny, and vindictive envy and malice from some of these vile, intriguing detractors, than from the most vindictive of our enemies on the side of the Irish and British Government, but I have ever treated them with the contempt they merit. We cannot help ordures to sully the earth, but we are masters to avoid looking on such disgusting objects.

If you see General Devereux, our old and good friend, give my love to him. I send you the inclosed for my excellent and beloved friend Hudson.

Believe me, my dear friend, your ever true and affectionate friend,

A. C. O'CONNOR.

PARIS, 2d Nov. 1828. Rue de Tortoni, No. 6.

[GENERAL DEVEREUX.—The writer would do violence to his own feelings, and injustice to his readers, if he did not embrace the opportunity offered in the letter of General O'Connor, to state a few particulars of General Devereux. He was quite a youth, not of age, when the rebellion of '98 broke out in the counties of Wexford and Wicklow. It never extended beyond those counties, yet the best authorities estimate that eighty thousand perished. Of these, fifty thousand were nearly unarmed rebels, and thirty thousand on the side of England. John Devereux had an estate of about ten thousand dollars a year; carried away by his principles, and the warmth of his heart, in 1798, he put himself at the head of his tenants, and soon found himself a rebel general, at the head of about two thousand men. They were defeated, and the general made prisoner. He was tried by a court-martial, found guilty, and ordered for execution, and his estate confiscated. He was greatly and generally beloved, and the most loyal and influential interested themselves in his favor. They represented his generous interference in behalf of many royalists, who had been taken prisoners, and who, but for his influence and activity, would have suffered death. In consequence of these exertions, the sentence was changed to banishment from the British dominions, and the confiscation of his estate.

He came where all the persecuted and devoted friends of liberty come, to the United States. He settled in Baltimore, where he soon found or made a host of friends. He made some commercial trips as merchant and supercargo to Bolivia, and there soon won the confidence and esteem of General Bolivar. When peace was made in Europe, and Napoleon banished to Elba, General Devereux obtained a general's commission, from President Bolivar, and obtained permission to return to Ireland, to enlist the troops which were then disbanding from the British service, in the service of President Bolivar. He soon after embarked with those troops for Bolivia, and at their head rendered eminent service to the President, who soon after became securely seated in the Presidential chair. The President was not ungrateful; he bestowed upon the general such a portion of a gold mine as made him wealthy for life. I regret to say that, soon after his return to the United States, his sight was so severely affected and endangered, that he went to Paris for advice. He, however, became blind, but went into society, where he was ever cheerful and welcome. He died some years ago. He was as generous and chivalric a soul as ever breathed.]

THE PASSPORT IN 1797.—The treasonable paper, for the having of which in his possession, with the intention to take it to France, the Rev. Mr. Coigley suffered death, purported to be "an Address from the Secret Committee of England to the Executive Directory of France." It stated that the bearer of that address had, on a former occasion, been the bearer of an address of a similar character. I have already mentioned that Mr. Coigley left with me, when he went to Ireland, in November, 1797, the passport under which he had travelled from Paris to Dunkirk, which passport was found in a pocket-book of mine, and was, on the Maidstone trials, admitted as evidence, in consequence of the name of "James Coigley," written upon it, being proved to be in the proper handwriting of the Rev. Mr.

Coigley, then on trial. From the time of my arrest, at Margate, I became sensible how important it was, to me, that the Government should not be able to prove that that passport had ever been in my possession, and, as far as in my power, I endeavored to prevent it from getting into their possession. To effect this, as we were brought prisoners from Margate into London, I sat as forward as I could in the post-chaise, in the hope of catching the eye of some friend who would have the good sense and the friendship to go to my lodgings and carry off my trunks. I was fortunate enough to succeed in my expectation; I saw Mr. Jones, a law-student, in Gray's Inn, who forthwith went to my lodgings and carried off my trunks, of which he retained possession for some time, and prevented the Government from being able to prove that the paper ever had been in my possession. If, when I was a prisoner in the Tower, and the wearing apparel, which had been in the trunk with the pocket-book, in which was the passport, had been received by me *as mine*, instead of being, as they were, repudiated and refused by me, *then* the passport would have been made evidence against me, in the same manner in which the cipher, by which Arthur O'Connor was to correspond with Lord Edward Fitzgerald, was made and admitted as evidence against him by Fugion, one of the Bow St. officers, who swore, on the trial, that while Mr. O'Connor was in the Tower, he, Fugion, took to him, O'Connor, a clothes-bag, in which were some silk stockings, which he, Fugion, took to the Tower to Mr. O'Connor, which stockings Mr. O'Connor received from Fugion as his property, and from one pair of those stockings he, Fugion, had taken a paper which he produced, and which was received in evidence. This paper was a cipher by which O'Connor and Lord Edward Fitzgerald were to correspond when he, O'Connor, should get to France; in the same way would the passport of Coigley have been received and read in evidence, to prove the traitorous confidence between Coigley and me, if I had received the clothes which were sent to me while I was in the Tower, which were in the same trunk with the passport; and thus would cause be given to the jury to infer that I was so thoroughly in the confidence of Coigley, that I doubtless must have been made acquainted with the object of his mission to France, and with the traitorous address of which he was the bearer.

ANOTHER LETTER FROM ARTHUR O'CONNOR.

My Dear Friend: I have just received your esteemed letter of the 10th ult., and hasten to answer it at the instant it has reached me.

I remember having had a letter from you a great many years ago, in which you desire I would contradict a calumny, that some Orangeman only could have uttered, to the purport that you had acted against Coigley. Those who spread then, or now, this odious calumny, must have been wholly ignorant of all that passed at our trial, at Maidstone, for never did the shadow of any fact transpire, on that occasion, which could, by any possible construction, impute to you the most distant intention to injure either Coigley or any one else.

I can, with the utmost truth, attest that it is impossible for any man to have conducted himself with more firmness, or more honor, in every particular, than you did during the whole of the time from our arrestation to our acquittal; and this testimony of your honorable conduct coincides with the opinion which Fox, Sheridan, Grey, and Burdett gave me, when they visited me in prison at Maidstone, the day after the trial; I remember, perfectly, their expressing the greatest praise for the firm and manly manner you had conducted yourself throughout the whole of the trial.

From first to last, you had nothing to do with Coigley, nor can I possibly conceive how any one could invent a calumny against you on the subject.

As far as my testimony can serve to cover your calumniators with shame and confusion, it is yours without the smallest reserve, and so lively an interest do I take in justifying an honorable man from such vile and utterly unfounded calumny, that I request you will regard yourself as perfectly free to make what use you think fit of this letter.

I am heartily rejoiced to hear that fortune has so justly rewarded your excellent qualities, by blessing you with the confidence of your fellow-citizens, and by proving it by the honorable posts you fill, by their choice, and by the prosperity of your numerous family.

It is with deep sorrow I learn, for the first time, by your letter, that my dear friend, Hudson, has been dead so long a time. I knew him well and nearly, and that in times of trying adversity, and never did I know a better or truer hearted man. He was an honor to the country that gave him birth, and to the country that adopted him.

I believe you know I married the only child of the illustrious martyr to French liberty, Condorcet; we had three boys, but have had the misfortune to lose two of them; he that remains, will tread in the steps of his ancestors.

Believe me, my dear Binns,
Your sincerely affectionate friend,
ARTHUR CONDORCET O'CONNOR.
PARIS, Rue de Lille, No. 3, Feb. 21, 1842.

General ARTHUR O'CONNOR expired at his residence, near Montargis, 62 miles from Paris, on the 25th of April, 1852, aged 89 years.

LETTER FROM JOHN BINNS TO ARTHUR O'CONNOR.

PHILADELPHIA.

MY DEAR FRIEND: For very many months I have been anxiously expecting to hear from you. I send you a copy of the letter which I wrote to you at the time it bears date, and forwarded by the Havre packet at that period. I have made many personal inquiries, all of which have been unsatisfactory. As I am now in my 74th year, and as I know you have, as we say in Ireland, the advantage of me, I have not been without apprehensions that you had paid the great debt of nature; I have gone so far as to write to our old friend, Lord Cloncurry, to Ireland, in the hope that he could and would give me some information; from him I have not yet heard. In your last letter to me, you mentioned that you then had but one son; may I not hope that, if you are sick, or unable to write, that that son will write to his father's friend, and relieve his anxieties; I would further hope that, if you have prepared for press, or put to press, any work in relation to your own life, that I may be favored with a copy of it. Attention to these matters will relieve me very much, and lay me under grateful feelings. I address this letter by the address you gave me in 1842, and shall, with deep interest, await the information which I cannot but flatter myself it will bring me.

Make my affectionate respects acceptable to your son, and be assured I am truly, affectionately, and firmly as ever, your friend,

JOHN BINNS.

ARTHUR CONDORCET O'CONNOR, *Rue de Lille, No.* 3, *Paris.*

DANIEL O'CONNELL, ESQ.

[The following letter Mr. O'Connell published in the "London Morning Chronicle," accompanied by his answer, in which he was so far from expressing any regret, that, in his answer, he emptied the hottest phials of his wrath upon the head of the subscriber, and with redoubled bitterness and hatred assailed the people of the United States as "the basest of the base, and the vilest of the vile." It was at that time that the British Government had made up their mind to emancipate their West Indian slaves, because they could not make them pay for their keep, and Daniel O'Connell was allowed to take the lead in the debates in Parliament on that subject, preparatory to receiving an offer of the peerage. Before that time he had denounced the United Irishmen as "weak and wicked," and his son, John O'Connell, had a patent place in the Bank of Ireland, for which he received annually fifteen hundred pounds [$6,000] a year, and is entitled to receive it so long as he shall live. J. B.]

TO THE HON. DANIEL O'CONNELL: 'The attention of the Repeal Association of Philadelphia has been imperatively called to a speech published in the "Dublin Freeman's Journal" of May 11th, 1843, as having been delivered by you, at the Loyal National Repeal Association of Ireland, on the 10th of May, 1843.

In that speech you have, in a bold, manly, and eloquent style, made known your utter detestation of slavery as you believe it to exist in these United States, as well as your indignation and abhorrence of slavery wherever, or by whomsoever countenanced, and poured upon all slaveholders, with no niggard hand, the phial of your hottest wrath.

To these annunciations no objection is offered. It would be against our judgment and principles to presume to interfere with your exercise of the right of freedom of speech, a freedom often exercised by you in defence of the emancipation of the Roman Catholics of Ireland, and which, while it has delighted the hearts of your countrymen in every clime, has carried alarm and terror to the ranks of their enemies. We desire to impress you, sir, with the truth that the Repeal Association in this country is made up principally of Roman Catholics, natives of Ireland, thousands of whom are your grateful and admiring friends. Having established this fact in your mind, allow me to claim for ourselves and fellow repealers the right you claim for yourself—freedom of opinion and of speech.

You, on all proper occasions, make known your loyal attachment to Queen Victoria; your determined resolution to obey the Constitution and laws of Great Britain and Ireland, and your anxious desire to secure the religious freedom of the Catholics of Ireland.

The repealers of this country, who are, nearly all of them, citizens of these United States, and have of course renounced all allegiance and fidelity to any foreign prince, potentate, State or sovereignty, and sworn to support the Constitution of the United States; and we, who are as determined as you are, faithfully to keep our oaths, are not a little mortified at the language you have thought proper to hold, in the speech before alluded to, not only to the great mass of our fellow-citizens, but more especially toward the natives of Ireland resident in the United States.

You declare that the Constitution of the United States, that which we have sworn to support, tolerates slavery, yet in the vehemence of your zeal, you pronounce every man in the United States "a faithless miscreant" who does not take a part to destroy that which our Constitution tolerates and our laws enforce. *Is this toleration?* Is this doing unto others as you would that others should do unto you? Is this doing unto us as we do unto you?

Why, sir, do you thus indiscriminately denounce, as the basest of mankind, hundreds of thousands of Americans, who, with a knowledge of your intolerant zeal on this topic have confided in you and have associated together in this distant land, and done all in their power to give effect to your labors, and emancipate Ireland from the bondage of submission to a foreign legislature. Yet, sir, you seem not content in this general and intemperate denunciation to include the natives of Ireland, but you have been pleased to select and set them apart to endure a furnace ten times hotter than that into which you have cast millions of our fellow-citizens. Our lips would curl with scorn and contempt at the puerile conceit which must inflate the man who should undertake to expatriate and disown, forever, a million of his country people because they did not violate their consciences and their oaths, and walk in the path which their supercilious contemner has chalked out for them.

The Repeal Association here are so satisfied of the honesty of your intentions, that they desire to overlook the blindness of your zeal. They cheerfully grant to you that toleration which you do not seem disposed to grant to them, and notwithstanding your intolerance, they will continue heartily and cheerfully to co-operate with you by all the means in their power, as American citizens, to emancipate Ireland and secure to her a national legislature. All they ask in return is that you will not cast reproach and dishonor on the hospitable land where millions of your country people have found a hearty welcome, and become part and parcel of the people among whom they dwell, and with whom they have married and intermarried, and become as one people. If you do thus cast reproach, you will sink, in our estimation, where fathom line can never reach. To show to you, sir, the facility of admission into our Repeal Association, we add the third article of the Constitution of the Philadelphia Society: "Every person, without regard to national, political or religious denomination, on subscribing to this Constitution and paying the annual sum of one dollar, shall become a member." At a Repeal Convention of the United States, held in this city on the 22d of July, 1842, it was "Resolved that they had no design or desire to interfere, either by action or opinion, in any matter of religion, politics or abolition connected with the social condition or governmental institutions of this country."

These extracts are made that you may be aware how entirely the Repeal Associations here desire to keep clear of every subject but the one, and to throw their gates as wide open as possible to obtain health and strength and means from every point of the compass to assist to accomplish the one thing needful, for which we have associated, a repeal of the legislative union between Ireland and Great Britain. These facts, we trust, will convince you that we ask no forbearance from you which we do not practise ourselves toward you. With our best wishes for your health and happiness in the unity and indivisibility of a great and good cause, with esteem, gratitude and respect,

YOUR WELL WISHERS.

CHAPTER XVI.

Church affairs—Intolerance—Selfishness rebuked—The question put—The old Congress in 1775—Hints to immigrants—Roman Catholic discipline—State of our music—Customs and manners—A reflection—Death of my wife—A death-bed scene.

CHURCH AFFAIRS.

It was not until after I had been some years in Philadelphia, that I became a regular member of a Christian church. It was about the year 1812, my wife and I were in the usual manner admitted members of the United Brethren's Church, in Race Street. That place of worship was one of the first five Christian churches which had been erected in Philadelphia. It was very small, and peculiarly constructed. It had a small steeple, and its internal arrangement was much smaller, and of a more primitive character than the one which in 1812 was erected on the ground where the old church stood. At that time, on the corner of Race and Bread Street, was a very large dwelling-house for the pastor and his family. That house was also taken down in 1812, and a smaller house for the same purpose erected in its place. All the buildings erected in 1812 have followed the fate of those which had been built early the preceding century—they had been previously sold by the church, and the elders, with the approbation of the members, purchased a building lot on the rear of their burying-ground, on Vine, Wood, and Franklin Streets. Some time after I had become reunited to the Moravian Church, I had, at one time, seven of my children baptized in it. It was an unusual sight, and the church was very much crowded.

The Moravian Church members, like those of the Society of Friends, the Methodists, and other Protestant churches, are in nowise so primitive as they were in my early days. They are none of them so plain in their dress, or primitive in their language or their manners. They have all conformed more to the world and its ways, than the world has conformed to them and their ways. *Quære.* Is not the world now as much in advance of these several sectarians as it was when these sectarians were most simple and primitive?

It may be doubted whether Friend Penn and Brothers Zinzendorff or Wesley would not now pass their followers without knowing or being known by them.

INTOLERANCE.

It may be well, so far as in my power, to note the progress of intolerance, and the effects consequent upon the desire of individuals, and combinations and associations of individuals to exclude other individuals and classes of citizens constitutionally qualified, from public offices or influence, to the end that they, the exclusionists, might the more certainly secure to themselves the offices and the influence from which they labored to exclude others. This shall be done as truly and as briefly as I can do it. It cannot fail to be observed that this desire to engross offices is not chargeable upon any particular party, but has gathered strength from all of them. Nothing but a union of honest and intelligent men of all parties will be able to prostrate the evils which have arisen, and will hereafter arise, from the desire of certain men and associations of men to monopolize the offices of the Union, the States, and Corporations.

In the year 1837-8, the writer was called upon by a committee of five—the late Joseph Diamond was their chairman. They were all natives of Ireland, and naturalized citizens of the United States. Their object was to state that for some time past a majority of the Democratic delegates to select candidates for office in the County of Philadelphia had refused to place on their ticket any naturalized citizen for any office whatever—that the Irish voters, to induce their fellow democrats to see the folly and injustice of this exclusive conduct, had determined to absent themselves from the poll. At their request, I drew up, and they published 5,000 copies of the following paper:—

"*Whereas*, The Constitution and laws of the United States all recognize, and are based upon an acknowledgment of the equal rights of every citizen, there is no privilege of any kind, no right whatever, which does not equally and as strongly attach to the naturalized as to the native citizen, save only the eligibility to two offices in the United States; and all burdens, taxes, and duties are equally imposed: We, the members of this Association, desire to perpetuate and carry out these constitutional principles and rights; and we cannot regard as a good citizen any man who would proscribe, and, so far as in his power, disfranchise any portion of his fellow-citizens; but more especially for an act over which they never had any control, nor as to which they never were, nor never could have been consulted—to wit, the place of their birth.

"The subscribers to this association have seen, with deep and unaffected regret, an evil and a proscriptive spirit growing up in our country, and seen it fed and cherished by influential politicians. We would wish to be distinctly understood that we do not complain of politicians of this party or of that party; we are of all parties, and represent the evil as it exists, without regard to any party, or to the influence which the facts we state may have upon party. Every party, all parties are willing to allow us to serve in the ranks, but no party is willing to permit us to wear even a worsted shoulder-knot.

"The subscribers to this association are natives of Ireland; of that island whose inhabitants have, from the dawn of the Revolution to this hour, at all times, and on all occasions, manifested affectionate respect and devoted attachment to these United States. Hundreds of thousands of her sons and daughters have left their homes, 'yea, where they were born,' the hearths of their youths, and the tombs of their fathers, to become inhabitants of this country. Hundreds of thousands of them have taken the oath of citizenship; how far they have proved themselves worthy, it is not for them to publish; yet they may be permitted to appeal to the war of the Revolution and the war of 1812, and to the American State papers and statesmen of those periods, as evidence that their countrymen did not dishonor the land of their adoption. There are no men more proud of being American citizens than the natives of Ireland; no men more proud to exercise the rights, and, they trust, not indifferent to the discharge of the duties which, as citizens, they have proudly and joyfully imposed upon themselves; they have been especially vigilant and faithful to exercise the right of suffrage. No matter what may be the party to which we have attached ourselves, we have been zealous and active to promote its principles and to advance into places of honor and profit the men who profess them.

"It is with sincere concern that we make known the fact that very many of these men who have been thus elevated by our zeal and our votes, are, when the election is over, nowise slow to turn scornfully upon their heel when spoken to by an Irishman, and to sneer at him and at the land of his nativity. If a native of Ireland, who has resided for a quarter or half a century in this country, conducted himself irreproachably, raised a large family with credit, and is of acknowledged talents, shall be named for a public station, then will these same public functionaries to whom we have alluded, and their minions, having nothing to say reproachful of the Irishman who is named for station, cast slanders upon the country of his birth and his countrymen.

"These wrongs, often wantonly inflicted, have wounded us deeply, and at length compelled us, in self-defence, and in defence of our own characters, and that of our country and our countrymen, to adopt a resolution no longer to consume our time and spend our money to elevate to office men who take a pleasure in speaking disrespectfully of us and of our nation. The course we propose to take is the least offensive, yet, we trust, not the least efficient, we can at this time devise. We will not only not go to any election, general or special, but we will not permit our names to be used as candidates for any office, or as committeemen to promote the election of any person or persons whatsoever; and we shall, and do earnestly recommend the same course of conduct to all our naturalized countrymen. When the wrongs, and the contumely, and the disrespect and injustice which have been heaped upon us shall be removed, and our fellow-citizens shall become sensible that we know and feel what is right, 'and knowing dare maintain,' then, *but not till then*, we shall be happy again cordially to unite with those of our fellow-citizens whose political principles are congenial with our own, and to go with them to the polls, and again cast our votes into the ballot-boxes. It is quite certain that for one year from this time we pledge ourselves not to vote at any election, and also to do all in our power to dissuade our friends and fellow-countrymen from voting.

"We know, and for many years have felt, the injustice which has been done us. We know the just cause we have for resentment, and we are not ignorant of our strength and ability to make the authors of these wrongs feel that we are not such dolts or blocks as to be proscribed and injured, and insulted, and trodden upon, and to continue to lick the feet uplifted to spurn us, because the wrongdoer thinks he may trample upon us with impunity. We will not invigorate the arms, and put lashes into the hands of our would-be taskmasters. We will, at least for a season, quietly withdraw ourselves from political contests, and, if defeat should follow, let those whose injustice and proscription have been the cause, be blamed for the consequence. If the spoils belong to the victors, why should we, among the most ardent on the battle-ground, and among the most attached of our fellow-citizens to the country, the Constitution, and the laws, and we alone, be prohibited from all share, and even insulted, if we shall presume to be claimants?"

The consequence of this determination was, as was expected—the great majority of the naturalized Irish being Democrats—their political opponents carried all the elective offices so long as the grievance complained of was inflicted. It was therefore removed, the pledge not to vote was abandoned, and the native and naturalized citizens united, and became, as they forever ought to be, a united party.

I now approach a period in which, I will not say that men associated, but they certainly gathered together, and inflicted deep and deadly injuries on the persons and properties of their neighbors and fellow-men; not, as it would seem, from personal or political hostility, but because they professed and believed in a different form of worship from the wrong-doers. It was acknowledged, it could not be denied, that those who inflicted the wrong, and those upon whom it was inflicted, acknowledged and worshipped the same God, and bowed their heads and bent their knees to the same Redeemer. But it was complained that they did not do it in the same manner, and for this cause the one party would destroy the party and take the lives of the others, and burn down their houses and places of worship, and cause the gutters and common-sewers of our streets to flow with the life-blood of their fellow-citizens.

We read that, in the early days of the church, the Christian world waged a bloody and destructive war, because one portion of its members would make the sign of the cross with *two* fingers, and the others insisted upon making it with *three*. In the same spirit the Spanish artists had a long and angry dispute as to whether the number of nails used in the crucifixion was three or four.

These acts, however wicked and barbarous, were the doings of an ignorant and savage people, whereas we live in an enlightened age, in a country where education is more general than it ever has been in any age or country of the world. The following reflections were written soon after the writer saw the roof of St. Augustine's church fall, where thousands of the worshippers of the Almighty had bowed down in humble adoration:—

REFLECTIONS ON RECENT EVENTS.

"Therefore all things whatsoever ye would that men should do to you, do ye even so to them: for this is the law and the prophets."

Within twenty years, a fearful pestilential disease passed over Asia, sweeping before it, with the besom of death, not less than sixty millions of human beings. The destroying angel then passed over Europe, consigning hundreds of thousands of men, women, and children, to their silent graves. We "the People of these United States," awaited its approach with humble resignation; yet, with "a firm reliance on Divine Providence," making such preparations as prudence and experience pointed out. At that awful period, a minister of the Gospel, in the city of Philadelphia, who had a large house and school-house adjoining, caused to be removed out of them every article of furniture which could be dispensed with, and converted the whole building into an hospital. He had it admirably arranged, fitted up with all the necessaries, and supplied with fearless and tender nurses; women, religiously devoted to the faithful discharge of their duties. I was acquainted with this benevolent individual; he was an Irishman and a Catholic. Although we thought widely different on many religious subjects of much moment, yet we worshipped the *same* God, and we adored the *same* Redeemer. I was, by him invited, and walked all over this new establishment for cholera patients. "The whitewashed walls, and the nicely sanded floors," exhibited its cleanliness and neatness. A plentiful supply of medicine and everything required, was provided. There were sedan chairs, with spring poles, of the easiest possible construction, to convey patients to this asylum, from wherever they might be found, in want of care, skill, and medicine. It was so judiciously adapted to the purposes to which it was devoted; its doors were thrown so hospitably wide open, and its superintendent was so intent on doing good, that many patients were collected within its walls. I examined the records. The whole number of patients was three hundred and seventy, of all ages and sexes. Of these, according to my best recollection and information, sixty-three were Catholics, and three hundred and seven were Protestants.

Having no faith, myself, in the infectious nature of the disease, I went through the rooms, and, "while memory holds her seat," I never can forget the impression made upon me by the affectionate solicitude of all who were in attendance on the sick. There are hundreds, now in this city, who have, more or less, knowledge of the intense and anxious care and untiring solicitude, with which the poor and the afflicted were there watched over, by night and by day. Many a parent, husband and wife were, through the instrumentality of that hospital, restored to their afflicted families.

This immense amount of good could not be done without attracting public notice, however unobtrusive and retiring might be the beings who dispensed these blessings. It not only commanded general attention, but the constituted authorities of the city, on the restoration of health, felt it their duty to tender amends for the expense incurred, and, as far as possible, for the eminent services rendered. All pecuniary remuneration was absolutely, and at once, promptly declined. The thanks of our City Councils were modestly accepted.

I would that I could here end my narrative: I feel, however, impelled to state what was the fate of the buildings which had thus been devoted to charitable purposes.

They had been a religious establishment, and near at hand was a church, dedicated to Almighty God. In that church, the regular inmates of this establishment daily performed Divine service. I have seen that church, and these houses—all that remains of them—within an hour of this time; they are soul-saddening ruins! Nothing of them remains but smoked and blackened walls!! Not a particle of wood, or any combustible substance, remains unconsumed!!! This deed was done, not by a foreign foe; not by an invading army; not by a tribe of savage Indians. No! it was done by that same people who, in the days of their calamity, when pestilence walked abroad in their streets, and carried away their relatives and friends—and who, within a few years, had been received and comforted, and healed and made sound, under the shelter of the very roofs which they have destroyed. The altar, before which millions had bowed down and worshipped the living God, has been consumed by fire! It is reduced to ashes, which are momently scattered abroad by the winds of heaven. The noble organ, which so often had warmed the hearts of a Christian people with love to their Redeemer; the melody of which had ascended in praises to the throne of the Triune God—is annihilated—not an atom of it can be found; every morsel of it has been devoured by the fierceness of the flames. The church bell, which for half a century had been suspended over that hall which is our city's pride, and which first proclaimed Independence to these United States, which had been attached to this church clock, was striking ten—"I felt the solemn sound, as if an angel spoke"—but it was quickly enveloped in the flames and silenced forever! Soon, the fire encompassed the steeple round about, and brought to the earth, in fragments, the most renowned and universal emblem of our holy religion —the sacred cross.

The surrounding churchyard, which should be the resting-place of the dead, is in sad confusion—the graves recklessly trampled under foot—the tombstones broken and defaced, and the urn, in which some pious Christians had enshrined the heart of their pastor, is cast down.

"Father, forgive them, for they know not what they do," were among the last words of Him, who, for a sinful world, perished on the cross—of that crucified Saviour, for whose garments the soldiers cast lots. May no heavy visitation overtake our city, for the sins of our people; but may their sins, and our sins, be mercifully forgiven!!! [J. B.]

PHILADELPHIA, May 10, 1844.

The men who at that time massacred their fellow-men, and burned their private property, and their buildings erected for the worship of the Creator, appear now in a kindlier form, animated by more human feelings. They seem no longer to be moved by a desire to destroy life or property. All they now insist upon is that no naturalized citizen, nor Roman Catholic, native or naturalized, shall hold any office or appointment under the United States, the States, or Municipal authorities. One of those authorities has avowed his determination to act upon those principles, and obey the behests of those self-appointed rulers of the land. This example, it is believed, will have little influence with men who know and respect the law.

Even this state of things is better, much better—yea, beyond all names of improvement better—than the days of 1844; and having taken up the march of improvement, who shall stay them? They may be glutted with offices, even to suffocation, and thus turn from them. Although this change is admitted to be an improvement, it is still a wretched and lamentable state of things in the only country under heaven where the rights of conscience are constitutionally guaranteed to all its inhabitants, and where such is the liberality of the mass of the people, that the creed a man professes has never been inquired after, even when he is a candidate for President of the United States. The people have elected fourteen chief magistrates, yet at no election has an inquiry been instituted as to the creed of any of the candidates. So entirely has the sectarian creed of candidates been uninquired after, that there is not a man in a thousand who, if called upon, could tell what was the creed of our elected chief magistrates.

Since the above was written, a flood of light has been shed on what is called KNOW-NOTHINGISM. Its oaths, its objects, and its organization are all, without any holding back, laid before the public. Its oaths are such as would become a band of conspirators, or a den of robbers—its object, to seize upon the public offices of the United States, the States and corporations, at the expense of truth, and to the manifest injury of all who do not join them, even though their union should sap and break down all the acknowledged obligations of religion and good conscience. Its organization is based upon disgraceful bonds, which can be binding only so long as the slave who wears them is content to despise and trample under foot the most sacred laws. No man can be a member of that society who is not determined, when sworn in a court of law, to disregard every legal tie which in any way shall interfere with the oaths they have taken as Know-nothingarians.

It may not be irrelevant to ask the citizens of Pennsylvania if they have forgotten that some twenty-five years ago all the high places in their State were filled by those who held it to be in a high degree criminal to belong to a secret society. Now, there is a disposition to fall at the feet of those who are banded together by unconstitutional oaths. Do they remember when anti-masonry was the ruling political creed, and our governor and other high officers were all anti-masons?

Anti-masonry has had its day, and been doomed to destruction. It will be the same with KNOW-NOTHINGISM, and its members will be ashamed to own it, and will join in the hue and cry against it and its followers.

My opinion is, that this new secret society, bound and kept together by illegal oaths, will have a ruinous influence upon the Whig party. The love of office, and the hope of obtaining it, will induce many active men among them to join the Know-Nothings, but those who are Whigs from attachment to the principles of the party will not band themselves with men, who, for the sheer love of office, take oaths against the peace and dignity of the Commonwealth.

SELFISHNESS REBUKED.

Soon after the inauguration of Gov. Snyder, in 1808, I was sitting with him in a room at his lodgings at Bausman's Tavern, in Lancaster. The room was up stairs, and the time evening, when the waiter entered, and said: "There are some gentlemen below stairs who desire to speak with the governor." "Tell them to walk up," said the governor. In a few minutes seven well-dressed persons entered the room. The foremost of them said: "We wish to speak with the governor on a matter of business." The governor made answer: "I have no objection that my friend, Mr. Binns, should hear anything you may wish to say to me, or anything I may have to say in answer." The person in advance then said: "We are all the applicants for the public offices in Chester County, except Charles Kenny; he is an Irishman. We have waited upon your Excellency to say that we shall be quite satisfied, and shall zealously support your administration, whosoever you may appoint, except Charles Kenny; we know that his appointment would be very unpopular in the county." The governor bowed, and made answer: "I shall consider, gentlemen, what you have said." The gentlemen applicants bowed respectfully, and retired. The governor turned promptly toward me, and said: "That's a selfish combination against an absent individual, and I shall appoint Kenny." He did appoint him Clerk of the Orphan's Court for Chester County, and he was as good an officer, and as acceptable an appointment as any he made in the county.

THE QUESTION PUT.

I do not recollect from whom I had the following statement, but I feel certain I had it from good authority: When the war of 1812 was declared, the then Secretary at War, Gen. Dearborn, made a contract with one of the Messrs. Dupont, of Wilmington, for gunpowder. At that time those gentlemen were the only extensive manufacturers of that article in the Union. The contract being completed, Gen. Dearborn, who was something of what is now called a Know-nothing, said to Mr. Dupont, who was a French gentleman: "My only regret in making this contract is, that I have been obliged to make it with a foreigner." "Pray, sir," said Mr. Dupont, "may I ask where were you born?" "Sir," said the general, "I was born in Boston." "Then, sir, you were not consulted as to your coming, and you came naked and helpless. I came of my own choice; I brought a sound mind and body, and the information and capital I had acquired, and have thus been enabled to establish the manufacture of an article of the first necessity. To which of us, sir, do you think the country is most indebted?"

THE OLD CONGRESS IN 1775.

I feel, as a native of Ireland, much gratitude to the men who, by their wisdom, their perseverance, and their valor, achieved the independence of "these United States," for the peculiar friendliness with which they, at all times, spoke of the people, yea, even of the Parliament of Ireland, and the promptitude with which they made known their zeal in the cause of America. At that time, and at all times since, the Irish have been prompt to gather round and defend the Star-Spangled Banner. I submit a few paragraphs from the address of the men of '76.

"As the important contest, into which we have been driven, is now become interesting to every European State, and particularly affects the members of the British Empire, we think it our duty to address you on the subject. We are desirous, as is natural to injured innocence, of possessing the good opinion of the virtuous and humane. We are peculiarly desirous of furnishing *you* with a true state of our motives and objects, the better to enable *you* to judge of our conduct with accuracy, and determine the merits of the controversy with impartiality and precision."

"Permit us to assure you that it was with the utmost reluctance, we could prevail upon ourselves to cease our commercial connection with your island. *Your* Parliament had done us no wrong. *You* had ever been friendly to the rights of mankind; and we acknowledge with pleasure and gratitude that *your* nation has produced patriots who have nobly distinguished themselves in the cause of humanity and *America*. We were not ignorant that the labor and manufactures of *Ireland*, like those of the silkworm, were of little moment to herself, but served only to give luxury to those who *neither toil nor spin*. We perceived that, if we continued our commerce with you, our agreement not to import from Britain would be fruitless, and were, therefore, compelled to adopt a measure, to which nothing but absolute necessity would have reconciled us. It gave us, however, some consolation to reflect that should it occasion much distress, the fertile regions of America would afford you an asylum from poverty, and in time from oppression also; an asylum in which many thousands of your countrymen have found hospitality, peace, and affluence, and become united to us by all the ties of consanguinity, mutual interest, and affection."

"Accept our most grateful acknowledgments for the friendly disposition you have always shown towards us. We know that you are not without your grievances. We sympathize with you in your distress, and are pleased to find that the design of subjugating us, has persuaded the administration to dispense to Ireland some vagrant rays of ministerial sunshine. Even the tender mercies of government have long been cruel towards you. In the rich pastures of Ireland, many hungry parricides have fed and grown strong to labor in its destruction. We hope the patient abiding of the meek may not always be forgotten; and God grant that the iniquitous schemes of extirpating liberty from the British Empire may be soon defeated."

HINTS TO IMMIGRANTS.

Immigrants, even those who come to the United States from principle, and a warm attachment to its constitutional provisions, insuring to them the free exercise of their religious, civil, and political rights, must expect, for many years after their arrival here, to grieve for the loss of the friends, and the want of the companions of their youth, and the friends of their riper years. Much time must pass away, new friends, nay, new relatives and kindred, must gather round them before they can cease regretfully to think of the playmates and the playgrounds, associated with the remembrance of the firesides round which they knelt, and prayed, and sported, and of the graves over which they had often wept. When many of those recollections have faded, and those whom the immigrant loved, and left in health, have sunk into their silent graves, even then, the remembrance of the mother-country and the father-land will cling to their hearts, and they will continue to feel a warm interest in the welfare of the old country! I feel it now, after an absence of more than half a century.

The love of country, at all times, in all nations, ancient or modern, savage or civilized, is universally and deeply implanted in the human heart, and its dictates as universally obeyed. In proportion to the ardor with which the love of country burns in the bosom of an immigrant, will become, in time, his love and attachment to the country by which he has been adopted.

> Ah! nowhere is the rose so red,
> And nowhere is the thorn so small,
> And nowhere is the down so soft,
> As those our childhood rested on.

ROMAN CATHOLIC DISCIPLINE.

About twelve years ago, an old woman who had long resided in the family of Mr. Hollahan, on Chestnut St., announced her intention of going to see her relations in Ireland, to whom she proposed taking what money she had saved, and then returning to the family with whom she had so long and so comfortably lived. She took and paid her passage to Ireland. A few days before the vessel in which she had engaged passage was to sail, she came to my office, in much trouble. She complained that she had put away, in what she thought a safe place, a leather bag in which were nearly four hundred dollars—the money she had saved to take to her poor people in Ireland, and that somebody had discovered and stolen it. After some conversation, I found that the old woman suspected the girl who had come to take her place of having stolen the money, and had charged her with the theft, which she bitterly denied. I gave the old woman the best advice I could, and she went home. The next morning she, and the girl she suspected, came to my office; the girl asked to be sworn, to the end that she might swear that she had no knowledge of the missing money, nor had ever seen it. I refused to swear her, on the ground that if she had been rogue enough to steal the money, she would be knave enough on oath to deny it. The old woman came over again to know what she should do. I then found the women were both Roman Catholics, and I advised the old woman to go and make her complaint, and take the advice of the priest. She did so, and the next day she got back her bag and her money, and took them, in a few days, to the old country.

There was a case of a very different character came to my knowledge, connected with the Catholic clergy, showing the inconvenience, not to say hardships, to which they are occasionally subjected. As I have good reason to believe in the truth of the whole statement, I commit it to paper in the hope that it may prevent scenes of a like character. A few years before the death of the Rev. Mich'l Hurley, when he was pastor of St. Augustine's Church, he was called up one stormy night, by one of his people, who came through a deep snow, and assured the priest that Paddy Murphy was in a dying condition, and sadly anxious that Father Hurley should see him before he died. It was in vain the priest represented his own delicate health, and the inclemency of the weather; nothing would do but he must forthwith do his duty, and go to the sick man who was said to be at the point of death. He only lives, said the messenger, in Vine St., above Eleventh. "Go," said Father Hurley, "and I will follow you immediately." Accordingly he put on as much clothing as he could, to shield him from the severity of the weather. It was snowing fast, and there were at least eighteen inches of snow on the ground when the good Father set out. He had made his way as far as Vine Street, between Eighth and Ninth Streets, when he heard a loud voice crying out: "Is that you, Father Hurley? I'm got better, you may go home. God bless you, Father Hurley." He returned home covered with snow, and perishing with cold.

STATE OF OUR MUSIC.

In 1807, and for the five following years, at the Democratic celebrations of the 4th of July, at the Wigwam in Spring Garden, near Sixth Street, the Committee of Arrangement obtained from Col. Miller, then in command at the Philadelphia Navy Yard, permission for the United States fifer and drummer, at that station, to play for the dinner party on that day. The fifer was quite deaf, yet I never heard the Dead March more effectually or correctly played than by that fifer and drummer. They were, *at that time*, the only public musicians in Philadelphia; now (1854), there are not less than sixty public bands of music.

The first musical celebration which arrested public attention, in the United States, was one in Philadelphia in St. Augustine's Church. It was got up about A. D. 1820, under the direction and superintendence of the Rev'd Dr. Hurley, the pastor of the church, and Messrs. Carr and Schitky, well known and respected teachers of music. The trombones, and those who played them, came from Bethlehem, and there were many other musicians and amateurs on that occasion from Philadelphia and other parts of the United States. The object of the pastor, which was accomplished, was to raise funds with which to erect an altar and to paint and embellish the church. The church, at the festival, was very full, and the vocal and instrumental music gave general satisfaction. It must be five-and-thirty years since that musical celebration.

Some years before that oratorio, that church had been built, under the superintendence of the Rev'd Dr. Carr, who had obtained a law authorizing a lottery to raise the funds for that purpose. There were other churches, not a few, in this State built, or the building of them much assisted, by money raised by lotteries. Public opinion, like that of individuals, fluctuates. March 1, 1833, the Legislature of Pennsylvania passed an act, the first section of which is in these words: "All and every lottery and lotteries, and device and devices, in the nature of lotteries, shall be utterly and entirely abolished, and are hereby declared to be unauthorized and unlawful."

CUSTOMS AND MANNERS.

Many well-informed, well-educated persons, male and female, who have published travels in the United States, have paid deserved compliments to the men of America for their uniform attention and respectful politeness to the women. I regret that the attentions thus praised do not appertain to all ranks of our men. We do not see so much attention paid by the working men of America as is paid in some other countries. We do not so often, as elsewhere, see these men and their wives and children walk out together, nor are there suitable places, at convenient distances from the city, for their recreation. In the environs of London there are innumerable houses of refreshment within from three to ten miles or more from the city. At these houses tea, coffee, cakes, &c. may be had at the shortest possible notice. To such houses mechanics and laboring men, with their wives and children, resort in great numbers. Not so frequently a man and his wife and children, as two or three neighboring families, who make parties and walk out or go in stages, of which there are an immense number, at low prices. The stages run every day, not excepting Sundays, from morning till night; on Sundays, a greater number of stages run than on any other day, except on holidays, of which there are many more kept in England than in the United States.

When a stage arrives at its destination, it is, with all expedition, discharged of its passengers, baskets and other lumber. The men attending to the baskets, and the women to the children. The women take tea, coffee, &c., and the men wine, cider, spirituous or malt liquors, and indulge in tobacco. There are many more women in Great Britain who take snuff to comfort their noses than there are in the United States, but I never beheld any women there indulge in the luxury of chewing tobacco or snuff, as do some of the ladies in our neighboring State of Delaware.

Horseflesh, of the better kind, is not so much in demand for pleasure or display in the vicinity of London, in proportion to population, as in that of Philadelphia. It is estimated, and I do not think it an over estimate, that on the Wissahickon road, not less than 2,000 pleasure-carriages and horses stop at two hotels on a fine afternoon in the summer season. There are other places in the vicinity of Philadelphia at which, if a stranger were to stop, he would suppose that nearly all the pleasure-horses and carriages in Philadelphia were there. There are many beautiful rides round this city, the roads are well made, kept in good order, of an accommodating width, and well fenced. These are temptations to use them.

In London, you may dine at eating-houses, taverns, or hotels at from three-pence [6 cents] to a guinea, at certain places at stated hours. Dinner, at most of these places, is set on the table at certain established hours, and at a certain price. At many of them the landlord presides. There is much freedom of speech allowed at all these places. I remember dining at an ordinary near the Strand, dinner one shilling and sixpence [30 cents]. The cloth being removed, such persons as chose called for a pipe, tobacco, and something to drink. The conversation was generally on public affairs and the news of the day. The person at the head of the table gave as a toast, "The King," which being drunk, he called upon the person at the foot of the table for a toast; "I will give you, said he, "Jack Ketch." There was a pause, when the person at the head of the table said: "That's an extraordinary toast." "Not at all," said the other; "I only carry out your toast; you gave the first executive officer, the king, and I gave the last executive officer, Jack Ketch." Nothing more was said on the subject. M. de Tocqueville, in his work on America, remarks that he was surprised to find in the United States so little of the conversation at public tables devoted to political affairs, or to the canvassing the principles and conduct of public men. He imputes this forbearance from these topics to the very general interest felt in the election of public officers, and to the number of candidates which are generally to be voted for. This reservedness not only arises, in his opinion, from a desire to avoid giving offence by any harshness of language against parties or individuals before the public for office, and thus making enemies who would remember those expressions to the injury of the individual who had uttered them, who might himself at some future time be nominated for office, and wish to conciliate all the voters he could.

There are, for several miles round London, many ordinaries, at which dinner is served at a certain hour, and at a certain price. The hour and the price are usually set forth on painted boards, to inform and to invite customers. I have heard it frequently asserted, and believe, there are men who live upon the activity and capacity of their appetites and stomachs. Thus, when the dinner is over at one of those ordinaries, and the price collected, a man who has dined and paid, will go to the bar and address the landlord in language like this: "I walk out this way very often, and dine at places on the roadside. I don't know how it has happened that I never dined at your table before; I like it very much, and shall frequently call and take dinner with you." The landlord having observed what a gourmand this man was, eating not only ravenously but selecting the dearest dishes to feed from, becomes rather alarmed at the thought of such a constant customer, and taking him aside, says: "There's a capital ordinary, same price as mine, half a mile further on the road; if you pass my house, I will make it worth your while to eat dinner there." The landlord and his customer soon understand one another, and come to terms; the landlord, for a certain sum paid to the gourmand, buying him off for the season. Thus some men make a living by being bought off by a number of landlords. I was so frequently, by men entitled to credit, told of the above arrangement being made, that I never doubted that it was extensively made on all the roads near London.

A REFLECTION.

I do not think I have ever done a generous, a charitable, or a kind act, no, not even from my boyish days, for which I have not been richly repaid by the after reflections of my own mind, and the warm glow of approbation of my own heart. I doubt, however, whether the reverse of this proposition be true. Surely I have done things I ought not to have done, for the doing of which I cannot say I have repented. Such a state of mind does not give birth to a proper state for prayer and humiliation. I am not aware that the things which have thus been done, and which I now think would have been better left undone, were, in my judgment, of such a nature as to injure others; nor am I aware that they did injure others. They were, however, for the most part, breaches of Divine law, and as such, required repentance. It is probable that if my most secret thoughts and actions were laid open to others, as they are to the omniscient eye of an all-seeing Providence, the judgment passed upon them would be in nowise so mild as that which the offender himself passes upon them.

DEATH OF MY WIFE.

Early in the year 1852, or rather late in the year 1851, the health of my wife became so delicate and alarming, as soon after to require the constant attendance of a physician. She had a bedstead put up in the room over my office. Our usual bedroom was one story higher than that where she had herself now located. Before these arrangements were made, very nearly about the same time, I had an attack of gout in both my feet, of a very painful character, which continued for eight weeks, without intermission. It was necessary to procure a cot, and to make it up every night in my office for me to sleep on. I sat at my desk all day, transacting whatever business was brought before me, in an easy-chair, on rollers. I was obliged to sit sideways to my desk, as both my legs had to be elevated to rest on pillows which ranged with the desk and seat of my chair; at night I was rolled, in the chair, to the cot, into which it was necessary I should be lifted every night, and from which, every morning, I had to be lifted into my chair, rolled to my desk, and placed as I had been the day before.

I could hear the movements in the chamber above me, from which, and the information I received, I conjectured the state of my wife's health. In the four weeks she was confined to the room over me, she had herself once a week been carried down to my room, sat by my side, talked with me a few minutes, and was then carried up to her sick chamber. Every visit she thus paid me I was more and more persuaded that she would not much longer be spared to be a blessing and a comfort to me, and to her children. Her daughter —her only daughter, Matilda, now came and tenderly watched over her by day and by night, until it pleased God to beckon her hence. So soon as my wife directed her usual bedroom to be put in order, that she might be removed to it, we who most dearly loved her apprehended, nay, greatly feared, that she was desirous to be removed to that room, there to die.

I was several times carried up to the room where she lay resigned to the will of her heavenly Father; she passed away so gently that even her daughter, on the bed with her, did not know the point of time she died. She had been, for more than six-and-forty years, my faithful, loving, and confiding wife. How, then, could it be otherwise than that she should be mourned over with the deepest sorrow? On the fourth day after her death, the funeral service was said, and sung, and joined in by members of the congregation, and by those who crowded the house from top to bottom. I was wholly unable to use my feet; the weather was very cold; I was warmly clad, and carried from room to room, and from place to place, until I saw her remains deposited in the silent tomb.

My son, having purchased a farm in Delaware, was,

with his family, obliged to remove to that State, and my daughter, having her own house and family to attend to, I should, on the death of my wife, and from my own situation with gout, have been left in a rather helpless state, had I not at that time, and for some years before, had in my employ a woman of industrious habits and good principles. She remains with me, and I have had no reason to think I have overrated her value.

A DEATH-BED SCENE.

Last night, September 27, 1854, as I was going up stairs to bed, my old friend, Mrs. Mary Caldwell, came into the house and said: "I am going up to Race Street, to sit up with Mary Hannah Geyer; she is very low, indeed. The holy sacrament was administered to her yesterday." I retired to bed, and there long thought on the condition of my poor sick grandchild, whom I had not seen for more than five years, whose mother was dead; she and her brother Charles, now a young man, and their younger sister, Georgiana, were living with their father and stepmother. I did not know this lady, but had always heard her spoken of as an affectionate and kind mother over her husband's children. I determined, early in the morning, to visit Mary Hannah. Having ascertained the house, I went in, and was soon introduced to Mrs. Geyer. I made known my name and business, and was kindly welcomed. "Indeed, Mr. Binns," said she, "I am very glad you are come. Yesterday I mentioned to Mr. Geyer that I thought we ought to send for you, our poor child is so anxious to see you. She is very sick. I will go and tell her you are here." She went to the sick-chamber, but soon returned, and I went back with her. On entering the room, my eyes turned to the bed on which lay the deathly-pale child. She put her hands towards me; I took them tenderly in mine, and gently pressed my lips to hers. "I am so glad to see you, grandfather; I love you; but I must leave you. I am ready to go to my Redeemer, and to my own mother." It took her some minutes to utter these words. I was unable to speak. She said: "I must go to my own mother." I put my hand on Mrs. Geyer's frock, and looked kindly from her to the child. She understood me, and said: "She is very good; but I am ready to go to my own mother." I was deeply affected. Mrs. Geyer, in the gentlest tone and kindest manner, said: "She is so gentle, resigned, and affectionate, that she reminds me often of her mother." I was fearful that my longer staying in the room would only oppress the child. I stooped, put my lips gently to hers, and said: "Farewell; I will come again." "You must come soon, then; I shall not stay long here; I will go to my own mother." She turned her eyes toward me, and pressed my hand. I turned from her, and between me and the door was my gentle Georgy, with her hand extended and her lips upraised. I kissed her affectionately, and she said: "Good-by, grandfather."

This scene has called up many remembrances of my first-born child, the mother of these children. I returned home, but with little hope to see Mary Hannah again before she departs this life. I have, indeed, no hope that she will ever be able to rise out of the bed on which she is lying.

It has just struck five o'clock; a young man enters the office, and says: "Mr. Binns, my mother sent me to tell you Mary Hannah died at ten minutes before two o'clock."

Never did a human being die more perfectly resigned, or with a firmer conviction that she was about to enter upon a life of never-ending felicity. Amen, and so be it.

Since the foregoing Recollections have gone to press, I have found the Memoir of Governor Snyder, which is there mentioned. It is altogether in his own proper handwriting. It is very brief, but it is truly characteristic of the writer. I give it word for word, as he gave it to me; not doubting but it will be most acceptable. I received the Memoir, of which the following is a copy, from Mr. Snyder in 1819.

"Simon Snyder was born at Lancaster, November, 1759. His father was a respectable mechanic, who had emigrated to Pennsylvania from Germany about the year 1748. The maiden name of his mother was Knippenberg; she was born near Oppenheim, in Germany. His father, Anthony Snyder, died at Lancaster. In 1776, Simon Snyder removed, and went and resided at Yorktown more than eight years; there he learned the tanning and currying business, serving an apprenticeship of four years without being bound by any indenture or written contract. At York, he learned at night-school, kept by John Jones, a worthy member of the Society of Friends, reading, writing, and arithmetic, and made some progress in mathematics. Often, at the midnight hour, after a hard day's work, Simon Snyder was found in the pursuit of knowledge, and his Sundays were also constantly devoted to his studies.

"He removed to the county of Northumberland, to that part which is now Union County, and became a storekeeper, and the owner of a mill. He soon became useful and respectable as a scrivener. He was ever the friend of the poor and distressed, modest and unassuming; he was unanimously elected by the freeholders of a large district of country a Justice of the Peace. In this office he officiated for twelve years, under two commissions. The first was granted under the Constitution of 1776, and the other under the present Constitution; and so universally were his decisions respected, that there was no appeal to the Court of Common Pleas, and but one certiorari sued out in all that time, though the inhabitants consisted of the precursors of all new counties, amongst whom quarrels and disputes are very frequent, yet his efforts to reconcile the contending parties so generally prevailed, that of the many actions brought before him for assaults and batteries, he made return to the Court of Quarter Sessions of but two recognizances.

"In 1789, he was elected a member of the Convention which formed the present Constitution of the State. Though but a mere novice in politics, his votes point him out as the steady supporter of those invaluable rights which protect the religious freedom, and the persons and property of the people of this free country. In 1797, he was elected a member of the State Legislature, and in 1802, was chosen Speaker of the House of Representatives. With him originated the arbitration principle just incorporated, with other wholesome provisions for the adjustment of controversies brought before Justices of the Peace, in a law commonly called the $100 law. He continued, after repeated unanimous elections, to preside in the chair until 1805, when he was taken up and run as the Democratic candidate for Governor, in opposition to Gov. M'Kean, who was elected. In 1806, he was again returned as a member to the House of Representatives and chosen Speaker. In 1808, he was again the candidate for Governor of Pennsylvania, and was elected by a very large majority."

THE END.

CPSIA information can be obtained at www.ICGtesting.com
Printed in the USA
LVOW02s0240071213

364231LV00006B/326/P